Louis Pasteur

BY

LAURA N. WOOD

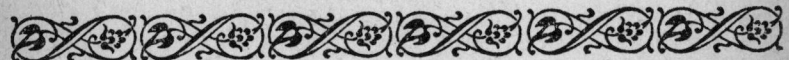

JULIAN MESSNER INC., NEW YORK

PUBLISHED BY JULIAN MESSNER, INC.
8 WEST 40TH STREET   NEW YORK 18

COPYRIGHT, 1948, BY
LAURA N. WOOD

Fifth Printing, April, 1956

PRINTED IN THE UNITED STATES OF AMERICA

ACKNOWLEDGMENTS

BUT FOR THE courtesy of the copyright owners, it would have been impossible to use some of the material which appears in this book.

For permission to reproduce copyrighted pictures, I am much indebted to the Carnegie Institution of Washington, Librairie Ernest Flammarion, Librairie Hachette, Harpers Magazine, Popular Science Monthly, W. B. Saunders Company and, finally, Professor Pasteur Vallery-Radot, Pasteur's grandson, whose collection is, of course, a valuable source of illustrative material.

Permission to quote from Pasteur's letters was kindly granted by Editions Bernard Grasset, publishers of Pasteur's *Correspondance*.

I am warmly grateful, also, to Dr. Henry E. Sigerist and Miss Genevieve Miller of the Institute of the History of Medicine, Johns Hopkins University, for enabling me to obtain copies of pictures done by Pasteur in his youth; to Dr. Alexander Sandow of New York University for carefully checking my manuscript; to W. Crosby Roper, Jr. and Miss Frances T. Schwab for valuable editorial criticism; to Mrs. R. Hall Pearson for editing my translations from the French; and to Mrs. Helen D. Bullock for assuming that final tedious task, making the index.

By the same author

RAYMOND L. DITMARS: HIS EXCITING CAREER WITH REPTILES, ANIMALS AND INSECTS

WALTER REED: DOCTOR IN UNIFORM

INTRODUCTION

Ask a hundred persons if Louis Pasteur was a scientific genius and every one of them, probably, will assure you that he was. But ask the same hundred in what his genius lay, and you will get a variety of answers, many of them inaccurate. You may hear, for example, that he was a genius because he discovered the microbic origin of contagious disease, or because he invented the pasteurizing process by which food is preserved. Actually, he did neither. For that matter, many of the discoveries with which his name is associated were foreshadowed or pioneered with more or less definiteness by other scientists.

There is, in fact, no easy answer to the question. It was certainly a part of his genius that early in his life he perfected that tool, the scientific method, by means of which he realized the vast possibilities of a powerful mind and character. In a time when religious and philosophical speculations often influenced scientific thought, Pasteur rigorously excluded both from his laboratory. When he had a problem to solve, he cared only for facts, demonstrable scientific facts. Collecting facts, facts, and more facts, he would formulate a theory; then, if further facts failed to conform to it, he would scrap it without a regret and formulate another into which they fitted. Always scientific theories had to be controlled by, and provable by, scientific facts; and because he was an unexcelled observer and an ingenious and accurate experimenter, Pasteur could distinguish a fact from an illusion with a precision that seemed uncanny to his admirers, suspicious to his opponents. All his work was scrupulously, laboriously, built on facts scientifically assembled, and that is the reason the foundations he laid are enduring.

It was a part of his genius, too, that he was a canny showman and an accomplished, unrelenting propagandist. Had he not been, he could not have won recognition for his theories in the face of the prolonged opposition of hostile doctors who sneered at him as a "mere chemist" and a medical dabbler. His demonstrations were not only striking but cleverly staged; his propaganda campaigns were unremitting. Nothing short of full acceptance of the truths he was advancing ever satisfied him, and, because he had a rare talent for presenting them tellingly, he eventually won it for them.

It was his good fortune, and it contributed to the expression of his genius, that he was born at the right time, when scientific ideas were already in the air for him to precipitate, define, document; and that he was born, too, in the right place, in a country whose industries were then presenting just the kind of problems that he was equipped to solve. A functionary all his adult life in the state-controlled school system, Pasteur was a public servant on the public pay roll. As such, he frequently found his services commandeered by government officials and by industrialists to solve biochemical problems that occurred in agriculture and industry. As a passionate patriot, too, he often volunteered his talents for the benefit of his country's economic health. Most of his great contributions to science evolved in the course of work in such relatively homely and unspectacular fields as the manufacture of beet juice alcohol and the culture of silkworms—an early example of a trend much more marked today, when many important discoveries are coming about as a result of industrial research.

At least one more factor contributed to the splendid flowering of Pasteur's genius: an absolutely tranquil family life. His wife's love for him was selfless, his children's devoted, and their prime and constant object was to protect his time and to conserve his strength and peace of mind. His success is the measure of theirs, as it was also the reward of their efforts.

The adventures and excitements of Pasteur's life were almost entirely intellectual; its sober drama unfolded slowly in the setting of the laboratory. It was a drama of unremitting work, work with which not grief, nor ill-health, nor fatigue, nor anything else, was allowed to interfere, until finally overmastering illness ended the labor before it ended the life which had always been dedicated to it.

CHAPTER ONE

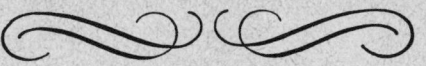

ATTRACTED by the cluster of men around the blacksmith's shop, the little boy joined them. They were unusually grave and quiet except for occasional murmurs of sympathy. Inquisitive, the child wriggled through them until he could see what was going on within the shop. The smith, looking tense and stern, was bringing a poker to a white heat in his forge. A peasant, one trouser leg rolled up to expose his mangled and bleeding calf, was supported, half-fainting, by two friends.

"We're ready now, Nicolle," the smith said, and Nicolle threw a look of pitiful, desperate appeal toward the knot of men in the doorway as the smith approached him with the glowing poker and his friends tightened their grip on him.

"Oh, poor M. Nicolle!" the child exclaimed. "The wolf has attacked him, too?"

One of the onlookers glanced at him. "Yes, Louis, the wolf got Nicolle, too," he said.

Louis watched in horrified fascination as the smith plunged the orange tip of the poker into the ragged wound and moved it slowly about in it. After a single cry of pain, Nicolle jerked frantically as the torn flesh seared, and his friends struggled to hold him still. In a few moments the agonizing treatment was over. Nicolle was helped to a waiting wagon by his friends; the little group, offering him good wishes for his recovery, dispersed; and the blacksmith went back to his horseshoeing. Louis hurried home to tell his mother that the wolf had attacked still another victim.

For weeks during the fall of 1831 the rabid beast had been terrorizing the Department of the Jura. It would skulk down out of the mountains and fall upon a peasant at work in his field, a tardy child hurrying to school, a woman walking along the road to market; it would tear its victim savagely and race away before his cries could bring aid. The only thing to do for the injured person was to cauterize his wound—burn away all the damaged tissue—or he would probably develop rabies and die. The treatment was frightfully painful and, more than that, it was unsure—already eight persons in the quiet little hill village of Arbois had died miserably in spite of it—but it was the only one then known that worked even part of the time.

Everyone watched Nicolle's progress with sympathic interest, and there was general relief in the town when, after many weeks, none of the dreaded symptoms of rabies had appeared. In his case, at least, the terrible remedy had succeeded. Nicolle was indeed lucky, it was agreed—but how the poor fellow had suffered!

It was more than fifty years before a safe and painless antirabies treatment was devised to replace the heroic, uncertain one to which Nicolle had submitted. The person who developed it was the same one who, as a nine-year-old child, had watched with horror and sympathy the treatment of his fellow townsman Nicolle. It was Louis—Louis Pasteur.

Peasants as well as princes can have pedigrees. Louis Pasteur, son of a tanner, could trace his father's family in an unbroken line from 1682, when Denis Pasteur married Jeanne David. Serfs of the Counts of Udressier in the Franche-Comté, a region bordering Switzerland, the Pasteurs worked their successive lords' lands, ground their flour, tanned their leather. They were an obscure peasant family, but they were fortified by the unspectacular qualities of industry, patience and independence. This independence reached a sort of boiling point in Claude Etienne Pasteur, grandson of Claude. He wanted to be his own man, and by the time he was thirty he was. Philippe Marie François, Count of Udressier, in a deed dated March 20, 1763, granted him his freedom for four louis d'or—or, very roughly, about twenty American dollars. It does not seem an excessive price.

Claude Etienne had ten children, and our interest—and sympathy—attach to the third, Jean Henri. He seems to have been unfortunate in almost everything: he was unsuccessful as a tanner at Besançon; his wife died at the age of twenty; he himself, after a second marriage, died at twenty-seven. The orphan son of his first marriage, Jean Joseph, went to near-by Salins to live, first with his grandmother, then with his father's sisters, whose husbands were in partnership as wood merchants.

If the personal events of little Jean Joseph's early years were melancholy, the public were cataclysmic—he was born in March, 1791. His childhood in the provincial town passed against a background of swift distant violence: the French Revolution, the execution of Louis XVI, foreign wars, the rise to supreme power of the brilliant young general, Napoleon Bonaparte. By the time he was thirteen Jean Joseph found himself the subject of the Emperor, Napoleon I, and by the time he was twenty he found himself one of his soldiers.

By that time Napoleon was having to keep an army in Spain to support his brother Joseph whom he had imposed on the resentful Spanish people as king. Jean Joseph Pasteur, tossed into this Peninsular War, served his Emperor with that ardent, wholehearted devotion that Napoleon knew how to inspire in his soldiers. His regiment fought guerrillas in the northern Spanish provinces until early in 1814, when it was recalled to France. Napoleon's luck was almost exhausted by then, and his popularity with it. Although the sadly depleted army was loyal, the nation was sick of battle losses and the lengthening string of defeats, and parents were sick of feeding sons into an insatiable war machine. By the time young Pasteur's regiment returned to France, abdication was only a couple of battles away. Before it came, however, Jean Joseph reached the rank of sergeant major and received, with his comrades, the Cross of the Legion of Honor from the Emperor for heroic conduct in the battle of Bar-sur-Aube. The soldiers' gallantry delayed Napoleon's collapse only briefly: in April the white cockade of the Bourbons, restored to the throne by France's enemies, replaced the beloved tricolor. His hero fallen, his country humiliated, even his brave regiment renamed *Régiment Dauphin*, Jean Joseph Pasteur retired from the army, an embittered man at the age of twenty-three.

His loyalty to the exiled Emperor remained proud and constant. When the mayor of Salins, an adherent of the restored monarchy, ordered all of Bonaparte's old soldiers to deliver their swords to the town hall, Jean Joseph grudgingly obeyed. But when he learned that these swords, which had served the Emperor and France in so many hard and glorious campaigns, were to be assigned to the detested Bourbon's police, it was more than he could bear. He leaped on the police agent who had received his, and snatched it from him. Shouts, threats, fighting, made a bedlam of the town hall. The outraged mayor pleaded with the colonel of an Austrian regiment, which was still quartered on the town, to make Pasteur restore the weapon. The colonel coldly refused, saying he respected the young man's loyalty. The mayor was discountenanced, and Pasteur, probably, felt almost as much so—he was naturally a retiring man, and he was not used to being seen home by a noisy crowd of sympathizers.

A healthy and reasonable man in his early twenties is unlikely to remain embittered indefinitely. It was only natural that Jean Joseph's attention, his fancy and finally his heart should be caught by an attractive and intelligent young girl in a family of gardeners whose plot bordered the mild little river Furieuse directly across from his own tan yard. Her name was Jeanne Etiennette Roqui, and she was one of a peasant family so ancient that their name was to be found in the local archives as far back as 1555, and so well known for their devotion to each other that "to love like a Roqui" was a common expression in the region. The young tanner asked her parents for her hand, they consented, and Jean Joseph and Jeanne were married.

The young couple established themselves in Dôle, near Salins, in a house in the rue des Tanneurs. The tanning pits were in the two-room cellar, the workshop was on the floor above, and on the top floor were three small rooms for living quarters. It was in this modest little place that four of the five Pasteur children were born.

In those days infant mortality was terribly high. If a baby failed to contract the "putrid sore throat," it was all too likely to fall victim to some other malignant disease that not even the best doctor knew how to avert or cure. When the Pasteurs' first child, Jean Denis, died in 1816 a few months after his birth, the young parents' misfortune was far from unique. Indeed, it was rather out of the ordinary that their next three children—Virginie, born in 1818; Louis, born, quite without portent, on Friday, December 27, 1822; and Josephine, born in 1825—succeeded, thanks to good management and good luck, in living through the precarious periods of infancy and early childhood.

By 1825 the Pasteurs were finding their living quarters almost intolerably crowded, so they moved to Marnoz, a near-by town surrounded by pear orchards and vine-covered hills, where Jeanne Pasteur owned a house which her widowed mother had given her. The road to Aiglepierre ran past the front of the house, and a stream at the back made it appear likely that Jean Joseph could pursue his trade satisfactorily. It proved to be too small a trickle for his use, however, so the family stayed in the Maison Pasteur—as it later came to be called—only long enough for little Louis to remember playing in the dust of the road, for the last of the Pasteur children, Émilie, to be born in 1826, and for the tanner, who had a taste for painting, to do a picture on one of the inside doors. It portrayed a peasant in an old uniform, leaning on his spade in a field and dreaming of the military glory he once saw and shared. However faulty its execution, the picture faithfully depicted the feelings of the former sergeant major who always remained loyal to his Emperor.

The next move, and the last, was to near-by Arbois, a hill town with brown roofs and tall poplars, where Louis Pasteur grew up and to which he returned throughout his life. The house to which they moved was a combination tannery and dwelling, containing a workroom and shop, and living quarters large enough for the family of six. It stood facing the rue Courcelles, just across the stone bridge at the entrance of the town. Beneath the bridge the river Cuisance rushed over a waterfall, then flowed broad and shallow over its pebbly bottom past the back of the house. Pits for the preparation of hides had been dug by some previous occupant behind the house, and in front of it a little garden flourished. Here the tanner found, at last, that with industry and thrift—not virtues, but necessities, in his circumstances—he could make a modest living for his family.

Louis by then was a stocky boy about five years old, with a

square forehead and gray-green eyes clear in color and direct in glance. He loved the tan yard, helped his father with the lighter work, and played in it with his companions. In good weather he would wade and fish in the Cuisance with the neighborhood children or ramble with them around the countryside. At bird trapping, however, he drew the line: the fright and pain of any wounded creature was intolerable to him. Except for this greater sensibility, there seemed to be nothing particular to distinguish the tanner's boy, in his early years, from the majority of his fellows.

Domestic life in the Pasteur household was calm and a little austere, but not joyless. Both parents worked hard, Jean Joseph at his trade, Jeanne over her house and family. The children loved their father with a touch of awe, and their mother with complete openness for her gaiety, enthusiasm and constant kindness. None of the roughness of his military life, however, had adhered to Jean Joseph. His speech, as well as his manner, was reserved and deliberate. He never spoke of his campaigns, but when on Sundays he put on his spotless frock coat, he always wore the conspicuous ribbon of the Legion of Honor. Then he and his entire family, devout Catholics, would attend Mass; and later in the day he would take a walk, on which Louis as he grew older was sometimes allowed to accompany him, along the road which wound through vine-covered hills toward Besancon.

The elder Pasteur had had no opportunity in his youth to acquire much education, but he was determined that his son should have a good one. Having a deep respect for it, he himself associated by preference with men of intelligence and culture. He never went to the village cafés, and guests, except the friends of the children, were few in the Pasteur home. Those who came, however, to spend pleasant evenings in conversation were such men as Dumont, the local doctor, a man of considerable learning and much goodness of heart, and Bousson de Mairet, who had spent most of his life compiling a sort of informal history of the Franche-Comtois. Perhaps it was he, with his heroic tales of the Franche-Comté, who first aroused in Louis that passionate love of country and admiration of her great men which so influenced his life.

Aside from the rather frightening excitement of the mad wolf episode, there were few memorable occurrences in the childhood of Louis Pasteur, although some of the stirring political events in the capital and larger cities echoed in the provincial town. When, for instance, Parisians on July 26, 1830, manned the barricades and raised the tricolor rather than let Charles X, who six years before had succeeded his brother Louis XVIII to the throne, make himself an absolute monarch, the excitement penetrated quickly to Arbois. Enthusiastic Arboisians sent the capital an address assuring it that every able-bodied man in the town was ready to fly to its aid. Paris, however, managed to get along without Arbois' assistance: Charles was overthrown with comparative ease. The liberal element among the Royalists maneuvered his Orléans cousin, Louis Philippe, onto the throne, and French political life settled down again, somewhat uneasily, for a time.

Echoes of another political disturbance filtered through to Arbois less than four years later when, one April night in 1834, a stagecoach traveler reported that the silkworkers of Lyon had staged an insurrection and declared a republic. Louis, hearing running in the streets, hurried to a window and watched men hastening toward the city hall to seize the arms stored there; and later, before they could accomplish anything in support of the Lyonnais, he saw the soldiers from Besançon march across the bridge and past his house to disperse them.

At this time, however, politics were well over young Louis' head. Who ruled France, how few were privileged to vote for the deputies to the National Assembly, how the newspapers were censored and controlled, how the teaching in schools and universities was regulated—all in the interests of the monarchy, of course—all these were matters which took up little of his attention.

It was the modest events of his private life that filled his time and his mind. There was the long illness of his sister Émilie, for instance, who at the age of three had what Louis later called a "cerebral fever," which permanently halted her mental development. There were, more happily, long walks and talks with his favorite schoolfellow, Jules Vercel, little jobs to do for his father about the tannery, and errands to run for his mother.

7

Often, in his leisure, he would get out his crayons and draw a picture. Some of the neighbors thought that the Pasteur boy had the makings of a fine artist, but his father did not take his work very seriously. Indeed, he did not like to hear his son referred to as an "artist." There was something frivolous-sounding about it that displeased him.

School, of course, took up much of the boy's time. He had first attended the primary school attached to the Collège d'Arbois, the local secondary school. There a monitor selected from among the students by the master recited the lesson to each group of pupils, who repeated it after him in a sort of chant. Louis often hoped to be selected monitor, but he was by no means an outstanding scholar. Then, when he was a little older, he entered the *collège*, and he still appeared, to the casual eye, to be no more than a satisfactorily average student. He did sufficiently well in his lessons to win an occasional prize, and he took an earnest kind of interest in his work, but he was diligent rather than brilliant.

There was one observer, however, who was not casual. He was M. Romanet, the headmaster of the school. He was the first to recognize that there were possibilities above the average in this industrious and deliberate scholar. Louis was slow to reach conclusions, M. Romanet realized, not through dullness but because he had a sound mind that insisted on certainty, and was not satisfied with anything short of it. This deliberation, he saw too, was saved from doggedness by being combined with stimulating qualities of imagination and enthusiasm.

"Your son will make a fine teacher," he told Jean Joseph. "I have been encouraging him to try for the École normale."

Jean Joseph looked dissatisfied. The École normale, reorganized by the Emperor in 1808 to train young professors for university teaching, was a long way off, in Paris; and Paris was a dangerous city, where innocent young boys from the provinces were likely to fall in with fast companions, or be taken in by some of those inveterate plotters who were always trying to assassinate the king. And besides, think of the expense!

"But why send him all the way to Paris? Why should he not study near by, at Besançon, and return as a professor to our own Collège d'Arbois, monsieur?"

"My friend, your son's career will take him far beyond a professorship in a provincial secondary school, if only you will give him the opportunity to educate himself for it."

Jean Joseph, with a troubled spirit, thought the matter over. The boy, of course, had his heart set on Paris, but when one's only son was involved, it was very hard indeed to make up one's mind to let him leave home. The anxious parents discussed the problem at length, finally decided to give Louis the opportunity for which he longed. But how could they meet the expenses, whom could they get to keep an eye on him?

Captain Barbier, of the Paris Municipal Guard, solved those minor difficulties. He always spent his leaves in Arbois, and he knew the Pasteur family well.

"I will watch out for him myself," he told Jean Joseph. "And my friend, M. Barbet, who is a Franche-Comtois, has a preparatory school in the Latin Quarter. He will do for Louis what he does for any boy from his own region—take him in at a lowered rate."

So, although his parents had misgivings, the matter was settled, and Louis, not yet sixteen, prepared to depart for Paris to study for an academic career.

CHAPTER TWO

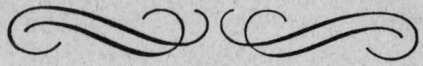

SINCE THE REVOLUTION, education in France had been a state monopoly. Every school in the country, from the primary schools in the rural districts through the most advanced schools in the big cities, dovetailed into an educational system which was planned, administered and supported by the government. The École normale, founded on the theory that "the starting point of the educational system is the instruction and inspiration of the teaching body," trained young men for teaching in advanced and professional schools. Its students were required to enter into a ten-year teaching contract with the government, and were exempt from military conscription. Only picked young men were admitted: the entrance examinations and other requirements were very difficult. Even more select were those who, after the three-year course either in science or letters, passed first the graduation examination and then the examination for the *agrégation* (a sort of teaching fellowship), which entitled them to be appointed assistant professors in universities or professional schools. One who succeeded in graduating but not in becoming an *agrégé* could look forward to a perfectly respectable—even distinguished—teaching career, perhaps as superintendent of an important secondary school; but one who cleared all the hurdles, including the agrégation, could expect to circulate at the top level of the French academic world for the rest of his life.

It was to this future that M. Romanet aspired for Louis Pasteur.

Louis gazed forlornly from the window of the steep old house into the Impasse des Feuillantines, dingy and dead-end, below. He had been at the Pension Barbet for more than two weeks, and every time he turned into the sunless impasse he felt as if he were poking his head into a noose. He was almost strangled with depression. Even the presence of his friend from Arbois did not comfort him; it only whetted his misery.

"Ah, Jules, what I would not give for even a glimpse of our bridge over the Cuisance, or for a whiff of the tan yard!"

Jules Vercel looked disturbed: Louis' homesickness was making him really ill. "My poor Louis! This will pass in a few more days. Try to control it."

"Yes," Louis agreed listlessly. He turned from the window with a sigh and sat down beside Jules at the table to make another effort to study.

The journey that had brought them both to the Pension Barbet—the journey that should have been so full of exciting novelties and stimulating new impressions—had been, on the contrary, an expedition full of unrelieved and mounting melancholy. A freezing rain had been falling through the October morning darkness as the little group of Pasteurs and Vercels gathered around the coach in the courtyard of the Hôtel de la Poste in Arbois. Lanterns flickered in the stable and the yard, and showed passengers, coachman and stablemen muffled to the ears against the penetrating chill. The breath of horses and human beings alike rose whitely from their nostrils and floated off in swiftly disappearing wisps.

"Work hard, Louis. Much depends on this."

"Oh, yes, Papa!"

"And do not fail to attend Mass regularly, my son."

"Of course, Mama. You will write me often?"

"Jules, Louis—stay close together, look after each other."

"We will, monsieur."

"Yes, Papa."

The five horses had been hitched to the coach, the baggage strapped on, a few more admonitions and farewells exchanged, and the passengers began to enter the coach. Perhaps because they had been the youngest travelers, perhaps because they had been the most polite, Louis and Jules had found themselves sitting uncomfortably under a tarpaulin behind the coachman instead of inside. As the coach rattled out of the cobbled yard the two boys had had a final glimpse of their parents, dimly illuminated by the little flame of Jean Joseph's lantern, waving good-by through the sleety rain. Altogether, it was not an auspicious way to begin a journey into the future.

The early morning darkness was barely beginning to lift as the coach rolled along the rue Courcelles, past the tannery and over the bridge. As home and familiar landmarks dropped behind, Louis felt his spirits fall sharply. He stole a glance at Jules —Jules, the cheerful, the unfailingly lighthearted companion. Well, this was one time his lightheartedness had failed. He looked ready to cry. Catching Louis' eye, Jules shrugged, and the two boys exchanged bleak little smiles of complete understanding. They were already homesick.

The trip to Paris, some two hundred miles distant, took several days. The coach road passed through some of the finest winegrowing regions of France, and through ancient towns associated with her traditional glory from Gallo-Roman times. Louis, who loved his country with a deep pride, would in his normal spirits have taken the keenest interest in the medieval buildings, the Roman remains, the historic towns, but on this trip he would willingly have exchanged them all for a view of the square tower of the Arbois church. The coach had lumbered through Dijon, Auxerre, Sens, and the sight of their antique glories had done nothing to disturb his melancholy indifference. Nights he had lain quietly in the bed beside Jules, sleepless with longing for home; and in the morning, pale and quiet, he had resumed the detested journey with sinking heart.

Even Fontainbleau, with its beautiful forest where the French court had delighted to hunt, and its magnificent palace where kings had reigned and an emperor abdicated, was little to the wretched traveler but another milestone that emphasized his increasing distance from Arbois.

When their coach finally had entered Paris, and lurched down the narrow streets of the Latin Quarter along the south bank of the Seine, the two young boys from the provinces had found that there was little about their first sight of the capital to appeal to them. Tall dingy houses with steep-pitched roofs flanked narrow, twisting streets, effectually shutting out the winter sunlight, so that to the gloom of the neighborhood was joined a permanent and unsavory dampness. Many of the streets were unpaved and dirty, and paving stones, when there were any, were those large, loosely laid limestone blocks which the Parisian populace knew so well how to convert into barricades. Pale gamins scrapped and squalled in these labyrinths and threw dirt at the passing stage, housewives shook their mops out of upper windows, and laborers and loafers stepped quickly into doorways as the coach passed, splattering filth. Nothing could have formed a more unpleasant contrast to the clean little hill town of Arbois, high in the transparent air of the Jura Mountains.

As the endless days passed, Louis had struggled stubbornly to adjust himself. There was much in his new life, he told himself, that was pleasing. Jules was with him, M. Barbet was kind, his work was interesting. He had a secure future ahead of him as a teacher—all he had to do was prepare for it. Why, then, could he not reconcile himself to Paris? Franche-Comtois have a deep and dogged love for their native region, and Louis was a Franche-Comtois. In Paris were strange people, strange sights, strange smells, strange ways—everything was strange, unbearably strange. He was sick for the sight of something familiar.

He stared unseeingly at his book, and sighed again.

"Now, Louis!" Jules exclaimed kindly.

M. Barbet was a perceptive man as well as a kind one. He recognized his new pupil's ailment, and, Franche-Comtois himself, sympathized with him. His kindly meant efforts to amuse and interest Louis, however, were perfectly useless, as useless as the classes at the Lycée St. Louis, the high school that he was attending, or the encouragement and good humor of Jules Vercel. Louis had character and determination, but the homesickness that overwhelmed him was too strong for a boy of fifteen. M. Barbet, realizing it, wrote to his father.

A few days later, as he was trying to study, a messenger brought Louis word that someone wanted to see him in the café at the corner of the Impasse des Feuillantines.

"To see me? But I know no one, except perhaps Captain Barbier. Is it he?"

"Go on, hurry! You will see."

Louis snatched up his cap and clattered down the stairs. Captain Barbier—that must be it. Or perhaps a neighbor from Arbois—but who in that little village would have business in the capital? He entered the café and glanced eagerly around the dark, clean room. There at a table near the back sat a man, a dearly familiar figure, with his head in his hands.

"Papa! Papa!"

Jean Joseph raised his head and looked at his son. "I have come to take you home, Louis," he said.

Louis Pasteur had had his own way: he had gone to Paris to study—and here he was back in a month, utterly routed by homesickness. It was an inglorious outcome. Little is known now of what he thought or did after the first happy excitement of his return wore off, but in any case it is evident that his self-confidence was not damaged. He could hardly have helped acknowledging his Parisian adventure for the fiasco it was, but neither could the adults involved have failed to accept their part of the responsibility. M. Romanet had urged him to an effort beyond his strength, his parents had consented against their better judgment. Very likely they let him feel that the fault was not entirely his, and that realization must have done much to neutralize his self-reproach. In any case, it is not disgraceful to love one's home and to miss it.

So Louis returned to the Collège d'Arbois. He resumed his art lessons under M. Pointurier, and amiably drew the picture of everyone who asked him to, elderly tradesmen, his mother in her Scotch shawl, even the mayor himself, elegant in embroidered uniform and the Cross of the Legion of Honor. He worked hard at his studies all that year, 1839, hard enough to win several prizes. M. Romanet was still encouraging his good student to go to the École normale, and the boy's own determination had not changed. The Collège d'Arbois did not offer all the necessary preparatory courses, but at the Collège royal de la Franche-Comté at Besançon Louis could prepare for the École normale examinations.

"That will be a good solution to your problem, Louis," the master said. "I do not think you want to risk Paris again soon, and Besançon is just a short journey from Arbois."

"Yes, Papa goes to the fair there several times a year to sell his hides."

"And you'll still be in your beloved Franche-Comté," M. Romanet added. "This time I do not think we will see you back so soon."

So Louis went to Besançon.

The next two and a half years of his life were dominated by one thing—study. He was working hard for the École normale and by now his parents, reconciled to his ambition, took it for granted that he was cut out for something bigger than a teaching position at the local *collège*. The whole family was wrapped up in the only son's future career, as Louis himself implied in his rather charming injunction to his sisters: "Love each other as I love you, while awaiting the happy day when I am admitted to the École normale."

The principal subject of his letters, as of his thoughts, was his schoolwork. The minute interest of his family in his scholastic affairs he satisfied with numerous details. In January, 1840, he wrote his parents that he was among the good students in his class, "but I hope that my rank will be much better in several months." With his real love of learning, it was not difficult for him to satisfy this hope. The following August he passed his examinations for his first degree, *bachelier ès lettres,* and he was reported to be "good" in Greek, Latin, rhetoric, medicine, history, geography, philosophy and French composition, and "very good" in elementary science. After the summer vacation he was able to tell his family that M. Répécaud, headmaster of the *collège*, had told him that he hoped to appoint him a preparation master early in the following year. While his examinations had been satisfactory, he was still considered a sound rather than a brilliant student, and the master's choice of him was as much a tribute to his character as to his scholarship.

In any case, he worked diligently, hard enough so that in his letters home he made occasional references to headaches, eyestrain and his need to wear his spectacles at least four hours a day. Eyestrain notwithstanding, one of his more frequent forms of relaxation was doing portraits of his friends. ". . . I am still doing the Bousson boy's portrait, but the resemblance is not as close as I had thought. . . . M. Pointurier would have been able to give me much advice."

He was even getting a little reputation in Besançon for his pictures, but was inclined to make light of it. "The first portrait I did is exhibited in the parlor, where a lot of people go, everyone who comes to see the students. But all that doesn't lead to the École normale. I prefer a top rank in the *collège* to ten thousand compliments. . . ." His esteem for poor M. Pointurier's talent, incidentally, seems to have fallen off sharply after an exhibit in Besançon in which his former teacher showed an "Adam and Eve": "Nothing is more frightful, whether for composition, or drawing, or color. Everyone cries out in protest on seeing this picture."

His family's interest in his affairs was fully matched by his in the home he had left. He was particularly concerned about his two older sisters—nothing, of course, could be expected of *"pauvre Émilie"*—who seem to have had little of their brother's enthusiasm for intellectual effort. A bad account of them—that they had been lazy, or perhaps quarrelsome—always distressed him deeply, and sometimes moved him to one of his very rare outbursts of displeasure. "They tell me that, more than ever, you never cease to argue, to fight, to be jealous of one another . . . nothing is better calculated to annoy and discourage me. . . ."

At a good report on Josephine and Virginie, however, he was delighted. A particular letter overjoyed him because it told him "that, for the first time, perhaps, my sisters have WILLED. It is much, dear sisters, to will; because action, work, always follow will, and almost always, too, work has for its accompaniment success. These three things, will, work, success, divide among them all of human existence: will opens the door to brilliant and happy careers, work conquers them, and at the end of the journey, success comes to crown the effort. . . .

"May my words be felt and understood by you, dear sisters. Engrave them on your hearts. Let them be your guide. Farewell, your brother."

This letter, coming from a seventeen-year-old schoolboy, has rather a solemn tone, but Louis, as the only son of a closely knit French family, had a responsibility toward the women in it second only to his father's, and he took it very seriously. To encourage his sisters to work was, under the circumstances, simply a matter of course.

He also took it to be his duty to defend them when he thought his parents were too severe. When Josephine was away at school, Louis received from his father another poor report of her, to which he replied:

"I was not at all satisfied with what you tell me on Josephine's account. Certainly, if you write her letters as you speak of her to me in yours, she cannot be much encouraged to work. You who are at home together, it costs you nothing to decry her; but when one is away at school like her"—and here surely he was remembering his own terrible homesickness—"it must not be very pleasant to hear it said of one that one knows nothing, that one is unwilling. It is not thus that you encourage industry. . . ."

Louis showed his affection for his sisters in many thoughtful and endearing small ways—drawing paper for Josephine, music for Virginie, bonbons always for poor Émilie—"she is not hard to satisfy"—warm and frequent letters, and an occasional book he had enjoyed himself.

He was able to afford such presents because of the small salary he began drawing when he became preparation master in January, 1841—three hundred francs a year, with board and lodging included. Usually he managed his studies and his extra duties without too much difficulty; sometimes they rather oppressed him. "One of the masters is sick at home," he wrote in November, 1841, "and I have to replace him: so that I am busy all day long, and will be for I don't know how long. If you have your troubles, I have mine, too, and I see them get bigger from day to day. I see that I am beginning to enter upon Life."

Jean Joseph, fearful that his son was overworking, admonished him frequently. "Be sure to get enough recreation! Health above all," he would urge—to which the earnest young master once soothingly replied: "I by no means work hard enough to make myself ill. . . . I go to bed early, and get up late, at five-thirty, with the pupils." It was the night watchman who used to arouse him, with words he never forgot and often quoted. "Come on, M. Pasteur, drive out the demon of laziness!" he would shout as he knocked on his door in the morning darkness.

Pasteur's recreations were innocent ones: he attended the fairs at Besançon with his father; visited in the homes of Besançon friends; read and walked and talked at length with his closest friend, Charles Chappuis. Chappuis, like Pasteur, was preparing for the École normale; but he was taking the letters course, whereas Pasteur was taking the science. When Chappuis went to Paris toward the end of 1841 to continue his preparation for the *École*, he left his friend quite bereft. Louis wanted to follow him there to continue his work. He was prompted not only by loneliness; it was freely admitted by the masters at Besançon that a pupil who had a year's preparation in the capital stood a better chance of being admitted than one who did all his preparatory work in the provinces. Urged on by Chappuis, Louis asked his father if he might finish the year in Paris. When the elder Pasteur refused, he was not surprised. He even said that he was not disappointed, but the rather brusque tone of his letter suggests that he was: "Let's not think of it further, and don't speak to me about it any more." Convinced, however, of the wisdom of working in Paris, Jean Joseph promised his son that he could go there the following year.

The lonely friends consoled themselves for their separation by exchanging long and melancholy letters. Louis confided to Charles that he was "sad as a nightcap," Charles to Louis that Paris was "infamous, debauched, disgusting." "Let your letters always be very long," Louis begged, and Charles obliged him with frequent ones, all of them taking up at least four closely written pages and filled with maledictions on the big city he loathed.

Louis, who planned to take the examinations for his scientific degree as well as the entrance examinations to the École normale in the summer of 1842, buried himself in his work. He was doing very well in physics, sometimes standing first in the class, but he admitted that, while it was less difficult and less dull than mathematics, it was also less important. "Nothing dries up the heart like this study of mathematics," he complained. His dried-up heart notwithstanding, he could still burst into tears over a "charming story" he was reading. He was, of course, not yet twenty.

The examinations for the *École* began August 6 at Besançon.

Pasteur approached them with fair confidence, and had no sooner finished them than he had to go to Dijon, on August 13, to take those for his *bachelier ès sciences mathématiques* degree. He passed both sets, neither brilliantly. The examinations for the degree, he told his family, were very difficult. He was no doubt right: this young man whose chemical discoveries were to revolutionize medicine was found by his examiners to be merely "mediocre" in chemistry! As for the entrance examinations, he was dissatisfied with his standing: he passed only fifteenth in a group of twenty-two. He would have been admitted to the *École*, but he did not care to enter in such an almost hairbreadth way. He felt that he would do better to have further preparation. The time had come for Jean Joseph to make good his promise—for Louis to try Paris again.

CHAPTER THREE

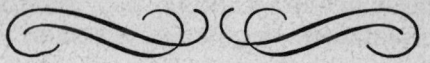

THE CURTAIN FELL to a wild outburst of applause. Rarely had even the Comédie française witnessed such enthusiasm. The playgoers stamped, clapped, wiped their eyes, cheered and shouted. The uproar lasted a full ten minutes. It had been touched off by a small dark woman in her early twenties. A street singer as a child, she now played in France's most celebrated theater and was everywhere recognized as the nation's greatest tragedienne. She was the superb Rachel.

Outside, once more, on the gaslit street with his friend Chappuis, Pasteur still felt the backwash of the emotions aroused by her performance as Mary Stuart. Rachel in 1842 was approaching the peak of her wonderful power, and that evening her characterization of the queen had moved to tears many a theatergoer more blasé than the inexperienced young provincials from the Franche-Comté.

"She is magnificent, magnificent," Pasteur murmured.

"She is indeed," Chappuis agreed.

"Ah, there, Charles," Pasteur teased him, "*there* is something wonderful in this repulsive Paris of yours that you would not find in the provinces."

"That is true," Chappuis conceded generously. "Paris has Rachel, and the Comédie française. How I should love to see her in something by Racine or Corneille!"

It was a fine night so the two friends walked from the rue Richelieu to the Latin Quarter, talking earnestly all the way, and separated with a quiet good night at the Impasse des Feuillantines. As Pasteur groped his way down the ill-lighted cul-de-sac he could not help reflecting with a little amusement how very different his second experience of Paris was from his first; and he was still smiling over the contrast when, fifteen minutes later, he got into his bed. Before pulling up the covers he leaned over to blow out the candle on the rough-surfaced table crowded with books. For a moment he was tempted to open his chemistry and get to work, but the chill from the stone floor, as well as the thought that he might waken his two roommates, made such industry seem ill-advised. He handled the book a moment, then resolutely put it down and blew out the light.

"Really, we must rent a stove," he thought, shivering. In a very few minutes he was asleep.

Nothing much had changed about the Impasse des Feuillantines in the past few years—it was still as cheerless and damp as ever—but a great deal had changed about Louis Pasteur. Instead of a miserable schoolboy, he was a self-confident young man of nineteen, taller, heavier, more self-possessed. Thick, straight hair framed his square forehead. His deep-set eyes were at once observant and kindly, and the expression of his smooth-shaven face was grave and pleasant. He no longer stared out the window of his austere and chilly room with the sick despair of intolerable homesickness, but every morning as he dressed he glanced out of it with anticipation—beyond the short dreary street lay the Lycée St. Louis he attended; the École normale to which he aspired; the Sorbonne, where he listened with the rapt attention of a disciple to lectures by France's leading chemist, the urbane and learned Jean Baptiste Dumas; and all the rest of the ancient and wonderful capital of his native country.

Pasteur's days, indeed, were too crowded now for homesickness. Every morning he got up "late," at quarter before six, and hurried the few doors from his lodgings to the Pension Barbet to tutor some of the younger students in mathematics. M. Barbet compensated him by reducing his tuition to one third of the usual amount, and it was not long before the schoolmaster rated his young assistant's help so valuable that he no longer required any tuition at all of him.

The elder Pasteur, with his deep-seated suspicion of urban ways, occasionally had to be reassured about his son. When he worried that the city boys Louis was teaching might put something over on him, Louis told him: ". . . be assured . . . that I will make myself liked and feared by the pupils I tutor. Nothing is milder than a Paris student as soon as you speak to him a little louder than usual." And when Jean Joseph warned him against frivolous gaieties and bad companions, he replied with simple finality: "I was never cut out for vice." It was entirely true; all his thoughts were on his family, his work, his ambitions. Early in 1843, in fact, he went to the expense of changing his room because he was annoyed and distracted by the conversation of his roommates, and felt that he could work better by himself.

Like most strong-minded young men, he had an occasional dispute with his father. Reproached for spending too much, he told Jean Joseph precisely where his money had gone—for a stove to heat his room, wood for the stove, a cloth to cover the bumpy table, writing materials, lessons in singing so that he could understand something of the art of music and of the physics of acoustics, four evenings at the theater, dinner once or twice a week with Chappuis. He thanked his father for admonishing him about his spending, because such a reminder would make him more careful; but he also pointed out that he had not been squandering money, and that it was he who had paid most of his tuition both at Besançon and in Paris by tutoring, and who had created for himself the opportunity for a lifetime job as a professor. Such collisions had no unpleasant aftermath. Father and son had such respect and affection for each other that they could discuss their disagreements, settle them, and forget them.

The dinners with Chappuis, who had been admitted to the École normale in the fall of 1842, were something that Jean Joseph himself insisted on. In every letter he expressed his constant worry that Louis might damage his health by immoderate work, and he urged him repeatedly to have dinner with his friend at the Palais royal on Thursdays and Sundays. They were days to which Louis looked forward all during the week. Although he was immersed in his scientific courses—chemistry, physics, mathematics—he was much interested, too, in philosophy, Chappuis' specialty, and in literature. Thursday afternoons and Sundays, when both boys were free, they made a habit of meeting in the library near the Pension Barbet to study philosophy together or read and discuss some literary work. The friends would work together in the library; then, tired from long sitting, they would go out for a stroll in the Luxembourg Gardens, and wind up at the Palais royal, where an acceptable dinner cost, moderately enough, about two francs. These evenings usually ended early, and Pasteur was in bed by his regular hour, before ten o'clock. Yet Jean Joseph, whose provincial distrust of the gay capital remained unabated, continued to bombard his son with warnings not to go out at night, or to go only with Chappuis. To Chappuis he wrote notes the burden of which always was: do not let Louis work too hard, do not let him undermine his health with study. After receiving one of these, Chappuis was always more solicitous than usual of his friend.

"Louis," he would say, after an hour or two of work in the library, "the light here is so poor. Let's quit now and go for a walk."

"But Charles, it isn't six yet!"

"I know, but my eyes are burning holes in my head."

Louis would close his book with resignation, and take off his spectacles. "Charles, you are a fraud! It is not your eyes—you have had another letter from my papa."

The school year passed quickly and profitably. The young physics instructor at the Lycée St. Louis readily fell in with Pasteur's wish to do extra work and gave him problems in addition to the regular classwork. Dumas' lectures at the Sorbonne were an inspiration. Paris itself, this time, was a constant source of interest and pleasure. Captain Barbier, mindful of his young acquaintance's earlier failure, made it a point to visit M. Barbet to inquire about his progress. He lost no time in reporting to Louis, with friendly satisfaction, that M. Barbet was thoroughly pleased both with his work and his conduct.

When the time came, at the end of the 1843 term, for Louis again to take the entrance examinations to the École normale, he passed high, taking a first prize in physics and two honorable mentions. By gaining admission to the *École*—this time he was fourth on the list—he safely passed another milestone on the road to his planned future.

Pasteur spent his vacation in Arbois, but in his zeal to get settled and get to work, he cut it short and returned to Paris a few days before the opening of the *École's* term. He was allowed to take up his lodgings in the empty dormitory. The *École* did not yet have quarters of its own, although they were being built, but shared those of the Collège Louis le Grand. The building was damp and barnlike, but it had symbolized the goal of all his ambitions and hopes for more than five years, and Pasteur could not have been better satisfied had he been moving into a palace.

The first year science students at the École normale attended about seventeen hours of lectures a week, divided between the *École* and the Sorbonne, which were given by the foremost professors in Paris. Much of the rest of their time they passed in studying. Tuesdays, all afternoon, they worked in the chemistry laboratory under the eye of the professor or an assistant. And, finally, there was another laboratory, wisely patronized by Pasteur, where for an hour a day they could blow glass, practice carpentry and lockmaking, and in general develop the manual skills valuable to physical scientists who must deal with delicate and complicated apparatus. Finding that about twelve hours of lectures and study a day did not satiate his taste for work, Louis also devoted two hours every Thursday, his half holiday, to teaching physics at the Pension Barbet, in appreciation of the kindness he had always received from its master.

Pasteur's spare time he spent in study in the library of the *École* or of the Sorbonne, and his holidays, too, were usually passed in work—reading biographies of scientists which fanned his ready enthusiasm into glowing resolution, solving problems in physics, doing additional experiments in the Sorbonne's chemistry laboratory under the benevolent direction of Dumas' assistant, Barruel. Chappuis was still delegated by the elder Pasteur to prevent the younger from overwork. Chappuis' technique was simple, although slow in taking effect. He would quietly enter the laboratory where Louis was working and sit silently watching him. He pretended that he was dying for air and exercise which he would enjoy only in Louis' company; actually, he waited without impatience, interested in watching the development of the skill his friend was already showing in chemical experimentation. Sometimes as he patiently sat there, Charles would be on the point of thinking that Louis had forgotten his presence; but finally Louis would take off his apron, look at him with his friendly and serious smile, and say:

"No, Charles, I have not forgotten you. Let's go now. I'm sure we both need a walk."

Strolling in the Luxembourg Gardens, they would discuss some philosophical problem, or a scientific one, or, with the intimacy of long and close friends, they would talk of their homes, their families, their ambitions.

By the fall of 1844, the walks in the garden were taken up principally with talk of a single subject: Louis had become fascinated by a problem which had been baffling the leading chemists of France and Germany for more than twenty years, and he discussed it tirelessly with his sympathetic friend. The problem, essentially, was: what was the difference between tartaric acid and paratartaric (or racemic) acid?

"To begin with, Louis," Chappuis asked when he first mentioned it, "what are these acids?"

"In 1770 a Swedish chemist named Scheele discovered tartaric acid in tartar, that thick crust that forms on the inside of wine barrels. It occurs in nature, too, in grapes. Paratartaric acid, or racemic acid, as it is frequently called, was discovered fifty years later by an Alsatian manufacturer, M. Kestner, at Thann. He produced it by some accident, and he has never since been able to duplicate it. The queer—and the interesting—thing about these two acids is that, in their crystalline form, they appear to be absolutely identical. Yet there must be some difference, because tartaric acid in solution is active in relation to polarized light—it deviates it to the right—and paratartaric, or racemic, is inactive, doesn't deviate it at all."

Chappuis looked bewildered. "I'm out of my depth."

"Polarized light? You know, don't you, that light throws off vibrations that travel at right angles to the direction of the beam of light itself, so that, if you could see the beam in cross section, it would look something like a dot vibrating in all directions?"

"Yes."

"Well, light is polarized when, by reflection or passing through some polarizing medium like a prism, these vibrations no longer spring off in every direction but are formed into a definite pattern. Let's take plane polarization—that's the simplest. If you could see a cross section of a beam of plane-polarized light, the light vibrations would not be oscillating, or dancing off in every direction; they would look like the hands of a clock pointing to six o'clock. See?"

"I think so. Go on."

"Now, you shoot a ray of plane-polarized light through a solution of tartaric acid, and the plane of polarization is deviated to the right—as though the hands of the clock had been moved to five minutes after seven. Shoot it through a solution of para-tartartic, and the plane doesn't change at all—the hands still say six o'clock."

"That's queer."

"It's a real mystery, because no one has yet discovered any difference whatever between the two crystals. Eilhard Mitscherlich, the German crystallographer, has studied them intensively and he can't find any physical or chemical difference at all—same crystalline form, same specific gravity, same double refraction, same everything."

"But there must be something, mustn't there?"

"There *must* be—but what is it? Jean Baptiste Biot, here in Paris, is a splendid physicist and very experienced in crystallography, but he can't find it either. It's a fascinating puzzle."

"Has it any practical importance?"

"No immediate one. Right now it's a problem in pure, not applied, science. But always, in science, any knowledge may turn out to have practical importance—you can't tell ahead of time. It's just that it's *always* important to find out, to explain. If we could crack this question, the solution might throw a light on something else—it might explain some one of the various unsolved mysteries of physical being, or structure, or something."

"Maybe you will be the one to track down this difference; it wouldn't surprise me at all."

"Succeed where Biot and Mitscherlich have failed? It would certainly be bold to expect that."

"I don't think so. But what a pity that work for your teaching examinations will keep you from concentrating on this problem!"

"Never fear, Charles, I'll come back to it—it fascinates me."

Charles looked at his friend's square-cut, rugged features, the expression of intelligence and disciplined imagination. "You know, Louis," he said seriously, "I expect you to become a great man."

Louis shrugged and smiled. "I don't care about being great, Charles. It will be enough for me if I am useful."

Not even Chappuis, who expected so much of his friend, could have imagined that, by solving this single small problem, Pasteur would open a whole new field to scientific investigation—that of stereochemistry, which deals with the arrangement of atoms and molecules in space; and that the answer to it would also serve as the starting point from which he would proceed to the solution of questions that had baffled the best minds in the long history of scientific thought. Years later, if he recalled the conversation, Chappuis must have smiled to think he had once asked: "Has it any practical importance?"

In addition to working for his teaching examinations, Pasteur found time to gratify the request of M. Romanet, who followed his old student's career with affectionate pride, that he select and obtain books on science and literature for the library of the Collège d'Arbois. Another extracurricular task he assumed was tutoring his father in mathematics so that he, in turn, could teach Josephine. Jean Joseph, as serious as his son about study, would sit up late nights working over the problems that Louis sent him, then the next day he would teach the newly learned lesson to Josephine. She still did not care to rack her brains, her father reported; nevertheless, she promised, he said, "that she would do everything to deserve the praise that you give her; one must admit that she has already given proof of some will."

Louis did not neglect his own work. With his characteristic passion for thoroughness and certainty, he conducted for himself experiments so long that they were merely described in class, with the result that Chappuis twitted him about being a "laboratory fixture." His showing in class was still something short of brilliant: when it came to taking the *licence* examination in August, 1845, he was seventh. His father, whose main anxiety continued to be his health, sensibly cared little about his making top marks, and said so; nor could he refrain from little homilies to the effect that eminence did not necessarily mean happiness. "In the practice of happiness, it [health] comes before everything. . . . I remain convinced that M. Romanet is more contented than the most learned of your Institute members who to maintain himself at the point he has reached must work night and day. But I believe," he added philosophically, "that on this point we are not in agreement."

They were not, indeed. To work day and night was Louis' idea of real satisfaction, and it was of just such satisfaction that his three years at the École normale were filled.

When, a year after the *licence*, he took the more advanced examinations for the agrégation, he was able to write Chappuis, by then the philosophy professor at Besançon, that of the four students who had passed he was third, and had been prevented from being second or even first only by having done badly in the natural history examination. His further news gave his friend much pleasure. Antoine Jérome Balard, the eminent chemist who lectured at the *École*, wanted him to stay in Paris as his laboratory assistant.

This gratifying plan of Balard's was almost upset by Pasteur's unexpected appointment to teach at Tournon; but Balard, a volatile southerner, made such vehement protests to the Minister of Public Instruction that the appointment was canceled. Triumphant, the professor installed his promising young protégé as curator of his laboratory in the fall of 1846.

CHAPTER FOUR

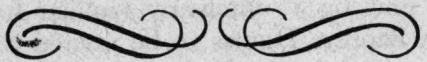

THE ÉCOLE NORMALE had by this time moved into its new quarters on the rue d'Ulm, although they were still unfinished. The building was large and handsome, reminding an English visitor of the colleges at Oxford and Cambridge. It had a chapel, a library, a beautifully neat garden, but its scientific equipment left much to be desired. While the students had laboratories for instruction in physics and chemistry, no provision had been made for research laboratories for the professors. They had to devise whatever makeshifts they could. Balard was struggling along with two tiny, ill-equipped rooms. He was so elated to have even that much, however, that he had set up a cot in one of them and often spent the night there rather than leave his precious work to go home to sleep. It was there that Pasteur pursued the researches that brought him his first scientific recognition.

The life of a student entirely devoted to science is usually a quiet one. Startling adventures have little place in it; both its excitements and its satisfactions are intellectual. Pasteur's life as Balard's curator was no exception. He worked early and late in the laboratory, grateful for the profitable experience of assisting the brilliant and still young scientist who, twenty years before, at the age of twenty-four, had earned a lasting reputation by his discovery of bromine.

By March, 1847, Pasteur had begun the theses for his doctorate, one in chemistry, and the other in physics, and his happiness in his work was unclouded. It increased, if possible, because of his increasing work with crystals. To become competent with the goniometer, an instrument for measuring angles, he began to study a series of easily crystallized combinations—tartaric acid and the tartrates. Ever since his first introduction to crystallography at the École normale he had loved it, and now he pursued this phase of it eagerly, keeping in mind the provocative problem surrounding tartaric and paratartaric, or racemic, acids.

He was by now on a sufficiently familiar footing with the celebrated Jean Baptiste Dumas to be invited to his Thursday evenings. He attended them with some regularity, mingling with students and professors and discussing with them topics of current interest in the scientific world. As for the theater Pasteur had so enjoyed during his early days in Paris, we hear no more about it—except from Jean Joseph, who wrote: ". . . follow the advice I give you not to run around the streets at night, skip the shows, read the plays, you will know them better than those who go to see them performed."

The advice not to run around the streets was, of course, superfluous. As always, Pasteur preferred more intellectual diversions. For his vacation, for instance, he dreamed of going to Germany with Chappuis for a month to learn German. Meanwhile he worked on his theses, the one in chemistry on the saturation capacity of arsenious acid, and the one in physics on an aspect of the rotary polarization of liquids. He dedicated them to his parents and, as soon as they were printed, sent them home, where they were received with a respectful admiration not at all dimmed by the fact that they were over their readers' heads. These first two scientific papers of his, although they won him his doctorate and were the source of a certain modest satisfaction to Pasteur, were also the cause of a great disappointment: the expense of printing them left him no money for his proposed trip to Germany. "I am more than ruined!" he lamented to Chappuis.

His father came to his rescue with two hundred francs. Perhaps, too, he raised Louis' spirits by reporting, a little later, that a local personage had told him: "Your son is in the finest position to make a brilliant marriage. . . . A refusal is not given to such young men except by fools." Louis had repeatedly said that he would not marry before he was thirty, however, so probably he was much more pleased by his father's own appreciation:

". . . for a long time, and ever, you have been all satisfaction to me."

His third scientific paper—he read it in March to the Academy of Sciences, one of the five learned societies that composed the academically exalted Institute of France—was, similarly, over the heads of his Arbois admirers. It was called "Researches on Dimorphism" and included a list, as complete as he could make it, of dimorphous substances—that is, substances which crystallize in two different ways, depending on the means by which they are melted or dissolved. M. Romanet, impressed and baffled, naïvely noted on the title page of the copy Pasteur sent him that dimorphism was a word not to be found even in the *Dictionnaire de l'Académie*, the standard French dictionary!

While Pasteur was quietly fitting himself for fame, Paris, rather less quietly, was working up to another revolution. The Bourbons' cousin, who had come to the throne in 1830 as Louis Philippe, had succeeded in the course of his eighteen years' reign in alienating almost all classes of the population. Working people, socialists and republicans felt cheated of the fruits of the 1830 revolution since it had deposed Charles X only to enthrone another ruler who had turned out to be almost as illiberal. Legitimists, who still hoped for a Bourbon restoration, despised this "citizen king" and plotted against him. Bonapartists—and there were many Frenchmen over whom the Emperor's name exerted an almost magical power—compared France's glory under Napoleon with her timidity under the July Monarchy and were ashamed. Only the rich *bourgeoisie*, whose manners ostentatiously and whose interests unaffectedly the king made his own, were really loyal to Louis Philippe. He himself had become increasingly conservative, and was by 1848 far out of touch with the majority of his subjects. Repressive measures were used against individuals, newspapers and groups critical of the government—measures which served, of course, only to breed more opposition. It did not at first occur to the king's ministers to forbid the device—banquets—by which republicans got around the ban on hostile political gatherings. When it did, in February, 1848, this one additional repression was all that it took to fan the smoldering resentment of the Paris populace into a hot blaze.

For the third time in two generations Parisians threw up their barricades and dragged down a monarchy. Louis Philippe fled to England, and France was through with him.

Pasteur, whose life revolved about the laboratory—"I am extremely happy here," he wrote Chappuis just a month before the February revolution, "and I attribute my happiness to the fact that I am at the laboratory every day studying chemistry" —still was far from indifferent to political events. He watched the moves of the provisional government and the birth of the Second Republic with an almost lyrical enthusiasm. He even joined the National Guard which was, he said, "full of ardor and ready to defend the Republic and make order respected. . . . They are beautiful and sublime doctrines which are unfolding here under our eyes . . . and if necessary I would fight with the greatest courage for the sacred cause of the Republic."

To this Jean Joseph, who had seen a revolution or two himself, replied heatedly: "If you owe something to order in Paris you owe a hundred thousand times more to your family, a fact of which nothing must make you lose sight." He had not reared a son with boundless love and care only to lose him in a street brawl incidental to some new political upheaval. Until the tension in the capital relaxed, his letters had a tone of almost frantic pleading: "I beg you, my dear child, do not leave your room. . . . One can let one's self be dragged along by imprudent friends, even by simple curiosity, and fall victim to an ill-considered move."

No theoretical patriot, Pasteur not only sacrificed his time and convenience by joining the National Guard, but he also contributed his entire savings—a hundred and fifty francs—to the republican cause. "That will show up some of our famous republicans hereabouts who would not, I believe, take two five-cent pieces out of their purses to save the Republic," Jean Joseph observed with satisfaction.

However much the events of 1848 stirred him as a patriot, Pasteur was in no danger of being distracted by politics from science. Even while the Second Republic was shakily establishing itself, he was working constantly in the crowded and inconvenient laboratory of the *École* with his goniometer, microscope, polarizing apparatus and crystals. He was, he felt with excitement, approaching the solution of the tartaric-paratartaric puzzle that had for so long held his interest.

He was intimately familiar, of course, with all the relevant literature on crystallography. He knew that the English astronomer, Sir John Herschel, had discovered that there was a relationship between a quartz crystal's rotary power and the dissymmetrical arrangement of the molecules composing the crystal— a dissymmetry expressing itself outwardly in the dissymmetrical shape of the crystal itself; and that there was, further, a relationship between the direction of the rotation and the direction of the dissymmetry. Pasteur was acquainted, too, with the work of Biot, who had found, by dissolving tartrate crystals, that the action of tartaric acid on polarized light was not due to the arrangement of the molecules in relation to each other—since that relationship was broken up by dissolving the crystals—but to the shape and constitution of the individual molecule itself. From these two earlier pieces of work, Pasteur guessed that in tartaric acid there must be some dissymmetry in the construction of the molecule, that is, in the arrangement of the atoms composing it. Close study of the tartrate crystals, he thought, might well yield some external indication of this inward dissymmetry.

In his intensive work measuring the crystals of the tartrates, Pasteur developed great skill, and he soon observed something which even Mitscherlich had perhaps not noticed, and had certainly not mentioned—the tartrate crystals, which deviated polarized light to the right, were dissymmetrical, or hemihedral. They had minute facets along one side of their edges which were not matched by corresponding facets along the opposite side of the edge. Tartrate crystals have a number of different aspects, all of them being more or less covered with facets cutting off their angles, and, in forming, fragments of one crystal may stick to another so that it is hard to know where one begins and the other leaves off; so this discovery of the tartrates' hemihedral, or dissymmetrical, form was in itself a very astute observation.

Studying the crystals of nineteen different tartrates, Pasteur found that the hemihedrism and the rotary power were in every case in the same direction—to the right. It was now clear that, in the tartrates, the dissymmetrical arrangement of the atoms composing the molecules expressed itself outwardly in the dissymmetry, or hemihedrism, of the crystals, and that hemihedrism and rotary power were always in the same direction. Therefore there was a direct relationship between the dissymmetry of the molecule and its rotary power.

Now Pasteur was ready to study the paratartrates. He suspected that Mitscherlich was wrong in asserting that the tartrate and paratartrate crystals were identical; there was probably some difference centering about the hemihedral facets. Careful examination showed that where the tartrates had a hemihedral facet on the right, the paratartrates had the same tiny facet—matched on the opposite side of the angle by one like it! In other words, the paratartrates—of which the solutions had no action on polarized light—were not hemihedral at all, but symmetrical.

This much Pasteur had foreseen, and he had been able to confirm his guess experimentally. Now he had a surprise: when he began working on the double paratartrates of soda-and-ammonia and soda-and-potash, he found that crystals were deposited in the mother liquor which were, unexpectedly, all dissymmetrical. Somewhat disconcerted, he set to work studying these new crystals, and quickly found that some were hemihedral to the right, others to the left.

His anticipation, as he reached this point after weeks of work, became almost oppressive. He hardly dared believe that he, a man of twenty-five, with only a few years of experience in crystallography, was on the point of solving the problem which had defied Mitscherlich's and old Biot's genius and experience. Painstakingly, he separated the crystals into left-handed and right-handed ones, and found that the right, in solution, deviated the plane of polarized light to the right, exactly like the natural tartaric acid of grapes. And the left-handed, just as he had dared to expect, turned the plane of light to the left.

The critical test was the last. Working with great deliberation, as much to control his mounting excitement as to insure against error, the young chemist measured out and mixed equal weights of the left-handed and right-handed crystals and placed them in an aqueous solution to dissolve. Hardly daring to breathe, he put the liquid in the polarizing apparatus. It had no effect on polarized light—the opposite rotary powers of the left-handed and the right-handed crystals had canceled each other out!

"I have it! I have it!" he shouted, and burst from his laboratory. In the hall he ran into another curator.

"Paratartaric! I have it!" he exclaimed, flinging his arms about him. "Come to the garden with me, monsieur! I am too excited to go back to my polariscope, but I must tell you about it!" Almost babbling in his excitement he dragged the astonished young man off into the garden, where he marched him back and forth in the spring dusk, overwhelming him with a torrent of explanation.

It was hours before he was calm enough to return to his laboratory. Looking down on the evidence of his long work, climaxed so happily by discovery, he thought of his friend at Besançon.

"Oh, if only Charles were here," he thought. "How I wish that he had taken up science. If we could work together, think what we might accomplish!" He was far from realizing it at the time, but he needed no partner to help him work a scientific revolution.

The journey to Arbois was a nightmare of apprehension to Pasteur, apprehension which, on his arrival, was sadly fulfilled. His mother was already dead. As soon as he had received word of her illness he had dropped everything and hurried home, but he had not been in time. The years of unending toil and willing self-sacrifice had not left her the strength to withstand the sudden attack of apoplexy.

The tannery seemed utterly changed to Louis. His father, always a quiet man, now was silent. Josephine and Virginie slipped around the house like tearful shadows. Émilie's dimmed mind was thrown pathetically into darker confusion by her mother's absence. Once or twice Louis caught his father looking at him sadly but without reproach, and realized that each had the same thought which neither dared express: that the terrible anxiety for her only son which had preyed on her ceaselessly during the recent revolution was largely responsible for Mme Pasteur's death. Louis' devotion to his mother had been intense, and for the second time in his life he found himself incapable of withstanding an overwhelming grief. It was several weeks before the thought of even his beloved crystals could arouse him.

While Pasteur was in retirement at Arbois, his name was being spread about in Paris scientific circles. Balard was loudly enthusiastic about the work Pasteur was doing in his laboratory. Members of the Academy of Sciences, gathered in the library of the Institute of France to read and gossip, listened to Balard with varying degrees of skepticism. It seemed unlikely that the modest young man, not yet twenty-six, who had recently read them a paper on dimorphism was *quite* as wonderful as Balard kept insisting.

Dumas, who had some acquaintance with Pasteur, listened without conviction to Balard's exuberant praises of his curator. Biot, old, dry and mildly misanthropic, was politely dubious.

"So you think, Balard, that this young prodigy of yours has solved the problem that Mitscherlich could not?" he said, cocking his gray head inquiringly.

"I am sure of it, monsieur!" Balard answered vehemently. "His solution is beyond question. Why, the boy is a genius!"

"It is hardly beyond question, when so many of us question it," Biot said with some asperity. The discussion had been long and was inconclusive; he was bored with it. "Send your M. Pasteur to me. I should like to go over his work myself."

"Very well, monsieur. And you will see!"

It was with some diffidence that Pasteur entered the elderly scientist's quarters at the Collège de France. He had written Biot asking him if he might repeat his demonstration for him, and Biot's letter bidding him come had been courteous but reserved. Now Biot's manner was the same.

"I will provide you with everything you need for your demonstration, M. Pasteur," he said, "since you are good enough to come here to show me your results privately."

"Thank you, monsieur," Pasteur said, but he realized perfectly that Biot's offer was at least as much of a precaution as a courtesy.

Biot's devotion to science and to scientific truth was rigorous, and for all he knew this young M. Pasteur might have achieved his "results" by sleight of hand or by innocent error. He intended to take no risk of being deceived, either by design or chance. So with his own hands he brought out soda and ammonia, and some paratartaric acid which, he knew from his own observation, was absolutely neutral to polarized light. After the three substances were mixed in a crystallizer, Biot put the jar where no one would disturb it.

"When crystallization begins to take place, I shall ask you to return," he said to Pasteur, almost warningly, in taking leave of him.

Now for the first time—and it was the first of many times—Pasteur went through one of those excruciating periods of waiting for his results to be verified by strict and impartial test. He was confident that he had made no slip; his own precision and self-criticism, he was sure, precluded accident. Yet, waking up suddenly in the middle of the night, he would anxiously ask himself if he could, conceivably, have left room for error, committed some slight carelessness that would invalidate all his findings. It was a weighty thing for a man of his age to subject himself to Biot's austere judgment, and fully realizing it, Pasteur tossed on his bed in anxious sleeplessness.

Fortunately, Biot did not keep him in suspense long. In two days crystallization began to take place, and when a number of crystals had taken shape he sent for Pasteur. Bringing out the jar in which the paratartaric crystals were forming, he offered it to Pasteur.

"And now, monsieur," he said, "continue."

Carefully Pasteur withdrew some of the best and largest of the crystals and wiped off the mother liquor, while Biot watched him closely.

"And now your microscope, M. Biot, if you please."

Biot uncovered his microscope, and Pasteur slipped a crystal under it and examined it for a moment. Then he straightened.

"This crystal, you will observe, monsieur, has the hemihedral facets I described to you along the right edges of its angles."

Biot peered into the instrument, twiddled it to adjust it, and studied the crystal carefully. "I do believe you are right."

Pasteur selected another crystal and put it under. "And this one has those facets along the left edges."

Soon he had separated the crystals into left- and right-handed.

"And it is your contention, is it, that the right-handed crystals will turn the plane of polarized light to the right, and the left to the left?" the old man asked.

"Yes, M. Biot, that has been my observation."

"Very well. Let me finish the experiment, and I will send for you when the crystals are dissolved."

Pasteur had some more anxious hours to get through before Biot again summoned him. This time when he reached the apartment in the Collège de France, Biot greeted him at the door and drew him quickly in.

"Both solutions are dissolved. Let us begin with the left-handed. That is the more interesting, since the right occurs in nature."

As he spoke he was getting out the solution and placing it in the polarizing apparatus.

"Now, monsieur, this is the critical test!"

Pasteur's heart was beating so hard he was sure it could be heard all over the room as Biot adjusted the apparatus. Then—one glance was enough! The deviation of polarized light to the left was so strong that there was not even need to measure it. His contention was established beyond further question!

The elderly savant turned to Pasteur and, grasping him by the arm, exclaimed in a trembling voice:

"My dear child! I have so loved science all my life that this makes my heart leap!"

Once convinced, Biot was wholehearted in his enthusiasm. For the next two or three weeks he and Pasteur worked together daily and, as Pasteur wrote Chappuis, Biot could think of nothing but the new facts so suddenly disclosed to him. He thought and talked of them so constantly, indeed, and with such eager excitement, that his wife more than once had to take Pasteur aside and beg him to change the subject; such intensity of feeling was not good for M. Biot.

Between the old scientist and the young one, so alike both in daring scientific imagination and in rigorous critical requirements, there developed a deep affection that was both to smooth Pasteur's way and to gladden Biot's last years.

CHAPTER FIVE

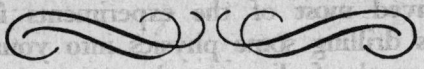

"I AM BORED at Dijon!" Pasteur wrote resentfully.

It was not remarkable. Although he was well qualified for a post in a more advanced institution, he had been appointed physics professor at the Dijon *lycée* at the end of the summer vacation. Biot and Balard were furious. Balard tried to have him made his assistant at the École normale; Biot railed against government officials who had no better sense than to waste such material as this gifted young chemist in a secondary school where he would be unable to pursue his researches.

"They are idiots!" he had exclaimed wrathfully. "Why, one or two more such beautiful discoveries, and you would find yourself in the Institute of France. Such studies are the most important thing you could pursue—and they send you to teach physics in a secondary school!"

"At least, monsieur, I have been allowed to report late at Dijon, so that I have had these weeks with you. That is something to be grateful for."

Biot's stern face had relaxed in a smile. Pasteur's passionate industry, his ardent love of science, and his personal character all had combined to dissipate completely, where he was concerned, the older man's misanthropy.

"It is something for *me* to be grateful for, my dear boy. To see my own researches climaxed by so brilliant a discovery—I can think of nothing but the new paths it opens up! The Dijon *lycée!* But don't worry. Your friends will not be idle in your absence, you may be sure of that. The Minister of Public Instruction will hear from us—frequently!"

At Dijon, Pasteur could only hope that his friends, as Biot had promised, were not being idle. Although it was a source of exasperation to him that his teaching schedule kept him from research, he gave conscientious attention to his lessons. He prepared them carefully in advance, striving for absolute clarity; and he devised a simple scheme to hold the attention of his too-large classes toward the end of the hour when it tended to wander—he saved most of the experiments for then. Even though he was drilling some physics into youthful heads, he could not escape the feeling that he was accomplishing little, and he longed for a change. He even thought of returning to Paris in his old capacity as Balard's curator, but his father, perhaps fearful of riots which might attend the forthcoming presidential election, persuaded him to remain at Dijon, with what patience he could muster, for a little longer.

His patience was not unduly strained. Early in January, 1849, the Minister of Public Instruction, responding to the pressure of Pasteur's friends, appointed the young man to the more advanced post of assistant professor of chemistry on the scientific faculty at the Academy of Strasbourg.

Pasteur liked everything about the ancient Alsatian capital. Not only was it full of those reminders of France's history which at once excited and gratified his lively patriotism, it was also, as the principal city of an industrial region, a center which offered many opportunities for chemical investigation. And it was not the city alone that pleased him. His lodgings, congenially, were with an old École normale friend, Pierre Augustin Bertin, now professor of physics at the academy, for whom he had a warm respect and affection. His classes, too, were a pleasure alike to him and his students, many of whom, the sons of local manufacturers, had a particular interest in the industrial applications of chemistry. Finally, like the rest of the faculty members, he was received cordially by the family of the rector of the academy, M. Laurent, a warmhearted and intelligent man whose ability and character made him generally admired. The provincial capital, in short, could offer attractions no less alluring than the national. M. Laurent's evenings "at home" ranked high among them, and the new chemistry teacher was soon attending them with suggestive regularity—M. Laurent had two unmarried daughters.

"What ideas you get in the provinces!" Pasteur wrote in a tone of surprise to Chappuis. "Here I am, thinking of getting married!" It had taken this young man, who was resolved not to marry until he was thirty, barely two weeks from the time of his arrival in Strasbourg to ask for the hand of Mlle Marie Laurent.

Naturally, Pasteur conducted his courtship in the French manner, but in his impulsive directness he short-circuited one of the conventions. He himself made his proposal to M. Laurent, instead of entrusting it to his father. Otherwise he was very correct. He set forth his family circumstances and his prospects to the rector; he consulted his own "*cher papa*"; when he wrote to Mlle Marie, he sent the letters to her mother, with the request that she deliver them for him.

In spite of the rather stately form of these negotiations, Pasteur was completely in turmoil. He had fallen in love with all the warmth of his openhearted and affectionate nature. He had one central thought—Marie—and a number of uneasy peripheral thoughts: what, in his modest and unimpressive exterior, was there that could please a gay young girl? might she not form an unfavorable first impression, to his eternal prejudice? if only he had a finer position in the world to offer! He begged Mme Laurent not to let her daughter judge him hastily because, as he said hopefully, since others who knew him well loved him well, perhaps Mlle Marie might too, in time.

By day he worked feverishly: he wrote to M. Kestner, the manufacturer who had first produced paratartaric acid, asking for some of the rare crystals for his continuing researches; he conducted his classes; he did all that his work required. But by night he lay awake and wept, tormented by the thought that Marie might never care for him.

His worry was excessive. There was nothing unpleasing about his appearance: he was a nice-looking young man of twenty-six, with spectacles, a fringe of whiskers all around his face, and a serious, kind expression. His position was promising: he had risen, by his own talent and industry alone, to a respectable scientific standing. As for his personal character, there was a kind of nobility about it which anyone who knew him at all well could recognize, and an appealing sensibility and ardor. Altogether, he was a better matrimonial prospect from a worldly point of view, and he was more attractive personally, than his modesty permitted him to realize; but in his anxiety he did not recall his well-wisher's opinion that only a fool would reject such a young man.

The Laurents were far from fools. Monsieur and Madame admired him, Marie found that she loved him, and his proposal was accepted. Pasteur walked on air. He felt that his personal happiness was assured, and, indeed, it was. He recovered his mental calm so promptly that, according to the story—and it is a story his wife did not deny—on his wedding day he had to be routed out of his laboratory and told to hurry or he would be late for the ceremony.

The marriage took place on May 29, 1849, at the Church of St. Madeleine in Strasbourg. A trip to Baden followed, where Pasteur and his wife were soon joined by her parents and unmarried sister; then the family returned together to Strasbourg, where Pasteur once more could apply himself with a quiet mind to his teaching and his beloved crystals.

Marie Pasteur, at twenty-three, had charm, kindliness, a gentle dignity—and but one aim in life: to make her Louis happy and advance his career. She had been brought up by her mother to be a thrifty and expert housekeeper, but that, she thought, was not enough under the circumstances—her husband needed a laboratory assistant.

"I want to study crystallography, too, Louis," she told him, "so that I can understand what you are doing, and be your assistant and secretary."

Pasteur joyfully welcomed her interest. "I will make you a reading list," he told her, "and at night, when I have finished work, I will hold private classes in crystallography, just for you."

Mme Pasteur was an enthusiastic and intelligent student, and the classes were so successful that she was soon able to qualify as her husband's assistant. Familiar with all the details of his researches, she worked with him in the laboratory and at night took notes as he dictated and copied his papers for him.

Biot, too, followed Pasteur's work closely; his interest and affection were so keen that he appointed himself Pasteur's mentor in all things having to do with his scientific career. He reviewed and criticized the young man's work; he scrutinized his scientific papers before publication; and, when Pasteur wrote an important one on the relationship between crystalline form, chemical composition and the direction of rotary polarization, Biot himself read it to the Academy of Sciences—prefacing it with such glowing remarks that, on reading them, "everyone here wept for joy, beginning with M. Laurent," as Pasteur wrote his father.

So that Biot could follow his researches without strain to his failing sight, Pasteur made large cork models of the crystals he was investigating, painted the critical facets, and sent them to his "venerable protector."

Biot was a severe as well as an affectionate protector. It was no part of his plan for his protégé that Pasteur should advance more rapidly than he deserved in the academic world, or receive honors too soon; all his efforts at this point should go into building his scientific reputation solidly and well. Biot therefore restrained him from applying for the vacant place in the general physics section of the Academy of Sciences because, while he was a brilliant innovator in chemistry, in physics he had used only known processes—it would be a mistake to strive for "a distinction which would be above your real and recognized claims." In every way that his unselfish devotion both to science and this young scientist could suggest, Biot watched over his career.

"I cannot tell you, my dear friend," Pasteur confided to Chappuis, "what a good adviser I have in M. Biot, what interest he takes in me. . . . I am too happy thus to have the esteem and friendship of such a fine intelligence and so fine a character."

He kept Chappuis abreast of his work, too, and often referred to his regret that his friend had not taken up science. "Why aren't you a professor of physics or chemistry! We would work together and in ten years would have turned chemistry upside down! There are marvels beneath the crystalline form, and through it the intimate constitution of bodies will one day be uncovered."

Although both his teaching and his research were progressing well, Pasteur's life was not without reverses. M. Laurent, his father-in-law, was ousted from his post for political reasons and, moving to Paris, retired from teaching rather than accept any of the inferior positions rather pointedly offered him. Then Pasteur's sister Josephine, whose education he had so affectionately supervised, died after months of pulmonary illness in November, 1850, leaving "*pauvre papa*" desolate, and her brother scarcely less so. Pasteur himself experienced what he called "*un petit chagrin d'amour-propre*" when the Cross of the Legion of Honor, which Dumas had asked the government to give him in recognition of his bold and ingenious pioneering work in the new field of stereochemistry, was withheld from him. In spite of such misfortunes, however, Pasteur could regard these Strasbourg years as happy ones: such exacting critics as Biot and Dumas were enthusiastic about his contributions to science; his domestic life was ideal; and his family was expanding—first a little girl, Jeanne, was born in April, 1850, and then a boy, Jean Baptiste, in November of the following year. Pasteur's joy at the birth of his son was made complete when his revered M. Biot consented to be godfather.

Between family and scientific demands, Pasteur had little attention to spare for current politics. But when Louis Napoleon Bonaparte, the Emperor's nephew, who had been elected President of the Second Republic, visited Strasbourg, Pasteur, something of a Bonapartist by inheritance, was enough interested in seeing him to tell his wife he would take her to the official parade. When the hour came, however, the laboratory exerted a stronger attraction than the politician. Mme Pasteur waited patiently all afternoon, and it was not until evening, at his customary hour, that Pasteur appeared.

"Louis, *where* have you been? You were going to take me to the parade."

"At my laboratory. I am sorry, but it could not be helped. I could not interrupt my experiments, could I?"

It speaks for both her good humor and her interest in her husband's work that Mme Pasteur wholeheartedly agreed that to interrupt the experiments would have been unthinkable.

A little later, Pasteur mentioned to Chappuis and to his

staunch old Bonapartist father that he was pleased by the *coup d'état* after which, in 1852, Louis Napoleon became Napoleon III, ruler of the Second Empire which replaced the short-lived Republic. Pasteur foresaw, hopefully, a fine future for his country with another Bonaparte at its head; the disasters it held failed to present themselves to his patriotic imagination.

CHAPTER SIX

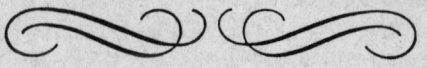

It was M. Biot's custom to take a daily stroll around the Luxembourg Gardens. On an August morning in 1852 the severe old man, so warm and so affectionate with Pasteur, was plotting an agreeable surprise for his friend. Mitscherlich himself, and his assistant, were in Paris, and Biot had arranged for Pasteur to meet them at his apartment and demonstrate some of his work for them. When he came to the Hôtel Joseph II, rue de Tournon, where Pasteur was spending a part of his vacation, he stepped inside and left him a note. Then the tall, stooped old savant resumed his walk, reflecting, as he often did, on the unexpected happiness that this young man, whose love of science was as ardent and disinterested as his own, was bringing into the final years of his life.

"What I gave them in silver, they returned to me in gold!" Pasteur exclaimed of his interview with the German scientists. They had arrived at Biot's apartment about ten in the morning, and had spent more than two hours discussing his work with Pasteur and examining his crystals. They had been astonished and delighted with his work, and they made no secret of it.

"Perhaps you have already heard, M. Pasteur, that the elusive racemic acid has put in another appearance?"

"No! Where? Who is getting it?"

"A manufacturer of tartaric acid near Leipzig, a man named Fikentscher. He thinks it comes from Trieste."

All Pasteur's considerable scientific ardor was fired. More of this remarkable stuff! And now the possibility of running it down to its source, of investigating on the spot the tartrates in which it was appearing, of studying both the type of grape that gave them, and the other acid fruits of the region! It was an irresistible prospect.

As soon as the Germans had taken their leave, Pasteur rushed to his father-in-law's house, where his wife and children were staying, and told Marie. Then he sat down and dashed off a long letter to Biot, who had gone to Auxerre, pouring out his plans, his hopes, his hesitation. The hesitation was caused by the thought of the expenses involved. Ever since his marriage his expenditures had exceeded his salary—not because he was extravagant but because the funds allowed by the government for his laboratory and researches were wretchedly inadequate and he had to supplement them out of his own pocket—and his wife, very naturally, was unwilling that he should undertake a trip of indefinite length at his own expense. Maybe the Minister of Public Instruction would finance him, he suggested excitedly to Biot—after all, the government ought to make it a point of honor to have a Frenchman solve this problem. Or maybe the Academy of Sciences would provide him with the money. Or, better yet, how about applying directly to Napoleon? What did M. Biot think?

M. Biot's reply was immediate, soothing and sobering. There was hardly need to set the Academy and the whole government in motion to obtain a thousand francs or so, he said mildly, and outlined the more modest steps he thought Pasteur should take. Dumas, as interested as Biot in seeing that Pasteur was enabled to go, asked the Minister of Public Instruction to finance the journey. Two weeks went by, while Pasteur seethed with impatience. The Minister finally said that he had no funds for such a purpose. Pasteur, utterly irritated by the delay and by the prospect of being entrapped in further red tape, decided to set off at his own expense, relying on the word of Dumas and Biot that they would see to it that he was reimbursed.

Intent though he was on reaching his objective, the factory of Herr Fikentscher at Zwickau, Pasteur was not too preoccupied to enjoy his first impressions of Germany. He was impressed by the beauty of the Rhine at Cologne; he reported that Hanover was a very fine city, Magdeburg a very curious one. The German trains were excellent, the second-class carriages being better than the first-class on French trains. Furthermore, he added with a touch of pride, he had not lost the least little thing during the whole journey, and that was saying a lot, what with all the changes and waits, and not knowing the language. When he reached Leipzig he did not even pause, but hurried straight on to Zwickau, registered at a hotel, and presented himself at Herr Fikentscher's factory. Just three weeks had elapsed since his interview with Mitscherlich.

He was fortunate in finding in Herr Fikentscher an intelligent man, and one who was entirely willing to expose to him all the processes of his factory. He was rather less fortunate in what he learned.

"We get very little paratartaric acid now," Fikentscher told him, "so little that we do not trouble to collect and keep it. It was about twenty-two years ago, when we were getting our tartrates from Trieste, in crude form, that we obtained it in quantity. I still have several pounds of the crystals left, incidentally, and I hope that you will accept a sample from me for your studies."

"I shall be happy to. You are very generous. But where are you now obtaining your tartrates?"

"They now come from Italy and Austria, and have already undergone one refining process before we receive them."

"One might guess, then, that the crystallization involved in the refining process eliminates the paratartaric acid, which, perhaps, remains in the mother liquor. Is there a laboratory connected with your plant, or in Zwickau, where I can examine samples of your tartrates?"

"Unfortunately, no, but you can surely use one at the University of Leipzig. No doubt the chemistry professor, Herr Erdmann, will place his at your disposal."

Pasteur looked doubtful. "I am a stranger to the gentlemen of the university."

"Indeed you are not, monsieur! They know your work well. Professor Hankel, the physics professor, has translated all your papers into German for a treatise that Professor Erdmann wrote."

It was as Herr Fikentscher said. The Leipzig professors welcomed Pasteur with interest, and Professor Erdmann lent him his laboratory, which was so well equipped—so far better equipped than anything Pasteur was accustomed to in his own country—that he called it magnificent. For days Pasteur worked intensively in the laboratory over Fikentscher's samples, seeing no more of the city than the street which led from his hotel to the university. Long letters to his wife kept her acquainted with the state of his work, but the loving family man was never submerged in the scientist. Had Jeanne's cold cleared up? And how were little Baptiste's teeth coming along? He had plans, now, for going to Venice, where there was a tartrate refinery, to see if racemic acid was left in the mother liquor after the first refining process; and he hoped, by practicing economies in his living expenses, to be able to afford some *point de Venise,* or perhaps a pretty coral pin, for his Marie—who had forgotten to pack a steel pen for him, so that he was having to scratch along with an old and abominable hotel pen. His enthusiasm was almost equally divided between his family and his pursuit—"yours and Science's for life," he closed one letter—and there was plenty for both.

After a little more than a week in Leipzig, Pasteur was on his way again, pursuing the trail of paratartaric acid to the south. He threatened to spend ten years looking for it, if necessary. By September 26 he was in Vienna, and, escorted by a well-known scientific man of the city, M. Redtenbacher, he visited two tartaric acid factories. There he got further confirmation of his theory: they had begun to operate with crude tartar about two years before—previous to that they had used tartrates which had undergone one refining process—and for about two years they had been getting a troublesome substance which they took for sulphate of potash. Pasteur promptly identified it as racemic acid crystals. He now felt reasonably certain that it was in the refining process that the tartrates lost their racemic acid. His trip was proving, to his satisfaction, to be very profitable.

He not only discovered paratartaric acid in Vienna, he also discovered the Viennese, and he was almost as charmed with his social find as with his scientific. The officers, the most handsome and elegant men he had ever seen, wore "bewitching" uniforms; the citizens had beautiful manners; and when he asked his way on the street he was answered in good French and with great amiability. It was quite a contrast to the French who, he said, were full of prejudices against foreigners and ridiculed their tastes, their manners, their civilization. This apparently reminded him, for he added:

"Don't tell my father too much of what I am doing. . . . He would be in torment if he dreamed I was so far from the beautiful land of France."

He gave up his plan to visit Venice, because a former student of M. Redtenbacher's offered to collect for him the information there that he had planned to get for himself, and went instead to Prague, where there was a large tartaric acid factory. There the chemist in charge, another old student of M. Redtenbacher's, confounded him for a moment with the news that he had been making paratartaric acid from tartaric for seven years. Pasteur thought such a transformation impossible in the current state of chemistry, and politely said so. He turned out to be quite right: the chemist had not obtained racemic acid from pure tartaric acid, he had merely been obtaining it in the same way that all the other manufacturers Pasteur had visited had obtained it, only he had been carried away by his enthusiasm—and by the fact that the Paris Pharmaceutical Society had offered a prize to whomever succeeded in manufacturing the one from the other. Pasteur by now was almost sure that racemic acid was formed in the mother liquor which remained after the refinement of crude tartrates. He was ready to go home.

After the scientific search came a domestic one: Pasteur had to go house hunting, since his family by now required more spacious quarters. Mme Pasteur was still at her parents' home in Paris with the children, but Pasteur had Chappuis, recently married and transferred to Strasbourg, to help him. The two friends combed the town without finding anything, possibly because they had so much to discuss after their separation that they found it hard to keep their minds on so practical and tedious a business as looking for lodgings. Eventually it was another friend who found something suitable for Pasteur, and he summoned his wife to join him. Because of the expense, he did not go to Paris to get her and the children, but he swamped her with traveling instructions: *"I expressly command you to take an express train, and travel first class. . . . Above all, take plenty of coats and covers. The nights are extremely cold. Mind your feet.* If you are cold when you arrive, I shall send you back."

With Mme Pasteur arrived to put their new home in order, just one more nonscientific task remained to her husband. It was to mollify *"cher papa,"* who had been greatly displeased by his son's foreign junket. The old soldier's only dealings with foreigners had been with the hostile Spanish guerrillas in the Pyrenees, and with his Emperor's enemies at Bar-sur-Aube. So far as he was concerned, what was not French was barbaric. Pasteur explained the importance and the success of his trip, and assured his father that he had been in truly civilized countries where he had enjoyed comforts and courtesies, and had made acquaintances both pleasant and useful. He added, however, in affectionate sympathy:

"But then, I understand you so much the better since I was made, or rather since you made me, in your image. There are days when you are annoyed, when you take the vexations of life hard. Well, I am the same way. . . ." But were the successes of his son nothing to him? ". . . great names know yours, and are made uneasy by it. If you persist in regarding all that as nothing . . . I will go to the laboratory to try to lift a new corner of the veil with which God has covered all His works. That will lead, perhaps, to successes . . . which will make you proud and happy."

Now it was possible to turn back to science. His work on racemic acid had so far led to these discoveries: that there was a correlation between the dissymmetrical arrangement of a molecule's atoms and its rotary power; that racemic acid, neutral toward polarized light, could be broken down into two acids, a dextro-rotary tartaric acid identical in all respects with the tartaric acid found in nature, and a laevo-rotary acid which was very similar to tartaric and differed from it in that it rotated polarized light to the left instead of to the right. One could also assume that the arrangement of the atoms forming the molecules of this second acid was the mirror image of those forming the molecules of tartaric acid, just as the arrangement of the fingers on one's left hand is the mirror image of the arrangement of those on one's right. He had concluded, further, as a result of his German trip, that racemic acid was formed in the mother liquor left after the first refining process, one of crystallization, of crude tartrates.

Now he wrote M. Kestner of Thann, the manufacturer who had first discovered racemic acid, urging him to take the necessary steps to prove this surmise. ("Racemic acid is your baby. You cannot abandon it.") M. Kestner, greatly interested in the problem, did as Pasteur asked and confirmed his conclusion in a letter to the Academy of Sciences in December. Pasteur himself, at Biot's urgent request, wrote an account of the results of his German trip, and Biot read both communications to the Academy early in January, 1853.

Each bit of ground gained led Pasteur, naturally, to further explorations into the chemical mysteries which so fascinated him. Just as he had hoped, new efforts led to new success. In May, 1853, he succeeded after long experimentation in converting tartaric acid into racemic by heating it.

He immediately telegraphed his big news to Biot. Biot, ever watchful of his protégé's reputation, withheld the announcement until he was convinced by several more detailed communications from Pasteur that there was no ambiguity, that he had actually transformed ordinary tartaric acid, absolutely pure and free of racemic, into racemic which was identical in all its chemical and physical properties with natural racemic acid. On June 6, Biot, gratified to the bottom of his heart, arose in the meeting of the Academy of Sciences and astounded its members with the announcement of this new triumph of his young friend's.

This piece of work finally won the Cross of the Legion of Honor for Pasteur. His father, completely dismissing his grudge against racemic acid for luring his son on a long excursion abroad, was in an ecstasy. He wrote an ardent letter to Biot thanking him for his part in securing it. Biot, characteristically, replied that a scientist's real distinction depended only on himself, not on the neglect or favor of a minister, and that, for the rest, the admission of Louis Pasteur to the Legion had honored the order more than the man.

A more practical reward was the fifteen hundred francs which the Paris Pharmaceutical Society had offered as a prize for the transformation of tartaric acid into paratartaric. Pasteur spent half of it on equipment for his uncomfortable and unhealthy laboratory at the Strasbourg Academy, but did not long enjoy his improved working conditions. A new baby, Cécile, had been born in October, then they had had to move again, and, in addition to the strain and anxiety of these domestic matters, Pasteur, as always, had been overworking. He ended by becoming so ill his family and colleagues were thoroughly frightened. It was necessary for him to take a long leave, and he was fortunate enough to get it with full pay, although a substitute had to be engaged to replace him on the Strasbourg faculty.

Early in 1854 the Pasteur family went to Paris and took lodgings near the Luxembourg Gardens. Pasteur, who refused to be alarmed about himself, passed the time pleasantly and restfully. He worked for a few hours each day with Biot, he attended Dumas' lectures "to learn how to teach," and he spent an hour or so daily, as he had once done with Chappuis, strolling with his wife and children in the gardens. Although his health improved slowly, he was obliged to ask the Minister of Public Instruction to extend his leave until the summer vacation. He offered, at the same time, to return to give examinations "so as not to increase the inconvenience of the faculty"—and, as he admitted to his father, "also not to let fall to someone else a sum of six or seven hundred francs" which was the examiner's fee. The salary of a professor was not so lavish that one with three children could afford to let such an amount escape him.

He could, however, let honors escape, when there was a question of tact and kindness involved. A corresponding membership in the chemistry section of the Academy of Sciences was open, and Pasteur decided to be a candidate for it. It was customary for candidates to make personal calls on members of the section to enlist their support. Pasteur began with Dumas.

Dumas received him with his customary suavity, but Pasteur, as he explained his errand, thought he detected a certain reserve.

"You seem doubtful, M. Dumas."

"I will be frank with you, my friend. I very much regret, on M. Malaguti's account, that you have decided to present yourself for this vacancy. You are almost certain to win, and that means that he will be defeated."

"I must confess that I have felt some reluctance to compete with a man who was a well-known chemist when I was still a schoolboy."

"If you defeat him—and, I repeat, it is practically certain that you will—it will be a real misfortune for him, not—as it would be for you—merely the failure to receive an unnecessary honor. He is very much fatigued by teaching, and I am hoping to get him into an administrative post—rector of Rennes, perhaps. You can readily see that this membership would enhance his reputation and be valuable to him, whereas you, who have recently received the Cross and a prize, have no need of fresh honors."

"You are entirely right, monsieur. I had not thought of it in that light. I shall withdraw my candidacy at once."

"That is good of you!" Dumas nodded approvingly "But you can still try for the vacancy in the physics section, you know."

"No, M. Biot is opposed to it. While I use physics in my work, I am first of all a chemist, and he thinks that it is on my merits as a chemist that I should apply to the Academy."

"There is reason in that. But have no doubt of it, my dear Pasteur—you will reach the Academy soon enough, in any case, with your ability. Meanwhile, you have done M. Malaguti a great service and," he clasped him cordially by the hand, "you have given fresh evidence of the goodness and sensibility which M. Biot and I have learned to expect of you."

By September Pasteur's health was restored, and he took his family to Arbois to visit his father and his sister Virginie, who by now was married and had two children. He had, meanwhile, been notified that he was to be dean and professor of chemistry on the newly organized Faculty of Sciences at Lille. His Strasbourg life, which had been on the whole both happy and successful, was over. So, although he did not know it, was the work he so loved with crystals. He was about to be diverted from it into new fields of research where he would achieve results which, in time, would have a profound and fruitful influence on medical science by replacing faulty concepts of contagious disease with true ones.

CHAPTER SEVEN

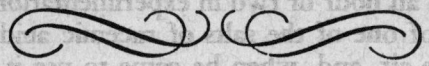

PASTEUR had taken great pains with his address. The students and teachers who heard him deliver it on December 7, 1854, at the opening ceremonies of the new Faculty of Sciences at Lille, received it with polite applause. Perhaps a few of the most perceptive among them suspected that the earnest and unassuming young dean who spoke to them was destined for greatness; they may even have guessed that one of the phrases he used that day was to have its own immortality: "Chance favors only the mind which is prepared."

It was almost two years before Pasteur himself was beautifully to demonstrate the truth of his statement.

Meanwhile, he attended to his new duties with his usual energy and efficiency, and the school flourished under his stimulus. Between two hundred and fifty and three hundred students, many of them the sons of local manufacturers, attended Pasteur's most popular lectures, and a score of boys were enrolled for his laboratory course which supplemented the lectures. In addition to carrying his administrative, teaching and research work, Pasteur also took his students on trips to factories, foundries and distilleries in the region, so that they could see for themselves the industrial applications of the chemical processes they were learning in the laboratory. He undertook, too, to test manures for the Department of the Nord, an extensive and important piece of work in that rich agricultural section. The Minister of Public Instruction was so pleased with the way the young man he had selected as dean was discharging his duties both to the school and the community it was intended to serve that he wrote the rector of the faculty a congratulatory letter especially commending M. Pasteur, who "justifies more and more the hopes I had placed in him."

In the evenings after supper, when the children had been put to bed, Pasteur, often accompanied by his wife, would descend from his apartment on the first floor of the school to the meagerly equipped laboratory directly beneath it on the ground floor and spend an hour or two in experimentation. He had once left a solution of one of the salts of racemic acid exposed for a few days to the air, and, when he came to use it, he had found it fermented. Even so trifling an accident as the spoiling of a beaker of racemic acid salts interested Pasteur, and he had examined the fermented material. He saw that it was only the dextrotartaric acid that had fermented; the laevo-tartaric remained unchanged in the solution. In the summer of 1856, while he was experimenting along the lines suggested to him by this strange observation, chance, in the person of a M. Bigo, presented itself to him and diverted—one might almost say wrenched—his whole attention over to the intensive study of the phenomenon of fermentation itself.

M. Bigo manufactured alcohol from beets. His factory was in Lille, and his son was one of Pasteur's students. When, during that summer, something went wrong with his manufacturing process—which of course involved fermentation—it was natural that he should consult the clever young chemist of whom his son spoke so admiringly. Pasteur, glad to be of service to him and attracted by the prospect of studying more deeply the then mysterious process of fermentation, readily agreed to investigate his failure.

Fermentation was a process widely used since very early times, but it was still little understood. Makers of wine and beer were among those whose products were a result of it. When fermentation proceeded normally, the beer and the wine would be good; when something went wrong with it, they would turn out bad. No one could explain this "something" or guard against it. Chemists, good ones, had studied fermentation, but none had succeeded in demonstrating its real character. Cagniard-Latour, some years before, had made the shrewd observation that the yeast causing the fermentation of beer was composed of cells that reproduced by budding, and he had suggested that it might be an effect of their growth that transformed sugar into alcohol. This opinion had received little support. On the other hand, a German chemist named Justus von Liebig held, and skilfully supported, an entirely different view. Fermentation, he said, was a phenomenon connected with decomposition: the yeast causing alcoholic fermentation was not growing but dead, and, as it decomposed, its molecules ruptured and set off a similar action among the molecules of the substance into which it had been introduced. The broken up molecules of that substance then regrouped themselves to form alcohol, and there you had the fermented end product—wine, beer or whatever. This was the view on fermentation which prevailed among mid-nineteenth-century chemists and which was taught in all the chemistry textbooks. It was quite wrong.

It was through his discovery of the real nature of fermentation that Pasteur was able to throw the first effective light on the cause and transmission of contagious diseases; so it is interesting to note that the theory had been cropping up, off and on, for several hundred years, that there was a connection, or rather a similarity, between the processes of fermentation and those of contagion. Among others who early suggested the idea was a sixteenth-century Italian physician, Frascatorius, who—more than a century before Leeuwenhoek first saw bacteria through a microscope—speculated that contagious diseases were spread by "seeds of contagion," invisible and living, which passed from sick to well to set up the disease process in the healthy body. A theory, however, has to have a certain amount of currency and credence to have any influence. This one of Frascatorius', resting as it did on logical speculation rather than scientific demonstration, had neither. About all it did have was curiosity value—and a sort of premonitory germ of truth.

Wholeheartedly interested in his investigation into the cause of M. Bigo's reverses, Pasteur passed day after day at the factory, thoroughly familiarizing himself with it and studying all its processes with the greatest care. In the evenings he would go downstairs to his laboratory and make prolonged microscopic examinations of samples of juice in various stages of fermentation which he had brought home with him. "Louis is now plunged up to his neck in beet juice," his wife philosophically wrote his father.

It was not long before he made an observation: as long as the fermentation was normal, he found, the yeast globules were round; when it began to go bad, they began to lengthen out; and when it had spoiled they were definitely elongated. By keeping track of the progress of the fermentation by frequent microscopic examinations it was possible to predict the outcome accurately, and by selecting healthy round globules to start new fermentations, it was a simple matter to avert failures. Now M. Bigo's problem was solved, and Pasteur was too interested in the larger chemical problems involved to abandon this line of investigation.

His work was not allowed to proceed without interruptions. The first, an agreeable one, was brief: the London Royal Society presented him with the Rumford Medal and a prize of 1,750 francs—an amount which made him feel gloriously solvent—for his work in crystallography. The other, brought about by his renewed candidacy to the Academy of Sciences, was a much less happy affair, although he tried to put a good face on it.

A vacancy had occurred in the mineralogy section of the Academy, and Biot and Dumas, considering that Pasteur's work in crystallography made him an appropriate candidate, urged him to enter the running. It was therefore necessary for him to go to Paris during the winter of 1856 and again the following spring to see members of the Academy and to press his candidacy. This kind of electioneering, although expected of all aspirants to the learned society, was entirely repugnant to Pasteur, and he had a miserable time. He entered into the competition with some energy, however, and even made a greater effort than he might have otherwise, because he felt that his leading rival—who, incidentally, was a former teacher of his—was undeserving of election. He had made little in the way of original contributions to science and was, in fact, rather a lazy man. It irked the hard-working and fresh-minded Pasteur to see him supported by "all the mediocrities" who, out of timidity or jealousy or stupidity, were snubbing his own much more important work. As the defeat of his candidacy began to seem more and more likely to him, he wrote to his wife in a tone of anger that belied his words: "I assure you that this failure means absolutely nothing to me. . . . This Academy, on the whole, is a shop, and what should I care whether I get in it or don't get in it." He needed thirty votes to be elected, thought he could count on twenty, and, when the election was finally held in mid-March, received only sixteen.

The expedition to Paris had not, however, been entirely without satisfactions. His work had been brought to wider attention in scientific circles; the minority which supported him had, he was gratified to know, comprised all the most eminent among the Academicians—and he had had the opportunity to witness one of the crowning honors of Biot's life, his admission into the French Academy. In spite of his sour-grapes remark about the Academy of Sciences, Pasteur had absolutely no cynicism about public honors; he took them literally and seriously, so just as he was chagrined by his own defeat he rejoiced over the success of his aged friend.

Determined to show the Academicians what a mistake they had made in rejecting his candidacy, Pasteur returned home burning with eagerness to get back to his fermentations. He was approaching the subject in a way entirely different from that of his contemporaries, a way made possible and even necessary by his long experience with substances having rotary power. There occurs as a by-product of various fermentations a substance having rotary power called amyl alcohol, and Pasteur became interested in that. Now in the contemporary view, as we know, fermentation was brought about by the decay of molecules, by their breaking up so that their debris formed new molecular structures which were the products of fermentation. According to that theory, the amyl alcohol's molecular structure must have been part of the framework of the sugar molecule. But, on examining amyl alcohol, Pasteur came to realize, for technical reasons, that it could not be a derivative of sugar. Yet all substances having rotary power, he believed at this time, were products of life, or cellular activity, rather than of death and decomposition; so the amyl alcohol must be, too. The first of these assumptions was wrong, but it led him in the right direction. Perhaps, he speculated, some living organism intervened between the sugar and the amyl alcohol. At this point Pasteur found himself led to think of fermentation as a vital act, and of ferments as living, growing organisms, not dead and decaying ones. It was his knowledge of crystallography, involving as it did knowledge of molecular structure and of the properties of rotary substances, that had enabled him to make his way to this conclusion.

Now that he had formed the theory that fermentation was a process "correlative with life," as he put it, he had to demonstrate it scientifically. He must sometimes have asked himself if it really was possible for him to fathom this difficult phenomenon which even the learned M. Dumas had called "strange and obscure." For months he worked in his laboratory day and night. When his wife, ever anxious about his overstrained health, persuaded him to leave his test tubes he would go on thinking about the problem, clarifying his ideas by expressing them to her, and dictating notes to her on the day's work.

Not all fermentations are alcoholic, that is, result in the formation of alcohol. That of butter is butyric; that of milk, lactic, etc. Pasteur, while working simultaneously on alcoholic and lactic fermentations, devoted his first written work to lactic, and for good reason. Liebig and his followers had practically admitted that yeast was necessary to alcoholic fermentation—if only to set it off—and that it might even be a living organism, but their most difficult argument to answer was: even so, what role can you possibly assign to this yeast, when related fermentations, such as lactic, proceed without yeast or anything that resembles it? Pasteur wanted to show that, contrary to Liebig's contention, there actually was a living organism in lactic fermentation analogous to the living organism—yeast—in alcoholic fermentation.

In his work on this fermentation Pasteur proved, as he was often to demonstrate again, that he was a more ingenious experimenter, a more astute observer and a more critical thinker about what he observed than his contradicters. Liebig and his school, thinking that the matter—cheese, let us say—in which lactic fermentation was going on was itself the ferment, had not been able to separate out the true ferment from the debris of decomposition. Pasteur, believing that the cheese was *food* for the ferment, conceived the idea of trying to identify the ferment and grow it in clear bouillon on which it could feed and in which he would be able to see it as it grew. Carefully he analyzed material in which lactic fermentation was taking place, and after some experimentation selected a certain organism as the probable ferment and set it to grow in bouillon. The upshot of his work was that he got a grayish deposit on the bottom of his flasks which he was able to identify as the lactic ferment. It was a homogeneous stuff, all the individuals of it resembling each other; it reproduced itself; with it he could start lactic fermentation in milk, bouillon or any other medium congenial to it. What yeast was to alcoholic fermentation, this newly discovered organism was to lactic fermentation. These two fermentations were plainly the result of the normal growth of living organisms, and each was caused by its specific organism. Why could it not be that *every* ferment was caused by its own specific organism?

Pasteur summed up his months of work, compressed his epoch-making conclusions, into a modest little paper about fifteen pages long which he called *Mémoire sur la fermentation appellée lactique*. With deceptive nonchalance, he tossed what he knew to be his bombshell into the scientific world, presenting it, tactfully, before the Lille Scientific Society in August, 1857.

This time he disregarded the advice that Biot had on an earlier occasion given him about including speculations in a scientific paper. With the calm boldness of a man secure in his facts and his logic, he confidently stated that fermentation was a process "correlative with life," and the still undemonstrated propositions that a specific ferment is the cause of each fermentation and that two living organisms can invade the same medium and engage in a death struggle in which the one best adapted to survive in the medium will be victorious. These ideas offered so calmly—so almost carelessly—foreshadowed the development of the new medicine.

This paper, and these ideas, naturally did not work any overnight transformation in scientific thought. The implications were too vast to be glimpsed, let alone grasped or developed, quickly; and the mode of thinking was so radically different from the prevailing one that it aroused hostility among that large group which prefers the security of old beliefs—however inaccurate—to the discomfort of adjusting to newly discovered truths. Sir William Osler, the great Canadian physician and scholar, has remarked that, when he was a student more than a decade later, Liebig's theory of fermentation was still being very fully presented in the chemistry lectures he attended. By that time, on the other hand, the Scotch surgeon Lister was already acting on the ideas suggested to him by the reading of this short paper of Pasteur's and practicing that antiseptic method which was to reform surgery.

As for Pasteur, discovery was not the novelty it had been to him at twenty-five—nor was it the climax. He knew instead that it was not the end but the beginning of a long, difficult way. To anyone who congratulated him on his new work, he conscientiously replied: "It is only a beginning."

One might have thought that the tasks of following such researches and of teaching and administration would be quite enough for Pasteur. He saw another one which needed attention, however, and offered to assume it. The École normale had been deteriorating for some years and had quite lost its eminent place in France's educational system. Its graduates were considered fit, by this time, to teach only in secondary schools. Pasteur, whose loyalty to his old school was intense, was distressed by its condition and felt it should be the first concern of the government to restore it to its former position. Its administration was undergoing a change so, although he was not sure that he was acting in the best interests of his scientific career, he offered his services to the school "in a modest position." The authorities snapped up his offer and made him administrator of the whole school and director of the scientific studies.

The kind of general administration entrusted to him included a rather staggering range of duties, among them supervising all economic and hygienic affairs connected with the school, and maintaining contact with the families of all the students. There was nothing about Pasteur of the absent-minded professor or the scientist incompetent in the practical affairs of the world. The minute care he brought to his scientific work he also applied to seeing that the school, down to its least details, was maintained in good running order. He was kept very busy, and work that he could not find time for in the day he would take home and, surrounded by his wife and children, he would finish it in the evening.

For the second time, Biot was angry that the authorities were putting the talents of his protégé—although by now, in fact, Pasteur had about outgrown the dependence the word implies—to pedestrian uses. His indignation was not softened when he heard of the kind of research facilities with which Pasteur was having to satisfy himself.

"Two rooms in the attic!" the old man—he was now eighty-five—exploded. "When will the government get it through its head that science is all-important? When will it stop this stingy, stupid practice of cooping up our best scientific men in noxious little dens to work? I could name you half a dozen—among them our incomparable Claude Bernard—whose health is being injured by work in damp cellars and ill-heated garrets. Dumas simply refuses to use his wretched little corner at the Sorbonne —but then, he had a father-in-law to give him a house which he has equipped as a laboratory. Sainte-Claire Deville for six years, ever since he replaced Balard at the *École*, has had to manage with those miserable, ill-equipped little rooms where you did your first work on tartrates. You cannot name a single French scientist who has acceptable equipment unless, like Dumas, he has provided it out of his own means!"

"Sainte-Claire Deville's situation is enviable compared to mine," Pasteur said with a sigh. "As for my two rooms under the eaves, only the rats wanted them—that's how I was able to get them. It is lucky that for my present work I don't need much equipment—a few measuring instruments, a microscope, some common chemicals and some glassware, because I've had to pay for them myself; the Minister of Public Instruction still cannot provide money for furnishing research laboratories. He can't even let me have a laboratory attendant."

"Well, my dear boy, I know you, and I know you will not allow yourself to become discouraged. And," Biot added grimly, "some day France's neglect of her best scientists will be recognized as a national disgrace—and a national danger!"

Inadequate and uncomfortable as his attic laboratory was, and pressed as Pasteur was by all his duties, he still succeeded in devoting a large fraction of his time to his research. He regularly toiled up the five dusty flights of stairs to continue his experiments on alcoholic fermentation, and by December he was ready to present to the Academy of Sciences his *Mémoire sur la fermentation appellée alcoolique*. Embodying experiments of great ingenuity, it established that alcoholic fermentation was a process, much more complex than chemists had theretofore realized, resulting from the healthy life and growth of the yeast, and corroborating his earlier conclusion that fermentation was a process of life rather than of decomposition.

CHAPTER EIGHT

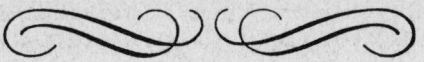

SETTLED in the suite in the École normale which was to be their home for the next three decades, the Pasteurs soon established a routine of life which changed little during the succeeding years. Pasteur rose early, breakfasted, and by eight-thirty was ready to leave the apartment with Mme Pasteur, who always went to Mass at the church of St. Jacques du Haut Pas at that hour. After a morning spent in classroom, office or laboratory, Pasteur would come home for lunch with his family and then take a short rest. The afternoons, passed in work or at some meeting of teachers or scientists, were usually followed by a quiet dinner at home. When the meal was finished and the children were in bed, Mme Pasteur would read *Le Temps* to her husband for a short time and, if he was not working that evening, she might continue to read to him from some biographical or historical work. More often than not, however, he would have brought home notes from which he dictated to her or he would want to go back to his laboratory. Before returning there he was likely to pace back and forth for awhile in the corridor outside his apartment, jingling the coins in his pocket and quite lost in thought. A passing student might meet the abstracted gaze that gave no sign of recognition and hear him mutter, as he abruptly set off toward the laboratory: "I must work!"

There was an expression he had picked up from Biot and frequently quoted because it so exactly expressed his own conviction: "Work is the only thing that is enjoyable." Sometimes, when he was upset by an untoward occurrence in the school, it was the only thing that could take his mind off his annoyance. Only a sharp crisis in his domestic life, such as the illness of his oldest child, could interrupt it. Jeanne, on a visit to her grandfather in Arbois in September, 1859, became ill with typhoid fever. No one had any clear idea of the cause of the disease, and treatments varied. The discoveries of Eberth, Widal and others on typhoid fever—discoveries which Pasteur's own made possible—were years in the future. The child died, and it was months before her father could drag his mind away from constant thought of his "poor little girl, so good, so happy in her little life."

Realizing that her husband's happiness lay in unremitting work, Mme Pasteur carefully protected him against interruptions. She taught the children early that nothing must be allowed to interfere with their father's work, and they quickly learned to regard the study with the padded doors at the end of the apartment as out of bounds unless he particularly invited them to enter it. Mme Pasteur also managed the family's financial affairs. Her husband's salary was paid directly to her, and she administered it thriftily. To Pasteur she gave a small allowance, a few francs a day, which suited him perfectly—his wife made all the purchases, he took his meals at home, and what did he need of money, except to pay for an occasional fiacre or to tip a messenger?

Casual visitors were not encouraged in the Pasteur household, and the scientist and his wife went out but rarely. Their own entertaining was confined almost entirely to their Sunday afternoons at home, when special friends, students at the *École* and, as he grew older, their son's schoolfellows were made welcome. These receptions were pleasant affairs: Mme Pasteur was a gracious hostess and Pasteur, kind and attentive, circulated among the guests, talking to each about what most interested him or her. The friends and students who came once found that they easily formed the habit of dropping in on the Pasteurs for a few hours on Sunday to enjoy the good conversation and to share the simple and excellent supper.

Pasteur had not been long at the École normale before his luck with laboratories began improving. Largely because of his unremitting insistence, he was allotted a little building, adjoining the *École* on the rue d'Ulm, which had been built as a concierge's lodge and was occupied by the school's architect. The two rooms in the attic were restored to their rightful inhabitants, the rats, and Pasteur moved his equipment into the comparative luxury of the tiny lodge. He was also allowed, at last, a laboratory assistant, and selected as his first an École normale graduate, Jules Raulin, a clear-headed and intelligent young man not at all alarmed by the terra incognita into which he at once found himself led by Pasteur.

As he pursued his studies of fermentations, Pasteur was raising several new problems for every one he solved. One in particular presented itself, very naturally and very insistently, to his mind: what was the source of the ferments, of these tiny yet potent organisms that could work such transformations in organic matter? Actually, he thought that germs must be carried in the air, fall into exposed liquids and develop there into ferments and infusoria, as microbes were then called. As the most meticulous of experimental scientists, however, he did not wish to declare himself until he could supply unanswerable experimental proof. As he said: "In experimental science it is always a mistake not to doubt, when facts do not compel you to affirm."

Others, less cautious and less exacting in their experiments, supported the theory of spontaneous generation. This theory went hand in hand with the old theory of fermentation: the same molecules which, breaking up through putrefaction, set off a similar movement in the molecules of fermentable substances and so brought about fermentation, also regrouped themselves to form living creatures, those infusoria which were found in decomposing organic matter, fermenting liquid and even stagnant water. One of the most active supporters of this theory of spontaneous generation was Félix Archimède Pouchet, a corresponding member of the Academy of Sciences and director of the Natural History Museum of Rouen.

This topic was no novelty: spontaneous generation had been the subject of philosophical speculation for centuries. The ancients had believed that eels were formed from river ooze, bees from the entrails of dead cattle. A later generation thought that anyone who wanted to could "create" mice by putting some grain or cheese and a few soiled rags in a quiet dark place, and that worms developed spontaneously in putrefying meat. In the seventeenth century Francesco Redi, an Italian naturalist, refuted this latter idea by a simple experiment. He covered a piece of meat with gauze, allowed it to decay and found that flies, attracted by its smell, swarmed over the gauze and laid on it their eggs from which hatched the worms previously thought to have formed spontaneously in the rotting meat.

This excellent observation by no means closed the discussion. It was not long before the microscope, coming into fairly common use at the end of the seventeenth century, disclosed the world of the "infinitely small," creatures visible only through its magnifying lens which appeared—nobody knew how—in any organic infusion, and even in rain water, exposed to the air. Where did they come from? Maybe flies and worms did not form spontaneously, as Redi had demonstrated, but what about these much lower forms of life?

The question dragged on, to flare in the middle of the next century into the celebrated debate between the two Catholic priests, Needham and Spallanzani. Needham, an Englishman, said the infusoria were formed by spontaneous generation, and conducted experiments which he believed proved his contention. He placed some putrefiable fluid in well-corked flasks, and cooked the flasks in hot ashes. When he took the flasks out of the ashes he found, after a few days, that they became cloudy, that they swarmed with microscopic beings. These must, he concluded, have formed spontaneously out of the putrescent matter. Spallanzani, an Italian, repeated Needham's experiment, only, not satisfied with merely corking his flasks, he sealed them hermetically and exposed them to long boiling. No microscopic life developed, no spontaneous generation occurred. Needham's answer to that was that Spallanzani, by using too much heat, had killed the "vegetative force"—an undefined concept—of the organic infusion.

The debate, like the experiments, was inconclusive. Philosophical and religious arguments—quite beside the point in experimental science, of course—were dragged in. New generations of scientists repeated and elaborated on the experiments of Spallanzani and Needham, with results which in general supported Spallanzani. But the partisans of spontaneous generation had to be confronted with experiments which should be irreproachable and always—not usually—successful. This had not yet happened.

It was at this point that Pouchet, a learned naturalist, a conscientious seeker after the truth, and an experimenter mediocre except in his own field of natural history, reopened the discussion by announcing in December, 1858, in a communication to the Academy of Sciences that he could demonstrate that microscopic plants and animals could be generated in a medium, absolutely free from atmospheric air, into which no germ of organic bodies could have been introduced by air.

Pasteur was both thunderstruck and amused on reading Pouchet's statement: "When by meditation it became evident to me that spontaneous generation was another one of the means which Nature employs for the reproduction of her creatures, I applied myself to discover by what processes one could demonstrate the phenomenon." Pasteur could hardly imagine a scientific man asserting his own opinion was the truth, and "evident" truth at that, when he had arrived at it by—meditation! Could even the clearest, most unanswerable demonstrations carry conviction to a mind which arranged facts to conform to a preconceived opinion?

His experience with fermentations had taught Pasteur that the cause of every fermentation was a specific ferment, each of which reproduced its own kind, and only its own kind, in any favorable medium. These facts naturally suggested the idea of some ordinary kind of generation. So Pasteur already had a good basis of fact for leaning toward his germ theory—the theory that germs were carried in the air and fell into exposed liquids to develop into ferments and infusoria. The problem of proving it by experiment remained; for that Pasteur, familiar with microscopic organisms and with the means of manipulating them, was certainly the best equipped man of his day.

Now the laboratory swarmed with the activity of the experiments by which he hoped, once and for all, to refute the theory of spontaneous generation. He was absorbed in his work, and, in the serious way peculiar to him, happy about it. Biot was less so. The mystery of spontaneous generation was not only unfathomed but unfathomable, in his opinion, and he did not want Pasteur to spend his time and his talents in a hopeless inquiry.

Dumas, too, in his Olympian way, maintained with urbanity a discouraging attitude. Distressed though he was at having to act against the advice of his two most respected masters, Pasteur took much comfort in Balard's encouragement.

Balard, content with the glory he had won when very young as the discoverer of bromine, was more sociable and less absorbed in work than Pasteur. He was always dropping around to the laboratories of his friends to see what was going on. Every few days he would appear in the little laboratory on the rue d'Ulm, and with several shrewd questions acquaint himself with the progress and aim of the work under way. Everyone was glad to see him, the laboratory boys because he was gay and kindly, Pasteur because he had inspired in him as a student a lasting respect and affection. In addition to that, Balard's great learning as a chemist enabled him to offer Pasteur valuable suggestions on the conduct of his experiments.

The first phase of the experiments involved the microscopic study of air. If germs existed in the atmosphere, as Pasteur believed, it must be possible to snatch them out of it. This Pasteur did by drawing air through a tube into which he had stuffed a bit of cotton wool. The plug acted as a filter on which the current of air deposited various kinds of debris—inorganic stuff such as soot, and, much more interesting, microscopic objects of organized aspect which were, he suspected, the spores and eggs of infusoria.

And were these particles alive or capable of producing life? Pasteur was sure they were, but to prove his point he had to devise an unassailable experiment which would demonstrate that they and only they were the source of the life found in organic infusions. He took a flask containing such an infusion, drew out its neck in a flame, and boiled it until every living organism in it was destroyed by heat. The air in the flask was removed, of course, in the current of vapor which was produced by the boiling and which also sterilized the inside of the flask. The vapor, on escaping the neck of the flask, was led out by way of a red-hot platinum tube. After some minutes of boiling, Pasteur extinguished the flame under the flask, the liquid cooled, the vapor condensed and the outside air rushed in to fill the flask through the platinum tube, still kept red hot, which killed everything organic it contained. Then Pasteur separated the flask from the rest of the apparatus by fusing its tapering neck with a blowpipe—and there he had a flask of corruptible fluid in which every living organism, whether in the liquid itself, or on the walls of the flask, or in the air in the flask, had been scrupulously destroyed. It did not surprise him to find that, no matter how long he kept this flask, no infusoria formed in it, no spontaneous generation took place. But when by another ingenious operation he put in the flask the cotton plug through which air had filtered, and on which it had deposited its dusts, within twenty-four hours the fluid would become clouded and in another day it would contain millions of living organisms. Pasteur performed this experiment, with variations, repeatedly, and after a year's work he felt justified in declaring positively that the only thing in the air to provoke the organization of life was the germs it contained.

Pouchet remained emphatically unconvinced, as did his two major supporters, Nicolas Joly, professor of physiology at Toulouse, and one of Joly's students, Charles Musset. It was absurd to think that the germs causing fermentation and putrefaction came from the air, they said; why, the atmosphere would have to be as thick as pea soup to contain so many germs. Maybe the cotton plug, itself an organic substance, had something to do with the development of these infusoria. Pasteur dealt with that objection by substituting an asbestos plug for the cotton, and then, at Balard's suggestion—one of those suggestions which made it so rewarding to the reticent Pasteur to keep him abreast of his work—made his flasks not with straight necks but with long curved ones. These flasks he did not seal hermetically. He did not need to: the air, moving gently into them, deposited its dusts and germs in the curve of the neck, and before any alteration in the fluid could take place the flask had to be tipped until the liquid reached the dust lodged in the crook of the neck. It was now impossible to attribute to the plugs, whether cotton or asbestos or whatever, any part in the development of the infusoria in the liquid of the flasks.

Pouchet, a vigorous opponent, was not through with the argument, and labored the point that most puzzled Pasteur himself: how could germs people the air in sufficient quantity to produce alteration in any or all exposed organic infusions without its being too thick to see through? Pasteur thought there might be more germs in some places than in others. To test this theory, he again took his little flasks, boiled the organic liquid they contained and, as the steam rushed out, fused the necks so that the flasks when cooled were not only sterile but also nearly empty of air. He took them to various places about Paris—the cellar of the observatory, the yard of the *École*, wherever it occurred to him—and with a pair of pliers which he had first passed through a flame to kill any germs which might be clinging to them snapped the necks. The air rushed in, he sealed them again with a blowpipe, and took them back to his laboratory where he kept them at a temperature suitable to the development of any life they might contain. In some of the flasks microscopic life developed; in some it did not. Most of those opened in the observatory cellar, for instance, where the air was still, showed no alteration; on the other hand, most of those opened in a busy yard or street, where the dust was constantly being stirred up, showed the expected alteration in due course.

So the air in some spots contained very few germs, in others very many? Pouchet and his friends inquired. A convenient explanation, indeed! They would undertake a series of experiments themselves, showing that air anywhere—whether in the midst of a city and loaded with dirt, or on a mountaintop and entirely free of it—was favorable to organic genesis. Pasteur planned to extend his experiments to prove just the opposite.

The long vacation of 1860 he decided to spend in the study of air on heights. It was late summer when he set out for his father's home, surrounded by his family and laden down with seventy-three sealed and sterile flasks of yeast water, a blowpipe and other apparatus. The old tanner, who followed all his son's work with an understanding made possible by the younger man's clear explanations, examined all this paraphernalia with wonder. Here was his Louis, not yet forty, already a well-known chemist. To think that he had discouraged him from going to Paris to study, that he had thought he would have achieved enough if he became a teacher at the Collège d'Arbois! And now he was qualified to attack one of the world's most formidable scientific problems, spontaneous generation! Jules

Vercel, too, viewed his former schoolfellow with all his old affection, and if there was a little awe in it at first it was quickly dispelled when he saw that the years which had left him in obscurity and brought Pasteur to eminence had not changed the simple friendliness of his heart.

Twenty of the little flasks containing yeast water, a corruptible liquid, Pasteur opened near Arbois on a little-used road to Dôle. With another twenty, he went to Salins and climbed near-by Mount Poupet where, even farther from human habitation and a half mile above sea level, he opened them. Of the first twenty, eight developed micro-organisms; of the second, five. So far Pasteur's theory that the higher and cleaner the air, the fewer the germs in it, was being borne out.

His final test was to be conducted with the remaining thirty-three flasks on the Montanvert, in the Swiss Alps. Pasteur arrived at Chamonix on September 20, and in the bright cold of the following morning he started the ascent of the mountain to its famous glacier, the Mer de Glace, where he intended to open his flasks. A guide led the way, a sturdy little mule carried the crate containing the flasks, and Pasteur and his assistant walked on either side of the mule, steadying the case nervously as the sure-footed animal picked its way up the trail. These scientists, no mountaineers, were more intent on the dangers precipices and crevasses offered to their precious little flasks than to those they offered to themselves.

When they had climbed as high as Pasteur thought necessary, the little party halted and the flasks were unpacked. With the cold wind stirring his short beard, Pasteur held one above his head, where no dust from his clothing could fall into it, and nipped off its neck with a pair of sterilized pincers. The clean mountain air rushed in with a hiss. When he tried to seal it with the flame of his spirit lamp, however, he ran into difficulties. The glare of the ice in the sunlight was so brilliant that he could not see the flame of the burning alcohol, nor could he judge where to direct the jet because the wind moved it constantly. After many attempts, during which he opened thirteen of the flasks, he was obliged to concede that he was, for the day at least, baffled; so with open flasks the thwarted expedition picked its way down the trail and back to the little Montanvert inn.

The following morning Pasteur got his party together again for a second attempt. He had had a tinker alter the construction of the lamp the night before and this time he was confident of success. He had twenty flasks left—twenty flasks which now are famous in scientific history. These he opened with every precaution to prevent the introduction of any dust other than that which was floating free in the air. He sterilized the neck of each flask before breaking it, he sterilized his nippers, he climbed to a little height above the rest of his party to avoid any dust they might have raised or brought with them, and he broke the neck of each flask while holding it as high as possible above his own head. This time his spirit lamp worked well; he was able to seal each flask without trouble. Satisfied that the experiment had been conducted with the most scrupulous care, and filled with impatience to find out the results, the scientific party descended the glacier for the second and last time.

In a few days the results were evident; one flask only developed infusoria, nineteen showed no alteration whatever. Pasteur could state with confidence that the dusts suspended in the air were the sole origin, and the necessary condition, of life in infusions, and that where the air was free of dust, no life would develop. Yet the matter was not settled: Pouchet, who had been collecting samples of air himself, had directly opposite results and continued to insist that air everywhere, absolutely everywhere, whether clean or filthy, was favorable to the development of life.

This scientific wrangle had by now attracted the attention of laymen. Newspapers commented on it, and the public followed their accounts, speculations and opinions with considerable interest. To many it seemed entirely fantastic, this world of Pasteur's, in which invisible micro-organisms floated around in the air and caused fermentations and decomposition in appropriate substances by falling into them. To the scientific students of the École normale, however, Pasteur was a great man, and many of them believed with an almost romantic ardor in the chemist who, by means of experiments that combined daring imagination with scrupulous precision, was opening up an undreamed of new world to science. The Academicians were less ardent. They were older, they were conscious of their own learning, and many of them had passed the time of life when the mind has the flexibility to adjust to new concepts. Biot, aged though he was, was not one of these. Because he cared more to see truth established than his own opinion borne out, he was quick to admit that his pessimism about Pasteur's new line of research was unjustified. Early in 1860, Pasteur had been given the Academy of Sciences award for experimental physiology for his work in fermentation; now, a year later, a vacancy existed in the botanical section of the Academy and Biot wanted his friend, almost a half century his junior, elected to it. Undaunted by the fact that Pasteur was not a botanist in the usual sense, he urged his election on the basis of his work in fermentations, which could be considered in the field of vegetable physiology. Much to the chagrin of Biot, and of Balard who seconded his efforts with his usual vigor, the Academy decided to be conventional about what constituted a botanist, and Pasteur, for the second time, failed of election. His margin of failure was shrinking, however; this time he received twenty-four votes.

CHAPTER NINE

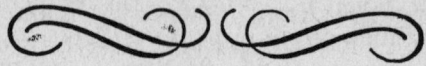

By 1862 Pasteur was attaining a certain celebrity. Savants, journalists, industrialists came to see him in his little laboratory, to talk to him and to get a glimpse through his microscope of the world of those infinitely small organisms into whose enormous activity and power he was beginning to penetrate. The government, impressed by his work, enlarged his laboratory and made it more comfortable, so that Pasteur no longer had to crawl on his hands and knees into the inconvenient little cubbyhole which had been the only place where he could set up his drying stove. A fine new room was built for him, well lighted, well equipped and appropriately ornamented with a bust of Lavoisier, the great French chemist who lost his head during the Revolution.

The year began badly, however, with the death of Biot in February. Pasteur, who loved the old man as much as he venerated him, could have been more grieved only by the death of his own father. Biot had, indeed, acted very much as a father to him all during his scientific life and had loved him like one.

Soon after Biot's death there entered Pasteur's laboratory, as Raulin's successor, a young man to whom Pasteur came to stand in much the same relationship as Biot had stood to him. Émile Duclaux had been born in 1840 in Aurillac, a town of gray stucco buildings and red roofs on a high plateau in southern France. His father, a clerk, was a man of scholarly inclinations who had devoted himself so fully to the education of Émile, his oldest son, that the child had been something of a prodigy. The two were inseparable until the elder Duclaux's death which occurred shortly after Émile went to Paris to study in the Pension

Barbet for admission to the École normale. In 1859 young Duclaux entered the *École,* and came under the influence of Pasteur, of whom he had heard frequent and glowing accounts from M. Barbet. Three years later, when he was graduated, he was taken into Pasteur's laboratory. Duclaux was small and slight, and had a long thin face with expressive, brilliantly blue eyes which could be melancholy, thoughtful, humorous. He had a fine quick mind, a joyous disposition, and a complete devotion to the master, as Pasteur was already being called by his students. He threw himself with energy and delight into Pasteur's researches.

The controversy with Pouchet, Joly and Musset was continuing and in the course of it Pasteur felt it necessary to reexamine some of his findings on fermentation. In doing further work on lactic fermentation, he observed that it was followed by another type of fermentation called butyric, and that the cause of this butyric fermentation was not an immobile globule, as it was in alcoholic fermentation, but was motile, an agile little rod with undulating movements that multiplied by elongating and coming apart in the middle. The barriers between the animal and vegetable forms were barely beginning to crumble at this time, and Pasteur was greatly surprised to realize that in this lively micro-organism he had discovered a ferment which was was not of a vegetable but of an animal nature. But there was an even more surprising fact about it: it lived in the absence of air; indeed, air killed it. Another new idea, that af anaerobic life, or animal life sustained in the absence of air, was thus introduced to science.

As the spontaneous generation controversy continued, both sides performed experiments. Pasteur's, so economical, so precise, so unanswerable, filled Duclaux with admiration. Those of Pouchet and his friends, conducted with queer pieces of apparatus that quite nonplused chemical observers, moved him to hilarity. Pasteur, however, was anything but amused at being confronted with experiments which were essentially naïve; he did not brook contradiction graciously, particularly when it balked the development of scientific truth. That certain members of the Academy of Sciences—either because they knew little of chemistry and the problems of chemical manipulation, or because they were frightened by the impact of new ideas—should hesitate in choosing sides on this critical subject exasperated him to the bottom of his heart.

When a vacancy occurred in the mineralogy section of the Academy and Pasteur came up again, late in 1862, for election, his irritation with some of his colleagues found vigorous expression. A question was raised about his study of tartrates. He had discovered, it will be recalled, that crystals hemihedral on the right side, when dissolved, bent polarized light to the right. In Germany the custom was somewhat different: the crystal was held in the opposite position, so that it was those hemihedral on the left which bent polarized light to the right. It was entirely a matter of convention, obviously, how one held the crystal; the essential result first announced by Pasteur was unchanged. Yet certain of his opponents tried to discredit him on this ground, although everyone who had any understanding of the subject knew that only usage was involved.

By the time that Pasteur realized that this trumped-up argument was being used, unscrupulously and with telling effect, against his candidacy, the election was less than a month away. The evening of November 8 the Philomathic Society, whose membership included a number of Academicians, was holding a meeting, and Pasteur succeeded in having the full time assigned to him for the presentation of his case. That morning he burst into his laboratory, where his assistant was already at work, and ordered:

"Duclaux, today we will make models of crystals. I am going to give the Philomathic such a demonstration that they will have no further excuse for not understanding my work on tartrates!"

"Good, monsieur," Duclaux agreed. He hurried out and bought the material for the models.

The two men spent the whole day cutting from wood a set, very large in size, of the crystalline forms of tartrates, coating them with colored paper, and pasting green paper over the hemihedral faces. There was going to be no mistake about identifying *those*.

Pasteur was warm with indignation as, that night, he addressed his audience. His demonstration was forceful and superbly lucid, and Duclaux, in the audience, smiled to himself as he listened to the master lecturing the learned gentlemen like so many schoolboys. Although he was of a more easygoing disposition than Pasteur, he approved his brusque inquiry: "If you know what you are talking about, what are you doing with your consciences? If you do not, why do you meddle?"

"That was good, very good," he told Pasteur afterwards, as they walked back to their apartments—or rather, to Pasteur's apartment and Duclaux's little room—in the *École*.

"It must be obvious now, even to an idiot, that it is entirely a matter of usage!" Pasteur answered, still with heat.

"Well," Duclaux remarked, with a hint of amusement in his tone, "I can think of one thing more you might have done to strike those gentlemen even more forcibly."

"Oh, no!" Pasteur stopped abruptly and turned aghast to his assistant. "What?"

"You might have hit them over the head with the models," Duclaux suggested, and smiled at Pasteur's laughter.

Pasteur's point, however, was sufficiently clear. On December 8, not quite three weeks before his fortieth birthday, he was elected to the Academy of Sciences with thirty-six votes. The next day Mme Pasteur entered the Montparnasse cemetery and laid flowers on the grave of Biot, who had had so large a part in guiding her husband's career.

Napoleon III was a handsome gentleman somewhat past middle age, with a magical name, a dashing set of whiskers, and an intelligent interest in science. News of the work being conducted in the small laboratory in the rue d'Ulm kept reaching him and, a few months after Pasteur's election to the Academy, the Emperor decided that he must meet this chemist whose novel and precisely documented theories were proving to be such a storm center in the scientific world. It was in March, 1863, that Pasteur, escorted by Dumas, had his first audience with his sovereign.

Pasteur, who took high position and honors seriously, was much impressed, but he forgot his awe in the interest of talking to this monarch who had been following his work from a distance with sympathy and sense. He spoke of his researches on fermentation, on putrefaction, on spontaneous generation. Napoleon questioned him closely, and he answered as fully as a scientist can answer a layman. At the end of the interview Napoleon gazed at him thoughtfully.

"And your ambition, M. Pasteur? What is that?"

"My whole ambition, Sire, is to arrive at knowledge of the causes of contagious diseases," Pasteur replied. He already understood the direction in which his studies of the infinitely small were taking him, and his ambition, however vast, was not beyond his achieving.

It is not every scientific man who is a good strategist, and without strategy it sometimes takes truth a long time to win acceptance. The history of medicine is full of illustrations of this painful fact, but Pasteur's career, fortunately, is not one of them.

His handling of the conflict with Pouchet was admirably canny. In a controversy of such scope, there were bound to be areas in which Pouchet, Joly and Musset were more at home than Pasteur. He did not allow them to draw him into their fields, but waited patiently until they intruded into his, where he could pounce on their weaknesses and expose them with all his authority. His opportunity came when, after the long vacation of 1863, they announced that they had repeated substantially the experiment he had conducted on the Mer de Glace—and had obtained precisely opposite results.

While Pasteur, during that vacation, was launching into some new studies on the fermentation of wine, his three antagonists had, indeed, conducted a conscientious experiment, and one fraught with considerable physical danger to them. Braving hardships which included exertion, fatigue and severe cold, they toiled with guides and scientific equipment up to the foot of one of the great glaciers of the Maladetta, almost ten thousand feet above sea level and more than three thousand feet higher than Pasteur had gone on the Mer de Glace. There they opened flasks similar to those Pasteur had used—except that they contained a decoction of hay instead of yeast water—with the most meticulous precautions. After the perilous climb came the perilous descent—during which Joly almost broke his neck through a misstep—but dangers, discomforts, weariness were all forgotten when, after a reasonable length of time, the three scientists saw that alteration was taking place in their flasks. They made haste to announce to the Academy their result, and the conclusion they drew from it: that new beings, without parents, could be formed spontaneously in putrefying organic matter. Pasteur, on his part, shrewdly seized upon this affirmation to request the Academy to appoint a commission to decide between him and his contradicters.

The Academy was quite willing to name a commission to pass judgment in so important a scientific matter, and selected Flourens, Brogniart, Dumas, Milne-Edwards and Balard. Pouchet, Joly and Musset, rather oddly, declined to take part in the test until the weather should become warmer. Pasteur, who thought that spontaneous generation, if it took place at all, should operate as well in winter as in summer, especially with the aid of a laboratory stove, nevertheless agreed to postpone the test to any time which his opponents thought suitable. It was not until June, 1864, that Pouchet and his supporters said they were willing to appear before the commission.

In the end, the decisive test was something of a fizzle. It was held at Dumas' estate. Pasteur, Duclaux and the other assistants from the rue d'Ulm laboratory came with all the equipment necessary to perform the experiments; Pouchet and his supporters arrived, as Duclaux later described it, "unarmed." They attempted to open lines of argument irrelevant to the experiment to be held. Dumas with some severity and Balard with his peculiar brand of mocking amiability kept dragging them back to the point. Finally, they declined to perform their experiment and retired. Pasteur ran his with his customary result. The commission, in an incisive report written by Balard, decided in his favor. It was a clear-cut triumph for the germ theory. Pasteur would have been astounded had anyone told him that it was also an empty one.

The victory was, actually, a mirage, but it was a dozen years before Pasteur and his supporters realized it. Pasteur was right, but the experiment of Pouchet, Joly and Musset was accurate even if the conclusion they drew from it was not. Pasteur used water of yeast in his flasks, Pouchet a decoction of hay in his. The truth was that flasks containing a decoction of hay, opened in even the purest air, were very likely to undergo alteration and fill with living organisms—simply because the germs which already existed in that infusion were of a kind which resisted boiling. As long as the flask was devoid of air they remained inert; when oxygen again entered it they resumed their normal functions. Had Pouchet gone ahead with his demonstration he would have held his ground, and Pasteur would have had to admit that he was wrong in some particular at least. Being the thorough laboratory man he was, and the imaginative experimenter, Pasteur might very well have discovered in reasonably short order this new type of heat-resistant germ, equally unknown at that time to him and to his adversaries.

In any case, the controversy subsided, except for a spate of popular discussion. There was some inquiry about how the first germ, the original ancestor of those Pasteur dealt with, came into being—by spontaneous generation? by an act of God?—but Pasteur, with humility, declined to attack that question. He was a devout Catholic, and speculation about the very origin of life, the first cause, lay not in the province of science but of religion, and so far as he was concerned it was going to stay there. He was a scientist and, as he said: "Science should not concern itself with the philosophical consequences of its discoveries."

The running fight over spontaneous generation had lasted five years, it had come out to Pasteur's satisfaction, and he was anxious to get on to something else. The previous summer he had started some researches into the diseases of wine; now he returned to them.

Pasteur always welcomed the long vacation; then, freed from administrative duties, he could devote himself entirely to his scientific work. Accompanied by his family—which by this time included two more small daughters, Marie Louise and Camille—assistants, and all the chemical apparatus he was likely to need, he regularly returned to Arbois where, if permitted by Mme Pasteur and his father, he could work from sunup to sundown.

Pasteur frequently said: "I should feel that I was committing a theft if I were to let one day go by without doing some work." So life at Arbois was, for him, much like life in Paris, except that his afternoons were not taken up with meetings of the Academy and other organizations. He worked all morning from about eight-thirty on; after lunch he might play a game of croquet with some of his family for perhaps an hour. At four every day he was supposed to take a little walk with some of his household, but it was often very hard to get him started. He had to be called several times, while his companions patiently and respectfully waited for him to lay aside whatever piece of work was occupying him. Dinner was a cheerful affair, and Jean Baptiste, who had a comic gift even as a youngster, could make his father laugh until he was helpless.

"Heavens! How silly you are!" Pasteur would exclaim, leaning back in his chair and wiping his eyes with his napkin.

Pasteur had one habit which filled his assistants with astonishment and respect. When he took a piece of bread from the breadbasket beside his plate, he would absent-mindedly pick out of it scraps which had fallen into it during the milling of the flour or the baking—a fragment of an insect's wing, a bit of chaff, any foreign particle which no one at the table noticed but he, and which no one but he, with his marvelously observant, trained eye, could recognize. Duclaux, Gernez and Lechartier, the three assistants he took with him to Arbois for his first study of wines in 1863, used to exchange wondering glances with each other as the master, absently making a little pile of oddments by his plate, consumed the portion of the bread he considered edible.

In some work on vinegar which he had conducted during the course of the spontaneous generation dispute, Pasteur had discovered that acetification—or the turning of wine to vinegar—was the work of a micro-organism which he called *mycoderma aceti*. The practical consequence of this discovery, as of so many of Pasteur's discoveries, was of considerable industrial importance. The manufacturers were then able to regulate the production of vinegar with security, instead of being at the mercy of circumstances they could neither understand nor control. Now that he had set the vinegar makers on the right track, logic suggested to him that other alterations in the taste of wines were probably caused by other specific micro-organisms, much as various fermentations were caused by specific ferments. This summer, 1864, Pasteur was back in Arbois to continue work along this line of thought.

The Emperor was encouraging him. France had about five million acres in vineyards, and commercial treaties allowing her to export to many foreign markets. The export of wine was an important source of revenue, but one that could have been much more important had it not been for the diseases that ruined many wines. Those of Jura became acid, those of Bordeaux turned, those of Burgundy became bitter, those of Champagne ropy. Naturally, Napoleon III was anxious to correct a condition that was damaging his country's prosperity.

Arbois, equally proud of its two most distinguished products, Pasteur and wine, welcomed the chemist this year with the offer of a laboratory equipped and supported by the town. Pasteur declined it, on the theory that his results might not justify the expense to his fellow townsmen. Instead, he obtained the use of an empty café, without either gas or water, and set up his laboratory there.

Duclaux was accustomed to doubling as charwoman. He washed the glassware and swept the floor in Paris, so he thought nothing of taking the utensils out the back door of the café to wash them in the Cuisance—the same Cuisance which was still wetting the hides for Pasteur's father and Virginie's husband who helped him at the tannery—and of stoking and fanning the little charcoal stove by hand. Since he did not get around to taking down the sign which announced that here was a café, he had also to shoo away the frequent callers who stopped in, hopefully, for a drink.

"No, no, monsieur," he would say good-humoredly, "we do not sell wine here. We only look at it."

As the would-be customer withdrew, baffled, Pasteur, if he noticed at all, would only look up from his work with a preoccupied frown.

Pasteur had boyhood friends in Arbois who had well-stocked wine cellars and they very willingly gave him samples of their wine for microscopic examination. It happened with a regularity which did not surprise him, so confident was he of the logic of his position, that each time a taster pointed out to him a particular defect in taste he would find a particular microscopic species at the bottom of the cask with the yeast. It was only the wines which contained no other micro-organism than yeast that were good. After examining a sample microscopically, it rather amused him to astonish his friends by saying:

"Oh, but this wine is acid."

"But Louis, you have not tasted it!"

"I do not need to. This little organism tells me as plainly as my own palate could."

And what could be done to outwit these little organisms, to keep them from invading and spoiling the wine? That was the next problem.

The vintners had the idea that wine, if it was to age properly, must be preserved from contact with the air. Therefore they painstakingly kept it away from air, except for the very short time needed to decant it, on the vague theory that oxygen in some way damaged it. Pasteur, who realized that there is often good observation behind popular usages, even if the explanation is faulty, knew that the practice was sound. In protecting the wine against air, they were also unwittingly protecting it against the germs carried by air, against those micro-organisms which caused the various diseases. As for the oxygen of which everyone was so suspicious, his researches demonstrated that the process of aging was, in fact, a process of slow oxidation. It was only when the wine had combined over a period of time with oxygen that it was properly aged.

The question of how to preserve wine from disease therefore boiled down to this: how prevent or halt the growth of these ruinous little parasites that got into it without damaging the wine itself?

First he tried tasteless antiseptics, but without satisfactory results. Then, after a very little additional experimenting, he found that by heating wine, protected from air, to fifty-five degrees centigrade, the growth of all harmful micro-organisms was arrested.

As a matter of fact, preserving foods by heating them was not a new process; it had already been in use for more than thirty years. Yet, like many other industrial processes, it was one which was not understood. It worked, or usually worked, but the reason—the science and theory—back of its working was unknown; it had not been developed by a scientific, but rather by a rule-of-thumb, method. Now Pasteur, by no hit-or-miss method but by strict logic and orderly experiment, developed it again, understanding each step as he took it, and understanding, too, what step he should take next. Thus he created (or re-created) and explained the process of pasteurization, a process now in common use to prevent the spoilage of foods and the spread of disease through contaminated foods. Pasteur's service to the wine industry of his native land was, in fact, a service to the whole world.

It would be pleasant to add that this work was at once appreciated, and its beneficial possibilities immediately realized—it would be pleasant, but it would be false.

For one thing, in 1865, the year before he placed in the Emperor's hands the three-part memoir describing his work on wine diseases and their prevention, the phylloxera, a destructive type of plant louse, appeared in the winegrowing region of the Gard, to spread so rapidly and so devastatingly in the vineyards that the problem for some years was not to preserve wines but to get any in the first place. The pasteurization of wines, therefore, was little practiced for a number of years.

For another thing, the claim was raised that Pasteur had merely rediscovered and plagiarized the previously used process, and an unhappily acrimonious dispute arose. It was, of course, by the coherence and logic of all his own earlier work that he had been able to proceed—that he had, indeed, practically been forced to proceed—step by step from the problem of the causes of the wine diseases to the discovery of their cure—and this truth was demonstrable. In the end he got the best of the controversy, but it was disagreeable while it lasted. The good-natured and devoted Duclaux thought Pasteur would have done better to disdain debate, letting his works speak for themselves, and grieved to see him diverted from his researches and overwrought, even temporarily. It was Pasteur's nature, however, to defend his work and scientific truth with an energetic directness which was often harsh, and Duclaux could still sympathize with his master, even in those heated and blunt replies which he himself would never have uttered. After all, as he said understandingly, "All profound faith is necessarily a little intolerant, and Pasteur had that faith."

CHAPTER TEN

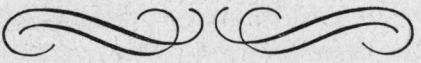

It was a day in the late spring of 1865 when Pasteur entered his laboratory and exclaimed in an agitated voice:

"Duclaux, do you know what M. Dumas wants me to do?"

"What, monsieur?"

"He's asked me to go south and study the disease of silkworms!"

"The disease of *silkworms!* Do silkworms *have* a disease?"

"Evidently."

Master and disciple gazed at each other, almost equally bewildered by the prospect opened up to them by Dumas' request.

Pasteur and Duclaux, whose lives were passed in a secluded laboratory on a little-frequented Latin Quarter street, might know absolutely nothing about the culture of silkworms and their diseases, but there was scarcely a child in the Department of the Gard, where sericiculture, or silk production, was a major industry, who could not have given a reasonably accurate account of them.

The silkworm is hatched from an egg, called the seed because of its resemblance to certain vegetable seeds; then it goes through four molts, or changes of skin. After the fourth molt follows a period of enormous voracity, known as the big gorge, which lasts two or three days. Then the worm ceases to eat and, if sprigs of heather are provided, it climbs up on them and spins the silken cocoon in which, during a period of about fifteen days, it undergoes the transformation from worm to chrysalis to moth. The moths mate as soon as they break out of the cocoon, and the female lays her eggs in batches of from six to eight hundred, eggs which, carefully collected by the cultivators, are saved for hatching the next spring. The evolution from egg to egg takes about two months, but it is only when the grower wants seed that the development is allowed to proceed so far. The cocoons are commercially worthless if ruptured by the emergence of the moth, so when he wants a harvest of silk the cultivator gathers the cocoons five or six days after the worm has spun them and puts them in a steam bath which smothers the chrysalis. The harvest of this lucrative product, a season of joyous festival, was known in the region as the time of the silkworm, and the mulberry tree, on which the worms fed, as the tree of gold. For some twenty years, however, the time of the silkworm had been not so much a time of rejoicing as one of increasing worry, disappointment and finally despair. A disease which had so far defied all efforts at control or cure was ravaging the nurseries, killing the worms, ruining the harvests and replacing plenty with poverty.

The disease was usually called pébrine, from the fact that the infected worms were covered with tiny dark specks as though sprinkled with black pepper (*pébré*). It was also frequently called the corpuscular disease because infected worms had been found to be full of unexplained cells, or corpuscular bodies. Some investigators, however, believed that the corpuscles were to be found in healthy worms as well as diseased, and no connection had been definitely established between the corpuscle and the ailment. The disease manifested itself in a baffling variety of ways, and its symptoms were not constant. Worms could be spotted without being sick, and on the other hand unspotted worms did not necessarily give healthy eggs. Various kinds of remedies had been tried—some growers sprayed the mulberry trees with wine or absinthe, some sprinkled sulphur, charcoal, soot or quinine on the unlucky worms—all without effect. After the first year of the plague, 1845, seed had been imported from Lombardy, but the new stock developed from that, too, fell victim. Within a few years the ruinous disease had invaded Italy, Spain, Austria, Greece, Turkey, even China, and by 1864 healthy seed could be obtained only from Japan. To silkgrowers, it was practically a world-wide disaster. The extent of the damage to French cultivators can be expressed quite simply: in 1853, before the disease had made alarming headway, their harvest was worth 130,000,000 francs; in 1865 they were expecting one worth only 4,000,000. The loss of some ninety-seven per cent of their revenue was, in effect, ruin. It was at this point that they addressed a petition to the Senate to appoint some qualified scientist to study the plague and develop a method of preventing it.

Dumas, born at Alais in the Gard, had the misfortunes of his native region much at heart. As a member of the Senate, he was in a good position to present and push the silkgrowers' petition, and he did it with such effect that it was quickly granted. As one of the most prominent scientific men of his country, he was also in a position to designate the investigator to work on the problem. He selected Pasteur, whose work he had watched from its beginning and whose qualities as a scientist he much admired.

"But M. Dumas," Pasteur objected, "I know nothing, absolutely nothing, about this subject."

"So much the better," Dumas confidently replied. "For ideas, then, you will have only those that you develop as a result of your own observations."

For a short time, Pasteur remained in a painful state of indecision. On the one hand, he had for some time thought that the new ideas he had introduced into science might one day be applied to the diseases of the higher animals; now that he had established that fermentations were caused by living organisms, might he not, perhaps, establish a similar cause for contagious diseases? He did not yet think of the idea in so definite and simplified a form, but a foreshadowing of it already existed in his mind.

On the other hand, he was no physiologist, and his attendance at the celebrated Claude Bernard's lectures, where he frantically scribbled notes, filled him with a kind of despairing irritation and convinced him that he would never become one. So naturally he hesitated to rush unprepared into a field where he would have to deal with the workings in health and in sickness of creatures so much higher than the micro-organisms with which he was familiar.

Still, he was even more attracted than frightened by the prospect. And besides, what shameful ingratitude it would be to refuse this urgent request of M. Dumas', after benefiting for twenty years by his kindness and friendship! There was, he decided, nothing for him to do but place himself at the disposal of the man whom he always called his master.

"Do what you like with me," he wrote the older scientist. It was probably the most critical decision of his scientific life.

"The athletes of old used to present themselves naked to combat. The genial warrior against the scourge of the nurseries, he similarly rushed naked into battle, that is to say, without the simplest notions about the insect to be snatched from peril. I was dumbfounded; better than that, I was wonder-struck." So spoke Jean Henri Fabre; and the wise entomologist added: "His arms were the idea. . . ."

He was quite right. Pasteur left Paris for Alais on June 6, still knowing almost nothing about the problem he was hoping to solve. He had watched the dissection of the larva of a May beetle; he had skimmed a few of the latest books on silk culture; he had attended a few meetings of the Imperial Commission on Silk Culture, by which he was more confused than enlightened. His knowledge was, to say the most, fragmentary; but he was armed with an idea—the idea that the corpuscle was somehow significant in pébrine—and he was armed, too, with the scientific method, that incomparable method by which he critically checked his guesses and ideas so that he was never long misled by a mistaken one but was always brought back to facts, to scientific truths.

One of Pasteur's first acts on arriving at Alais was to call on Fabre, then assistant professor of physics at the Avignon *lycée*, who already had a reputation as an expert on insect life. The son of poor and almost primitive peasants, Fabre himself was a man of learning and wisdom, and he was thoroughly familiar with Pasteur's work on crystallography and spontaneous generation. They exchanged a few remarks about the silkworm disease, then Pasteur came to the point. He wanted instruction.

"I should like to see some cocoons. I have never seen any and I know them only by name. Could you get me some?"

"Nothing simpler. My landlord is a cocoon merchant, and he lives next door. Wait a minute, and I'll come back with what you want."

Fabre clapped his black, flat peasant hat on his head and hurried next door. In several minutes he was back, his hands full of cocoons. Pasteur took one and examined it curiously, turning it over and over in his fingers. Fabre opened one to show him the chrysalis, and explained the creature's life cycle. Pasteur questioned him closely, and Fabre was much surprised by the almost naïve ignorance of his distinguished caller. By the time Pasteur was ready to leave, however, Fabre was even more impressed by the serene assurance of this man who, ignorant of the most elementary facts about silkworms, was planning to put the ruined industry back on its feet.

Now that he had some notion of the silkworm's life cycle, Pasteur could start to work. He established himself in a little nursery near Alais and looked, first of all, for the corpuscle, the microscopic body to which he instinctively attached importance. It was easily enough found: all the cultures he first examined, already approaching their end, were diseased and worms and moths were riddled with corpuscles. Then he made an observation on two broods of silkworms in a neighboring nursery. One of these broods had finished the big gorge, climbed the twigs of heather and was spinning; the insects appeared to be admirably healthy, and the cultivator was planning to let the harvest go and keep all the cocoons for eggs. The other brood, just emerging from the fourth molt, appeared to be diseased. The worms languished, ate little, and were stunted; and there was every reason to suppose that the harvest of cocoons would be negligible. The strange thing was that, under microscopic examination, Pasteur found that the chrysalises and moths developing from the successful culture were swarming with corpuscles, whereas in the worms of the less advanced, diseased brood, corpuscles were to be found only rarely. Was this an exceptional fact? Examination of other broods quickly showed him that, far from exceptional, it was very usual. So then, what did it mean?

Were the corpuscles and the silkworm disease unrelated? Could healthy-appearing and healthy-acting worms develop into corpuscular chrysalises and moths? Could the worms be obviously sick, yet not be corpuscular? Pasteur set to work investigating, misled, in his innocence, by the fact that he was confronted with *two* silkworm diseases, the one in which corpuscles figured, the other in which they did not.

He had been in Alais little more than a week, and his work was only beginning to take shape, when he was overtaken by the first of those stunning misfortunes which so saddened his life during this period. A wire came telling him that his father was desperately ill.

He must have felt that he was moving in a dreadful recurring dream as he made, with all possible haste, the journey to Arbois. More than twenty years before a similar message had summoned him to his dying mother. Again there was the same rending anxiety, the same sickening foreboding. Again, too, there was the same confirmation of his fears. When he got out at Arbois the first persons he saw at the station were some of his cousins, dressed in funeral black, who had come from near-by Salins. Again, he was too late.

Pasteur's devotion to his parents was deep and so fervent that, even when he was an old man and a very famous one, tears would come to his eyes when he spoke of them. Yet his love of family, country and science were so intermingled and so interdependent—his work he regarded as a sort of tribute to his family, a duty to France—that, even on the night of his father's funeral he closed a touching letter to his wife, who had remained in Paris, with mention of the progress of his work in Alais. He must return there at once, he said; otherwise his work, and the national benefit resulting from it, would be delayed a whole year, since the silkworm season was already almost over.

Back in his nursery, he resumed his observations. He especially wanted to see what would become of the cocoons of the ailing brood which he had first observed as worms emerging from the fourth molt. What happened to them, as he learned by daily microscopic examination, was that the number of chrysalises containing corpuscles kept increasing the older the chrysalises grew; and by the time the moths had formed, not a single one but was thoroughly infested. Pasteur concluded promptly, and inaccurately, that there was a disease that could affect the worm in the absence of the corpuscle, and that the corpuscle was simply the tardy evidence of the disease.

This theory accounted, to his temporary satisfaction, for the behavior of the two broods he had studied. Both had been diseased: the first had been attacked only as the worms approached the spinning stage, so the disease had not had full scope; the second had been earlier and more thoroughly infected.

The theory pointed, too, to a practical preventive measure: if the presence of corpuscles was evidence of the advanced stage of the disease, it would obviously be better to obtain eggs from moths having a few or no corpuscles than from heavily infested ones. The former might be diseased, but they would have been so for a shorter time.

Although it was Pasteur's instinct and his practice to shroud his work in austere silence, communicating his ideas not even to his assistants until he was ready to confront the scientific world with a new theory buttressed with experiments confirming it, in this case he had to act differently. It was his duty to let it be known as soon as he found out anything useful, to excite public opinion and influence industrial usage at once, even before the problem was solved, the disease fully and clearly explained. So on June 26, after spending only fifteen days in researches on the spot, he announced to the Agricultural Committee of Alais his method of egg selection, a method which, although founded on the faulty idea that the corpuscle was a belated symptom of pébrine, was nevertheless correct and was strengthened both in theory and in practice when the defective foundation was replaced by the sound one: that the corpuscle was not *evidence* of the disease, but itself the sole *cause* of it.

The substitution, however, was one which Pasteur did not feel compelled to make for another two years. He continued to hold his mistaken belief about the nature of the corpuscle because of a defective technique which is worth mentioning. In examining a moth for corpuscles, he would snip out a bit of the skin of the abdomen and examine it under the microscope. The trouble with this method was that corpuscles, far from being evidence, everywhere present in the moth's body, of the pébrine, were in reality parasites in the moth which might or might not have invaded the abdominal tissue. It was only when Pasteur realized that, and ground up the moth in a mortar to study a drop of the pap microscopically, that he had a reasonably sure method of detecting the presence of corpuscles.

In any case, he had thus far devised a system of egg selection, and now he was going to use it himself, so as to have sound seed for the next year's experiments. After a search that was long and difficult, since the region was thoroughly infected, he finally obtained a few cocoons from a culture that had appeared healthy. These he took back with him to Paris, where he set up a miniature silkworm nursery.

He found much to do on his return besides cultivate his silkworms. There was his share of the administration of the École normale to resume; there was a voluminous correspondence with the silk cultivators; there was an article on Lavoisier, to be prepared at the request of Dumas—Dumas to whom he could refuse nothing—who was about to publish the famous chemist's works. There were all of these things, and many others, to fill his time, but none of them could take his mind off his one overshadowing preoccupation, the illness of his youngest child, two-year-old Camille. Thanks to his powers of concentration, he could work when he had work to do, and he had a great deal. When he was home, however, he spent most of his time with his little girl, trying to entertain her, soothe her, make her comfortable. And he had also to try to reconcile himself to the fact, finally quite clear, that she was not going to live.

It was September when she died. Her father, worn out both by grief and the weariness of her long illness, took the small coffin to Arbois to be buried in the cemetery with his parents and his first child. Then he returned to Paris and to work, exhausted but resigned. His philosophy was, as he said himself, not of the head but of the heart; besides, he was deeply religious.

CHAPTER ELEVEN

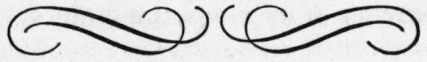

PASTEUR was the last man on earth to aspire to social success, but when it came his way he knew how to take advantage of it. Napoleon had long been well disposed toward him; even had the Emperor been indifferent to science, he could hardly have remained indifferent to the scientist whose work on vinegar, wine and silkworms held such promise for French industry. His interest was so much whetted, in fact, that toward the end of the year he invited Pasteur to spend a week with him at the palace of Compiègne. An invitation from the Emperor, of course, could not be refused; Pasteur, however, accepted it with real pleasure. He had long felt strongly about the niggardly budget allotted by the government to scientific work, and he wanted a larger, more convenient laboratory for his own work. Here was a chance to press the cause of science.

In between stag hunts, performances of Racine, excursions to a restored castle, torchlight processions and similar diversions, Pasteur got in his work for science. Standing with Napoleon by the fireplace of the big drawing room, somewhat apart from the rest of the company, the scientist discussed crystallography, the diseases of wines, spontaneous generation, the application of science to industry, fanning the imperial interest with his own enthusiasm.

The Empress Eugénie, handsome as she approached forty, a fine sportswoman, and leader of the world of fashion, had several talks with Pasteur. She had married Napoleon for love and, naturally, interested herself in what interested him. She was particularly concerned about the silkworm disease, the ravages of which Pasteur described to her. It was probably with some surprise that he found her so alive to the misfortunes of the silk-growers and so sympathetic to his own confusions, which he outlined to her.

"You must not become discouraged, monsieur," she told him earnestly. "This is a great and beneficial work you are engaged in. Science is never more splendid, I think, than when it is seeking to extend the range of its practical usefulness."

Pasteur, however little he needed her admonition, was pleased by her good will. As he showed her and her husband samples of wine under the microscope, discussed various scientific problems with the other guests, and one afternoon even gave a simple lecture to them while the Empress acted as his laboratory attendant, he was glad that he had moved for a time out of his quiet orbit to propagandize for science in this fashionable and politically powerful circle.

The Emperor, who had once asked him what was his ambition, had another question for him:

"Monsieur, some of your discoveries and the processes you have invented have greatly increased the revenues of French industrialists, yet they have never put a sou in your own purse. It would be entirely legitimate for you to seek to turn them to your own profit. Why do you never do so?"

"Sire," Pasteur answered with a shade of severity, "in France a scientist would think he demeaned himself to do such a thing. We who are devoted to science do not pursue it for personal gain. A scientist should let his mind range freely, not confine it, in the hope of gain, to the problems of any one industry."

Courtiers and politicians do not usually accustom rulers to disinterestedness. Napoleon and his empress were quite impressed.

Back in Alais again, early in 1866, with two congenial young assistants, Gernez and Maillot, Pasteur resumed his investigation of the silkworm disease. The difficulties under which they worked were irritating and obstructive: the hotel where they lived was uncomfortable, the meals were poor, and the impromptu laboratory, which they had set up in a silkworm nursery in the town, was far from satisfactory. The two younger men were not greatly inconvenienced by their discomforts, however little they liked them, but it worried them to see their master, energetic and uncomplaining but visibly tired, push his plate away before he had half finished the unappetizing food on it, or come down in the morning with the unmistakable look of a man who has passed a bad night.

"He sleeps too little, works too constantly, and does not eat enough," Gernez remarked one day to Maillot.

"Yes, madame would be terribly worried. I wish we could make him take better care of himself."

"I'm going to ask him for the Sunday off—maybe I can find a better place for us to live outside the town."

Gernez got his Sunday off, and undertook to search the countryside. In the evening he came back triumphant.

"An ideal place for us, monsieur!" he reported to Pasteur. "A big comfortable house with plenty of room for madame, the children and the rest of us; an *orangerie* which can be made into a laboratory without trouble, and a silkworm nursery. There is a gardener, too, rather a cranky old fellow, but not badhearted. He was furious at first when he found me wandering around the grounds, but I explained that I'd knocked and shouted without being able to rouse him, and then I admired his garden, and he ended in quite a good humor. He thinks the owner, who lives elsewhere, would be willing to rent the place to us."

The owner was, and eight days later Pasteur and his assistants were installed in the villa at Pont Gisquet. Comfortable at last, they launched into a period of intensive work.

Pasteur, whose passion for precision made him always apprehensive of slips in technique, undertook the large number of necessary tests himself, entering the results, in great detail, in his laboratory notebooks. The principal work of his assistants was to repeat and check his experiments, and, as usual, they knew no more of the master's thoughts than they could deduce from the work he assigned. Pasteur carried not only the full burden of the experimental work, but also that of dealing with callers and correspondents, most of them importunate, and most of them critical. How much easier his life would be, he must often have thought, if ignorant or selfish objections were not so often opposed to the scientific theories he advanced! Still, the research was proceeding well under congenial conditions and he pressed both his work and the campaign for his method of egg selection with equal energy.

It was just at this point, when everything seemed favorable, that the last in his series of misfortunes occurred. In May his twelve-year-old daughter, Cécile, contracted typhoid fever. With her mother and younger sister, Marie Louise, she was visiting one of her mother's sisters, Mme Zévort, wife of the rector of the Academy of Chambéry. Pasteur, who had already lost one child from this painful and still baffling disease, was alarmed by the news of her illness and hastened to Chambéry. Cécile was better when he arrived and the relieved father, putting his duty to his work ahead of his longing to remain with his sick daughter, returned to Alais. Even as he was deluding himself with hope of her recovery, Cécile had a sudden relapse, and on May 23 she died. For the second time within a year, Pasteur, heartbroken, made the melancholy journey with a little coffin to Arbois.

The only antidote for his grief was his work. In devoting himself sternly to the silkworm disease research, and to editing the book he had written on the diseases of wine, he was able to keep his mind from dwelling constantly on this new calamity.

By the end of the silkworm season he had made encouraging progress in unraveling some of the problems posed by the disease. For purposes of comparison, he had cultivated diseased as well as healthy eggs, and he found that his method of selection maintained the difference between the eggs. Various other important facts were established by this year's experiments. For one thing, the eggs of corpuscular parents resulted in a more or less meager harvest of cocoons in proportion as the moths which laid the eggs were more or less infested with corpuscles. At last, therefore, the connection between the presence of corpuscles and the disease was definitely established.

For another thing, he found that the eggs laid by corpuscular moths did not necessarily miscarry, and might produce a good harvest of cocoons. Never, though, would they produce good eggs, because all the moths hatched from them were heavily infested with corpuscles. This observation explained why growers so often got disappointing results when they selected eggs from apparently successful cultures: the success of the harvest did not guarantee the health of the eggs.

One of the season's most interesting findings was this: that even in very heavily infested broods, in which a great many deaths had occurred among the worms and the chrysalises, there were always a few noncorpuscular moths which would produce healthy eggs. The practical importance of this fact was great and obvious: even a thoroughly diseased strain of moths could be regenerated by careful selection. It was necessary only to keep each pair of mating moths separate from every other, examine them for corpuscles after the egg laying, and retain only those eggs produced by noncorpuscular moths. These eggs, in their turn, would produce noncorpuscular moths which would also lay healthy eggs.

"But such a difficult instrument!" protested an egg merchant, overawed by the microscope and reluctant to undertake the extra labor involved in the new process of egg selection. "You, monsieur, have been using one for more than twenty years, and are very expert. But a peasant, even if he could get a microscope, could not use it. It takes years to develop such skill."

"It is not necessary for every grower to have a microscope, monsieur," Pasteur patiently explained. "He can pickle his moths in brandy immediately after the laying and send them to some central point to be examined. And as for the difficulty of using the microscope, you overrate it. Let me show you something."

He led his skeptical visitor to the door of the laboratory.

"Look, monsieur," he said softly.

At the laboratory table sat a little girl, her eye to the eyepiece of the microscope, absorbed in the inspection of a slide. She moved it a little, then took it out, laid it to one side and slipped another under the microscope.

"That, monsieur," said Pasteur, "is my little Marie Louise. She is examining the abdominal tissue of moths for corpuscles. She has recently learned how to detect them, and is very competent at it. And," he added, "she is only eight years old."

Absorption in his work could keep his mind off his own troubles, but Pasteur did not allow it to harden him to those of a friend. Claude Bernard, suffering from a serious gastric complaint, had been obliged to retire from work and devote himself exclusively to caring for his health. Idle, ill and compelled to weigh every action in the light of its possible effect on his sickness, the great physiologist slipped into a deep depression. Pasteur, concerned as much about the mental as the physical state of his friend, wanted to make some sort of affectionate and cheering gesture. It occurred to him to write an appreciation of his work for publication in *Le Moniteur Universel*. At the same time Henri Sainte-Claire Deville had the kindly idea of editing a collective letter to Bernard from his friends. These two tokens of loving concern cheered the ailing savant immeasureably. Pasteur's article, which appeared in November, actually made him blush. He was too modest to think that he deserved so much praise, but he was delighted and touched to receive it from so authoritative a source.

Pasteur's principal scientific preoccupation remained the silkworm disease, and in January, 1867, he was back again in Alais, resolved that this year should be the last to witness failures among the silkgrowers. He had a large supply of eggs, selected by his own method and free from corpuscles; he had rented Pont Gisquet, and his wife and daughter were to be with him while Jean Baptiste remained in Paris at school; Maillot and Gernez again were to be his assistants. All that was lacking was Duclaux, now assistant professor of chemistry on the Faculty of Sciences at Clermont-Ferrand, who of all his affectionate and devoted disciples was perhaps the most affectionate and devoted—and Duclaux was coming soon.

Assured now of having a strain of silkworms free from corpuscles, Pasteur was ready to perform experiments on corpuscular contagion. At the same time he was continuing the propaganda for his method of egg selection through every possible channel. He wrote letters to egg merchants and to cultivators. He sent communications to scientific and agricultural journals. Tirelessly—or at least uncomplainingly—he journeyed under the hot southern sun to visit nurseries far and near for the purpose of explaining his method and giving away seed. Always he gave away with the good a little diseased, with the plea that the cultivator raise it, just to check his precise prediction of its development. It was nothing to him that the grower, while politely promising to cultivate both lots, was probably saying to himself: "What nonsense the man talks! He must take me for a fool, to think I'd believe he can forecast the harvest like that!" Pasteur wanted to arouse attention and interest, which would be followed, when his prediction came to pass, by astonished and full acceptance of his method. The unworldly scientist with the soaring imagination gave place to the practical man determined to compass a practical object: the total elimination of pébrine. His assistants were filled with admiration for the masterly way in which he conducted his propaganda campaign, all the while planning and executing an exacting series of experiments on the transmission of the disease.

In those experiments he fed noncorpuscular worms mulberry leaves onto which water containing fresh corpuscles had been sprinkled, he fed them leaves soiled by the excreta of corpuscular worms, he inoculated them with fresh corpuscles—and in every case he produced pébrine. These experiments brought him face to face with the fact that the corpuscle, far from being belated evidence of the disease, was itself the sole cause of it. Now at last, after three seasons of patient and exacting research, Pasteur realized the full perfection of the method he had so boldly recommended after his first two weeks' work: to eliminate the corpuscle was to eliminate the disease, not merely to reduce its strength as he had at first thought. Even more important, he had assigned the cause of a contagious disease scientifically—not logically, speculatively or by inference—to the infinitely little. This particular finding was a clear forecast of the bright new day in medicine.

Pasteur is sometimes, and wrongly, thought of as the first to have discovered the role of micro-organisms in contagious diseases. He was not. Agostino Bassi, an important pioneer bacteriologist who died in 1857, had demonstrated that muscardine, another disease of silkworms, was caused by a micro-organic fungus, and he had further suggested that "contagious materials . . . are actually living substances, that is to say, animal or vegetable parasites." Pasteur was anticipated, then, in his discovery of the micro-organic origin of contagious disease, just as he was in some of his other discoveries. But a fact is almost nothing in itself; it is the application made of it, and the facts beyond itself to which it leads, that give it meaning.

It was Pasteur's genius—and he is one of the small handful

in history to whom genius can truly be attributed—that he took his discoveries as starting points—starting points, on the one hand, toward some such eminently practical end as the restoration of an ailing industry, and, on the other, into splendid vistas of speculation and further discovery. His finding that a living micro-organism was the cause of pébrine was such a starting point. It not only led to the elimination of the disease, but also to the development of the germ theory of contagious disease, a theory which, to be sure, had already been advanced in a vague form, and almost casually, by others. Pasteur, however, did more than advance it; because he was a thorough and convincing propagandist, he documented it, demonstrated it and finally forced its general acceptance. In that great and very difficult work he was anticipated by no one. But all that still lay ahead of him.

Now that the cause of the disease was definitely settled, the moment of infection could be recognized and its course defined. Pébrine, the destructive blight of the silk cultivators, was a menace no longer. Its cause was understood, its course traced, a means of prevention found. Pasteur had again served his country well, and science better.

Before this happy solution was reached, however, Pasteur had one disturbing setback. As the silkworm season advanced, letters in increasing numbers reached him every morning, notifying him of the results of cultures for which he had supplied the seed. He would sit at the breakfast table, surrounded by family and disciples, and read each one with interest.

"Ah, good! That is excellent!" he would exclaim, smiling. Or sometimes—and as the season progressed it was more and more often—he would say:

"Ah, *Dieu!* What a misfortune!"

"Is it bad news, Papa?"

"Yes, my child, I am afraid it is. The seeds I furnished a certain grower have unaccountably failed. What can have gone wrong!"

"Don't worry, Papa. There is some reason, and you will discover it."

Marie Louise's confidence in her papa's ability was no more

than that of the young men who worked for him. When Pasteur made the discovery that brought him to the brink of despair, his assistants felt none of his consternation. They had realized for some little time that something was troubling him, but he was always so uncommunicative of his thoughts that they did not know what it was until he hurried into the laboratory one morning, his customary composure quite gone, and sank into a chair. In a voice trembling with tears he exclaimed:

"Gentlemen! Nothing is accomplished. There are *two* diseases. Nothing, after so much work!"

Duclaux, Gernez and Maillot gaped at him openmouthed for a moment. Then their wits began to function.

"But, monsieur, what if there are two diseases? That means only that your work is not finished, not that you have accomplished nothing."

"Of course, my dear master! Your accomplishment stands. Now you simply have a new fact to work with. There is nothing in that to dismay you."

"Come, monsieur, cheer up! We have been investigating pébrine—now we will investigate this new disease of yours. We will end by solving even more problems than we had expected."

"You have a great deal of confidence, you young men," Pasteur said with a touch of bitterness.

"We have all the confidence in the world, monsieur," Duclaux answered calmly. "It is not in ourselves, however—it is in you!"

Heartened by his associates, Pasteur quickly shook off his depression and attacked the new disease. It was not, in fact, new. It was called flacherie, and he had observed it during his first season in Alais. Its symptoms were so constantly associated with pébrine, however (simply, as it turned out, because pébrine was all but universal at the time), that he had supposed some necessary or at least close connection existed between the two diseases. The next year he had given less thought to flacherie because it was comparatively rare, and it was not until the 1867 season, when a large number of cultures surely free from corpuscles failed, that he was forced to recognize the fact that behind the conquered pébrine there lurked another formidable disease.

Pasteur, whose passion for exactitude led him to keep very detailed notebooks on all his work, had only to consult these records to obtain a considerable amount of information on the new disease, now that he recognized it as such, even before beginning experimental work on it. It was now too late in the season to start a new series of experiments, but he obtained cocoons from some silkworm cultures which had been attacked by flacherie. Satisfying himself that the moths which emerged from them were free from corpuscles, he saved the eggs they laid for his experimental cultures the following year.

In spite of harassments, irritations, reverses, it had been a good year. Pébrine had been solved. Now no less than ten microscopes were set up in Alais alone to which growers were sending their moths for examination. The more enlightened and conscientious of the seed merchants, convinced by Pasteur's powerful demonstrations, were examining dead moths so as to avoid the distribution of bad stock. Flacherie, too, had been distinguished from pébrine, and a start had been made on studying it.

Most important, a luminous new idea had been brought to bear on the problem of disease, the idea of the micro-organic—the word microbe and its derivatives had not yet been invented—origin of contagious diseases. It was an idea whose searching brilliance was to throw a great light on questions which, throughout the whole history of scientific thought, had seemed hopelessly obscure.

CHAPTER TWELVE

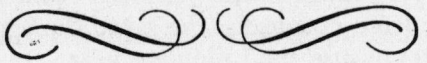

RECOGNITION ordinarily lags behind accomplishment. In Pasteur's case this was almost necessarily true because he progressed so steadily from one valuable discovery to the next that it was hard for the lay mind, and indeed for the scientific, to keep up with him. He had been awarded the Cross of the Legion of Honor well after he had finished the work by which he had earned it, and he had been admitted to the Academy of Sciences, principally on the basis of his work in crystallography, long after he had given it up and had advanced far into the study of fermentations. Now that he had triumphantly concluded his researches on pébrine, he was notified that he was to receive a Grand Prize of the Exposition of 1867 for his work on the diseases of wines.

The presentation took place on July 1, 1867, and, in all the ceremonial pomp, the middle-aged scientist in the black coat attracted little notice. It was not surprising that he should almost escape attention among the brilliant uniforms, the potentates domestic and foreign, and the more publicized recipients of Grand Prizes, such as the painters Gérôme and Meissonier and the engineer de Lesseps, who had built the Suez Canal. Pasteur's work, however much appreciated by scientists, savants and industrialists, was still little known to the public, nor was there anything in the gravity of his personality or the seriousness of his life to catch the popular imagination. It was, in all probability, no more than a handful of the seventeen thousand persons who gathered in the splendidly decorated Palace of Industry to watch the Emperor distribute honors who had any inkling that the fame of the stocky, dark-haired scientist with the air of modest dignity would outlast and eclipse that of all the princes and soldiers assembled there.

Politics were not Pasteur's forte, and where political maneuvers were concerned, he was as uninterested as a child and not much more competent. It was through a political incident, touched off by the well-known man of letters, Sainte-Beuve, that Pasteur was removed from his post at the École normale.
The Senate, of which Sainte-Beuve was a member, had approved a petition of certain citizens of St. Etienne in which they protested against the presence in their libraries of the works of some of France's greatest writers—Voltaire, Balzac and Rousseau, among others—which they considered politically or morally dangerous. Sainte-Beuve arose in outraged liberalism and in a speech which vastly irritated most of his hearers—one august hothead afterwards challenged him to a duel and was contemptuously refused—castigated the Senate for its judgment. The students of the *École*, delighted with Sainte-Beuve's spirited defense of "the independence and the rights of thought," congratulated him in a letter which was published in a newspaper. Since all political demonstration was forbidden to the students by the government, Nisard, the director of the school, punished the writer by sending him home to his family. This action provoked his comrades to rebellion. Pasteur, who had implicit respect for authority in general and for that of the Second Empire in particular, took, rather innocently, the side of authority and discipline: he addressed the students in an effort to make them see their duty as he saw it—and did it with such poor effect that they marched out of the room and into the streets, where they paraded in protest. To his own students on the scientific side of the school he was a great man, a venerated genius; to the *littéraires*, however, who were naturally the most exercised, he was, for the time at least, simply a government functionary who was trying to justify an intolerable act of suppression.
The incident created such a storm that the government closed the school temporarily, and opened it again only when its three chiefs, Nisard, Jacquinet and Pasteur, had been replaced. After eleven years—years in which his patience, his genius for detail and his diligent and brilliant work had helped bring the

École normale back to its early high place in the French educational system—Pasteur's official connection with it was severed.

It was, in spite of everything, a relief to him. What he above all wanted was time for research in his laboratory. Now he no longer had to apply himself to administrative details—the doors could squeak, the students could complain that they were receiving too little meat, the court could need sanding, and it would not be he who would have to order oil for the hinges, calculate how many grams of meat per man per meal were being served, send out for sand. Somebody else would have to do all that, and he could go right on working, undisturbed, in his laboratory. It was a relief, but he never quite forgave the *littéraires*. The word itself became a term of opprobrium in his vocabulary.

"Oh, come, monsieur! You are talking like a *littéraire*," he would sometimes say, and by it he would mean, "You are being inaccurate, thoughtless."

His administrative connection with the school was severed; but he kept his apartment in the rue d'Ulm building and he kept, too, as a neighbor, his loved and valued friend, Bertin. Bertin, after eighteen years in Alsace, had been transferred the year before to the École normale; now he succeeded to Pasteur's position, and to all his administrative problems. Easygoing as a young man, he had not become more ambitious with the years, and he had been reluctant to leave Strasbourg. He had a real talent and love for teaching, however, and was a capable administrator, and Pasteur knew that his old duties had been placed in good hands.

Bertin usually dropped in on Pasteur in the evening, two or three times a week, for a call. Mme Pasteur would lay aside *Le Temps* and take up her knitting, while the two friends, the one always grave and serious, the other full of jolly amiability, talked about the school, the state of science, or whatever.

"Louis, how did you keep those young rascals off the roof in the warm weather?" Bertin asked plaintively.

"That, my friend," Pasteur said blandly, "is your department now. I am sure you will devise a way."

"I wish I had stayed in Strasbourg! There I did not have all these problems. And besides, the beer was better."

"Really, Pierre!" Pasteur exclaimed, with mild reproach.

"You think I am being frivolous? Well, let me tell you, my friend, beer is a serious matter. You are a genius, of course, so you cannot understand little things like that, but take my word for it, beer is *serious!* And besides," Bertin added slyly, "it is a national disgrace that French beer is so far inferior to German."

Pasteur rose to the bait. "Is it really so bad? Ah, poor France, what a pity!" he exclaimed, stung in his ever-sensitive patriotism.

"A national disgrace!" Bertin repeated solemnly. "But then, what is France's shame to *you*—*you* do not drink beer."

Pasteur laughed. "Now you are teasing me. But it is true, I dislike beer, and have no taste for it—I can scarcely tell good from bad."

At the moment, beer to Pasteur was nothing more than the subject for pleasantries with Bertin. Within four years, however, it was no longer a joke; by then he was as serious about it as Bertin himself.

Toward the end of the year, Pasteur was nervously poised between hope and despair. He had appealed directly to the Emperor, ever well disposed toward him and toward science, to build him a large and well-equipped laboratory, with several outbuildings in which he could safely conduct experiments on contagious diseases.

The Emperor immediately told the Minister of Public Instruction, Victor Duruy, who was a warm admirer of Pasteur's, that he wanted M. Pasteur to have his laboratory. Duruy was delighted, and in short order plans for the new laboratory were being drawn up. Then, suddenly, Pasteur's hopes received a painful blow: credit was refused for the building.

"Millions of francs are being spent on the new opera house!" he exclaimed bitterly to his wife, "and they will not spend fifty or sixty thousands to advance science—to investigate the splenic fever, for instance, that costs the neighborhood of Chartres four millions of francs every year. What imbecility! Things have not improved a bit since M. Biot's day—most French scientists still have to work in cellars or cramped dens, and pay for their equipment out of their own pockets. This parsimony is simply strangling all progress—but you cannot make shortsighted politicians see anything beyond their own noses!'

The matter of the laboratory hung fire until well into the next spring. While Pasteur was brooding over France's neglect of science, he was somewhat consoled that Germany took occasion to honor it through him: the University of Bonn conferred on him the degree of M.D. for his work on micro-organisms. Early in the next year, he went back to Alais to resume his research on flacherie. On his arrival, he was delighted to find that the nurseries that had strictly followed his seeding instructions had met with complete success; others, misled by the healthy aspect of their broods, had not bothered to examine their moths for corpuscles and had experienced failures.

He was a good deal less delighted to find that he was viewed, in some quarters, with ferocious dislike. It was no great surprise, however; he was trying to establish a method of breeding which transformed commercial and industrial usages, and he expected to be assailed by those whose interests were threatened. His aging father-in-law, now living in Lyons—where the Silk Commission skeptically questioned Pasteur's method—even heard that he had been chased out of Alais by an angry mob. The rumor was false, but the unpopularity it suggested was a fact. Pasteur, although sensitive and kindly, steeled himself to face it with indifference and pushed his campaign unflaggingly, all the while conducting his experiments on flacherie.

His work was exacting and tiring. He would spend hours in the laboratory watching his worms with that minute attention that made him an unsurpassed observer. More hours were spent traveling, under the sun's hot glare, to and from nurseries. When he should have been resting, he was writing answers to the attacks leveled against him—not so much that he cared what slanderers said about him personally, as that he was relentless in the defense of scientific truth and of the interests of innocent and confused cultivators. He was straining his health to the cracking point, but what good, he thought, was a man unless he rendered every ounce of service he was able?

In July came the word that made him, for the moment, forget his fatigue: his laboratory, after all, was to be built. Rejoicing, he returned to Paris, and wrote jubilant letters to Raulin and his other disciples telling them the good news, describing the progress of the plans, asking their advice about details, speaking of his schemes for research. They were as happy as their master, now that at last his genius was to be provided with the proper tools.

And there was more good news to tell his well-wishers: decisive tests of the pasteurizing process had been undertaken on French ships, and had succeeded completely. The *Jean Bart* and *La Sybille* had set out from port with both heated and unheated wines aboard, and when they returned after long voyages the pasteurized wines were mellow and limpid, the unpasteurized scarcely potable. Pasteur had had no doubt of the outcome of the experiment, but he was gratified by the force of the practical demonstration.

This brief turning back to his earlier work, incidentally, revived its full fascination for him. Leaving an Academy of Sciences meeting, where the discussion had run on the possible relationship between fermentation and contagion, Pasteur exclaimed to Dumas: "Ah, monsieur, I made you a great sacrifice back in 1865!" It seemed to him that he was always having to leave work he loved to take up something new. And his cherished crystals, his first love! Would he ever again go back to them? he sometimes wistfully asked himself.

In Paris he had much besides his new laboratory to occupy him. On leaving the École normale, he had been appointed professor of chemistry at the Sorbonne. Twenty-five years earlier, as an awe-struck young enthusiast, he had listened to the great Dumas there; now, a middle-aged man, he succeeded to his master's place, he spoke from the same platform, he in turn packed the same hall with reverential young men whose love of learning he was stimulating with his own. He had his course of lectures to organize—lectures which he prepared still, as he always had, with endless care. Nor could he relinquish his spirited campaign on behalf of his seeding method, and that took time and energy. He had, also, the next year's work to plan on flacherie, which had already revealed itself to his quickened understanding as another disease due to a micro-organism, one which lodged in the worm's intestinal tract.

With all his duties and interests, he was working so hard and looking so worn that his wife and his friends began to worry.

"Really, Louis," Mme Pasteur remonstrated one evening,

"you are going to make yourself ill, and what good will that do science, or the silkgrowers or anyone else?"

"Madame is right, Louis," Bertin, for once completely serious, agreed. "You cannot go on like this—you are not strong enough. Even if you care nothing for your own health, think of the loss to science should you have to stop work even temporarily."

Bertin's argument had exactly the opposite effect from the one desired.

"I must work," Pasteur answered with simple finality, and left them to return to his laboratory. To him the need to work required no explanation, no justification. Work was an obvious, a self-evident, a completely compelling duty.

He did, finally, become ill, even more alarmingly than anyone had feared. On October 19 he was seized with a shivering fit and a curious tingling that extended over his left side, but with his customary self-discipline he did not allow his symptoms to interfere with his morning's work. After lunch he attended a meeting of the Academy of Sciences, where he read an article by an Italian scientist confirming his work on pébrine; he walked home with Sainte-Claire Deville and Balard who, aware that he was not feeling well, saw him to his door; he went to bed after a light supper—and, when his symptoms came on again, he found himself unable to utter a sound. He had had a cerebral hemorrhage.

For the first few minutes that he remained speechless his mental anguish must have been intense. To be paralyzed at forty-five, at the peak of his superb powers! To be an invalid—perhaps a lump, without speech or motion—for the rest of his life! To be transformed, between one day and the next, from the mainstay of his family to an unwieldy burden on it; and, perhaps worst of all, to have all his promise of future usefulness erased at one quick sweep! With an effort Pasteur opened his mouth and called for help.

Help came immediately. First madame, then doctors, then friends. Henri Sainte-Claire Deville, summoned in the first anxious hours of Pasteur's illness, entered the sickroom softly.

"My dear Pasteur, I am so grieved to learn that you are unwell!"

Pasteur, who could again speak a little, with difficulty, smiled sadly. "I am sorry to die—there is so much more I wanted to do for France."

Affecting a cheerfulness he did not feel, Sainte-Claire Deville protested: "But you are going to get well! You have long years of usefulness ahead of you, in which you will make more wonderful discoveries for France and for science. Now listen—I have a favor to ask of you. You are younger than I, and you will live longer—I want you to be the orator at my funeral. You will think of such nice things to say about me. Will you promise me?"

"Of course, my dear friend—if I am here," Pasteur answered thickly, and Sainte-Claire Deville left the room with tears running down his handsome face.

The following days were ones in which hope and despair trod on each other's heels. At one point Pasteur appeared to be dying, then he slipped into a deathlike sleep—and when he aroused from it, he wanted to discuss science. When it became clear that his mind and his courage were unimpaired, everyone dared to hope that he would recover. His study with the padded doors, the room farthest from the sickroom, was crowded from morning to night with his colleagues, his disciples, his friends, his relatives, all anxiously waiting for bulletins. Every morning the Emperor and Empress sent a footman for news, which Pasteur's doctor gave him in a sealed envelope. Dumas, friend as well as Olympian, took his turn watching by the bedside. Gernez scarcely left it for a week. There was always some friend, whether master or pupil, ready to help with the nursing. Pasteur had become not only one of the most important men in the French scientific world, but one of the most loved.

His recovery, like Claude Bernard's, was encouraged by constant evidences of affection. Soon his speech became clearer, and motion began to return to the paralyzed side. Gernez, trying one night to distract him with gossip about trifles, gave up in the face of Pasteur's insistence on talking about flacherie, and found, with astonishment, that the master was expressing himself with his usual clarity and precision. He had even, as he lay sick and supposedly dying, worked out an ingenious new technique for detecting eggs predisposed to flacherie. A mind of such disciplined power could ignore the distress of the ailing body that housed it.

"And my laboratory, how is it coming?" Pasteur would ask every day.

"Papa, you are not to worry about anything!" his daughter would answer severely, or madame, after a glance out the window, would make some evasive answer. The fact was that all work on the new building in the rue d'Ulm courtyard had been stopped immediately after Pasteur's seizure. Why build a laboratory for a man who would soon be dead?

When the Emperor heard of this misplaced thrift, building, after a flurry of official buck passing, was quickly resumed. Pasteur, who had not been deceived by his family's vagueness, began to feel happier. He was going to recover, he was going to have his laboratory. What more could anyone want?

And the silkworm season, the time for forcing sample broods, was drawing on. Pasteur refused to miss it. Doctors, family, friends, all advised him to rest for a few months, to try to recover his health in undisturbed quiet.

"And let another whole year go by, when two or three months' work now will mean the difference between success and ruin for many growers? Certainly not!" Pasteur answered all arguments.

There was no denying the truth of what he said and, since personal considerations did not count with Pasteur, there was nothing to do but fall in with his plans. On January 18, just three months after the stroke which nearly killed him, he was on his way south with Mme Pasteur, Marie Louise and Gernez in anxious attendance.

The house at St. Hippolyte-le-Fort, near Alais, to which he went for the first part of his work, was uncomfortable and cold. His disciples—Raulin and Maillot followed him down—did their best to make it habitable for an invalid, and his wife and daughter did everything to protect him from overexertion. He complained that his brain was "still weak," but there was little evidence of mental weakness in the notes for a book on the diseases of silkworms that he dictated to his wife in the afternoons, or in the plans for work that he outlined to his three young collaborators every morning when they came to ask for his instructions. For the rest, he moved about very little—indeed, a fall on the stone floor disabled him for weeks—and spared himself as much as possible.

Early in April, at the beginning of the commercial season, Pasteur moved with his family and assistants to the Pont Gisquet villa near Alais to observe the industrial cultures, and his young men made expeditions to Corsica and elsewhere to distribute seed and collect data on the results of the seeding process—data which established beyond any reasonable doubt the merit of his method—in two hundred broods not a single failure had occurred. Reasonable doubts, however, were not the only things that Pasteur had to combat. As Dumas, who came to Alais for the harvest, told him, he had "quacks to fight and envy to conquer," no simple task. Pasteur, who could never be philosophical about frivolous or interested contradiction, was upset and embittered, but he tried to console himself with the reflection that everyone who had followed his method intelligently had been converted to it. Furthermore he had the loyal support of competent scientists, his disciples and his family. Even the cross-grained gardener who had scolded Gernez for climbing the wall had been completely won over; now he trapped with fanatical diligence the mice that loved to prey on the silkworms, and in the emergencies brought on by sudden changes of weather he was as prompt as Madame, Marie Louise or the scientists themselves to rush out and gather in the worms.

While Pasteur was studying the results of his seeding process and continuing his work on flacherie, a benevolent notion had entered the head of the aged Marshal Vaillant, Minister of the Emperor's Household. A man of scientific bent like the Emperor, he had followed Pasteur's work on silkworms with such interest that he had set up for himself, in his study in Paris, a little silkworm nursery. Following Pasteur's method, he met with complete success and took considerable pride in his healthy worms and fine cocoons. It occurred to the old gentleman that he could do both Emperor and scientist, whose health was still very feeble, a good turn by having Pasteur offered lodgings at Villa Vicentina, a property of the Prince Imperial near Trieste, where the silkworm nursery had been losing money for the past ten years. The Emperor was charmed by this happy thought and the Minister of Agriculture, who also had to be consulted, agreed grandiloquently: "It would indeed be well that M. Pasteur should find peace, rest and a return to the health he has so valiantly compromised in his devotion to his country in the midst of the lands which will be the first to profit by the fruit of his splendid discoveries and where his name will be blessed before long."

Accordingly Pasteur established himself, late in November, at Villa Elisa, the main dwelling on the property, a comfortable white house surrounded by acres of lawn shaded by fine trees. He did not rest, because rest was foreign to his temperament, but he was able to work with tranquil regularity. The book on silkworm diseases, which he had begun dictating to his wife at St. Hippolyte-le-Fort, he developed to impressive length. Ready for publication in April, 1870, it incorporated all his findings on pébrine and flacherie up to that time.

The micro-organism of flacherie, peculiar to the digestive tract, was present not at all or only in very small numbers in the intestines of healthy worms, he had found. That the disease was contagious he had readily discovered by spreading the excreta of sick worms on the leaves on which healthy ones were feeding. The healthy worms then became diseased, but all those infected at the same time did not become sick at the same time; death might come in twelve hours, or in three weeks—or not at all, for the disease was not necessarily fatal. Here was clearly expressed a notion new to Pasteur and almost as new to science —the idea of the *receptivity* to germs, differing from individual to individual of the same species.

He had observed, too, that worms infected with germs taken from an artificial fermentation of mulberry leaves died in eight to fifteen days, while healthy worms infected with material taken from the intestinal tract of those first worms died in six to eight days. The virus, therefore, had gained strength in passing through its first victim.

The germ itself, he had discovered, was very common, a fact which accounted for the spontaneous appearance of the disease in nurseries. If one left a bit of bruised mulberry leaf in a flask at summer temperature, micro-organisms in every way identical with those found in the intestines of sick worms appeared in it. The disease was not chronically raging simply because a healthy worm could devour a contaminated leaf and be none the worse for having consumed the flacherie germs with it, since its digestive tract would normally halt the development of the micro-organisms. But if some accident occurred in the nursery—if a leaf had been warmed to the fermentation point and so was very heavily contaminated, or if the worms' resistance had been lowered by storm or chill or unusual heat or bad ventilation—the micro-organisms could take advantage of their hosts' comparative weakness and lay them low.

Flacherie, then, Pasteur stated, was both contagious and spontaneous, requiring for its spontaneous development certain unfavorable conditions to set the stage for it. It was also hereditary but not in the same sense that pébrine was: its germ could not be passed from moth to egg; what passed was a hereditary disposition to the disease, some hereditary weakness that made the offspring, like the parent, easy prey to the germ.

All this was explained in the *Studies on the Diseases of Silkworms* which Pasteur dictated to his wife in the peaceful setting of the Villa Vicentina. He had set out toward a circumscribed, practical goal: the restoration of the silkworm industry. He had achieved it, and far overshot it. He had placed on an experimental basis the great questions of contagion and heredity that are central to pathology.

Remembering the Empress' interest in his assignment, and appreciative of the imperial household's concern for his health, Pasteur dedicated this critically important work to her. With Gallic courtesy he wrote:

> In dedicating these studies to Your Majesty, I fulfill a duty. I had just undertaken them . . . and I was frightened, discouraged by the numberless difficulties that I had glimpsed, when Your Majesty did me the honor to speak to me of them at the Palace of Compiègne. The Empress, touched by the miseries dragged in the wake of this disease which for fifteen years had been decimating the silkworms and ruining one of the finest agricultural industries of France, deigned to take an interest in my first observations and to invoke me to follow them. . . .

Capable of Gallic gallantry, Pasteur was also capable of Gallic wrath. When the time for hatching seed arrived, he distributed among the tenants of the estate twenty-five ounces of guaranteed seed which he had procured from Alais; then he heard that the steward of the villa, who had been keeping an old box of Japanese seed, had sold this dubious seed with the rest. None of Pasteur's pupils and assistants had ever seen him angry in the laboratory, even over a serious mistake, but this piece of callous greed threw him into a memorable rage. The steward, summoned to face the storm, shrank under a thundering torrent of denunciation. When it was finally over, and he could collect his battered wits, the only thing he could remember with any satisfaction was that the gentleman from Paris never wanted to see his face again.

In spite of this misadventure, the seeding process led to a successful harvest. When Pasteur left the Villa Vicentina in July, after living there for more than seven months, he had the pleasure of knowing that, at the same time that he was restoring his own health, he had been restoring the economic health of the silkgrowers on the Prince Imperial's estate. For the first time in a decade it showed a profit—twenty thousand francs.

CHAPTER THIRTEEN

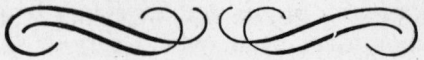

NAPOLEON III had troubles, however, that neither twenty thousand francs, nor twenty million, could assuage. At once rash and irresolute, in the course of his reign he had committed errors in the conduct of domestic and foreign affairs that had played into the hands of his opponents at home and France's enemies abroad. "There are no blunders left for us to make!" exclaimed a French statesman after a particularly resounding one, but he was unduly optimistic. The government, with the sick and aging Napoleon at its head, succeeded in 1870 in making the supreme blunder of being led, unprepared, into war with Prussia.

It was not until he stopped at Strasbourg, early in July, 1870, on his way home from Villa Vicentina, that Pasteur realized the acuteness of the political situation. He had been deeply occupied with a problem in practical science, and a little with one of personal health, and political affairs had not been much on his mind. Politics, in any case, was not his field, and he brought to the contemplation of it little but the high-minded and very general idea that progress and peace were to be attained through scientific advances.

His disillusion was profound and bitter. Within two months this humane and gentle man, whose dealings with German scientists had always been cordial and stimulating, was writing to his pupil Raulin: "Every one of my future works will bear on its title page the words 'Hatred to Prussia! Revenge! Revenge!'"

They had been terrible months to work such a transformation in his spirit. His forebodings had been sharpened to alarm on his arrival in Paris by Sainte-Claire Deville's warning that invasion was certain, France helpless to resist it. Then the

Normaliens, although exempt from conscription, enlisted to the last man, and his own son, the cheerful and amusing Jean Baptiste, joined the *chasseurs*. The young men had spent their last evening together in Bertin's apartment, with Bertin, Pasteur, Sainte-Claire Deville and Duruy. Patriotism, enthusiasm, optimism, all were evident, but behind these gallant and indeed necessary emotions was the somber knowledge that France was in no condition to wage war, and that there were some of these boys whose promise would be brutally extinguished for a cause already compromised. After the departure of the students, the big school building lapsed into echoing silence.

Then followed the news of defeats, defeats which came with appalling swiftness. Weissenburg, Forbach, Gravelotte, Sedan—each name filled Pasteur's heart with anguish. For once he could scarcely work; personal grief he could dominate, but the immensity of the national disaster was too much. After the capture of MacMahon's army and of the Emperor on September 1 at Sedan, the government collapsed and the Second Empire with it. France was finished with the Bonapartes now, just as she was with the Bourbons and the Orléans.

The new government's efforts to end the war failed: Prussia wanted more than heavy indemnity in money, as some French statesmen had innocently supposed; she wanted Alsace as well—and that was too much. The Government of National Defense continued the desperate struggle. Paris, empty of troops and unprotected, prepared to stand siege.

"You must leave the city, Louis," Bertin insisted. "A man in your physical condition cannot fight, and everyone who cannot fight is simply a useless mouth to feed."

It was against every instinct to turn his back on a fight, to leave his friends to face the danger, but Pasteur realized that Bertin was right. On September 5 he and his wife and daughter set out for Arbois. Bertin saw them off; then, with his invincible good humor, he went about converting part of the school building into a sort of hospital and lodging for the *Normaliens* stationed in Paris. The rest of Paris battened down for the siege.

In his childhood home, Pasteur did what work he could, and followed the disheartening progress of events. Watching his sister and brother-in-law at their baking and tanning, he would ask them questions about these homely occupations, seeking the scientific reason for every operation. It was hard for him to work steadily, so he read a great deal, philosophical as well as scientific books, to try to maintain some kind of mental balance in the general wreck of his hopes and illusions. But when the town crier blew his trumpet, and everyone rushed into the street to hear his announcement, Pasteur would fling down his reading and limp hastily outdoors, his philosophical thoughts brought abruptly down to earth and to the sufferings of France.

The news was generally bad: other European powers refused to intervene; Paris, invested on September 19, was isolated from the rest of France; Bazaine treasonably surrendered his army at Metz toward the end of October. Thinking of his friends and countrymen working and fighting in the half-starved capital, Pasteur could hardly contain himself. The Germans began shelling the city on January 5, and when their bombs dropped into the Garden of Medicinal Plants, founded by an edict of Louis XIII and never before injured during wars and revolutions, he wished more passionately than ever that he had stayed in Paris to suffer with his colleagues and with them sign their defiant protest over this damage.

The only thing he could do to express himself he did: he wrote the head of the medical faculty of the University of Bonn, which only two years before had conferred an honorary M.D. upon him, demanding that he revoke the diploma. It was only a gesture, but it was one eloquent of "the indignation inspired in a French scientist by the barbarity and hypocrisy of him [Wilhelm I] who, in order to satisfy his criminal pride, persists in the massacre of two great nations." The solace of righteous anger and pride was the only one left to him, and he collected anecdotes illustrating courage and sacrifice on the part of the French, brutality and oppression on the part of the invader.

And there was no word of Jean Baptiste. His regiment of *chasseurs* had fought at Harlicourt with Bourbaki's Eastern Army Corps, which had then been ordered to withdraw to Besançon and which was retreating, under the most lamentable conditions, even farther back toward Pontarlier. Wretched stragglers, half frozen, ravenously hungry, often sick or wounded, lost from their regiments and hopelessly confused in the strange region, could be encountered around Poligny and Lons-le-Saunier; and the snow-covered roads more directly in the line of retreat were swarming with more coherent, but scarcely less miserable, groups of soldiers. Anything might have happened to Jean Baptiste. He could be dead, or wounded, or still alive and suffering from cold and hunger and despair among these unfortunates. Toward the end of January Pasteur could bear the suspense no longer and made up his mind to look for his son.

"Marie," he announced, "I have hired a carriage, and tomorrow I am going to set out for Pontarlier to find our boy."

He may have intended to go alone. If so, it was one of the few times in his domestic life that his decision was not final. On Tuesday, January 24, a tumble-down old carriage rolled almost silently—for the road was deep with snow—out of Arbois toward Montrond, carrying Louis Pasteur, his wife and his daughter on their anxious search.

The going was heartbreakingly slow and hard. The roads were almost impassable because of the snow, which continued to fall quietly and ceaselessly in enormous flakes, and the carriage, creaking and floundering, often had to be pushed. The half-paralyzed man, the middle-aged woman and the child were upheld principally by a sort of desperate hope through the grueling journey. The first night they slept in a primitive little inn near Montrond, the next at Censeau, the next at Chaffois. It was not until Friday that the battered carriage, by then ready to fall to pieces, creaked with its weary passengers into Pontarlier.

The small town, close to the Swiss border, was crowded with soldiers who were doing whatever they could to wring a little physical comfort out of their desperate situation. Fires burned in the streets around which tattered groups, scarcely recognizable as remnants of the imperial army, huddled. Soldiers went from door to door, begging for a bit of food, a little straw to lie on. Many had taken refuge from the weather in the church, and lay in the careless and uncomfortable postures of exhaustion on the floor; others, wakeful with pain, were trying to wrap rags around their frozen feet. The Pasteurs, passing through the midst of these pitiful figures, scanned every face. Sergeant Pasteur was not among them. They did encounter, however, Sainte-Claire Deville's nephew, Commandant Bourboulon.

"No, monsieur," he said, "I cannot tell you where your son's battalion is. You can see for yourself," his gesture was apathetic with fatigue as he waved his hand to take in the scene, "how things are with us now."

"The retreat from Moscow can have been no worse!" Pasteur exclaimed.

While he was talking with Bourboulon, Mme Pasteur approached a soldier in the battle-stained uniform of a *chasseur* and was questioning him.

"Only three hundred out of the twelve hundred men of that battalion remain alive, madame," he told her.

"And my son, Sergeant Pasteur, you know nothing of him?" she asked him imploringly.

"Nothing, madame, I am sorry."

"Pasteur?" interrupted another soldier who had overheard the conversation. "A young sergeant? I slept beside him only last night at Chaffois. He is ill, but not seriously. Return toward Chaffois, madame. You may meet him on the road."

Electrified by this good news for which they had scarcely dared to hope, the Pasteurs prepared to retrace their steps the next morning. The only thing that withheld them from starting immediately was consideration for their tired horses and the fear of passing their son without seeing him in the dark. Fortified by hope and rest, they set out early the next morning. As they left the town they looked eagerly into every face, peered into every conveyance they passed. On one of the first carts they met after going through the city gate sat Jean Baptiste.

Jean Baptiste, catching sight so unexpectedly of his parents and sister, gave a silent gasp of surprise. Then, with his greatcoat flapping clumsily about his thin figure, he leaped over the tailboard of the cart. Pasteur halted the carriage and scrambled limpingly down, followed by his wife and daughter. The reunited family embraced without a word in the snowy road.

M. Loir, Pasteur's brother-in-law, was now head of the Lyons Faculty of Sciences. The Pasteurs had frequently stopped at his home on their way south for the silkworm season, and a cordial affection existed between the two families. It was with the Loirs that they stayed after seeing Jean Baptiste safely to Geneva, where he could recuperate from the illness brought on by the hardships of his military service.

Pasteur had intended to return to Paris—the city, reduced to eating rats and the animals in the zoological garden, had finally capitulated on January 28—but Bertin advised him not to. The south wing of the school had been demolished by shellfire, he wrote, dormitories and classrooms were given over to sick and wounded, and Pasteur's laboratory—from which he so rigorously excluded everyone but his chosen assistants—was full of national guardsmen who had nowhere else to go. There was, in short, no place for him to work.

Pasteur spoke of his mind as lying fallow, but even in the absence of a laboratory he occupied it. He wrote an article explaining why France, in her extremity, had found no superior men: it was the "forgetfulness, disdain even" that she had for intellectual men, especially those in the realm of exact science. The cost of the government's parsimonious policy toward education and science had at last, in his opinion, made itself frightfully clear. "Great discoveries—the manifestations of thought in art, in science and in letters, in a word the disinterested exercise of the mind in every direction and the centers of instruction from which it radiates, introduce into the whole of society that philosophical or scientific spirit, that spirit of discernment which submits everything to severe reasoning, condemns ignorance and scatters errors and prejudices. They raise the intellectual level and the moral sense, and through them the Divine Idea itself is spread abroad and intensified."

Philosophical reflections, however, did not help him to contain his anger when he received the answer of the principal of the faculty of medicine at the University of Bonn. It read:

> SIR, the undersigned, now Principal of the faculty of medicine of Bonn, is requested to answer the insult which you have dared to offer to the German nation in the sacred person of its august Emperor, King Wilhelm of Prussia, by sending you the expression of its *entire contempt*.
> DR. MAURICE NAUMANN

> P.S. Desiring to keep its papers *free from taint*, the faculty herewith returns your screed.

The stupid, almost juvenile, arrogance of this response provoked from Pasteur the answer:

> I have the honor to inform you, Mr. Principal, that there are times when the expression of contempt in a Prussian mouth is equivalent for a true Frenchman to that of *Virum clarissimum* which you once publicly conferred upon me.

But this harsh and intemperate chauvinism was too unlike Pasteur for him to let it stand unmodified, and he added:

> And now, Mr. Principal, after reading over both your letter and mine, I sorrow in my heart to think that men who, like yourself and myself, have spent a lifetime in the pursuit of truth and progress should address each other in such terms. . . .

Patriotism had been outraged on both sides, but expressions such as they had used had outraged something superior to patriotism—a sort of ideal of international decency and good will—and Pasteur was quick to mourn the fact.

So the small and depressing episode was concluded, and lost among more important events. Germany demanded the cession of most of Alsace and part of Lorraine, and France, unable to resist further, had to yield the territory. The victor also exacted the indemnity, enormous for the time, of five billion francs. Most flagrant humiliation of all, the Germany army marched into Paris. The Paris populace, which had been armed for the siege, and never disarmed, arose two weeks later, on March 18, and established the Commune; fighting raged between communards and anticommunards, and the city was not recaptured by the government for two months.

Meanwhile Pasteur, deprived of a laboratory, fretted quietly at Lyons. He could not return to Paris—the intellectual world, incompetent to deal with such disorders, had scattered to the provinces and to neutral Switzerland—nor could he return to

Arbois, which had been converted to a Prussian depot. He occupied himself as well as he could with writing, reading, playing with the Loir children—and practicing stoicism. Little Adrien Loir, his nephew, particularly remembered one day at dinner when the call to arms sounded in the street, summoning the national guardsmen to assemble in the square of the city hall, over which floated the red flag of the Commune. M. Loir sprang up from the table, and hurried out of the room to change into his uniform. On his re-entry Mme Loir flung herself into his arms, begging him to take care of himself, and the frightened children clung to him. There were tears and farewells, and through them all Pasteur sat, quietly eating his soup. From his behavior one might have thought that his brother-in-law was going out for a walk, rather than on a perhaps dangerous military mission. The fact was that his emotions over everything concerning the war and its aftermath were so intense that he could have expressed them adequately only by going up in smoke; therefore he behaved with severe calm.

His calm cracked, however, when he considered the possibility of helping to restore his beloved country to her previous dignity and prosperity. He wrote impassioned letters to Duclaux, exclaiming: "I have a head full of the most beautiful projects for work. . . . Oh, why am I not rich? A millionaire! I would say to you, to Raulin, to Gernez. . . . Come! We will transform the world by our discoveries! . . . Oh, that I could begin a new life of study and work! Poor France, dear land of our fathers! Why can I not help to lift you up once more from your disasters?"

Duclaux, realizing how frustrating it was to his master to be without a laboratory, suggested that Pasteur come to Clermont-Ferrand, where he was still teaching chemistry, and make use of his. Duclaux's affection embraced Pasteur's family as well. He rearranged his own household—he was now married and had a baby—so that not only Pasteur but Mme Pasteur and Marie Louise could stay in his home. It was small wonder that Pasteur, referring to his pupil, was accustomed to speaking in an accent of tenderness of "my dear Duclaux."

Surrounded by a congenial domestic circle and provided with the means of working, Pasteur, for the first time since the outbreak of the war, felt sufficiently at peace to return to his researches. But what should he work on? He wanted to get back to fermentations, and he wanted to do something of practical importance, something that would help to restore the ruptured French economy. It was then that he remembered Bertin's strictures on French beer, his comments on its inferiority to German. If only he could improve it, through the application of science to its manufacture, so that it equaled or even surpassed the product of the detested enemy! There would be an appropriate, a dignified revenge! Pasteur at once applied himself to the study of beer.

At Chamalières, near Clermont-Ferrand, was a large brewery. Pasteur went there to inquire on the spot into all phases of the manufacture of beer. He found, as he had found in other industries he had investigated, that the processes of production were not clearly understood; sometimes they turned out well, and sometimes, for unexplained reasons, they turned out badly and the beer became acid, putrid, slimy or otherwise unfit to drink. When that happened, the brewer, assuming that something was wrong with the yeast he had used, ordered yeast from another source and started over again.

What made these unfavorable alterations? Pasteur had exploded the theory of spontaneous generation, and he had found that each type of fermentation he had examined was due to its own specific germ. He began with the assumption, therefore, that each type of change to which beer was subject was due to the introduction of germs at some stage of its manufacture. In spite of the technical difficulties in the way, he succeeded, with the co-operation of Duclaux and the brewers of Chamalières, in protecting beer from the introduction of outside dusts. Early in August he was writing Dumas, sending him a dozen bottles of "my beer," as he proudly called it, and hoping that he would find it compared favorably with the best obtainable in Paris.

Before leaving Duclaux and returning to Paris, which was by that time enjoying a sort of exhausted quiet, Pasteur wanted to go to London to visit the big breweries there. He was received courteously, and shown around the various breweries when he explained his errand. He confounded the managers, as he had once confounded his Arboisian friends when he was studying the diseases of wines, by pointing out defects of taste after only microscopic study of the beer. He was happy to find that several of the breweries, quick to take advantage of the information he gave them, installed microscopes for the regular examination of their product. And why should that make him happy—what did he get out of it? "We must make some friends for our beloved France," he explained. That was what he was doing.

On his return to Paris in the fall he continued his work on beers. The problem was not merely to keep ferments causing disagreeable changes out of beer—a beer protected against them is not necessarily a good beer. The question of taste entered in, and taste is variable and difficult to grasp. Each brewery had its own to which its patrons were accustomed and which depended on the original material used, such as the yeast and the water, and on the varying processes of manufacture as well. Pasteur would have been happier if he could have conducted his studies exclusively through a microscope and never tasted the stuff, but he strove valiantly to cultivate a taste for the nuances of the general taste which he disliked. Bertin, who loved beer and had an exquisite palate for it, watched with amusement the struggles of France's foremost scientist who, out of patriotism and nothing else, forced himself to consume quantities of beer.

"I have found a new café, Louis, and you must go there with me this evening—the beer is beautiful!"

"Indeed, Pierre? Very well, I shall be interested to examine it."

" 'I shall be interested to examine it!' " Bertin mimicked, and threw up his hands. "My dear man, when will you learn that one does not 'examine' beer—one *savors*, one *enjoys* it!"

Pasteur, conscientiously and with resignation, studied all the beers recommended by his enthusiastic friend, and conducted long experiments on them. At the conclusion of this work he announced that every unfavorable alteration in beer was caused by some micro-organism which was the ferment of a specific disease; that these micro-organisms were introduced into the beer by the air, by one of the ingredients used in its manufacture, or by the apparatus employed in the breweries; and that beer free of living germs is unalterable. The same heating process which he had applied to wines could be applied to beers to keep them indefinitely.

Thanks to Pasteur's investigation, the best French beers became as good as the best German ones; France was freed from her dependence on her recent enemy across the Rhine for one of the amenities of life.

And Pasteur, who always saw beyond the immediate accomplishment into the distant prospects it opened to his imagination, wrote:

"When we see beer and wine subjected to deep alterations because they have given refuge to micro-organisms invisibly introduced and swarming within them, it is impossible not to be pursued by the thought that similar facts may, *must*, take place in animals and in man. But . . . let us endeavor to remember . . . that the greatest disorder of the mind is to allow the will to direct the belief."

The application of his theories to human and animal diseases was becoming clearer to him, but he did not intend to be betrayed by enthusiasm into reckless statements. As he had said much earlier, "In experimental science it is always a mistake not to doubt unless facts compel one to affirm."

CHAPTER FOURTEEN

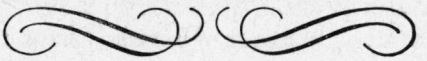

THE NARROW majority—one vote—by which Pasteur was elected in 1873 to the Free Associates of the Academy of Medicine was hardly compatible with the impact of his researches on the medical world, but it was an impact that was making itself felt only gradually. His work was not highly regarded in that Academy; it was, on the whole, a tradition-minded body of men and, although some of his firmest and most effective champions developed in it, he met there opposition that was violent, dogged and prolonged. The traditional doctors of the day believed that disease was something that sprang up in the body when, for some reason or other, certain of its elements got out of balance, certain of its chemical processes operated faultily. The microorganisms which were undeniably present in some cases were, they held, the by-product, not the cause, of the disease. Many members of the Academy, practicing physicians, took it as an impertinent affront that a "mere chemist" should contradict the opinions of qualified practitioners, and their distaste for Pasteur's upsetting theories was not moderated by the impetuous bluntness with which he defended them.

However the conservatives of the Academies of Medicine and Sciences reacted to the germ theory of contagious disease, medical students and young doctors eagerly attended meetings of both academies to hear Pasteur advance and defend his views. His novel theories, sharply scouted by those to whom old ideas were sacrosanct, were taking hold in the receptive and flexible minds of a younger generation of medical men.

In spite of ridicule and hostility, the theory that certain germs caused certain infections and contagious diseases was making headway and proving its worth by its fruitfulness. The most striking example was the work of the Scotch surgeon, Joseph Lister. After reading Pasteur's early *Mémoire sur la fermentation appelée lactique* it had occurred to him that, if germs floating in the air could drop into organic fluids and cause fermentations, they might also be getting into the wounds of surgical patients and causing the infections that made even the most trifling operation a dangerous risk. Lister thought that it would be worth while to try to eliminate germs from air, instruments, dressings and operators' hands, and he did so by the lavish use of carbolic acid. The results he got were startling. Like all other surgeons, he had been accustomed to losing nearly all of the few amputations he undertook; then, between 1867 and 1869, thirty-four out of forty of his patients, operated on under the antiseptic conditions he devised, survived amputations. Yet his results—where they were known—were sneered at and he was treated with sarcasm by surgeons who, in the established tradition, continued with unshaken self-confidence to lose most of their patients. His work was almost unknown in France, even at the time of the Franco-Prussian War, and the mortality among the soldiers—not only from wounds but from surgical interventions that resulted in infections—was a source of horror and bafflement to French surgeons who never for a moment imagined that with their unsterile hands and instruments and dressings they were bringing death to the men they were working valiantly to save.

In February, 1874, Lister wrote to Pasteur, making cordial acknowledgment that his method was inspired by the fertile thought of the French scientist. Still, however, members of the Academy of Medicine were so far from grasping the importance of germs and germ-free operative techniques that Pasteur had to explain in some detail the reason and the method for putting an instrument through a flame before operating with it.

However slow was the appreciation of the medical implications of Pasteur's work, recognition of its practical consequences was by now widespread. Winegrowers, vinegar makers, silkworm cultivators, brewers, all could testify that the application of his techniques to their industries had added millions of francs yearly to their revenues. The English scientist, Thomas Henry Huxley, declared that Pasteur's discoveries had contributed more to the French national income than the Franco-Prussian War indemnity had drained off. This same year, 1874, the National Assembly, acting on the report of Paul Bert, one of its members and a colleague of Pasteur's, voted Pasteur, as a "national recompense," a life annuity of twelve thousand francs—by the large majority of five hundred and thirty-two to twenty-four. Enthusiasm for France's leading scientist was probably the one sentiment which the Assembly held anywhere nearly unanimously.

The senatorial electors of his native Jura were probably just as grateful to Pasteur as the members of the Assembly, but they still did not want him for Senator when, on the persuasion of some of his Jura friends, he ran for the office in 1875. Perhaps there was an element of we-knew-him-when in their attitude; perhaps they preferred a political figure; perhaps they misunderstood his somewhat distant manner. Certainly he kissed no babies during his campaign; he could hardly, at any time, bring himself to shake hands. The man who had demonstrated the omnipresence of germs was especially conscious of those clinging to hands. He usually met people with his right hand held behind his back, and if he was unable to avoid a handshake he seized the first opportunity to wash. In any case, he was not elected. Pasteur took his defeat in good part, agreeing with his daughter that he could serve his country better in the laboratory than in the Senate.

Glad to be done with campaigning, Pasteur returned from the Jura to Paris and to his customary routine of hard work—lectures, attendance at scientific meetings, brief journeys on scientific missions, long experimentation in his laboratory—which was still broken only by his Sunday receptions. Now that he was so prominent, he could, like a king or a president, invite to them men whom he did not know but wished to meet. He always considered it one of the happiest impulses of his life that, after reading a book that pleased him, *Le journal d'un volontier d'un an*, he asked its author to dine with him one Sunday in 1876. Pasteur's modesty prevented him from guessing it, but young René Vallery-Radot received the invitation with mixed feelings: he was almost as much frightened by it as flattered. For fear of appearing an ignoramus to his host, he studied zealously for several days to familiarize himself with the main features of Pasteur's work, and when Sunday came and he knocked on the door of the apartment in the École normale, he was more in the mood of a student going to an examination than a young man going to a party.

But he had a wonderful time. Madame welcomed him warmly. Pasteur, too good a host to talk about his own interests, said: "We so much enjoyed your book, monsieur. Tell me, do you intend to make literature your career?" And Marie Louise was charming. Captivated equally by parents and daughter, the handsome young man forgot his original shyness and became a frequent visitor. Within several years he was more than that— he was the husband of Marie Louise and the intimate friend of her parents.

Sometimes it seemed to Pasteur that he would never hear the end of the spontaneous generation theory. From time to time its advocates reared their addled heads and reopened the old argument. Facts, in this case, compelled Pasteur to affirm that spontaneous generation was an illusion, and no compromise was possible. When a young Englishman, Dr. Henry Charlton Bastian, revived the discussion, Duclaux, whose genial good heart tempered but did not blunt a sharp critical faculty, said of him that he had "tenacity, fertility of mind, and love, if not understanding, of the experimental method." Thus he summed up Dr. Bastian; and Pasteur disposed of him in his usual way— by demonstration. Repeating Bastian's experiments and devising variations on them, Pasteur discovered that the microscopic organisms which Bastian believed had developed spontaneously in a supposedly sterile organic infusion were, in fact, organisms which had resisted boiling. This, of course, was the phenomenon which Pouchet and his supporters also had thought was spontaneous generation. Pasteur, with whom there was no such thing as a sterile and repetitious discussion, was the first to interpret it correctly.

He felt it imperative to defeat Bastian completely, to establish it firmly that each ferment was a living being, arising not spontaneously but as the normal offspring of like living beings which produced its own and only its own kind of fermentation. If spontaneous generation was left a leg to stand on there would then be some room for belief in the spontaneous origin of contagious diseases—and that theory, Pasteur was positive, was wrong. Medical science could advance to new knowledge, and medical treatment could extend its usefulness only when doctors accepted the fact that contagious diseases, far from developing spontaneously in the body, were always implanted in it from without, by the agency of an invading micro-organism.

In 1865 Pasteur, with many misgivings, had taken up the study of the diseases of silkworms, insects vastly higher in the scale of creation than the germs and ferments he knew. Now, a dozen years later and without any reluctance, he went to work on anthrax, a disease that raged fatally among sheep, cows and horses.

Anthrax, which was also called splenic fever and charbon, was a mysterious scourge ruinously costly to agriculture. In the plain country surrounding Chartres, known as the Beauce, farmers were losing a fifth of their sheep to it, and in a bad year they might lost half. In its choice of victims the plague was erratic. One farm would be a "charbon farm" and suffer a high mortality among its animals, and the flocks of the farm neighboring it would be entirely free of the disease; a field or a hillside would be "cursed" and a large number of the animals grazing there would die, while those on adjoining ground would remain in perfect health. The pest, widespread in France, was active in other countries; nor was it confined to livestock—human beings, too, had fallen victim to it by the hundreds, and had died as promptly and painfully as the domestic animals.

Such a challenge to veterinary medicine had not been ignored. Onésime Delafond, a professor at the Alfort Veterinary School, examined anthrax blood in 1838 and found some "little rods" in it, but attached no importance to them. In 1850 Casimir Davaine observed the same threadlike, motionless micro-organisms and called them bacteria; thirteen years later, after reading a paper on fermentation by Pasteur, he decided that they must have an action similar to that of ferments—that they were, in fact, the cause of anthrax. When he inoculated rabbits with some fresh charbon blood, he found these same bacteria in the blood of the dying rabbits.

Two other investigators, however, apparently refuted Davaine's experiment: Jaillard and Leplat took blood from an animal dead of anthrax, inoculated rabbits with it, examined the blood of the rabbits, which had promptly died—and found it free of the suspected bacteria. More discussion and experiment followed, and none of it was conclusive.

Then, in 1876, a young German, Dr. Robert Koch, a genius at devising techniques for studying micro-organisms, published an important paper on the life history of the bacterium, which was by then beginning to be known as *bacillus anthracis*. Having discovered a medium in which it grew well, he had been able to study it in isolation, outside the body of an animal. Growing in the aqueous humor of oxen's eyes, it developed rapidly to ten or twenty times its original length and, in time, small round spots appeared in it, rather suggestive of peas in a pod. These were the spores of the bacillus and, injected into a susceptible animal, they produced anthrax quickly and infallibly.

Just when this much seemed clear, Pasteur's friend, Paul Bert, again threw the subject into doubt by announcing that the *bacillus anthracis* in a drop of blood could be destroyed by compressed oxygen; the drop—now entirely free of bacilli—could be injected into a laboratory animal, and the animal would die of anthrax.

At this point Pasteur entered the field. It was just the kind of problem he liked, since it had both a theoretical and a practical side. To approach it, however, he had to change his method of work to a certain extent. Without training in medicine or veterinary medicine himself, he was going to need assistants—collaborators, rather—trained in those fields and experienced in new experimental techniques that he would need.

During his recent discussion with Bastian, he had, on Bertin's advice, taken into his laboratory Jules François Joubert, physics professor at a Paris *lycée*, who was particularly interested in the action of physical agents on micro-organisms. Early in the course of his work on anthrax he also admitted Charles Édouard Chamberland, a young École normale graduate whose mechanical ingenuity was to prove valuable to the laboratory and at least one of whose inventions, the Chamberland filter, came into wide use. Thus it was that, for a time, the papers on anthrax coming out of Pasteur's laboratory were signed by Pasteur, Joubert and

Chamberland. Later, when Pasteur gave up the study of the action of physical agents on micro-organisms—a study suggested to him in the first place by Bertin—Joubert, seeing that the work was leading away from his own interests, left the rue d'Ulm, and the work of the laboratory was then signed by Pasteur, Chamberland and Roux.

Émile Roux, brilliant and incisive, was one of the new generation of medical men. Delighted by the logic and fruitfulness of the Pasteurian theories, and by the scrupulously precise methods of the master, he as a student had eagerly attended meetings of the academies to hear Pasteur explain and defend his work. Later Duclaux, under whom he had studied, had presented him to Pasteur, and Pasteur, some time afterward, admitted him to the rue d'Ulm laboratory, where he worked for ten years, from 1878 to 1888.

Pasteur's first step was to try to determine finally whether the bacillus, or something else in the blood of which the bacillus might be a by-product, was the cause of anthrax. He took a drop of blood from an animal dead of anthrax and placed it in a suitable culture medium. Within a few hours the bacilli, growing fast in the favorable medium, had lengthened to form long, entangled threads. Pasteur then took a drop of this culture and placed it in a fresh medium, and when the process of growth had repeated itself, he sowed a drop of that new culture into yet another fresh medium. This operation he repeated forty times—and a drop of the fortieth culture, injected under the skin of a rabbit, was as fatal as a drop of fresh charbon blood. The spores, likewise, sown in broth, produced bacilli which then were found capable of producing anthrax. By this prolonged culture of bacilli outside the body, Pasteur was able to prove that it was the bacillus and it alone—for the original drop of blood had been too diluted through forty successive cultures to retain any obscure property or virulence—which caused anthrax.

There was one point settled. But how explain the findings of Jaillard and Leplat—how had they produced death by injecting charbon blood, yet found no bacilli in the blood of the experimental victims? Reviewing their experiment, Pasteur seized on the salient point: the blood which the two investigators had used had been sent to them from a distance at the peak of the summer's heat. It must have been taken from the dead animals at least twenty-four hours before they used it. The time lapse, he was sure, was important; the blood must already have been decomposing when they received it.

Anthrax had broken out again around Chartres, and Pasteur decided to go there to conduct some experiments. He wrote to the knacker—the dealer in worn-out animals, hides and bones—from whom Jaillard and Leplat had obtained blood, asking him to keep for several days the carcasses of animals dead of anthrax. On June 13 Pasteur arrived at Chartres and went to the knacker's yard where three carcasses were being kept for him. One was a sheep dead sixteen hours, another a horse dead the previous day and the third a cow dead for two or three days. The blood of the sheep, most recently dead, contained anthrax bacilli only; that of the horse revealed, on microscopic examination, both anthrax bacilli and septic vibriones, the bacilli of putrefaction; and in the blood of the cow was found an even larger proportion of the putrefaction vibriones. In the inoculations on guinea pigs which followed, the sheep's blood alone produced death with the anthrax bacilli in the blood of the experimental animals; the blood of the other two animals produced prompt death—but no bacilli. It was now clear to Pasteur that the vibrio of putrefaction, the septic vibrio that lives harmlessly in the intestinal canal during life and penetrates only after death into the organs and the blood, was the micro-organism responsible for the deaths of Jaillard's and Leplat's experimental animals.

Two points now had been cleared up. There remained only Paul Bert's objection to answer. Pasteur did it quite simply by demonstrating that, while compressed oxygen destroyed the bacillus, it left the much tougher spore uninjured, and quite capable of developing, once it was in an animal's blood stream, into the fatal bacillus. Paul Bert, convinced of his error, freely admitted it.

It was in March, 1878, that that eminently convenient word "microbe" was introduced into the language of science by Dr. Charles Emmanuel Sédillot, an elderly surgeon whose age had not suspended his critical faculty or the receptivity of his keen mind. He read a paper to the Academy of Sciences called "On the Influence of M. Pasteur's Work on Medicine and Surgery" in which, for the first time, "microbe" replaced the more unwieldy "micro-organism." Having gone through the Franco-Prussian War and suffered in helpless distress while the wounded all around him died not of their wounds but of infections, he welcomed with enthusiasm the application of the germ theory to surgery. While Sédillot was praising Pasteur in the Academy of Sciences, others, less susceptible to new ideas, were attacking him in the Academy of Medicine. Professor G. Colin, of the Alfort Veterinary School, particularly, continued to insist that anthrax was caused by some virulent agent in the blood other than the bacillus. He seemed, in fact, to be under a sort of compulsion to contradict Pasteur at every turn. This perversity got him into an embarrassing situation.

Koch had found that birds, especially hens, were immune to anthrax, and Pasteur, who had verified this curious fact, one day mentioned it at a meeting of the Academy of Medicine. Colin at once asserted that Pasteur was wrong. It was, he declared, quite easy to give a chicken anthrax. Pasteur suggested that Colin try it, and Colin nonchalantly accepted the challenge. For weeks thereafter Pasteur, every time he saw Colin, asked if he had yet produced a diseased hen. Colin was full of excuses: he had been too busy, his first effort had failed, a naughty dog had gobbled up his experimental birds, etc. Finally, he said he had changed his mind; it was not possible to give anthrax to a hen.

"But my dear colleague," said Pasteur with polite surprise, "surely you are mistaken! I have myself recently succeeded in infecting hens with charbon."

Poor Colin was almost speechless with annoyance at this chemist who had lured him to abandon his first position, and now said it had been sound all along—and all to show, as Pasteur expressed it before the Academy with infuriating condescension, "that our colleague's contradictions of our observations on charbon have never been very serious."

Pasteur had, in fact, produced anthrax in a chicken, and to demonstrate the fact he took a step that might have abashed a less single-minded man. The stocky elderly scientist, who was always careful about his appearance to the point of being almost dapper, unself-consciously presented himself before his astonished colleagues at the next meeting of the Academy of Medicine tenderly carrying an unusual burden—a cage containing three hens, one of them dead. The dead one, he said, had been injected with pure anthrax bacilli two days before.

But how had he given the disease to this admittedly immune creature? he was asked. It had been easy, he explained. It had occurred to him and Joubert and Chamberland to see if the body temperature of chickens, which was several degrees higher than that of animals susceptible to anthrax, had anything to do with their immunity. He had inoculated the white hen—now a corpse—and to lower her temperature had tied her, half immersed, in a cool bath for several hours. Sure enough, she died of anthrax. To meet the objection that the long wetting alone might have killed her, Pasteur had kept in the same bath for the same length of time another hen, a lively gray one, which turned her beady eyes, bright with curiosity, on the learned men gathered around her. The third hen, as active and healthy as the second, had been inoculated with a double dose of the same culture that had killed the first hen, but she had not been kept in the bath.

Pasteur had still a fourth experiment, and performed it a few days later. He wanted to see if the course of charbon could be reversed simply by removing the chicken from the bath and allowing her temperature to rise again to its normal height. Inoculating a hen and placing her in a cool bath, he left her there until the disease was well advanced. Then he lifted the sick, wet creature out, and took her to a warm room where he wrapped her in cotton wool. The anthrax bacilli, unable to withstand the rising temperature, disappeared from her blood and the lucky bird recovered entirely.

Colin, with his perverse skepticism, could not leave well enough alone, and remarked insinuatingly that it was a pity Pasteur had not let the Academy witness a necropsy on the dead hen, instead of having whisked her away. Pasteur indignantly demanded that the Academy appoint a commission to examine microscopically a hen dead of anthrax which he would provide. Colin, Davaine, Henri Bouley, a veterinarian and pathologist who was a member of the Academies of Medicine and Sciences, and Edmé Félix Alfred Vulpian, dean of the Faculty of Medicine, accordingly met with Pasteur on July 20, 1878, in the Council Chamber of the Academy of Medicine. Pasteur produced three dead hens, and one which, inoculated and removed from her bath after the disease was well started, was recovering from anthrax. At the end of the examination of the first hen, Colin was obliged to concede that Pasteur had been right—she was full of anthrax bacilli. The demonstration was so convincing, indeed, that Colin, whose skepticism had eventual limits, said it would not be necessary to examine the other two dead hens—he was satisfied. Bouley drew up the report declaring that Pasteur had produced anthrax in hens, and Colin, with no one knows what feelings, was obliged to affix his signature to it beside those of the other commissioners.

The skirmish over anthrax had dragged on for about six months without, of course, filling them. Pasteur had also been studying the septic vibrio and formulating far-reaching ideas on germs and disease. Some of them he expressed in a lecture to the Academy of Medicine in April. Speaking in the name of Joubert and Chamberland as well as in his own—for he was scrupulous about giving credit to his collaborators—he described how they had discovered the anaerobic nature of the septic vibrio and explained the apparently contradictory fact that it could thrive in an open wound or in blood exposed to air. In the recess of a wound inaccessible to air, or in blood providing it stood in a vessel of enough depth, the vibriones on or near the surface die; those farther down, however, protected against air by the layer of dead ones above, continue to reproduce for a while and to form spores. Eventually the vibriones themselves are absorbed, but the hardier spores, immune to the action of oxygen and as fine as dust, continue to live indefinitely and need only a congenial culture medium to develop, themselves, into vibriones.

"Here, then," said Pasteur, "is the septic dust, living the latent life of germs, no longer fearing the destructive action of oxygen, and we are now prepared to understand what seemed at first so obscure: the sowing of septic dust into putrescible liquids by the surrounding atmosphere, and the permanence of putrid diseases on the surface of the earth."

Pasteur was no longer groping or hesitant. The suggestive glimmer he had glimpsed early in his study of fermentations was now a clear bright light.

CHAPTER FIFTEEN

THE ANTHRAX work continued; when summer came, Roux and Chamberland went to Chartres to pursue it, and Pasteur, with his family, returned to Arbois. The young men mailed him almost daily reports of their observations in farmyards, sheepfolds and knackers' yards, and Pasteur studied them and wrote out lists of suggestions for experiments which he sent by return mail. Frequently he joined his colleagues for a day or so. Master and disciples would meet at the Hôtel de France and have lunch; then in a hired carriage they would set out for the farm of M. Manoury who had, out of interest in the problem, put his flocks at their disposal. Rattling along the country road in the bright August sunshine, the three scientists would discuss the work accomplished and plan what was to come next.

Arrived at their destination, they would go at once to the sheepfold. Perhaps a sheep would be falling sick; Pasteur would watch it for hours with an intentness that overlooked nothing. Or perhaps he would notice a sagacious-looking shepherd; he would question him closely and at length, realizing that the observations of a lonely man who had nothing to do from one day's end to the next but watch his flock were probably worth hearing.

When it began to get dark, Roux and Chamberland, having labeled and packed their phials of charbon blood, would try to get Pasteur started homeward.

"A little longer," he would say, scarcely glancing at them. "This is most interesting—I cannot leave yet." And he would resume his conversation with the shepherd, or his staring at the sheep, and forget them.

A little later Roux would try again.

"Look, monsieur," he would gesture toward the town in the distance, "it is getting dark—you can hardly see the spires of the cathedral any more. If we are to have dinner before you catch your train, we must start at once."

With a sigh Pasteur would shake off his absorption and reluctantly return to the world where youthful assistants got hungry and trains ran on time.

By mid-September Pasteur was ready to write a report on his anthrax studies for the Minister of Agriculture. He had found, in the course of his summer's experiments, that when anthrax spores were scattered over a small field on which sheep grazed, a mild outbreak of the disease would follow. But add to the diet of the experimental animals some prickly plants, like thistles, which would stick them in tongue and throat, and the deaths among them would increase greatly. From this experiment it was clear that the disease usually gained access through small wounds in the mouth and throat, and it was equally clear that a simple practical measure would reduce it—keep from the flocks all harsh food that might cut them as they ate it.

This same summer, while he was in the midst of anthrax work, Pasteur was obliged, greatly against his will, to revert to the study of fermentations because of an unexpected—and ghostly—challenge. Claude Bernard, who had died in 1878, had left among his papers some incomplete notes which several of his friends ill-advisedly published in *La Revue Scientifique* as "A Posthumous Work of Claude Bernard."

This posthumous work, which was merely a fragment, set forth certain startling and radical statements—that anaerobic life was an illusion, an impossibility; that ferments were not caused by exterior germs—but it gave no indication how the prudent and powerful mind of the great scientist had been led to conclusions squarely at variance with Pasteur's most fundamental work which, Pasteur had always supposed, Bernard accepted fully. It was Pasteur's guess that these conclusions represented merely speculations, speculations which Bernard had never mentioned to him because he had never had the opportunity to test them experimentally. Such speculations, coming from a man of lesser stature, Pasteur might have ignored; since, however, they were those of a fine scientist and a good friend, he felt it necessary to refute them. Out of respect for Bernard's memory he decided to undertake new experiments on fermentation.

Toward the end of July, therefore, while his associates were busy at Chartres, Pasteur covered some of the vines in his vineyard at Arbois with three tightly fitting small glasshouses. His strange activities no longer caused much comment in the village; his friends, knowing that he was always doing queer things that produced remarkable results, merely agreed that if Louis wanted to put up hothouses in his vineyard it was certainly his own affair—no doubt he had some reason.

He had, of course, a good reason. It was his theory that yeast appeared only about the time that the grapes began to ripen, and that its germs were not to be found on green grapes. Since spring and early summer had been cold and rainy in the Jura, the grapes were still green—and presumably free from yeast—when he erected his glasshouses. If all went well, he thought, the grapes under glass—some of which he tied up in thick sterile wads of cotton wool as an extra precaution—would ripen in an atmosphere to which yeast germs had not had access and so would not ferment.

By the time he finished his anthrax report, which he wrote at Arbois, the harvest was approaching. Every day he would walk to his vineyard, accompanied by his fifteen-year-old nephew Adrien Loir who was visiting him, by some member of his family or by Jules Vercel.

Vercel enjoyed teasing his old friend.

"At last you are interesting yourself in the grape harvest, Louis," he said. "When you were a boy you hardly knew it existed. It was the high point of the year for most of us, but you never used to come near the vineyards. Now in your old age, I suppose, you will want to take up bird snaring, too."

"You may laugh at my belated interest, Jules," Pasteur answered smilingly, "but I am driving one more nail in the coffin of that mischievous theory, spontaneous generation."

When the grapes were ripe, Pasteur told Adrien he could help with the experiment. Adrien could hardly believe in his good fortune. Thanks to his father's instruction, he appreciated better than many of Pasteur's own colleagues the discoveries that were revolutionizing medical science, and his admiration for his uncle was boundless. Carrying sterilized test tubes, scissors and other apparatus, Adrien accompanied Pasteur to the vineyard. They snipped grapes from the open-air vines and dropped them in the tubes, and, with every precaution, gathered them from the protected ones, too. Returning to the laboratory that Pasteur had equipped in the old tannery, they placed the open-air and the protected grapes in a stove at a temperature favorable to fermentation. Within forty-eight hours, all the open-air grapes were fermenting with grape yeast—and not one tube containing protected grapes, whether free or swathed, showed a trace of fermentation. To be sure that the protected grapes were, under the right conditions, capable of fermenting, Pasteur removed some bunches from under glass and tied them to exposed vines. When he crushed them after a few days, they fermented normally. Altogether, it was a very satisfactory demonstration.

"You are a good helper, Adrien," Pasteur told his nephew, and Adrien walked on air. He would have been even more excited had he known that Pasteur intended to ask his father to train him to enter his laboratory as an assistant.

In an Academy of Medicine meeting, Pasteur had promised to bring "our colleagues who are still able to believe in the spontaneous generation of yeast" a few bunches of ripe grapes that would not ferment. To get them from Arbois to Paris was something of a problem, but no consideration of convenience could balk him when there was a scientific end to be accomplished. His wife and daughter shared his feelings perfectly—nothing was too difficult, too tiresome or too bizarre for them to do if it would forward his work. So mother, father and daughter, looking in every respect but one like any normal middle-class French family, rode all the way to Paris taking turns holding upright, with the tenderest care, vines from which dangled the bunches of grapes wrapped in cotton wool which were to confound Academy skeptics.

This experiment on fermentation was only one of several which Pasteur undertook to test the ideas advanced by Claude Bernard's posthumous note. When he had thoroughly satisfied himself that his conclusions still stood and that Bernard's were wrong, he wrote, not without some feelings of pain, a rebuttal to the speculations of the friend who could no longer reply. Yet he did not hesitate to speculate himself. The fact that "those few cubic yards of air, those few square yards of soil, were there [under glass] in the midst of a universal possible contagion and were safe from it" was too suggestive to pass without remark. "Is it not permissible to believe, by analogy, that a day will come when easily applied preventive measures will arrest those scourges which suddenly desolate and terrify populations; such as the fearful disease (yellow fever) which has recently invaded Senegal and the valley of the Mississippi, or that other (bubonic plague) which has ravaged the banks of the Volga?"

Looking back, it seems more than permissible—it seems necessary. In Pasteur's day, however, it still took daring and vision to believe in such a future.

As the field of his investigations widened, Pasteur became more than ever intolerant of interruptions. He had more work in mind than he could possibly encompass in another full lifetime, and he was always fearful of time-wasting lapses of technique. Émile Duclaux, who had returned to Paris in 1878 as professor of biological chemistry on the Faculty of Sciences and had been granted by Pasteur the use of a small upstairs laboratory in the rue d'Ulm building, was one of the very few persons, other than his collaborators, whom Pasteur would admit to his laboratory. The younger man stopped in almost every afternoon to see his master and discuss Pasteur's work. Other would-be callers were usually intercepted by Roux or Chamberland or Eugene Viala, the faithful laboratory boy whom Pasteur had educated and trained from childhood to be his assistant. Sometimes one would succeed in penetrating to Pasteur's office or laboratory and Pasteur, trapped, would have to see him.

"Please, monsieur," he would exclaim imploringly, "do not interrupt me now! The work on which I am engaged is very important, and I do not have time to see you, truly!"

No one could be offended by such an ingenuous plea, and few were hardhearted enough to resist it. The rare ones who were, however, finally had to be barred by the simple device of keeping the street door locked.

By this time Pasteur was spending as much time in the Paris hospitals as in his laboratory. Accompanied by Roux or Chamberland, he would go into wards and operating rooms where at his direction his assistants—for his crippled arm made actual manipulation difficult for him—would collect various morbid materials in their sterile pipettes and culture tubes. He could never harden himself to suffering, so these visits were always harrowing to him. He would flinch at another's pain as if it were his own, and autopsies literally made him sick. Still, the inquiring mind always dominated the recoiling body, and he persisted in his distressing visits.

Possibly because the wife of "dear Duclaux" had recently died of it, puerperal fever was one of the contagious diseases that now most interested Pasteur. For years it had been one of those taken-for-granted horrors—like the high percentage of deaths in surgical cases—that a certain number of the pregnant women brought to hospitals to be delivered should die of this unexplained infection. Sometimes the rate was low, sometimes it rose to one out of five, or four, or even three. Occasionally a hospital would have to be closed to give the "miasma"—or whatever it was that caused the disease—a chance to dissipate. The measure was, needless to say, ineffective. In 1843 Dr. Oliver Wendell Holmes in Boston, and about the same time Dr. Ignaz Semmelweiss in Vienna, had announced that scrupulous cleanliness of the doctor's hands, of the instruments used in delivery and of the delivery room minimized the melancholy mortality. Both were jeered and ridiculed—Semmelweiss so viciously that he eventually sank into mental illness and died insane.

M. Stephen Tarnier, director of the *Maternité*, which had been the scene of distressing losses, was convinced of the contagious nature of puerperal fever. When he learned that Lister's antiseptic surgery was being practiced with success in maternity hospitals in various European countries, he introduced it at the *Maternité* with excellent results. At the same time, Pasteur was making his painful rounds among sick and dying women and taking blood samples back to his laboratory for study. In a badly infected woman he could demonstrate the microbe causing the disease in a drop of blood from her finger.

He loosed his findings, after his usual fashion, like a thunderbolt on his unprepared colleagues. Tired, one afternoon, of listening to a pontifical and pointless speech on the causes of puerperal fever by one of the members of the Academy of Medicine, he interrupted impatiently:

"Forgive me, my dear colleague, but none of the things you call 'causes' has anything to do with causing puerperal fever. It is caused by a micro-organism that is carried from a sick woman to a healthy one by the doctor on contaminated instruments or hands."

His dear colleague smiled with condescension. "I fear, M. Pasteur, that this hypothetical micro-organism of yours will never be demonstrated."

Pasteur sprang up from his desk and limped quickly to the blackboard. With a few strokes he diagramed an organism in the shape of a chain.

"There! That is what it is like! And *you* say it will never be demonstrated!"

Such blunt tactics won Pasteur friends only among those who cared more to see science advance than to see their own opinions confirmed. More than one doctor, in showing Pasteur around his well-kept ward, experienced a moment of chagrin when the chemist, who had never set foot in it before, criticized its appliances, and said that it was criminally careless not to sterilize all bandages. His earnestness, however, his assurance, the painful solicitude for the patients which was plain on his kind, lined face, all were disarming, and conviction not infrequently displaced resentment.

CHAPTER SIXTEEN

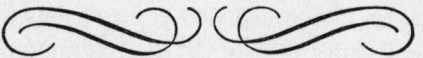

STILL WORKING steadily on anthrax, Pasteur was beginning to feel that he and his assistants were slowly closing in on it. The cause of the disease had been identified as *bacillus anthracis;* its method of invading the victim had been discovered; the very durable nature of the bacillus had recently been established in an ingenious experiment; and a way of reducing the frequency of the disease had been recommended. Could they figure out any sure preventive measure? That was the remaining problem.

Pasteur usually had several related problems on his hands at one time, and work on one sometimes suggested a solution to another. Toward the beginning of 1880 he was drawn into the investigation of another costly farmyard disease, chicken cholera. In the course of it an accidental observation—one of those chances that "favors only the mind which is prepared"—led him to a principle of enormous importance in combating not only anthrax but some other contagious diseases, both animal and human.

The microbe causing chicken cholera had already been identified and its connection with the disease clearly established by other workers when Jean Joseph Henri Toussaint, a young professor of veterinary surgery at Toulouse, sent Pasteur the head of a rooster which had died of it. Pasteur isolated the microbe and after several failures found a culture medium—broth of chicken gristle—in which it flourished. The virulence of the micro-organism grown in this very favorable medium was such that a minute drop of it, mixed with a chicken's food, would produce death in short order.

When he tried to communicate chicken cholera to guinea pigs by injecting the laboratory-raised microbe under their skins, Pasteur found that the little animals, unless inoculated in a vein, rarely succumbed to the disease, or even became particularly ill, although an abscess usually formed at the point of inoculation in which the microbe was present. Chickens kept in the same cage with them, however, would quickly sicken and die. The guinea pigs, in short, could transmit the disease while themselves remaining impervious to it. "How many mysteries in the history of contagions will one day be solved as simply as this!" Pasteur remarked prophetically.

It was in continuing his experimental inoculations that Pasteur stumbled on—and seized on—an observation of the most far-reaching consequence. He had been sowing fresh culture media daily with the chicken cholera microbe, and the virulence of all these had been the same. Then, on returning from an absence during which no one had remained in the laboratory to sow cultures, he found that all those left there had become sterile. In an effort to revive them, he made transfers from the sterile cultures into fresh bouillon and into chickens. Many of the cultures were unable to grow in the fresh medium, and none produced any evident effect on the chickens.

It occurred to Pasteur, whose experimental method always involved trying as many combinations as he could think of, to test the reaction of these chickens, which had resisted the sterile culture, to a very virulent fresh one.

They withstood it.

Had they turned to solid gold, the astonishment and excitement in the laboratory could not have been higher. A vaccine had been discovered for a disease of microbic origin! The microbes, their strength impaired—or, as it was later expressed, their virulence attenuated—themselves acted as the vaccine, inducing a feeble form of the cholera which made the chickens immune to the violent common form. What might such a discovery not lead to, who could tell what other microbial diseases might yield to this marvelous new method? Full of enthusiasm, Pasteur continued his experiments. He quickly made a second discovery: these enfeebled microbes produced offspring which had just the same degree of virulence as themselves. In other words, the attenuated virus could be perpetuated through generations of microbes, the vaccine could be manufactured quite simply in a series of little glasses in the laboratory by raising generation after generation of microbes of attenuated virulence.

Pasteur for a long time had had the deepest admiration for the English doctor, Edward Jenner, who a hundred years earlier had learned to vaccinate for smallpox with the material taken from a cowpox sore, and who later developed the technique of vaccination from arm to arm. Now he wanted his new technique to be known, like Jenner's, as vaccination. "I have lent," he said, "to the expression vaccination an extension that I hope science will consecrate, as a homage to the merit and immense services rendered to humanity by one of the greatest men of England, Jenner."

It was a very generous tribute, but the fact is that there was little resemblance between the two discoveries. Jenner's discovery, great as it was, was an isolated one, a chance observation of genius, which had no further development, because no one knew just what it meant or how to go on from there. Its one result in a century had been its application: it had led to nothing more, no further scientific advances had stemmed from it. Pasteur, on the other hand, using as a starting point the microbe causing the very disease he was seeking to suppress, had developed a method of producing the vaccine—and producing it, moreover, in the laboratory, under controlled conditions—which might be applied equally well, there was reason to think, to other microbial diseases. He had told the Emperor almost twenty years before that his whole ambition was to fathom the causes of putrid and infectious diseases; now he was getting not only at the causes but at the means of prevention. It was more than he had dared to hope.

These were happy days for him, and he was entirely wrapped up in his work. With single-minded absorption he thought of it morning, noon and night. Even the conversation at meals, which he always took with his family—a family now expanded by the marriages of his son and daughter—was given over almost entirely to the wonderful new technique he was developing. His mind was buzzing with ideas set off by his observation; he made notes on them, drew up programs of study, made the precise and painstaking experiments by which he habitually checked the hypotheses he reached by logic and intuition.

More and more dominated by the idea that contagious diseases would prove conquerable if his doctrines were accepted and his principles put into practice, Pasteur was relentless in advocating them. Chagrined by the obstructive atmosphere of the Academy of Medicine, he would often return home from its meetings thoroughly angry, to be met by the gentle reproaches of his wife.

"Louis, you must not become so excited! Just reflect—you are right, all the contradiction in the world cannot alter that fact, and the judgment of time will vindicate you. Proceed quietly with your work, and ignore this ill-founded opposition."

"Yes, monsieur, with truth for a guide, you will vanquish all your contradicters! Ignore them—pursue truth!" René Vallery-Radot exclaimed earnestly. He was a serious young man and he frankly adored his father-in-law.

At these well-meant admonitions Pasteur would smile reassuringly. "Yes, you are right. Next time I will keep calm."

And next time, of course, he became just as angry, just as excited, in spite of his good resolutions. On one occasion, provoked by remarks of the eighty-year-old surgeon Jules Guérin, Pasteur replied with such harsh ridicule that the old man, enraged, leaped up from his seat to attack him. Somebody stopped him, and the assembly disbanded in an uproar more appropriate to a street brawl than to the sitting of a scientific society. Guérin, made bloodthirsty by insult, challenged Pasteur to a duel. Pasteur, who scarcely knew a pistol's butt from its barrel, sent his challenger's emissaries to see the secretaries of the Academy of Medicine. Together the gentlemen agreed that M. Guérin would probably be as well satisfied to accept an apology from Pasteur as to shoot him. That arrangement, a satisfaction and a relief to everyone, was consummated and the episode was closed. It was merely a somewhat exaggerated version of the skirmishes that Pasteur was always engaging in. Perhaps another man could have conducted this intellectual warfare with more suavity—but then, he would not have been Pasteur. "It is," as Roux said, "a characteristic of exalted minds to put passion into ideas."

It was not until the end of 1880 that Pasteur felt justified in announcing that he had successfully attenuated the virulence of the chicken cholera microbe and had vaccinated with the attenuated virus. By that time, he was already trying to develop a vaccine for anthrax.

As he worked on this problem his face wore an expression at once abstracted and inspired, "the face of approaching discovery," as his daughter called it. "Ah, what a wonderful thing it would be," he often exclaimed, "if one could show that this new method of producing vaccine has a general application!" But when members of his family asked him about the state of his researches he would refuse, almost superstitiously, to tell them.

"No, I cannot discuss it. I can tell you nothing. I dare not express my hopes aloud."

There was a difficulty in attenuating the anthrax microbe that had not occurred in the work on the chicken cholera organism. Whereas the chicken cholera microbe reproduced by fission—that is, one microbe simply came apart in the middle and became two—the anthrax microbe reproduced by forming within itself tiny, tough spores, impervious to conditions which killed or weakened the microbe itself, and it formed them faster than Pasteur could attenuate it.

The difficulty was not insurmountable. Pasteur soon succeeded in preventing the formation of spores by maintaining the charbon microbes at a certain temperature, and he found that cultures, kept at that temperature and exposed to air, gradually lost their virulence just as the chicken cholera cultures had done.

He told the great news to his family with tears of joy in his eyes. "Ah," he exclaimed, as he embraced them repeatedly, "I should have been inconsolable if this discovery which my assistants and I have just made had not been a French one!"

He announced his discovery of the anthrax vaccine before the Academy of Sciences on February 28, 1881. The reaction was mixed: Dumas, Bouley and others of his audience agreed that he was destined for immortality; the Society of French Agriculturists, convinced that the discovery would save flocks and money for its members, presented him with a medal; and many veterinarians were skeptical. H. Rossignol, one of the editors of a widely read veterinary journal, sped shafts of not ill-natured ridicule at the "microbiolatry" of which M. Pasteur was the "prophet." He had doubts of the genuineness of Pasteur's discovery, but he was open to conviction. A large-scale demonstration would settle the matter for him one way or the other. He was willing, he said, to place his farm at Pasteur's disposal and offered to raise money by subscription to cover the costs of experimental animals.

Rossignol's idea of a public experiment appealed both to skeptics and believers—and to that firmest believer of all, Pasteur. When some of his colleagues warned him against committing a "scientific imprudence," he said: "If it will work in the laboratory on fourteen sheep, it will work just as well outside it with fifty," and calmly went ahead with his plans for the demonstration.

Rossignol's farm, Pouilly-le-Fort, was near Melun, and the Melun Agricultural Society, intensely interested in the outcome of the experiment, was furnishing sixty sheep for it. Twenty-five of them were to be vaccinated with two inoculations given about two weeks apart. Later they, and twenty-five more, were to be given an injection of very virulent charbon culture. Pasteur predicted, with serene confidence, that the twenty-five vaccinated sheep would live, the twenty-five unvaccinated ones die. The survivors would be compared with the ten remaining sheep, so that everyone could see that vaccination had in no way interfered with the normal health of the sheep. As plans for the demonstration progressed, the experiment was extended somewhat: Pasteur agreed to include ten cows in it, although he had not as fully tested the vaccine for cattle as for sheep.

All over France attention—friendly, hostile, skeptical, curious—was focused on the preparations. Discussion, speculation, gossip were rife: Pasteur was about to make a public demonstration; Pasteur was in a position from which there was no retreat; Pasteur would have to have full success or admit to one of the most resounding failures in the annals of science. Some of his adversaries did not conceal their satisfaction that "that chemist" had gone out on a limb—he and it would crash together, and then medicine could return to the good old days, the pre-germ days when disease was spontaneous and not the result of some little air-borne organisms that nobody could see without a microscope.

In the midst of the growing agitation, Pasteur kept calm. Any misgivings he had, he smothered: they were due to nerves, stage fright, not doubt. He knew that there were some who, perversely, hoped for the failure of this method that held so much promise in it for humanity, but he was too busy supervising all the details of the coming demonstration to allow himself to be ruffled.

It was a little harder, though, on May 5, 1881, in the yard of the Pouilly-le-Fort farm, to ignore the smug looks, the sly smiles, the whispers of ill-wishers. The yard was crowded with farmers, doctors, druggists, veterinarians, journalists, and there were few among them who had faith in Pasteur and his new method. Composed and concentrated, Pasteur, followed by Roux, Chamberland and a new assistant, Louis Thuillier, separated the animals, collected under a large shed, into two groups, those to be vaccinated and those not to be. Twenty-five sheep here, thirty-five there; six cows here, four there. Soon they were ready to give the first inoculation.

At the last minute somebody wanted to replace two of the sheep with goats, and one of the cows with an ox. Pasteur, willing, waited patiently while the substitution was made. Then his three assistants, with practiced skill, injected the charbon vaccine into the thirty-one animals, and marked each vaccinated beast on ear or horn. The performance—the first act—was over. There was certainly nothing about it to suggest that the last would institute a new epoch in veterinary—and human—medicine.

The second inoculation, this one made with a culture of greater virulence, took place on May 17. There was nothing dramatic about it, either. The drama was reserved for the third inoculation, on May 31, when the virulent charbon culture was administered.

Colin, whose misanthropy prevented him from believing in Pasteur's competence as an experimenter, and perhaps even in his good faith, had warned another veterinarian named Biot, who was interested in the experiment, to watch Pasteur like a hawk during the last inoculation.

"You know, the culture he will use is in two parts—all the

virulence settles to the bottom, and the top part is quite harmless. He will inoculate his vaccinated animals with that, and use the virulent part on the unvaccinated ones. I suggest you make some excuse to get hold of the phial and give it a good shake—then we will see what becomes of his discovery!"

Biot had been somewhat impressed—impressed enough to act on Colin's suggestion. As Pasteur and his assistants, in the presence of a large crowd, prepared to make their final inoculation, Biot approached him.

"May I, M. Pasteur?" he asked, extending his hand toward the phial of virulent charbon culture.

Pasteur, with a questioning look, handed it to him. Biot shook it with violent energy and returned it. Had Pasteur been capable of irony, he might have made some comment, or smiled ironically. He was not, however, and merely received the phial back without any change of expression.

If Biot was a little abashed, he concealed it. He proceeded doggedly, still acting on one of Colin's incomparable suggestions:

"Another thing, monsieur, so that there may be no question as to whether or not you injected a quantity sufficient to produce charbon—will you consent to give a larger dose than you originally planned?"

At this request which, although politely phrased, contained a plain insinuation, Roux darted an angry glance at Biot. Pasteur answered, however, before his assistant could speak.

"I will triple the dose, monsieur," he said coolly. "Will that satisfy you?"

Another veterinarian, who feared some sleight of hand might contribute to Pasteur's results, asked that he give these inoculations alternating vaccinated with unvaccinated animals. Pasteur agreed. He had had his first experience of distrust when, as a young student, he had performed his racemic acid demonstration for J. B. Biot. Then it was not unreasonable. He was unknown, without reputation, and the discovery he claimed seemed far beyond a young man's powers. Now, however, when his great reputation and his known probity should have protected him from suspicion, he was again obliged to meet it. He did it as he had done it long before—calmly, and with apparent indifference to everything but the demonstration itself. He accepted all proposals that the skepticism of his witnesses suggested, and by midafternoon the inoculations were over. Many of those doubting witnesses found something almost convincing in his confident bearing; others, hoping for a failure, found it disquieting. They still expected, however, to enjoy their ungenerous triumph on June 2, the day appointed for the final rendezvous.

The next day a crack appeared in Pasteur's confidence. Roux, Chamberland and Rossignol reported from Melun that some of the unvaccinated animals were already refusing to eat and standing about listlessly with hanging heads; several of the vaccinated ones, however, were not in satisfactory condition. Later in the day came word that all the unvaccinated ones were sick, and thoroughly sick; but several of the vaccinated beasts—those beasts on which Pasteur's hopes were so passionately set—had increased temperatures and one, indeed, was expected to die.

In his laboratory where he received the news, Pasteur paced back and forth, muttering in distress: "*Mon Dieu . . . ah, 'mon Dieu!*" Some of his "immunized" sheep were ill, they would die, his discovery was an illusion, his method a chimera. "*Ah, mon Dieu!*" he groaned repeatedly, anticipating the failure of all his beautiful hopes.

Roux, who had returned from his trip to Melun, became anxious too—about Pasteur, not about the outcome of the demonstration.

"Look, monsieur—the experimental method *cannot* betray you. You know it. You are almost ill with strain, or you would not doubt."

Pasteur glanced at him out of haggard eyes and continued his pacing and muttering.

That evening he could not eat, and Mme Pasteur's reassurances were as futile as Roux's. Pasteur brushed them off. Finally, with a desperate exclamation, he went off to bed, where he spent a sleepless night.

By the next morning, resignation had begun to set in. The experiment had failed. Well, that meant there had been a mistake somewhere. He would study his laboratory books, repeat his work, find it. No great work was accomplished without great pains, and this one was certainly worth infinite efforts.

With recovered composure Pasteur went to the laboratory at his usual hour, eight-thirty.

At nine came the telegram from Rossignol. The "dying" sheep had recovered, all the vaccinated beasts were well, all the rest dead or dying. "Stunning success!" the once skeptical veterinarian concluded enthusiastically. Resignation was out the window; jubilation took its place. Viala, Thuillier, Roux, Chamberland, Pasteur—everyone from laboratory boy to master was wild with joy. Madame was notified at once; letters were rushed off to the children.

Pasteur and his collaborators reached the farm of Pouilly-le-Fort early that same afternoon. A large crowd had collected—delegates from agricultural and medical societies, farmers, newspapermen, veterinarians—and this time there were cheers instead of sly looks, applause in the place of whispers. Twenty-two dead sheep were stretched out in the farmyard, and the remaining three, dying, showed all the characteristic symptoms of splenic fever. Former skeptics openly and warmly proclaimed their conversion, Rossignol and Biot foremost among them.

"What a pity Colin is not here!" remarked one veterinarian. "This would convince even him."

"No," Pasteur answered with asperity. He could not forgive Colin his chronic carping. "He contradicts out of perversity. It is a neurosis with him, and no demonstration on earth could cure it."

An autopsy of two of the dead animals showed that anthrax was indeed the cause of death—not that anyone doubted it, but there was no use in marring an otherwise perfect demonstration by leaving a loose end. Pasteur's triumph was complete. The cheering crowd, tumbling all over itself to do him homage, accompanied him back to the station and saw him onto the train.

"Well, my dear master," Roux said as they settled into their seats, "you have left behind you many a convert."

Pasteur's tired face lighted up happily as he waved to the crowd on the platform.

"Yes. Biot even says that he is going to undergo a similar test," he said smiling. "His wife will probably have something to say about that."

Biot did, in fact, later take the first two inoculations, and it was only by the most strenuous opposition that his wife prevented him from receiving the third and virulent one.

The sensational success of this demonstration aroused boundless enthusiasm not only in those who witnessed it, but also in the French scientific world and indeed throughout the whole country. Now, stimulated by success and appreciation—he could also be stimulated by failure and opposition, but he liked it better this way—Pasteur worked at top speed. He read papers before the academies of which he was a member, and he worked in his laboratory on some of the problems he had taken up in the course of his anthrax researches. Much more than before, his activities took him out of the laboratory. He traveled to and fro, explaining his method and the advantages of practicing it to scientific and agricultural societies just as he had done when he was propagandizing for his method of silkworm seed selection.

Government recognition—the Grand Cordon of the Legion of Honor for Pasteur, and, at his suggestion, the Cross for Roux and Chamberland—capped the popular acclaim, but criticism was not entirely quieted. He had immunized animals against his laboratory-cultured anthrax bacillus, but would the outcome have been the same had fresh charbon blood been used? Another experiment, conducted near Chartres, established the fact that the vaccine worked equally well in either case. Less and less ground was being left to carping, or honest, criticism.

Only one thing marred Pasteur's happiness in this productive period: the death of his dear friend Sainte-Claire Deville. Pasteur discharged the promise exacted from him years before to deliver the funeral oration, and he ended it in tears. Sainte-Claire Deville had been right in thinking that Pasteur would say "nice things" about him. He probably had no more loving and understanding friend, nor any who felt his loss more deeply.

Recognition was not merely national, but international now; Pasteur, however, never quite accustomed himself to fame. At the International Medical Congress held in London in August, 1881, his entry into St. James' Hall was greeted with a storm of applause.

"We are late, we should have come earlier," he said anxiously to his son and son-in-law who were escorting him to the platform reserved for the illustrious. "The Prince of Wales must be arriving."

"It is not the Prince whom they are cheering, M. Pasteur," said Sir James Paget, president of the congress, as he smilingly rose to greet him. "It is *you*."

Pasteur had interrupted his work to attend this congress because he was an enthusiastic believer in the value of international scientific meetings; understanding among nations was advanced by the mingling of their citizens in an intellectual atmosphere, he thought, and scientific progress was stimulated by the discussions and the exchange of knowledge. He himself, at this congress, learned a very useful new technique, invented by Koch, for separating one type of microbe out of a culture in which there were several. At one of the meetings when the German scientist demonstrated his method, which was both very simple and very ingenious, Pasteur rushed forward to congratulate him. "It is a great advance!" he exclaimed warmly. He, perhaps better than anyone else, could appreciate its value, since his own experiments had sometimes been thrown into confusion by the impurity of his cultures.

He attended every meeting and he was, according to a French journal, the outstanding success of the congress. There was probably more truth than chauvinism in the claim. Pasteur himself, however, was a little bewildered by all the homage. "What an unexpected success!" he said in surprise. He, perhaps, was the one person to whom it was really unexpected.

CHAPTER SEVENTEEN

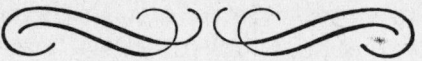

IN THE MIDST of success and acclaim Pasteur's mind returned longingly, as it had occasionally done for years, to his early love, crystallography. During the vacation this year, 1881, he and his family spent a month near Lyons with the Loirs, who had rented a house in the country. Young Adrien's questions on crystallography awakened all Pasteur's old enthusiasm for it.

Holding the cork against his chest with his disabled left hand, he carved models of crystals for the boy and explained them to him. He strolled with him in the garden and took him on walks in the neighborhood, describing all the while the mysteries he had fathomed almost forty years earlier and pausing, whenever illustration was necessary, to draw diagrams in the dust with his cane. Every once in a while he would say wonderingly about one aspect or another of this old research: "How beautiful it is! And to think it was I who discovered it!"

"How beautiful it is, monsieur, and how beautiful a book could be written about it and about your succeeding discoveries!" exclaimed René Vallery-Radot, who often accompanied the uncle and nephew. With the ardor of a disciple, although he was not a scientist, he had familiarized himself with all the work of his beloved father-in-law, and he had an excellent understanding of it.

"There is no need for a book—it is all recorded in the transactions of the Academy of Sciences," Pasteur objected.

"Who sees it there? Only savants. I mean a book which the public would read, which would tell them the history and logic of your discoveries, describe the importance of your method, show how you arrived at your scientific principles."

"My dear René, I have no time to waste writing about something already behind me."

"Of course not, monsieur. It should be written by someone else, someone who is an intimate of your household, who is impregnated with your method and ideas, who has the happiness of understanding your life and accomplishments and who wishes to make that joy available to others," René replied.

Pasteur laughed at his earnestness. "And where, my dear boy, is this man, at once so happy and so impatient to share his happiness with the rest of the world?"

"It is I, monsieur."

René ended by getting Pasteur's permission to write a popular account of his work. Since Pasteur was already reviewing it for Adrien's benefit, he dictated to his nephew, and Adrien took each day's notes to René, who recast them into a more popular form. The young editor would then present his new version to Pasteur and stand anxiously by while he read it. Sometimes Pasteur was satisfied, sometimes he could scarcely recognize his text.

"No, no, René!" he would say. "That's not it at all! In trying to popularize the scientific language, you have quite distorted what I dictated. Really—this is the work of a *littéraire*."

Poor René, crestfallen, would go back to his editing and try to earn a kinder epithet. Being called a *littéraire* by his father-in-law kept him very modest. When the book was finished and edited to Pasteur's satisfaction, it appeared as *M. Pasteur: Histoire d'un savant par un ignorant*.

Pasteur's little excursion into the past could not last long and he soon returned to Paris and to his current studies. In the laboratory preliminary researches on *rouget*, a disease of swine, and on rabies kept him busy; and out of it his chief preoccupation was his candidacy to the French Academy. It was natural that he should have expected to become a member of the Academy of Sciences, and even, although he was not a doctor, of the Academy of Medicine; but that he might scale the sacred height on which dwelt the Forty Immortals was an idea that had never entered his head. Friends, however, urged him to stand for the place made vacant by the death of Émile Littré and, as he told the Academicians on whom he was obliged to pay the usual ceremonial calls, he could not decline an invitation "so glorious for science and so flattering to myself." That was as nearly as he could bring himself to soliciting their votes. One member, Alexandre Dumas the younger, thought the process of the calls should be reversed, and went himself to call on Pasteur, to "thank him for consenting to become one of us." Far from indifferent to this sincere bit of flattery, Pasteur was from that time on cordially devoted to the playwright.

The election was held on December 8, and Pasteur was the successful candidate. He had to prepare a careful speech, arrange to have J. B. Dumas and Nisard act as his sponsors, send a ticket of admission, along with a couple of hundred francs for train fare, to young Adrien, purchase the green-embroidered Academician's suit, attend to a dozen other things in connection with his reception—and not neglect his laboratory. It was no wonder that on April 27, 1882, he looked pale and tired as he confronted the thirty-nine Immortals and the larger crowd of fashionable mortals who were gathered to witness his reception into the scholarly fastness considered the most exclusive and august in France.

Pasteur had studied his predecessor's work—his translation of the Hippocratic writings, his biography of his friend the Positivist philosopher, Auguste Comte, and his great dictionary. He had made a pilgrimage to Littré's home, the small humble house, surrounded by a garden, where the poor scholar had worked and lived happily with his wife and daughter. He had studied, as well, Littré's character, and found it saintly, his philosophy, and found it wanting. With all the merits of Positivism, it omitted one idea of crucial importance in Pasteur's system of thought: "Positivism does not take into account the most important of positive notions—that of the Infinite." In his speech Pasteur sincerely praised his predecessor, and frankly dissented from his philosophy. The large audience listened with silent attention as he asserted his own religious idealism in moving terms.

Ernest Renan, the noted historian—and skeptic—welcomed Pasteur to the Academy. Sitting at his desk, he smiled benevolently, and a little ironically, and in his soft deep voice began his address. The Academy, he said, was not entirely competent to evaluate Pasteur's scientific work. "But," he said, "there is, monsieur, a greatness on which our experience of the human mind gives us a right to pronounce an opinion; something which we recognize in the most varied applications, which belongs in the same degree to Galileo, Pascal, Michelangelo or Molière; something which gives sublimity to the poet, depth to the philosopher, fascination to the orator, divination to the scientist. That common basis of all beautiful and true work, that divine fire, that indefinable breath which inspires science, literature and art—we have found it in you, monsieur: it is Genius."

Renan, whose thought was accurate and whose expression was precise, did not use the word genius lightly. He had a superb control of the French language, and expressed difficult ideas with exactness, suppleness and force. His speech was masterly, and it was marked, in those parts which alluded to Pasteur's direct and ardent statement of faith, by a sort of gentle and graceful irony.

Pasteur might have been pleased at being called a genius by such a man; instead, he was outraged by the skepticism with which Renan spoke of his dearest convictions. He did not forgive his courteous contradicter. The day was a triumph, but in discussing its details that evening with his family, he fell on Renan with unusual rancor. Skepticism, irony, amiable levity were qualities utterly foreign to his character; he could not view them in another without distrust and real dislike.

Pasteur's indifference to money remained complete, and instead of accumulating wealth he was accumulating honors. The Melun Agricultural Society struck a medal with his effigy on it in recognition of his work on splenic fever. Aubenas, a town which was erecting a statue to Olivier de Serres, the founder of the French silk industry, invited Pasteur to attend the ceremonies and swamped him with grateful attentions. In Nîmes and Montpellier meetings of sericiculturists, agriculturists, veterinarians were held in his honor. The round of activity was trying, but, far more, it was rewarding; he could see how widely his doctrines were spreading and what fruit they were bearing.

The most treasured praise was J. B. Dumas'. He arrived at Pasteur's apartment in the École normale one Sunday afternoon in June, 1882, at the head of a delegation representing several scientific societies, and in an informal ceremony he presented Pasteur with a handsome medal from "his colleagues, his friends, his admirers." Pasteur, who used almost to weep with exaltation when he left Dumas' lectures at the Sorbonne as a student, almost wept now at the aged scientist's warm and affectionate words. The approval of his masters had always seemed to him the most desirable reward possible, and a fortune could not have made him as happy as Dumas' praise.

Another honor was the invitation to present a paper on the attenuation of viruses before the International Congress of Hygiene at Geneva, in September. The whole of one meeting was set aside for Pasteur, and the applause of doctors, professors, even sightseers, was tremendous. He hardly knew whether to be more pleased by the acclaim—which as usual he assigned to France and to science—or by the fact that Dr. Koch, who from his laboratory in Berlin had loosed a barrage of criticism against his latest work, found that he did not care to renew it from the platform.

By mid-September Pasteur was able to devote himself more fully to his work. *Rouget*, or swine fever, headed the list of subjects under investigation just then. Louis Thuillier, a meditative and silent young man, devoted to science and to Pasteur, had for several months been applying all the energy of his fine mind to the research. He had isolated the microbe the previous March, established its connection with the disease, and found a suitable culture medium for it. What remained was to try to attentuate its virulence and develop a vaccine.

Twenty thousand pigs had died in 1882 in the Department of the Vaucluse; some farmers had lost every one they owned. M. Maucuer, the young veterinarian who lived at Bollène, appealed to Pasteur to come to the stricken region and there press his search for a preventive.

Shortly after his return from Geneva Pasteur, accompanied by Thuillier and Adrien Loir, whom he had just taken into his laboratory as an assistant, arrived in Bollène. Adrien, coached by his father within an inch of his life for his new responsibilities, felt their weight gravely. He had been trained to blow glass, he had taken lessons in penmanship so that he could write his uncle's letters for him, he had been put through all kinds of laboratory manipulations until he could do them in his sleep, he had repeated long series of Pasteur's experiments so that he knew them by heart. He had been thoroughly equipped to be Pasteur's assistant—and now he found he had to be his valet as well. Mme Pasteur had given him a long list of instructions before they departed on the care and feeding of his uncle.

"He is very particular about his clothes, Adrien. Brush them each night when he takes them off, and hang them up carefully. You will have to help him in the mornings with his cravat—he puts it on himself, but he cannot tie it. And his shoes—he needs to be helped on and off with them. And be sure that he changes them *at once* if he gets his feet wet. Otherwise he is sure to catch cold. And. . . ."

Adrien's expression stopped the flow of directions.

"Now, do not worry, my child. He is particular, but he is also patient. Just do your best. Oh, another thing. . . ." and she resumed her instructions in detail.

Adrien, as his aunt advised, did his best, and Pasteur, with ready tact, soon gave him to understand that his best was very satisfactory.

The weeks at Bollène passed pleasantly and successfully. M. and Mme Maucuer did everything for their guests' comfort that they could. Pasteur had a room with a cheerful fire in it, Adrien and Thuillier shared a pleasant bedroom, and the Maucuers squeezed themselves gladly into some corner or other. Every day Pasteur and his assistants drove into the country in an open buggy, and brought back with them either dead pigs on which they performed autopsies or, later, little ones—more manageable than big ones—which they vaccinated experimentally. Each day's work clarified their problems more, and Pasteur confidently predicted success. By early December, *rouget* was whipped— Pasteur again had developed a vaccine by culturing the microbe and attenuating its virulence. In the note to the Academy of Sciences in which he announced this new success, he had the kindly thought of mentioning the work of his young assistant, M. Adrien Loir—a courtesy that made Adrien more completely than ever his slave. Pasteur was one of those rare men who was a hero even to his valet.

To his wife Pasteur made a slightly shamefaced confession: he, who had never cared greatly for animals, was captivated by little pigs. "They are very young, and quite charming," he wrote. "One cannot help getting fond of them."

In spite of successes, embroilments with unbelievers continued to interrupt Pasteur's work. Dr. Koch changed his mind about the attentuation of virus. He no longer doubted that it had been done and was theoretically important, but he questioned its practical value. Pasteur answered him with a broadside of statistics: instead of the average yearly prevaccination mortality of nine per cent among sheep in the Eure et Loire Department, it was now less than one per cent; for cattle, the figures were even more impressive.

He was maintaining, too, a running fight with the professors of the veterinary school at Turin. They had repeated his Pouilly-le-Fort experiment—and the vaccinated as well as the unvaccinated animals all died. They concluded, therefore, that M. Pasteur's method of vaccinating by attenuated virus was no good, and made haste to tell him so. In vain Pasteur pointed out to them that the charbon blood they had used, twenty-four hours old, was septic, so that all the animals died not of splenic fever but of septicemia. The professors replied, haughtily, that it seemed incredible to them "that a scientist should affirm the presence of septicemia in an animal he has not ever seen. . . ." Pasteur answered, in a tone of controlled politeness, offering to repeat the experiment. The Turin professors side-stepped the offer, Pasteur publicly renewed it, they made an absurd counter-proposal, and the whole matter petered out, in an atmosphere of ineffaceable ill will, after they published a pamphlet with the provocative title *Of the Scientific Dogmatism of the Illustrious Professor Pasteur*.

Meanwhile Pasteur had to cope also with a new outburst of hostility in the Academy of Medicine. It started as a row over a new method of treating typhoid fever, and ballooned into a ferocious assault on the germ theory of disease. M. Peter, a clinician who was married to Adrien Loir's cousin, spearheaded the ranks of traditional medicine and minimized the value of Pasteur's discovery of the microbial origin of the contagious diseases he had investigated. His work had only a natural history interest, Peter asserted, and could have no effect on medical practice. "After so many laborious researches, nothing will be changed in medicine—there will only be a few more microbes." In the course of the discussions, which lasted for weeks, Pasteur made one of his frank and far from conciliatory retorts—and another exponent of the good old times joined the ranks of his enemies. Finally, Pasteur stopped attending the Academy of Medicine meetings, since they served only to anger and upset him, and left his defense in the very capable hands of Bouley. Adrien Loir, whose friendship with the Peter family was very affectionate, regretfully gave up seeing them. So far as Pasteur was concerned, an enemy of his work was a personal enemy, and with such his assistants could not consort.

Appreciation, however, outweighed vilification. It was expressed in its simplest form by a peasant who met Pasteur in a village street. "Long live Pasteur!" he shouted, and rushed up to seize his hand, saying feelingly, "You have saved my cattle!" It was expressed more elaborately by the Department of the Cantal, now by the use of anthrax vaccine spared a yearly loss of three million francs, which welcomed him enthusiastically to its agricultural show and presented him with a cup of silver-plated bronze commemorating his anthrax work. The physicians of the department, more enlightened than many of their Paris confreres, gave him a banquet, and the toastmaster hailed him, quite without exaggeration, as "the illustrious Pasteur, the precursor of the medicine of the future, a benefactor to humanity." Such incidents did much to soothe the feelings ruffled in the Academy of Medicine. Even more soothing was the knowledge of the lives saved by the antiseptic method in surgery founded on his early work, and by the virtual elimination of puerperal fever that had for so many years made the maternity hospital too often the vestibule to the grave.

The grateful Republic, feeling that Pasteur's services to France had considerably outstripped France's expressions of gratitude to him, raised his national recompense to twenty-five thousand francs a year.

The town of Dôle soon joined the procession hastening to confer honors. On July 14, the national holiday marking the fall of the Bastille, the village unveiled a statue to Peace, and a plaque on the modest house in the rue des Tanneurs where Pasteur was born. Pasteur, accompanied by his family, attended the ceremonies. He was greatly moved, not so much by the flowery speeches, sincere as they were, as by the sight of the humble house he had not revisited since childhood where his beloved parents had lived and toiled. In his speech of thanks he protested that the town was doing him too much honor.

"Oh, my father, my mother, dear departed ones!" he exclaimed emotionally. "It is to you that I owe everything." He meant it. He was quite unable to take credit to himself. His parents, his masters—it was always to them that he attributed responsibility for his accomplishments. Similarly, he could never really believe that it was Louis Pasteur who was being honored —it was always science, or France, or both, in his person.

Rather strangely, it was with some difficulty that Pasteur got laboratory assistants. The reason was that in his laboratory new ground was being broken all the time, unclassified subjects broached. One did not go into it to do advanced work in physics, chemistry, veterinary medicine, or physiology, and to emerge from it more accomplished in a special field. The work of an assistant cut across the old classifications, and his career, when he left, had to take a new direction. When working, Pasteur noticed his assistants only to make use of them, and more than one young man, fresh from the École normale, after spending a few bewildering days—days during which no one paid any attention to him—among the strange apparatus, quietly left the laboratory in the rue d'Ulm, glad to escape into some less rarified atmosphere.

Those who stayed, and accommodated themselves self-effacingly to Pasteur's ways, formed a sort of family. Viala and two assistants, Arcony and Député, kept the laboratory in order, cared for the experimental animals and attended to some of the simpler operations. Adrien Loir functioned as his uncle's secretary, manipulator, representative, errand boy, factotum. Chamberland, Roux and Thuillier held more the position of collaborators, although subordinate ones. Duclaux was a confidant and a stimulating influence to Pasteur. Pasteur's interest in all of these younger men was almost paternal. When Adrien arrived in Paris to be his assistant, Pasteur had him installed in a room in the old Collège Rollin, 14 rue Vauquelin, now an annex to the laboratory, next to Chamberland's apartment; he saw that his room was equipped with rug, stove and other comforts; himself selected the eider down for his bed and accompanied his nephew to buy a gasoline lamp—a wonderful novelty for the boy who had always used kerosene. Adrien was a close relative, to be sure, but Pasteur's interest was scarcely less in the other members of his staff. It was of course, then, a deep grief to him when Louis Thuillier, only twenty-seven, died, one of that honorable army who risk and lose their lives in the war against disease.

Pasteur had long suspected that the cause of cholera would be found in some microbe. Almost twenty years before, during a light epidemic in Paris, he, Claude Bernard and Henri Sainte-Claire Deville had gone into the attic above the cholera ward in the Lariboisière Hospital and drawn air through a ventilator connected with the ward in the hope of snaring the microorganism responsible for the disease. The effort had come to nothing. In the summer of this year—1883—there was an epidemic in Egypt and Pasteur wanted to send a French scientific mission to Alexandria to study the outbreak. His suggestion was approved by the proper government committee, which asked him, also, to select a group of young men whose experience and courage would be equal to the work.

The young men were easy enough to find—he had only to speak of the matter in his laboratory. Roux, Thuillier and two others who had recently obtained permission to work in the rue Vauquelin annex—Isidor Strauss, a professor on the Faculty of Medicine, and Edmond I. E. Nocard, a professor at the Alfort Veterinary School—volunteered. Pasteur himself, because of the pressure of other work, reluctantly decided not to accompany them.

The French scientists reached Alexandria in mid-August and immediately went to work. The epidemic had also attracted a German mission, headed by Dr. Koch, so some of the best scientific brains in Europe were assembled in the Egyptian city, trying to crack the problem of cholera. Frequent reports reached Pasteur, who had gone to Arbois: Roux and his associates had been so fortunate as to get two perfectly fresh corpses (often they had to work, rather horribly, with decomposing ones); there was a baffling variety of microbes in the intestinal tract of the victims; methods of culturing the various micro-organisms were proving difficult to discover; they had so far found nothing significant in the blood; the epidemic was tapering off suddenly, and until it reappeared they would study a very prevalent cattle disease.

And then, without warning, came Roux's telegram announcing Thuillier's death from cholera. Pasteur was stunned, inconsolable. He reproached himself bitterly with having sent his young friend to his death, with not having shared the risk himself. Efforts to comfort him were futile—he could only cover his eyes with his hand and shake his head, speechless. The whole day the house was hushed. The family moved quietly and spoke in whispers, Pasteur did not speak at all. Chamberland, realizing what Pasteur's feelings would be, hurried from Paris to be with him, and the two men shut themselves up in Pasteur's study and wretchedly asked each other which, of the multitude of precautions they had prescribed, Thuillier could have neglected.

Roux's letter, a few days later, told everything there was to know. Thuillier had neglected no precautions, so far as anyone knew; he had gone to bed the night of September 14 apparently in perfect health, become ill toward morning, and presented, by eight o'clock, all the symptoms of violent cholera. Five days later, in spite of the frantic exertions of his doctors, he had died. His funeral had been very impressive, and the German mission, headed by Dr. Koch, had paid him affecting tribute.

"Science loses in Thuillier a courageous representative with a great future before him. I lose a much-loved and devoted pupil; my laboratory, one of its principal supports. I can only console myself for this death," his grief-stricken master wrote Dumas, "by thinking of our beloved country and all he has done for it."

The French mission, incidentally, accomplished little. It was Koch who finally discovered the cholera bacillus.

Dumas himself died not long after, in April, 1884. Unlike poor young Thuillier, he was past eighty, and his life closed in serene dignity. Pasteur had once said to him: "There has not been one important circumstance in my life or in that of my family, either happy or painful, which you have not, as it were, blessed by your presence and sympathy." Now he felt bereft as he had not since the death of Biot and his father. He was past sixty, and the men whom he had known as his masters were all dead. In their lifetime he had joined their gradually thinning ranks, and now he was the foremost among those whom a younger generation of scientists called master.

His reputation was by now so great that no international gathering of scientists could be considered complete without him. When Edinburgh University, celebrating its three hundredth anniversary, invited the Institute of France to send representatives from each of its five academies, the Academy of Sciences selected Pasteur and de Lesseps as its delegates. Pasteur would infinitely have preferred to attend the funeral of his beloved master, but he was persuaded that he could better honor Dumas' memory by representing France and French science on this official mission to a foreign country than by representing nobody but himself at a funeral.

At Edinburgh Pasteur received—and in the name of France enjoyed—the by now usual ovation. There were speeches, banquets, entertainments. Two things, especially, gratified him: he had the opportunity to pay a tribute to Dumas in his address to the assembly, and he discussed with Rudolph Virchow, the fine old German who was a founder of cellular pathology, the question of rabies.

Rabies was a subject on which he had been working for almost four years, and by this time it was his central preoccupation.

CHAPTER EIGHTEEN

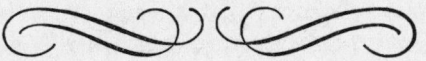

It was the public demonstrations of the worth of the anthrax vaccine which first dispelled the general skepticism about Pasteur's new doctrines; but it was the successful development of a treatment for rabies, on which he was by now far advanced, that was to establish them firmly in public confidence. This may at first appear strange, since rabies was not an important disease. Death was not inevitable after the bite of a rabid animal, and those deaths that did occur were numerically few. Yet it had a powerful grip on the popular fancy. The mere mention of it suggested raging victims, foaming and snapping at frightened attendants, or struggling with vain fury between the mattresses with which terrified and guilty relatives were smothering them.

The fact that no sure remedy had ever been found had much to do with the horror rabies inspired. Cautery immediately applied to the bite of a rabid animal was a very ancient one, and it was better than the rest of the ancient remedies in that it often worked. Crayfish eyes, the livers of mad dogs, magic and religious rituals—all such fanciful and recommended therapeutic measures had proved inferior to the simple and desperate measure of destroying the injured tissue by burning. Pasteur for four years had been working to discover some less drastic, more certain remedy.

Doctors were generally agreed that the saliva of mad animals contained the agent of rabies—whatever it was; that the disease was passed from animal to animal, and from animal to man, by bites; and that the incubation period might be short or long, depending on some factor that nobody had yet discovered.

That was about all that was known about hydrophobia when Pasteur went to work on it in 1880.

His first step was to try to give rabies to laboratory animals—rabbits, in this case—by injecting under their skin the saliva of an unlucky five-year-old child who died of the disease in a Paris hospital and of two mad dogs given him by a veterinarian interested in finding a preventive. These efforts to produce rabies were not always successful, and the method was unsatisfactory since the incubation period was of such variable length that he sometimes had to wait several months for a purely negative result. Patient and searching examination of the saliva of rabid animals revealed no microbe on which the disease could definitely be pinned, and similar work on the blood was equally barren. After months of work and dozen of experiments, Pasteur decided that success did not lie in the direction of those first efforts; he would have to tackle the problem from another angle.

The close observation of several months had suggested strongly to him that the nervous system, particularly that part of the brain called the medulla oblongata, was the seat of the disease. It was not a new theory, but it was one which had never been experimentally confirmed. Pasteur, by one of those precise experiments of his in which not a motion was wasted, confirmed it. The brain of a dog, just dead of rabies, was laid bare and the surface of the medulla oblongata scalded to destroy any dust that might have settled on it during the operation. Through a sterilized tube a bit of the medulla was drawn up and deposited in a sterilized glass, where it was mixed with a sterilized rod into a sterile liquid. This material, from which all morbid matter had been excluded except what might be peculiar to the medulla, was then injected into experimental animals. Most of them developed hydrophobia and died of it. Thus Pasteur demonstrated that the virus was to be found, in greater strength even than in the saliva, in the brain of an afflicted animal. He had taken the first great step in his conquest of rabies.

The next thing was to shorten the incubation period. A delay of several months between inoculation and result was not unusual, and it meant that the experiments would probably drag out over a period of years. It occurred to Pasteur that if the injection could be made directly into the brain of an experimental animal, the process might be greatly speeded up. It was a fine idea, but it was also one that repelled him. His horror of suffering was not confined to human suffering.

"But I can trephine a dog under anesthesia, monsieur," Roux told him, "and he will feel nothing."

"No, no! It would probably damage his brain," Pasteur protested. "I will try to work out some other way."

Roux did not argue. He had seen Pasteur many a time, during inoculations, anxiously caress and console an animal that squealed at the prick of the needle as though it had been a child. He quietly decided that he would perform the operation some day in Pasteur's absence. A few days later he had an opportunity, and when Pasteur came into the laboratory, Roux said:

"Monsieur, I trephined a dog this morning and injected some of the prepared virus beneath the dura mater."

"Oh, Roux! Was it painful to the poor animal?"

"No, monsieur," Roux said soothingly. "He was anesthetized and felt nothing."

"But his brain must have been injured. Can he walk? Is he suffering?"

"Not the least in the world—just a minute, and I will show you."

Roux went to the basement where some of the experimental animals were kept and returned with a lively little dog at his heels. It hurried up to Pasteur and sniffed, then, wagging its tail with interest and pleasure, made the tour of the room. Pasteur's relief was enormous. He lavished extravagant endearments on this animal that had set his scruples at rest, and patted and fondled it as though he could never do enough to express his thanks. Roux, smiling at the scene, reflected that anyone who knew no better might take the master for a dog lover.

From then on, dogs were regularly trephined in the laboratory, but Pasteur, although he realized perfectly that anesthetized animals could feel nothing, suffered nervously through every operation. He would stand, as he habitually did during every manipulation, behind and a little to the left of the operator, draw in his breath sharply and screw up his face in sympathy as the saw went into the bone, and exclaim:

"Easy, now! Take care, take care! Oh, la la!"

He hated having to experiment on living animals and he never sacrificed one needlessly. The only thing that enabled him to subject one to an operation at all was the idea of his goal—immunity for animals and human beings alike to rabies.

The little dog which had so greatly accommodated Pasteur by not suffering from trephining became rabid after fourteen days. Pasteur repeated the experiment several times, and always with the same results—after fourteen days the inoculated animal developed rabies.

The problem of culturing the organism causing the disease still presented an obstacle. It could not be found, therefore it could not be isolated. Yet, obviously, it existed. An alternative suggested itself to Pasteur: if it could not be isolated and cultivated outside the body, he might cultivate it, unisolated, within a body—within the body, say, of a living rabbit. When the rabbit died of rabies, a scrap of its medulla could be planted in the medulla of a fresh rabbit, and when that one died, the process could be repeated.

Pasteur found that as the inoculations progressed from rabbit to rabbit the period of incubation of rabies became shorter and shorter. When it had decreased to seven days, it remained constant. He had achieved a rabic virus of fixed and predictable virulence.

The next move was to attentuate the virus. To see how long they retained their virulence, Pasteur suspended by a thread scraps of rabic spinal cord in flasks which had two cotton-plugged tubes, one at the bottom and the other at the top, to allow air filtered of all germs to pass through it. In the bottom of each flask was some caustic potash to keep the air dry. The virulence of the suspended scraps, experiments showed, decreased day by day, until at the end of fourteen days it had entirely disappeared.

Now began the test. Some of this dried-out fourteen-day-old cord, mixed with sterile water, was injected into several dogs. The next day the dogs received an injection with thirteen-day-old cord, and so on, until the last and very virulent injection with fresh rabic spinal cord. The inoculated dogs, then exposed to the bite of a rabid dog, or trephined and receiving an injection of rabic material directly into the brain, were found to be immune to rabies. The general principle of vaccination with attenuated virus had found another and striking application.

The research and experiments that have taken a few pages to outline took three and a half years to perform. It had been a complicated and difficult task, but the goal was now in sight—a preventive for rabies.

Long experience with critics who threw doubt on every announcement he made moved Pasteur to demand at once a commission to verify his results. It was formed in May, 1884, with Bouley, Vulpian, Paul Bert and Tisserand, Director of the Agriculture Office, among its members. For three months it conducted a variety of tests and controlled experiments and by August Bouley, who drew up the report, was able to declare that the first series of experiments had been wholly successful.

The commission also thought that Pasteur should have better facilities for keeping his animals than the courtyard of the rue Vauquelin building and the basement of the rue d'Ulm laboratory. The gentlemen of the commission were not the only ones who wanted to see Pasteur's experimental animals sent elsewhere. Faraboeuf, anatomy professor of the Faculty of Medicine, who conducted classes in dissection in part of the rue Vauquelin building, was exasperated to the bottom of his heart at sharing the old school with chickens, pigs, rabbits and dogs that howled. He had once even sent Adrien, who, being a medical student, had a class with him, to tell Pasteur that a simple operation which he, Faraboeuf, would gladly teach to one of the rue d'Ulm workers, would render the dogs voiceless and a good deal less annoying when rabid. Adrien, with a straight face, delivered the message to his uncle, who received it impassively. It had never occurred to Faraboeuf that the rabic voice might be of interest in diagnosing the disease in its early stages.

When Adrien in his room heard the rabid howl of an inoculated dog, he would tell Pasteur as soon as he arrived at the laboratory the next morning. Rarely thinking, in his haste, to remove his laboratory coat, Pasteur would put on the high hat he always wore and thus incongruously clad, hurry with his nephew along the rue d'Ulm and the rue Claude Bernard toward the rue Vauquelin. He was never too interested in his errand, however, to keep a sharp eye trained upward for housewives shaking dustmops out of upper windows. When he saw one, he would abandon the sidewalk for the middle of the street, dragging Adrien with him, and hold his handkerchief over his nose to avoid breathing in any of the dust and germs cascading over him from above.

Arrived in the courtyard where the animals were kept, he would inspect the dog. When it was not necessary to the experiment to allow the disease to proceed to its inevitable conclusion, Pasteur would have the animal chloroformed at once.

"Poor beast!" he would say pityingly. "It is pointless to allow him to suffer longer."

Député would bring out the zinc-lined box and the paralyzed dog would be lifted into it and mercifully chloroformed.

On the way back to the rue d'Ulm, Pasteur, who was very neat about his clothes, might at length notice the incoherence of his costume.

"Adrien!"

"Yes, Uncle?"

"We need not mention it to your Aunt Marie that I forgot to change my coat when I went out."

"No, of course not, Uncle."

"Of course not—she would scold me." Pasteur smiled contentedly. There was not a detail of his existence which she did not lovingly supervise.

Faraboeuf merely complained and made impractical suggestions about the beasts in the rue Vauquelin. The commission on rabies did something more constructive. They recommended that a large kennel be built somewhere so that the duration of the immunity conferred by the treatment, as well as other unsettled questions, could be studied under more convenient conditions.

The first spot, near Meudon, that these friends and admirers of Pasteur's investigated could not be purchased because the inhabitants protested vigorously. Next, the park of Villeneuve l'Étang, a state property which nobody wanted to buy, was considered for the use of the workers in the rue d'Ulm. There were in it a ruined pavilion, partially destroyed during the Commune, where Napoleon III and Eugénie had spent their honeymoon, and a big building which had once served as a barracks. Pasteur quite favored it, but there was again the problem of the neighbors, who visualized their peaceful community overrun with mad dogs.

While the matter was being negotiated, Pasteur attended the International Medical Congress at Copenhagen where his son, incidentally, was secretary to the French legation. It was another triumphal appearance. The meeting, attended by sixteen hundred delegates, the King and Queen of Denmark, the King and Queen of Greece and other notables royal and common, opened on August 10. There were the usual speeches about science, progress and international amity, with Sir James Paget speaking for England, Virchow for Germany, and Pasteur for France. At the end of the opening meeting, Pasteur was presented to the masculine Majesties, and, as one of his entourage reported with awed snobbery, the Queens, disregarding etiquette, walked toward him to be introduced, "a signal proof of the esteem in which our illustrious countryman is held..."

Evidence of esteem more valuable to Pasteur than royalty's was the silent attention, followed by the roar of applause, with which his paper on hydrophobia was greeted by all the assembled scientists. It seemed scarcely possible to them that even the benign wizardry of Pasteur could accomplish this miracle that had been sought for ages; yet he had climaxed his long, logical list of wonders by discovering a method of immunizing animals to rabies.

At the close of the meeting a French doctor, Jacques Joseph Grancher, a professor on the Faculty of Medicine, whom Adrien knew in Paris, came up to him as he stood near his uncle and asked to be introduced to Pasteur.

Adrien had already mentioned Grancher to Pasteur, adding that the medical students referred to him as the "Grand Vicar" because of his pontifical manner. Now he led him up to Pasteur and said:

"Uncle, may I present M. Grancher? You have heard me speak of him."

"Ah, yes," Pasteur said pleasantly. "I know of M. Grancher.

This young man"—he nodded toward Adrien—"tells me that at the Faculty you are known as the Grand Vicar."

"Indeed!" remarked Grancher, eying Adrien thoughtfully.

Adrien merely looked resigned. Pasteur was noted for saying whatever came into his head, and this was not Adrien's first experience with his embarrassing bluntness.

Grancher, it developed, wanted to be admitted to the rue d'Ulm laboratory. Pasteur, whose routine had not become more flexible with the years, would not hear of it, but allowed him to work with Strauss in the laboratory in the rue Vauquelin building. Adrien used to stop in there, after his day's work was done, on his way to his own room. What impressed him most about it was the comfortable chairs, particularly the rocking chair, which Grancher had introduced into it. He used to sit in it, rocking luxuriously, while Grancher and Strauss worked, and wonder to himself what Pasteur, who sometimes, with lofty austerity, spoke of laboratories as "temples of science," would say to this one. Finally, one day, when Pasteur accompanied him to the rue Vauquelin to look at a dog Adrien showed it to him. Standing in the doorway, Pasteur looked all around it. He took in everything, and said nothing. Adrien got the impression that the master—who all his life had worked standing up at a desk—thought he had done well to bar from his own precincts a man capable of installing such frivolous equipment in a laboratory. Yet he liked and respected Grancher; it was merely that he knew his working habits would be incompatible with his own.

By May everything was ready at Villeneuve l'Étang. The neighbors had been soothed with assurances that only immunized dogs were to be kept there, and had withdrawn their opposition. Kennels for the accommodation of sixty dogs were ready; rabbit hutches and guinea pig pens were finished; a comfortable, simply furnished apartment for Pasteur, who would frequently have to spend days at a time there, was arranged in the old barracks; and a retired policeman named Pernin was engaged to care for the animals. Pernin soon promoted one of the more appealing dogs to the post of household pet, and the two of them presided happily over the new domain.

In addition to the sixty immunized dogs at Villeneuve l'Étang, Pasteur still had forty dogs at the rue Vauquelin, and another twenty-five quartered on veterinarians interested in the rabies work. With these hundred and twenty-five dogs he was multiplying experiments. Sure now that he could render an animal immune to rabies *before* it was exposed either to a bite or an injection, he was now working principally on preventing the onset of rabies by inoculating animals *after* exposure. His work was so promising that to his old friend Vercel he confidently wrote:

"I am demonstrating this year that dogs can be vaccinated, or made refractory to rabies, *after* they have been bitten by mad dogs."

He added, significantly, that he had not yet dared to treat a bitten human being, but that he was already so sure of his results that he was much inclined to put them to the test—on himself.

CHAPTER NINETEEN

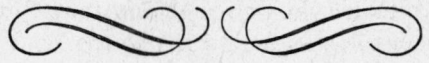

The vaccine worked on dogs after they were bitten, but would it work on man?

That was the big, the crucial, question about the attenuated rabic virus. Just as some animals were immune to diseases fatal to others, so also one species might be killed by an attenuated virus that immunized another. Pasteur thought the antirabic vaccine that protected dogs would protect human beings; Roux doubted it. There was, of course, only one way to find out.

Yet when the chance presented itself, Pasteur shrank from it. Had he refused, however, to try his new remedy, he would have been condemning a fellow being to certain death. The fellow being, too, was a little boy eight years old, and Pasteur always found children infinitely appealing. "When I see a child," he once said, "he inspires me with two feelings: tenderness for what he is now, respect for what he may become." He ended by doing the only thing that might save the boy's life.

Now that the street door of the rue d'Ulm laboratory was usually kept locked to discourage callers, Adrien, when anyone knocked, would inspect the visitor from a window. If it was someone unknown, he would open the door and ask his business; if it was someone he knew, he would go directly to Pasteur, at work in laboratory or office, to tell him. There was a technique for approaching the master in these cases. Adrien would stand beside him and say softly:

"Uncle, M. So-and-so wishes to see you."

Usually he received no answer, so he would say it again after a short pause. He might have to repeat himself several times before Pasteur, with the air of a man awakening reluctantly but without irritation from a dream, would answer:

"M. So-and-So? Bring him to my office." Or, "Oh, no, I am too busy. Beg him to excuse me today."

This morning—Monday, July 6, 1885—Adrien, peering from the window in response to the bell, saw a man, a woman and a child at the door. He opened it to ask what they wanted, and what the woman told him sent him fairly flying to Pasteur.

"A Mme Meister, Uncle, from Alsace, and her son Joseph want to see you. The boy was attacked and badly bitten by a mad dog two days ago. Their local doctor told her that you could perhaps save her son. M. Vône, the dog's owner, is with them."

"Ah, poor child! I will see them at once." Pasteur closed his notebook and limped quickly into his office.

Always distressed by suffering, Pasteur was shocked at the sight of Joseph's wounds. His bites were deep and numerous—there were no less than fourteen on his hands and arms and legs—and he was in great pain. As Pasteur examined the weeping child, Théodore Vône, who introduced himself as a grocer of Meissengott, told him what had happened. Little Joseph had been on his way to school when Vône's dog leaped on him and knocked him down A laborer, seeing the attack, rushed up and drove off the animal, which then returned home and bit its master on the arm. Vône at once shot it, and took the body to a veterinarian who, finding the stomach full of straw and scraps of wood, did not hesitate to pronounce it rabid. Joseph's rescuer, meanwhile, had taken him, covered with blood and saliva, to his parents. When Vône brought them the terrible news that the dog had been mad, they took the injured child to a doctor who advised them to start at once for Paris. Vône, feeling responsible for the accident and worried on account of his own bite, decided to escort them.

It was plain to Pasteur that no one injected so deeply and repeatedly with the rabic virus as this child could fail to contract the disease. It was equally plain to him that if he tried his vaccine and Joseph died, he would be accused of having caused or hastened his death with an untested remedy. Failure would discredit him—and how some of his colleagues in the Academy of Medicine would love that!—and, worse than that, it would discredit the vaccine. Should he let the boy die, or should he risk a grave failure?

"I am going to ask one of my colleagues to see your son, madame," he said. "He will help us decide what to do. As for you, M. Vône, you have nothing to fear. Your shirt sleeve was not torn by the dog's teeth and the saliva did not even reach your skin. You may go home this very day, with a quiet mind."

Pasteur, after giving Adrien instructions for the Meisters' comfort, left for the Academy of Sciences meeting where he knew he would find Vulpian. Vulpian agreed to return with him to the rue d'Ulm after the meeting to see Joseph.

He examined the child with a grave face, and Joseph, fascinated by his big white beard which waggled as he talked, stared at him wonderingly.

"Well," Vulpian said finally, "first let us hear what madame thinks of testing this vaccine on her son."

Mme Meister had but one idea. "Try anything—anything that may save him!"

Vulpian nodded approvingly. He drew Pasteur to one side and said in a low tone:

"That is the way I feel about it, too. Try your vaccine."

"I do not need to point out to you, monsieur," Pasteur said a bit drily, "that I am not a medical man—our colleagues in the Academy of Medicine do that often enough. But think what they will say if I, a chemist, treat that child and he dies."

"And how will you feel if you do *not* treat him? You will wake up nights, and you will say to yourself: 'I might have saved a life by lifting my hand—and I did not lift it!' You are in a painful position, my friend. Whether you act or refrain from acting you assume a great responsibility. In my opinion, it is your duty to try the vaccine. Otherwise," he shrugged not unsympathetically, "it is all up with the poor child."

"Very well," Pasteur agreed. "I had hoped that you would feel that way. And you—you will give the inoculation, will you not?"

"I? Vaccinate? Heavens, no! I am a physiologist, not a practitioner."

"Then I must ask Grancher," Pasteur said. He knew there

was no use in asking Roux who, feeling that the vaccine was not yet ready to try on human beings, would certainly refuse to administer it.

Grancher, routed out of his lodgings and brought to the laboratory by Adrien, got ready to make the inoculation. At the sight of the preparations and the instruments, and especially of the hypodermic needle which he knew was going to stick him, Joseph broke into tears. He had already had so much pain, and now these solemn men with beards were going to hurt him again! With renewed howls he flung himself on his mother.

It was not enough that Pasteur should make his wonderful discoveries—he was always having to reconcile the beneficiaries to them. This time he took Joseph on his knee and soothed and reassured him. Finally Joseph, half convinced, asked:

"Really, just a little prick, monsieur? You are sure it won't hurt?"

"Just a little one, Joseph. And you will scarcely feel it. I promise you."

Pasteur nodded to Grancher, who, his preparations completed, slipped the needle under the skin of the boy's abdomen and injected the vaccine.

Joseph wiped his tear-stained face on his sleeve with smiling surprise—the old gentleman with the kind face had told him the truth, after all!

There was then the problem of finding lodgings for the Meisters. Pasteur undertook it, as much out of kindness to the distraught mother as out of his desire to keep Joseph under observation. He took a fiacre and drove with Adrien to a store in the Boulevard Saint Michel where he bought two beds and bedding which he ordered sent to 14 rue Vauquelin. Adrien helped Mme Député, wife of the laboratory helper, to clean a room next to his own and to set up the beds. Thus Joseph and Mme Meister were established in private quarters, free of charge, under the constant and friendly observation of Adrien. The poor mother began to feel that her troubles were falling away from her.

Pasteur's, on the other hand, were just beginning. He gave Adrien careful instructions: he was to take Joseph's temperature four times a day—in the morning after the inoculation, at noon, at five o'clock, and when he went to bed after the supper that Mme Député would prepare for him; he was to observe his actions closely; and he was to make a note of everything the child said to him. Daily Pasteur listened to the reports that Adrien brought him, usually while he was having lunch in his apartment with his wife, and entered notes on them in one of his books. Often he was at Joseph's side in the morning when he got up, to see how he felt and acted on arising; often he came to the rue Vauquelin during the day to watch the little boy, soon as happy and busy as though he had never been bitten, at play among the harmless experimental animals; sometimes he would allow Mme Meister to take Joseph into the Luxembourg Gardens and he, with Adrien, would follow along at a distance, watching all his movements.

Joseph presented himself each morning at the laboratory for his inoculation with trustful cheerfulness. Nobody was going to hurt him, and his "dear M. Pasteur," who had given him a rabbit for a pet, was so kind and good to him that he often kissed him good-by.

"He is still well today," Pasteur would say as Joseph skipped out of his office. "Let us hope that he may be tomorrow!"

As the days passed and the inoculations became more and more virulent, Pasteur's anxiety increased painfully. What if the stuff failed to work, and the disease developed in its usual time? Worse, what if it not only failed to prevent rabies, but precipitated it? What if—oh, what if a thousand things! Joseph, meanwhile, was having the time of his life. He received the last, most virulent, inoculation with perfect unconcern.

When the treatment was finished, Pasteur was so worn with anxiety that he went to a quiet country place in Burgundy, where his daughter and son-in-law were staying, to visit them for a few days, but he could enjoy no peace. His apprehensions about Joseph were too keen. He awaited Grancher's daily report on his health, wired from Paris, with impatience and dread. When it arrived, announcing that the little patient continued well, he would experience a momentary relief, then he would begin to worry what the next day's telegram would say. He spent hours walking in the woods, without a word, while René, sharing his anxiety and wrung with sympathy, paced silently beside him.

When the climax came, it was a negative sort of thing: Joseph Meister simply failed to develop rabies.

Pasteur was in no hurry to make public this wonderful result; he did not intend to give his detractors the chance to say that he had not allowed the disease time enough to develop. Word of it got around unofficially, however, and on October 20, Jean Baptiste Jupille, a shepherd boy fourteen years old, presented himself for the new treatment.

Six days before, on October 14, Jupille and several younger children had been watching their sheep near the Jurane town of Villers-Farlay when they saw, running erratically toward them, a rabid dog. Jupille commanded the others to run, and grasping his long whip placed himself between them and the mad dog. The animal attacked him, and he struggled with it, succeeding finally in getting it down and kneeling on it while he held its jaws closed with his hands. Only then did he shout for help, and one of his companions ran up with the whip he had dropped. Jupille twisted the long thong around the dog's muzzle, and beat it over the head with his wooden sabot. Then the two children carried the stunned beast to a near-by stream and held it under water until it was drowned. During the struggle Jupille had been severely bitten on the hands.

Pasteur heard the story, and saw the large and by now infected wounds with horrified sympathy. Must this brave boy die? Was there justification for giving him the vaccine? It could already be too late—the virus, injected a full six days ago, was perhaps even now at its deadly work in his nervous system.

"Adrien, get Vulpian and Grancher," Pasteur ordered.

Adrien got them, and a long and somewhat sharp discussion ensued. Might not the vaccine, used so long after the bite, precipitate the attack, might it not intensify it, might it not be, at best, useless? In the end it was decided to risk failure and all its consequences. Grancher, as before, made the inoculations, and Jupille was established in the room lately occupied by Joseph Meister where Adrien could keep an eye on him.

On October 26, while the outcome of Jupille's treatment was still in doubt, Pasteur described to the Academy of Sciences the case of Joseph Meister, and told his colleagues of the brave shepherd boy then undergoing treatment. This announcement of the first successful treatment of a human being with the new antirabies vaccine made a profound impression. Vulpian rose to voice his solemn admiration. Bouley, the chairman, who had so often and so well defended Pasteur, offered him a tribute that was the more affecting since it came from a man who realized he was dying and weighed his words accordingly.

The period of Jupille's treatment was one of anxiety, but it was not as trying to Pasteur as Joseph Meister's. He had more confidence in his method now. Finally Jupille was discharged, in perfect health. The vaccine had worked again, and this time, in view of the six days that had passed before it was given, under much more difficult circumstances.

The wizard in the rue d'Ulm had done it again! The dreaded hydrophobia could be prevented! Word of the miraculous treatment—for it seemed no less than miraculous—now spread rapidly, and more victims of rabid animals appeared in the office in the rue d'Ulm begging to be saved from the consequence of their bites. While the victims were trusting—or were, perhaps, willing to catch at straws—Pasteur's critics in and out of the Academy of Medicine were far from it. Some questioned the new method because it was foreign to their temperaments to find any progress tolerable. Some few others strongly doubted the wisdom of using the preventive on human beings until its action was better understood; they feared that a few successes might be followed by catastrophe. Among these was Roux. Almost daily in the laboratory he discussed his many and not unreasonable doubts with Eugene Viala and Adrien Loir. He ended by making such an impression on Adrien that Adrien confided his apprehensions to his father and Duclaux.

"Just keep your opinion to yourself, my boy—certainly do not thrust it on M. Pasteur," was the substance of their advice.

So Adrien, with an anxious and divided mind, continued to assist at the inoculations that Grancher, under the supervision of Pasteur, performed every morning in the master's office. His faith in his uncle's method was badly shaken, and he wondered how Grancher could, with a clear conscience, inject into person after person this vaccine which might at any moment produce disaster. He soon found out.

Grancher, while preparing to inoculate someone under treatment with a four-day-old—that is to say, a very virulent—injection, pricked himself with the hypodermic. He proceeded with the vaccination and when he had finished Pasteur, whose short-sighted eyes missed nothing, said to him:

"You will have to submit to the treatment now yourself, Grancher."

"Just as you say, M. Pasteur," Grancher agreed, almost with indifference.

The next morning, Adrien, full of the misgivings stimulated by Roux's objections, seized an opportunity to speak to Grancher alone.

"You aren't really going to let yourself be inoculated, are you, monsieur? We still do not know what this treatment may do to human beings."

The Grand Vicar, from his superior height, looked down on the student. "And do you imagine, young man," he asked drily, "that I would inoculate those people every morning as I do if I was not confident of the method?"

Adrien was rebuked but not satisfied. Grancher was living in a fool's paradise, that was all! Far removed from the backstage workings of Pasteur's laboratory, he had no notion of the uncertainties, the disappointments, the reverses that surrounded these scientific techniques still in their embryonic stage. But he, Adrien, and Roux and Viala who were intimate with every detail of the laboratory understood these things better. Grancher must not be allowed to take the risky treatment! Adrien went to the animal room to talk the matter over with Viala.

It took the two assistants no great time to figure out that they—a laboratory attendant and a medical student—could not successfully oppose Grancher and the great Pasteur.

"Well," Adrien finally said desperately, "I know one thing—we can't let M. Grancher go through with this alone! We must have ourselves inoculated along with him!"

"If you wish," Viala agreed equably—much as Grancher had earlier agreed with Pasteur.

It was a generous decision, however little reason it had to recommend it.

The following morning after the regular inoculations, which Grancher performed as usual, Adrien, Viala and Grancher were left alone with Pasteur in his office. Pasteur closed the door behind the last patient, and turned to them.

"And now, Grancher, before you are inoculated, you will first inoculate me."

"No, M. Pasteur. You have not been exposed to rabies, and there is no reason to vaccinate you. I absolutely refuse to do it."

Adrien and Eugene goggled. One did not "absolutely refuse" to do anything the master commanded—it was unthinkable! Pasteur turned abruptly to his nephew and ordered:

"You, Adrien, inoculate me—since Grancher refuses."

"Oh, no, Uncle. No, I have no right. I—I am not even a doctor," Adrien babbled. He had never dared—never dreamed of daring—to disobey Pasteur, and he was so appalled that he could scarcely believe the sound of his own voice. "I cannot, unless M. Grancher orders me to"—he and Grancher exchanged a look—"and M. Grancher isn't saying anything."

If it was a new and shocking experience to Pasteur's assistants to defy him, it was fully as novel and shocking a one to Pasteur to be defied. He said nothing, but flushed with mortification while he cast about for some way to handle this unprecedented situation. In the embarrassing silence, Adrien said loudly:

"Viala and I wish to take the preventive inoculations, Uncle."

"I accept," Grancher said quickly. "The boys are right—they are in daily contact with rabid animals."

Outmaneuvered, Pasteur could only consent. Viala loaded the syringe in silence, in silence Adrien took it from him and inoculated Grancher, and still in silence Grancher inoculated the two assistants.

From then on the inoculations took place daily. Every morning, after the regular patients had been treated, the three younger men would shut themselves in his office with Pasteur, and under his eye inoculate each other. Roux, who had observed this routine from the laboratory once or twice, became suspicious. One afternoon when he and Adrien were alone in the laboratory, he began to question him. Adrien tried to evade answering, but he was no match for Roux, who seized him by the arm and said fiercely:

"You are inoculating someone in there—I know it! Who is it? Is it M. Pasteur?"

"No, no, M. Roux. Truly it is not M. Pasteur. M. Grancher and Viala and I—it is we who are taking the treatment."

Roux was furious. "You are all crazy!" he shouted. "Do you want hydrophobia? This has to stop—if you do not stop at once I will tell your father!"

"Please, please, M. Roux, don't!" Adrien begged, almost in tears. "Papa knows what you think of the treatment—I have told him—and he would be wild with alarm. Anyway, it is too late now. We are on the twelfth day. I must go on to the fourteenth. How can I stop now? What good would it do?"

Roux stood still for an instant, then strode angrily out of the laboratory. A moment later Adrien heard the street door savagely slammed. He relaxed with a sigh. He knew that Roux, as soon as he became calmer, would realize that he could not stop the inoculations by whatever means. It was far too late—the experimenters had already used virulent injections.

Roux, in fact, said nothing, and Adrien's parents remained happily unconscious of their son's inoculations. They remained unconscious, that is, until Pasteur himself exploded the information at them.

It was the custom of the two families to get together occasionally on Sundays for dinner. The sisters exchanged notes on their households, M. Loir and M. Pasteur discussed science or some other elevated topic, and the children joined in whichever conversation interested them the more. This Sunday, about two months after the conclusion of Adrien's inoculations, the Loirs and the Pasteurs were at dinner, and in a pause Pasteur turned to his sister-in-law and suddenly asked:

"Well, Mme Loir, how has your son seemed to you in the last couple of months? Hasn't he been in fine shape?"

Adrien saw what was coming. "Please, Uncle, don't say it, don't say it!" he exclaimed.

Mme Pasteur, who knew all about her nephew's inoculations, cast her husband a pleading look. "Louis, be still!" she commanded.

But Pasteur, once launched, could not be stopped by a mere wife or nephew. He continued blandly:

"Didn't he tell you, then, that he has been inoculated, that he has taken the antirabic treatment?"

The electrified Loirs dropped their spoons into their soup from horror-stiffened fingers. A frigid silence fell over the table. Adrien looked miserably around. No one had a word to say. Perhaps the Loirs had a few, but if so the mannerly training of a lifetime prevented their utterance. Pasteur went on eating his soup as though nothing had happened, and one by one the other members of the family gathering began to go through the polite motions. The rest of the visit, however, was not a success and the Pasteurs took their leave very soon after dinner.

That night Mme Loir tucked her son into bed and fussed over him as though he were a small child.

"Oh, come, Mama, there is nothing to worry about. The treatment was finished weeks ago—there is no danger now, and what little there may have been was past long ago!"

But Mme Loir only half believed him. She was by no means sure that she was not taking her last look at her boy before he should be carried out, foaming at the mouth, to die a wretched victim to his uncle's overconfidence.

CHAPTER TWENTY

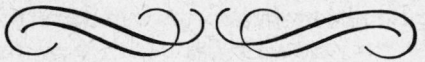

WITHIN a few months the celebrity of the antirabies treatment had spread so that persons bitten by rabid animals were coming to Pasteur from all over France. There were more inoculations than Grancher could perform alone—Roux, doubting and disapproving still, refused to have anything to do with the vaccination of human beings—so that two young graduates of the Faculty of Medicine, André Chantemesse and Albert Charrin, came every day to help. Another graduate, Terrillon, who was a surgeon and a friend of Grancher's, was always in attendance to dress the wounds of the bitten, some of which were severe.

Daily at eleven o'clock Pasteur would open the door of his office, where the treatments took place, and call the patients, each in turn, from the anteroom in which they were waiting. Viala had spent the morning preparing the rabic spinal cords for inoculation, and the vaccinal liquid for each person was ready and labeled. Under Pasteur's sympathetic eye the young doctors performed the inoculations while the master himself reassured parents, and comforted children with kind words and with the candies and new copper coins he kept in his desk for the purpose.

The morning of November 9, however, he could offer no reassurance to the parents of one patient. Louise Pelletier, ten years old, had been badly bitten on the head by a mad dog—and it was not until that morning, thirty-seven days later, that her parents brought her to Pasteur. Aside from the fact that the wound was infected, she appeared to be in normal health, but Pasteur did not doubt that rabies would develop in a short time —in a very few weeks at the most: the rabic virus, he thought, must already be working its way along the nervous system toward the brain. The vaccine, to be effective, had to get in its work before the nervous tissue was attacked.

Because he was practically certain that vaccination would not succeed, Pasteur did not want to use it in this case. A failure would cast doubt, however undeserved, on the method, which was already under violent attack in the Academy of Medicine; it would frighten those who were undergoing treatment; and it might altogether scare away bitten persons who could be saved by it. There was every argument against attempting the treatment, and only one for it—pity for the distracted parents. Pasteur's tenderness of heart made him helpless; pity outweighed colder considerations. The vaccination was started, the wound dressed; and with a heavy heart Pasteur saw the parents, daring to be happy in their renewed hope, lead the little girl away.

It was, as he knew it must be, useless. Louise remained well for about a week after the final inoculation; then all the terrible symptoms—breathlessness, spasms, tormenting thirst, inability to swallow—appeared. Although he had expected nothing better, Pasteur was disconsolate. Every moment he could spare from his work he spent by Louise's bedside, and the little girl, choking and convulsed, clutched his hand and begged him not to leave her. At night he posted Adrien beside her to watch in his place. Several times during Adrien's vigils Roux, in spite of having dissociated himself from the antirabies work, climbed the stairs to the Pelletiers' apartment and stood quietly by the sick girl's bed, his intelligent face grave with compassion. The hopeless, horrible illness dragged into early December. On the day Louise died, Pasteur, who had been attending Bouley's funeral, hurried to her side. Overwhelmed with sorrow, both for his dead friend and for the child he could not help, he wept bitterly on leaving the sickroom.

"I had so hoped to save your little girl!" he said.

His opponents seized on the death of Louise Pelletier and called it failure. Her father took a juster view of it. He could not imagine another man, he said, "capable of sacrificing long years of work, of jeopardizing a universal reputation as a savant, and of walking knowingly into a grievous failure—simply out of humanity."

Competent critics were filled with admiration for the method that was saving lives by the score, and the public, with hope and good judgment, continued to apply for treatment. Patients were beginning to come from foreign countries by this time. From across the Atlantic came four children to be saved by the miracle-worker of the rue d'Ulm, sent by a public subscription raised by a New York newspaper.

Official French statistics on the mortality from bites of rabid dogs had ranged from sixteen to forty per hundred; by March, 1886, Pasteur had treated three hundred and fifty patients, and had lost but one, Louise Pelletier. Inspired by this striking success, he was now dreaming of setting up an organization for the treatment of rabies and of the contagious diseases for which he had developed vaccines, and for the continuance of his research work. It should be supported, he thought, not by the French state, but by voluntary gifts from all countries, since its work would be of international benefit. A wealthy and generous Frenchman set the ball rolling with a gift of forty thousand francs, and subscriptions were opened at home and abroad. When the donations came in from Alsace, Pasteur was touched to see the name of Joseph Meister on the subscription list.

While money was being raised for the new establishment, Pasteur continued to treat—or rather to have his young men treat—patients at his office in the rue d'Ulm. In March nineteen Russians who had been attacked by a mad wolf arrived from Smolensk. Several of them had been shockingly mauled and were in such critical condition from their wounds that they were at once hospitalized at the Hôtel Dieu. The others Pasteur lodged in the neighborhood of his laboratory. The wounds of all of them were the more serious for having been inflicted a full two weeks earlier. Pasteur decided to speed up the treatment, giving inoculations not once a day, but morning and evening. Every morning those who could came to the laboratory, enhancing by their foreign dress and speech the already international air of the waiting room, and every evening they again presented themselves. Pasteur, accompanied by Charrin or Chantemesse or Grancher, went twice a day to the hospital to give inoculations to the invalids. The bite of a rabid wolf was much more virulent than that of a mad dog; eight out of ten of a wolf's victims could expect to die. Yet Pasteur saved sixteen of the nineteen Russians. Over the three who died he was inconsolable. It was not that his faith in his method was shaken; it was that he interested himself so tenderly in each individual he treated that a death was a real blow to his affections. The Czar of Russia, however, looked on the bright side. Deeply impressed by the treatment his subjects had received, he presented Pasteur with a hundred thousand francs for his proposed institute and with a diamond-studded decoration, the Cross of the Order of St. Anne of Russia.

By April so many persons were applying for treatment that the laboratory could not accommodate them. Pasteur therefore had a small building erected in the courtyard at 14 rue Vauquelin and the patients, while awaiting their turn, amused themselves among the cages of the experimental animals which had aroused old Faraboeuf's wrath.

Pasteur had not been to the theater since, as a student, he had gone to see Rachel and had brought down on himself a torrent of anxious admonitions from his father. His life for many years had been too busy, too serious and too regular for him to spend an evening being amused. A theatrical performance for the benefit of his new establishment, however, was a good deal more than just an evening's entertainment, and when one was organized he took his usual interest in every detail of the plans. The performance was to take place at the Trocadéro, and some of the most popular of the contemporary French actors and musicians had offered their talents. Sitting at the desk in the library of his apartment, Pasteur inscribed in his small, legible hand the stack of programs to the participating artists, to his friends and to his family, and smiled to think that, after so many years, he was again going to the theater.

He went in much more style than he had in the old days: instead of sitting obscurely in the cheapest seats, he and his family had a box; and ministers, senators, scientists and others enjoying varying degrees of contemporary greatness stopped in during the intermission to pay their respects to the man whose greatness eclipsed them all. Perhaps at the banquet later, some of the celebrated performers were astonished to learn that he saw them that night for the first time. If they were, they could feel no pique, for he said guilelessly: "But I can have no regrets now that you have given me, in a few hours' interval as in an exquisite synthesis, the feelings that so many others scatter over several years."

There were problems connected with the new organization. What, for instance, should it be called? Where should the building be erected? Someone suggested Pasteur Laboratory for the name, but that sounded flat and inadequate. Pasteur, besides, objected to having his name appear in its title. The objection was vigorously overruled—of course it had to carry the master's name, the committee in charge insisted. How about Pasteur Institution? That didn't sound right, either—it sounded like something for the care of the feeble-minded. Well, what about Pasteur Institute? No, protested Pasteur. To use the term "institute" was almost sacrilege: it was never used in that sense, and to Frenchmen it meant but one thing, the Institute of France, the great learned society that comprised the five academies. Pasteur might as well have argued with the wind: Pasteur Institute was the name chosen in spite of him.

Nor did he care for the site that was finally selected: it was in the rue Dutot, away from the Latin Quarter and the narrow, friendly streets in which he had passed most of his life. The original spot chosen, on the Boulevard Port Royal, had pleased him better, but Duclaux, whose influence with him was very great, had not approved of it. It was too small and would not permit the physical expansion that pursuit of the Pasteurian doctrines, which touched so many branches of science, would make necessary. Pasteur had finally yielded, without much resignation, to having the building erected in the rue Dutot. The Right Bank seemed almost another world to him, and a trip to it a veritable expedition. Occasionally he would hire a fiacre and drive over there with Adrien to look at the big truck garden, soon to be replaced by the fine stone-faced building in which he and his colleagues and disciples would work.

"Ah, it is so far!" he would sigh regretfully.

In spite of the fact that far less than one per cent of the patients who underwent the Pasteur treatment had died of rabies,

Pasteur continued to be hounded by hostile critics. Between chronic overwork and the anxiety caused by these assaults, many of which were conducted with bad temper and bad faith, Pasteur's health began to suffer. He was only sixty-three, but his life had been strenuous: singlehanded, he had launched a profound revolution, and he had been in the forefront of all its battles. Grancher, seeing him almost daily, recognized symptoms of heart trouble. Toward the end of November he persuaded Pasteur to go for a rest to Bordighera, where one of his admirers, M. Raphael Bischoffsheim, had offered him his luxurious Villa Margharita. The work of the laboratory and of the rabies service could be continued in his absence, and he could be consulted by mail about the plans for the Institute. Pasteur, accompanied by his wife, Marie Louise and René, and their two children, wearily departed for rest and sunshine in the South. His loyal collaborators prepared to carry on.

Almost the first thing that happened to them was a crisis: a child who had undergone the rabies treatment died. The father distractedly accused the laboratory of having killed his son, the police were called in and an autopsy was ordered. Roux, aloof up to now, threw off his air of indifference: the master was away, the laboratory was threatened, and it was his business, as the medical man longest associated with it, to conduct its defense.

The coroner, a reasonable official, on learning that Paul Brouardel, dean of the Faculty of Medicine and a friend of Pasteur's, was familiar with the work of the laboratory, appointed him to perform the autopsy and report on it. Roux had Adrien Loir and Grancher attend it and bring a piece of the dead child's spinal cord back to the laboratory. When Adrien returned with it Roux had everything in readiness to make a preparation from the cord and inject it into rabbits to test its virulence. The test, in due course, came out positive: the child had indeed died of rabies. The length of time that passed before the disease developed in the experimental rabbits showed, however, that he had died of street rabies, that his death had not been brought about by vaccination. Roux at once sent Adrien on a flying trip to Bordighera to get all of Pasteur's laboratory books containing the notes of his rabies work. On Adrien's return Roux applied himself intensively for several days to catching up on the work he had for so long snubbed and, thanks to his brilliance and to much hard work, he was prepared when Brouardel sent for him.

Brouardel was grave and anxious. Feeling among the old guard physicians had mounted high against Pasteur and the laboratory, he said; one of the most influential professors on the Faculty of Medicine had brutally demanded of Grancher if he was prepared to go to the penitentiary, where he would soon find himself since he could hardly expect to pay the thousands and thousands of francs damages that would be claimed against him for his part in the fiendish new treatment.

"I know, M. Roux," Brouardel continued, "that you have all along been opposed to the application of the treatment to human beings. Now you say that your tests show conclusively that the child died in spite of, not because of, the vaccination. I have great faith in your judgment, and I want to know if, despite the caution that motivated your opposition, you think the treatment is justified now."

"Yes, I do! I have reviewed in detail the whole course of M. Pasteur's work, and I am now so convinced that it is justified that I would not hesitate to put it to the test on myself."

"Well, in that case, I will confide in you. There is about to be another fierce attack on the method in the Academy of Medicine. Your partisans may be overborne—and medicine set back fifty years—if I do not throw my weight on your side."

"And what do you intend to do, monsieur?" Roux asked sharply.

"I will support you, naturally!"

The attack, spearheaded again by Peter, developed as predicted. Brouardel and Grancher took the brunt of it, and Jean Martin Charcot, the great neurologist, sustained them with his enormous authority. The clash was violent, the polemics were heated. When it was over, the Pasteurians were in possession of the field. Once again the workers of the rue d'Ulm, from master to laboratory boys, could congratulate each other that the new medicine had turned back another assault in its long war with the old. It was a skirmish, too, with a unique and happy by-product: harmony between Pasteur and Roux was completely restored.

Although peace and rest were now absolutely necessary to

Pasteur, echoes of the conflict over the antirabies treatment could not be kept from reaching him at Bordighera and, reaching him, could not fail to agitate him. Even had there been nothing of the sort to worry him, he would still have had to work hard on plans for the Institute. Duclaux had had the idea of starting a monthly publication called *Annals of the Pasteur Institute*, and in the *Annals*, he had grimly decided, should be published a list of those undergoing the treatment, with a bulletin of their condition, to silence ill-natured hints that Pasteur concealed his failures. Details important and unimportant in connection with the Institute and the new magazine had to be referred to the master, who devoted his usual careful attention to each one. In short, worry and work between them prevented his vacation from being as restful as his intimates had hoped—and an earthquake brought it suddenly to an end.

It was six-thirty on the morning of February 23 that Pasteur noticed the first shock. The earth rumbled and shook, the ceiling of his room cracked and began to sprinkle down and the glass in his windows rattled furiously. Within a minute his family was clustered around him and the second shock, more violent than the first, took place. By the time the upheaval was over the handsome villa was scarcely habitable: ceilings were fallen, plaster dust lay over everything, windows were shattered. There was nothing for Pasteur and his entourage to do but join the other refugees from the town on the trip to the nearest railway station and depart for France. In Arbois, perhaps, his worn heart and tired body would recover some of their spent strength.

There, after the strenuous journey, he was able to recuperate somewhat. It was always relaxation to him to return to the congenial atmosphere of his childhood home, to hear, as he walked slowly down the village street, the harsh Arboisian accent—an accent no longer distinguishable in his own speech—and to talk to old friends of old times, and of the new he had done so much to introduce. He worked more than he should have, but he had always overworked and it was too late now to try to change the fixed habit of a lifetime. Not only did he keep up with the affairs of his laboratory and the Institute, but he applied himself to all the problems that friends, neighbors and strangers brought him. Pasteur heard everyone out, no matter how rambling or inarticulate his complaint. He took a deep, serious pleasure in his ability to resolve their difficulties, to help them through science to a more secure and a happier life. To exercise his kindness, to observe the fruitful function of his good will and wisdom, seemed to refresh him.

Considerably restored after a few weeks, Pasteur returned to Paris and to his old routine: breakfast at eight, the laboratory at eight-thirty, the rabies service at eleven, luncheon at home and, after a short rest, the laboratory again or a meeting of one of the societies or committees of which he was a member. When his health permitted, he continued to receive on Sundays, and his *salons* now had something of an international character. Doctors from foreign countries, attracted to Paris by the opportunity to study and do research under him and the men he had trained, frequented them. Knowing few of the other guests, and perhaps speaking French with some difficulty, they might, in the beginning, be ill at ease, but Pasteur's tact as a host smoothed over any awkwardness. When Élie Metchnikoff, the Russian scientist, misled by the unassuming air of Pasteur whom he had met only once before, appeared at a Sunday reception wearing simply a frock coat, he was mortified to find all the other guests in formal dress.

"Please, monsieur," he begged, as Pasteur started to draw him into the *salon*, "let me go back to my rooms. I will change, and return more suitably dressed."

"Of course not! No one cares what you are wearing. It is you we are interested in, not your clothes."

"But I must appear discourteous to your other guests. Really, I shall not be comfortable."

"Oh, if you are uncomfortable, that is different. But do not go away—wait here a few minutes, and I will fix everything."

Pasteur disappeared and Metchnikoff waited in the hall, wondering what his host was going to do. In a few minutes Pasteur returned—wearing a frock coat.

"Now, monsieur," he said smilingly, as he took the Russian's arm, "I do not think anyone can find fault with your costume. Come meet our other guests."

Although he continued to follow his established routine, Pasteur could not conceal from himself, or from friends and family, that his health was seriously impaired—so seriously, in fact, that he did not expect to live long. What time remained he hoped to spend in the new Institute, "on the one hand in encouraging to research and in training for scientific studies—the future of which seems to me most promising—pupils worthy of French science; and on the other hand in following attentively the work incited and encouraged by the Academy of Sciences." He was frail and ill, and looked it, and it was no surprise but rather the fulfillment of apprehension when, one day late in October, he suffered a light stroke and found himself unable to speak. The paralysis passed after some hours, only to recur a few days later. The second attack, more serious than the first, left his speech slightly thickened and his voice weak and without its customary resonance.

Yet although his health was declining, his mind was as active, his spirit as indomitable, as ever. One evening toward the end of 1887, Adrien Loir, now a full-fledged doctor, dropped in to see his uncle after dinner. Madame was reading *Le Temps* aloud to him, as she had every night for years, and Adrien sat down to listen. The paper carried an announcement that the Australian government was seeking some method of exterminating the wild rabbits that were multiplying at a fantastic rate and destroying the vegetation on the sheep ranges so completely that sheep raisers were having to abandon their land. When his wife had finished reading, Pasteur said:

"Adrien, when you leave, go to the laboratory, take a flask and sow in it some chicken cholera germs."

"Yes, Uncle." Adrien wondered why, but knew better than to ask for an explanation. The next day Pasteur dictated to him a letter to *Le Temps* which explained his order of the previous night. It was the custom to try to kill rabbits, when they became a pest, by chemical poisons; how much more sensible, Pasteur suggested, to counteract them with a living poison, a poison that would reproduce itself even faster than the rabbits could reproduce themselves—a poison that was, in short, an epidemic disease. Chicken cholera would be the ideal disease to sow among rabbits, he concluded, since they were very susceptible to it; and other domestic animals, except chickens which would normally be kept out of the infested fields, took comparatively little harm from it.

In the midst of illness, plans for the Institute and the press of his regular routine, Pasteur's fertile mind could apply itself to a new problem like this and conceive, apparently effortlessly, a novel solution that, in fact, had in it the germ of the idea of bacteriological warfare. A month later he sent Adrien to Reims to try out the method on the property of a Mme Pommery who was much afflicted by a plague of rabbits. It worked successfully, and early the next year Adrien was in Australia. Because of political rivalry between two ministries, he was not allowed to apply the new method of controlling rabbits, but he remained to organize a Pasteur Institute and to direct it for several years.

Pasteur had never had any particular desire to be a great man; to be of some service to science, France, humanity had been his ambition. His service had been so spectacular that he had achieved international fame, but it was hard for him to realize what a celebrated figure he had become. His country, his colleagues, scientific and industrial societies, foreign nations had all conferred high honors on him. He valued more than those the faithful love of his family and friends, and the grateful affection of the thousands he had benefited, most of them not even known to him by name. If he was still vulnerable to the yelping of detractors, he was even more sensitive to the good will and gratitude that flowed toward him from every part of the world where his name was known.

The big vegetable garden in the rue Dutot was gone now, and in its place was the tangible evidence of this good will. Behind a tall iron grille and hedge stood a handsome and well-equipped brick building faced with stone—a center for the treatment of hydrophobia and for the study of contagious diseases, and a training school for young scientists who would carry on the tradition, the method and the work of Pasteur. More than two and a half million francs, the sum of gifts magnificent and modest from all conditions of men, ranging from kings to peasant children, had gone into the establishment of the Pasteur Institute.

Pasteur, who appreciated clearly and with a sort of grateful humility the magnitude of his contribution to science, could not but be moved by the ceremonies which, on November 12,

1888, inaugurated the great new enterprise. In the library of the new building were gathered political figures, colleagues, disciples, friends, family. Joseph Bertrand, chairman of the Institute Committee, whom Pasteur had several years before inducted into the French Academy, spoke of the past and of those masters now dead—Biot, Balard, Dumas—who had guided and influenced the young provincial who was to become the glory of nineteenth-century French science. Grancher described his innovations, his struggles to establish them, his revolutionary accomplishment. The treasurer of the committee, M. Christophle, told of how these discoveries had aroused the hopes and touched the hearts of people all over the world who had, with disinterested generosity, financed the new Institute. By the time all the speakers had finished praising him Pasteur was so close to tears that he had to ask Jean Baptiste to read his speech for him.

He was close to tears because the great men of science who had been his masters were dead, many of the colleagues—Bouley, Paul Bert, Claude Bernard, Vulpian, Sainte-Claire Deville, Bertin—who had sustained him in his conflicts were gone, too, and he himself was old and ill. He had discovered a marvelous new territory, he had charted some of its most prominent features, but, "vanquished by time," he would not live to explore it in any detail. That would be the work of his disciples; aided by the up-to-date facilities and the endowment of the Institute, and guided by the principles of its founder, they would press forward the frontiers of knowledge, penetrate farther and farther into the promised land, and claim for science and humanity regions which a few years before had been distantly visible only to the creative imagination of their master.

CHAPTER TWENTY-ONE

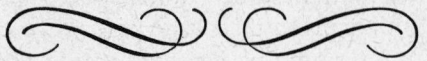

The declining years, for Pasteur, moved by serenely. The doctrines he had established were developing in practice with a beautiful fruitfulness. The time for the hot and hostile debates was over: it was now a mark of eccentricity or of stubborn old age to deny the function of the infinitely small. The personal griefs and losses that had plagued his middle years were past; the memories of the parents, children, friends who had died had lost not their clarity but only their sharpness, and, devoutly religious, he believed that his separation from them was a transient affair. The friends and family who remained surrounded him with a love as reverent as it was familiar. He was active mentally, as ever. The single cloud on his happiness was his inability to continue his researches—his physical strength, forced and strained since his early manhood, was too far gone. His halting step was slower, the deep timbre was gone from his voice, and his worn face, set with the still luminous eyes, carried the plain marks of illness.

With the opening of the new building, he had moved from the quarters he had occupied for more than thirty years in the École normale to the apartment prepared for him in the Pasteur Institute. From the suite of high-ceilinged rooms, furnished with a homely and solid comfort that reminded one American caller of a well-to-do New England home, he directed the establishment he had founded.

Every morning he arrived at the laboratory on the ground floor in time to supervise the preparation of the material to be used in the day's antirabies vaccinations. When the vaccines were ready, the sixty or seventy patients were summoned from the big waiting room, equipped with benches and decorated only by a photograph of the Pasteur Institute in Rio de Janeiro and the two maps with the cities marked on them where other Pasteur Institutes were established; or they were called in from the lawn where they were looking at the bronze statue of Jupille struggling with the mad dog, or strolling around behind the hedge and tall iron grille that set apart the place of science from the rushing activity of Paris beyond. Frenchmen, Arabs, Italians, Americans, Russians, Spaniards; men, women, children; rich and poor, timid and confident—all would take their turn in the inoculating room where, with a quick, painless jab of the hypodermic needle, the marvelous saving fluid was injected beneath their skins. For each one Pasteur had an encouraging and friendly word; for the very poor—and many who came from a distance found themselves friendless in Paris, except for him, and almost penniless—he often had material help; and for the frightened, always, comfort. Toward children, as ever, he felt a special tenderness; when he took them on his knee with gentle and reassuring words their wails subsided and, after the inoculation, they departed smilingly, clutching one of the trifling gifts that Pasteur always kept by him for them.

Some time during the afternoon his familiar figure, stocky and draped in the cloak that had come to be almost his trademark, was to be seen moving limpingly along the halls to one or another part of the building. He might inspect the laboratories on the ground floor where vaccines for charbon, chicken cholera and *rouget* were being prepared. Frequently he visited Roux, under-director of the Institute, and his brilliant young collaborator Alexandre Yersin, in Roux's laboratory on the second floor—that laboratory from which was to issue such striking work on diphtheria and other diseases. Or he might find Roux in his office, where the worktable, congested with culture tubes, blowpipes, bottles, glasses, a microscope, perhaps a cage of guinea pigs, testified to the activity of the small, energetic man who, ever since his medical school days, had been Pasteur's ardent disciple. Or he might seek out his "dear Duclaux," who held his classes in microbiology on the same floor, and then, climbing to the third floor, call on the scientists—Metchnikoff, Albert Calmette, Chamberland and the rest—who were conducting their independent researches in the private laboratories there.

Unless prevented by illness, Pasteur saw his two grandchildren daily, either at his own apartment or at the house of their parents, the Vallery-Radots. Often callers—a journalist, an old friend, a foreign doctor, a fellow member of one of the academies—would be admitted to his library or sitting room, where the aging savant, a black skullcap on his iron-gray hair, would receive them with friendly sincerity. No one could talk to him even briefly without realizing that here was a very great man, and a very good one. "One has to have lived in close association with him," Roux once said, "to know all the goodness of his heart." To know all of it, perhaps, but even those whose contacts with him were slight could feel the quality of that goodness, if not its whole range.

Although his age and his frailty might have excused him, he continued to appear at public functions as a matter of duty and of patriotic pride. In 1889 he attended the opening of the new Sorbonne—a Sorbonne equipped with excellent laboratories and other facilities that reminded him, by vivid contrast, of those inconvenient and unwholesome crannies where earlier generations of scientists had worked. In the fall of the same year he insisted—"I am alive, I shall go," he said—on making the fatiguing journey to Alais where he had been invited to witness the unveiling of a statue to his old master, Dumas.

The greatest public function, however, was the one held in his own honor, on his seventieth birthday. Foreign countries, as well as France, formed committees of scientists to do honor to the master whose disciples, as Paul Brouardel said, they all were. On the morning of December 27, 1892, the big theater of the new Sorbonne was crowded with delegates of French and foreign scientific societies, members of the Institute, professors of the various faculties, ambassadors, government and municipal officers, and rank after rank of students from both the advanced schools and the *lycées*. There were speeches, glowing not only with appreciation but also with real affection, by the Minister of Public Instruction, the President of the Academy of Sciences, such foreign delegates as Sir Joseph Lister, and many others. Pasteur, as on an earlier occasion, was too moved to reply in person; in any case, his voice was now too weak to be heard in a large gathering. His son read his response for him. It was very short, and the precepts which he addressed to the assembled students were a sort of distillation of the principles by which he had regulated his own life.

"Young men . . . say to yourselves first, 'What have I done for my instruction?' and, as you gradually advance, 'What have I done for my country?' until the time comes when you may have the immense happiness of thinking that you have contributed in some way to the progress and to the good of humanity."

Pasteur, more fortunate than many scientific innovators, had lived to see the triumph of his doctrines, and each new conquest filled him with happiness. Roux's contribution to the development of an antitoxin for one of the most dreaded diseases of childhood, diphtheria; Yersin's work in discovering the plague bacillus; Calmette's in developing antitoxins for the bites of venomous reptiles; Metchnikoff's on the action of the white corpuscles and their role in immunity—these were some of the beautiful researches, based on the foundation he had laboriously and securely laid, which Pasteur lived to see.

Still, his regrets for his abandoned crystallographic career were never entirely quieted. Toward the end they were, indeed, keener, because he could no longer indulge himself in the charming hope of some day returning to it. Past seventy, ailing and weak, he knew that there was, for him, only today, and the past, but not "some day." So, unable to beguile himself with the prospect of resuming those researches, he instead reflected on the work he had done with crystals so long before. Visitors with whom he discussed it, whether old friends like Chappuis, later associates like Chamberland and Roux, or colleagues whose interests lay in entirely different directions, were all captivated by the interest with which his clarity and enthusiasm clothed this difficult subject, and recognized the regret which Pasteur could not conceal at having had to abandon that field so promising of scientific enlightenment—Pasteur to whom the world already owed an immeasurable debt. Yet it was characteristic of his spirit, which sought only to serve, that concern over the service left unrendered should shadow his joy in those he had superbly performed.

In November, 1894, not long after his return from Arbois, Pasteur had an attack of uremia and became seriously ill. Friends and disciples again, as during his first stroke more than a quarter of a century earlier, rallied to assist his family in nursing him. By the beginning of the year he was enough improved to receive the old *Normaliens* who, on the point of celebrating the centenary of the founding of their school, asked to call on him and to visit the Pasteur Institute.

After the reception Pasteur, still too feeble to move about unaided, was carried into the downstairs laboratory. There Roux had arranged a sort of museum in miniature, containing souvenirs of Pasteur's career and of his pupils' work. On exhibit were the flasks he had used in his spontaneous generation experiments, the tubes he had employed during his researches on the diseases of wine, various kinds of culture media with bacteria thriving in them, a large variety of microbes on slides, to be viewed through the microscope, including the two sinister ones most recently captured—those responsible for plague and diphtheria. Pasteur's work, recapitulated in this display, had demolished the old and laid the new foundation for medicine and surgery; he and his disciples had, by their discoveries, opened up the fertile new field of public health and preventive medicine; almost a score of Pasteur Institutes, in various parts of the world, were dedicated by this time to expanding their work. All these things might, to another man, have seemed a sufficient accomplishment. But Pasteur, who always saw the past as prelude, clasped Roux's hand and exclaimed:
"There is still a great deal to do!"

Spring came on, and the chestnut trees in the garden of the Institute flowered. Pasteur spent many hours under them, in a small tent which had been set up for him, reading, talking to family and friends, playing with his grandchildren. As the season advanced toward summer, the blossoms dropped and the heat came on; the ill savant, with his family and several of his disciples, left the city for Villeneuve l'Étang. In the park there he passed the time much as he had in the Institute garden, interrupting his conversation or reading occasionally to watch the horses, part of a herd of a hundred which Roux was using for the production of diphtheria antitoxin, grazing quietly in the adjoining field.

He had once remarked: "In point of doing good, duty ceases only when strength fails." His paralysis was increasing and his strength had so far failed that there was nothing he could do but read, talk, keep posted on the progress of his disciples' work. For that matter, he had nothing that required doing: in the course of his serious and well-ordered life he had never left undone anything which duty suggested and strength permitted. Even his will, a document as straightforward and simple as the character of the man who signed it, had been prepared years before. It read:

> This is my testament.
> I leave to my wife all that the law allows me to leave her. May my children never depart from the path of duty, and keep always for their mother the tenderness she deserves.
>
> L. PASTEUR

It was there at Villeneuve l'Étang, in the midst of the beneficent activities launched by his genius, that, late in the afternoon of September 28, 1895, Louis Pasteur peacefully died, surrounded by his family and by the disciples he had trained and inspired.

He was buried, after an imposing state funeral, beneath the Pasteur Institute, in a marble crypt—a memorial less durable and less impressive than the indestructible heritage he left to science and to humanity.

SELECTED BIBLIOGRAPHY

So much has been written about Pasteur that a full list of books and articles on him would be as tiresome to read as laborious to draw up. The short list which follows, therefore, is intended only to suggest to anyone interested in further reading where he or she can most interestingly begin.

Duclaux, Émile, *Pasteur: The History of a Mind*. Translated from the French by Erwin F. Smith and Florence Hedges. Philadelphia and London, W. B. Saunders Company, 1920.

Loir, Adrien, *A l'ombre de Pasteur* (souvenirs personels). Paris, Le Mouvement sanitaire, 1938.

Metchnikov, Ilia Ilich, *The Founders of Modern Medicine*. New York, Walden Publications, 1939.

Pasteur, Louis, *Oeuvres de Pasteur*, Réunis par Pasteur Vallery-Radot. Paris, Masson et cie., 1922–1939. 7 volumes.

Pasteur Correspondance 1840–1895, Réunie et annotée par Pasteur Vallery-Radot. Paris, B. Grasset, 1940. Volume 1.

Vallery-Radot, René, *The Life of Pasteur*. Translated from the French by Mrs. R. L. Devonshire. Garden City, Sun Dial Press, 1937.

Louis Pasteur, His Life and Labors. Translated from the French by Lady Claud Hamilton. New York, D. Appleton and Company, 1885.

Madame Pasteur. Paris, Flammarion, 1941.

INDEX

Academy of Medicine, 181-2, attacks on LP, 137-9, 150, 165-6, 186, 196-7; LP addresses, 111, 139, 146; LP elected to, 77-9, 129, 160-1; LP's demonstrations to, 138

Academy of Sciences, 36, 43, 47, 53, 67, 69, 74-5, 110, 170, 202; LP admitted to, 105; LP appeals for commission from, 81; LP campaigns for election to, 58-9; LP's papers to, 31, 111, 164; 185-6; on LP's germ theory, 81-2, paper on LP at, 136-7; tribute to LP, 205.

Acids, 46-9; LP's interest in, 25-6, 30

Agriculturists, honor LP, 162

Aigleperre, 5

Air, miscroscopic study of, 70-2

Alais, 89; Agricultural Committee of, 93; LP in, 90-4, 96-7, 113-4, 205; mobs in, 109; Pasteur family in, 109

Alcohol, 77; chemistry of, 56-61; LP's study of, 59, 64

Alexandria, cholera in, 168-70

Alfort Veterinary School, 137, 168

Alsace, 119, 124, 181, 193

Amputations, early dangers of, 130

Anaerobic bacteria, 139-41

Animals, experiments on, 136-9, 152-5, 163-5, 172-8, 194

Annals of the Pasteur Institute, 198

Anthrax, 108, 133-9, 157, 204; bacillus, 136-9; LP's report on, 141, 144; LP's work on, 135-9, 147, 151-5, 165-6; vaccine discovered by LP, 151-2

Antirabies treatment, LP's attacked, 194-8; success of, 191; trial of, 186-90

Antisepsis, development of, 130

Antiseptics, 85

Antitoxin, diphtheria, 206-8

Antivenins, 206

Arbois, 123, 125, 207; in revolution of 1830, 7; LP in, 23, 36, 73, 92, 169, 198; Pasteur family in, 54, 82, 119, 140-4; rabies in, 2; wines of, 84

Arcony, 167

Aubenas, honors LP, 162

Australia, rabbit plague in, 200-1; Pasteur Institute in, 201

Austria, silkworm disease in, 88

Auxerre, LP in, 12

Avignon *lycée*, 90

Bacilli, effect of oxygen on, 136

Bacillus anthracis, 134, 147

Bacteria, 133-9

Baden, LP in, 42

Balard, Antoine Jérome, 29, 39, 63, 70, 75, 111; appointed to Committee of Academy of Sciences, 81; praises LP's work, 36; sponsors LP, 28; tributes to, 202

Balzac, Honoré de, 106

Barbet, M., 23; aids LP's education, 9, 13; pension of, 76-7; pension of, LP at, 11-3, 22-4

Barbier, Capt., 9, 23

Bassi, Agostini, 101

Bastian, Henry Charlton, 132-4

Bazaine, Achille, 120

Beauce, anthrax in, 133

Beer, 107-8, 126-8

Beer-making, chemistry of, 56-7

Bernard, Claude, 63, 89, 168, 202; LP's tribute to, 99-100; on fermentation, 141-3

Bert, Paul, 131, 202; on anthrax, 134, 136; on rabies commission, 176

Bertin, Pierre Augustin, 40, 111, 119, 202; LP's friendship with, 107-8, 119, 134-5; on beer, 126-7
Bertrand, Joseph, 202
Besançon, 3, 6, 120
Bigo, M., manufacturer in Lille, 56-7
Biot, M. accepts LP's theory, 156-7
—— Jean Baptiste, 39-40, 47, 53-4, 75, 108, 154; and LP, 36-8, 43-4, 46, 61; criticizes government's aid to science, 63; death of, 76; elected to French Academy, 59; Mme. Pasteur decorates grave of, 79; tributes to, 202; work in crystallography, 26, 37
Bischoffsheim, Raphael, 196
Blacksmith, treats rabies, 1
Bollène, LP at, 164
Bonaparte, Louis Napoleon see Napoleon III
Bonapartists, 31
Bonn, University of, honors LP, 109; LP's controversy with, 120, 123-4
Bordeaux, wines of, 84
Bordighera, LP in, 196, 198
Botanists, 75
Bouley, Henri, 138, 202; funeral of, 192; on LP, 151, 166, 186; on rabies commission, 175; report on anthrax, 138-9
Bourbaki, Charles, 120
Bourboulon, Commandant, 122
Bourbon restoration, 3-4, 31
Bousson, LP's portrait of, 15-6
Bousson de Mairet, M., 6
Brain, as seat of rabies, 172
Breweries, LP's studies in, 126
Brewers, use LP's methods, 130
Brogniart, A., 81
Bromine, 70
Brouardel, Paul, 196; tribute to LP, 205
Bubonic plague, 144
Burgundy, LP in, 184
Butyric acid, 60

Cagniard-Latour, Charles, 56-7
Calmette, Albert, 204, 206
Cantal, Department of the, honors LP, 166
Carbolic acid, 130

Catholic Church see Roman Catholic Church
Cattle, anthrax disease of, 133-9
Censeau, Pasteur family at, 121
Chaffois, 121-2
Chamalières, 126
Chamberland, Charles Edouard, 144-5, 168-9, 206; assists LP, 134-5, 153, 155, 167; at Pasteur Institute, 204; award to, 157; on anthrax, 138-40
Chambéry, Pasteur family at, 98
Chamonix, LP's experiments at, 73-4
Champagne, wines of, 84
Chantemesse, André, 191, 193
Chappuis, Charles, 20, 22-5, 30, 35, 53, 206; LP's friend, 18; LP's letters to, 32, 38, 40, 43
Charbon see Anthrax
Charles X, 7, 31
Charrin, Albert, 191, 193
Chartres, 108; anthrax in, 133, 136, 140; experiments at, 157
Chemistry, 29; LP's experiments in, 24
Chicken cholera, 200, 204; LP's work on, 147-8, 151, 168
Chickens, anthrax in, 137-9
Christophle, tribute to LP, 202
Clermont-Ferrand, 100, 125-6
Colin, G., 137-9, 153-4
Collège d'Arbois, 72; LP at, 14; LP selects books for, 27
Collège Louis le Grand, 24
Collège Rollin, 168
Collège royal de la Franche-Comté, Besançon, LP at, 14-5
Commune, 177
Comte, August, 161
Contagion, LP's discoveries in, 57
Corpuscles, LP's work on, 91-4, 99-104
Corsica, 114
Cows, vaccination of, 152-5
Cuisance river, 6, 84
Cross of Legion of Honor, LP awarded, 105
Crystallography, 31, 46, 48-9, 110, 159-60; LP's demonstrations in, 36-8, 78-9, LP's discoveries in, 33-6; LP's interest in, 25-6, 206; LP's medal in, 58; Marie Pasteur studies, 42; LP's work on, 29-30, 105

Davaine, Casimir, 133-4, 138
David, Jeanne, 2
Delafond, Onésime, 133
Député, assists LP, 167
Dijon, LP in, 12, 19, 39-40
Dijon *lycée*, LP at, 39
Dimorphism, LP's work on, 34, 36
Diphtheria, 204, 207; antitoxin, 206-8
Disease, germ theory of, 165; LP's theory of, 57, 80, 145-6, 150; silkworm, 87, 96-7; theories of, 101-2, 127-8, 165
Dogs, experiments with, 172-9; rabid, 181-2, 193, 204
Dôle, honors LP, 166; LP's experiments at, 73; Pasteur family in, 4
Duclaux, Mme., death of, 145
—— Émile, 78-9, 81, 83, 87, 89, 100, 103, 126, 132, 198; assists LP, 76-7, 84; at Pasteur Institute, 204; introduces Roux, 135; LP's friendship with, 144, 167; LP's letters to, 125; on LP's defense of his theories, 86; on site for Pasteur Institute, 195
Duels, 150
Dumas, Alexander, *fils*, 161
—— Jean Baptiste, 44, 53-4, 60, 63, 70, 110; appointed to Committee of Academy of Sciences, 81; death of, 170; friendship with LP, 30, 94, 112; lectures of, 21, 23; LP's letters to, 169; on LP, 36, 151, 161-3; on silkworm disease, 89; tributes to, 202, 205
Dumont, Dr., 6
Duruy, Victor, 108, 119

Earthquakes, 198
Eberth, Charles Joseph, 66
École normale, 10, 14-5, 18, 21-2, 39, 74, 79, 110, 134, 162-3; Bertin at 107-8; course of study, 24; liberalism of, 106; LP dismissed from, 106-7; LP enters, 23-4; LP in, 132; LP leaves, 203; LP's administration of, 62-4, 94; LP's assistants from, 167; LP's laboratory at, 66-7; LP's life at, 29-30; Pasteur family life at, 65-6

Edinburgh University, honors LP, 169
Education, in France, 9, 37-40
Edward VII, Prince of Wales, 158
Egypt, cholera in, 168-70
Entomology, LP's work in, 87-94, 100-4
Erdmann, Karl G. H., Professor, 48-9
Eugénie-Marie de Montijo de Guzman, and LP, 95-6, 112, 116, 177
Exposition of 1867, awards prize to LP, 105-6

Fabre, Jean Henri, on LP, 90-1
Faraboeuf, 175-6, 194
Fermentation, germ theory of, 71; Lister's theory of, 130; LP's study of, 56-62, 64, 67, 69, 77, 83-4, 88, 105, 141-4; LP's theory of, 61-2, 64; of beer, 127-8; organic nature of, 60, 64; types of, 60-2, 64
Fikentscher, manufacturer of acid, 46, 48-9
Filters, Chamberland's, 134
Flacherie, 103-4, 112, 114-6; LP's theory of, 115-6; LP's work on, 109-10
Flourens, Pierre Jean Marie, 81
Fontainbleu, LP in, 12
Forbach, 119
"Forty Immortals", LP joins, 160-1
Fracastorius, Hieronymus, 57
France, Revolution of 1848, 31-2; Roman ruins in, 12; Second Republic, 32, 44
Franco-Prussian War, 118-126, 130-1
French Revolution, 3
Fungus, 101-2
Furieuse river, 4

Galileo Galilei, 162
Gard, vineyard disease in, 86
Garden of Medicinal Plants, Paris, 120
Geneva, LP in, 163
Genius, LP's, vii-viii, 101-2, 162
Germ theory, 69, 165; LP's, 73, 81, 128-9, 133, 139
Germany, 30; LP in, 47-9
Germicides, 130
Germs, 70-2; as cause of fermentation,

71; heat-resistant, 82; LP's avoidance of, 131, 176; receptivity to, 115
Gernez, Désiré, LP's assistant, 83, 96–7, 100, 103, 112, 114, 125
Gérome, Jean Léon 105
Goniometers, 29
Grancher, Jacques Joseph, 177, 185, 193; attacked by Academy of Medicine, 197; protects LP's health, 196; tribute to LP, 202; work on rabies, 182–4, 186–8, 191
Grand Cordon of the Legion of Honor, awarded LP, 157
Grapes, yeast germs in, 142–4
Gravelotte, 119
Greece, silkworm disease in, 88
Guérin, Jules, challenges LP to duel, 150

Hankel, Wilhelm Gottlieb, 48–9
Harlicourt, 120
Heat treatment of foods, 85–6
Heredity, LP's theory of, 115
Herschel, Sir John, discoveries in crystallography, 33
Hippocrates, 161
Holmes, Oliver Wendell, on puerperal fever, 145
Horses, 207
Hôtel Dieu, 193
Huxley, Thomas, on LP, 130–1

Immunity, 206
Impasse des Feuillantines, Paris, 21
Imperial Commission on Silk Culture, LP's work for, 90
Infusoria, 70–2, 74
Inoculation, 148; anthrax, 136–9; of animals, 153–5, rabies, 172–9
Institute of France, 39, 195, honors LP, 170
International Medical Congress at Copenhagen, LP attends, 177
International Medical Congress, 1881, honors LP, 157–8
International Congress of Hygiene, Geneva, LP attends, 163
Italy, silkworm disease in, 88

Jacquinet, of Ecole Normale, 106

Jaillard, Pierre François, on anthrax, 135–6
Japan, mulberry seed from, 88
Jean Bart, (ship), 110
Jenner, Edward, LP on, 149
Joly, Nicolas, 71, 81; LP's controversy with, 77, 80
Joubert, Jules François, assists LP, 134–5; on anthrax, 138–9
Le Journal d'un volontier d'un an, 131
Jupille, Jean Baptiste, 185, 204
Jura, Department of, 1, 131; wines of 84

Kestner, Alsatian manufacturer, 25
Koch, Robert, 134, 158, 163; on anthrax, 137; on cholera mission, 168–70; opposes LP, 165

Lactic acid, 60
Lariboisière Hospital, 168
Laurent, M. rector of Strasbourg Academy, 40–4, 47, 109
—— Marie, see Pasteur, Marie (Laurent)
Lavoisier, Antoine, 76; LP's article on, 94
Lechartier, Georges Vital, LP's assistant, 83
Leeuwenhoek, Antoine, 57
Legion of Honor, 6; awards cross to LP, 52; awards Grand Cordon to LP, 157
Leipzig, LP in, 48–9
Leplat, F., on anthrax, 135–6
Lesseps, Ferdinand de, 105
Liebig, Justus von, theory of fermentation, 60, 62
Life, anaerobic, theory of, 77; nature of, 70–2; organic genesis of, 71–2; spontaneous generation of, see spontaneous generation
Lille, LP's address at, 55; LP appointed to faculty of, 54–5; Scientific Society, LP's paper to, 61
Lister, Joseph, *1st Baron*, LP's influence on, 62, 130; surgical technique, 145; tribute to LP, 205
Littré, Émile, 160–1

Loir, M., 122-3, 125, 189-90
—— Mme., 125, 189-90
—— Adrien, 125, 161, 165, 175-6, 180, 183, 185, 195-200; assists LP, 142-3, 163-4, 192; early work of, 167-8; goes to Australia, 201; introduces Grancher, 177; interest in crystallography, 159-60; rabies treatment of 186-90
—— family, 159, 189-90
Lombardy, silkworms, 88
London, LP in, 126-7; Royal Society, awards LP medal, 58
Lons-le-Saunier, 121
Lorraine, 124
Louis Philippe, 7, 31-2
Louis XIII, 120
Louis XVI, 3
Louis XVIII, 8
Luxembourg Gardens, 22-3, 25, 184
Lycée St. Louis, LP at, 13, 21
Lyons, 109; Pasteur family in, 124, 159-60; Faculty of Sciences, 122

M. Pasteur: Histoire d'un Savant par un Ignorant, 160
MacMahon, Marie Edme Patrice de, 119
Maillot, assists LP, 96-7, 100, 103, 113
Maladetta, experiments at, 80
Malaguti, François, 53-4
Manoury, M., aids LP's experiments, 140
Manures, LP's work on, 55
Marnoz, Pasteur family in, 5
Maucuer, M., 163
Medicine, LP's contribution to, 61, 207
Meissengott, 181
Meissonier, Ernest, 105
Meister, Mme., 181, 184
—— Joseph, 193; and LP's rabies treatment, 181-6
Melun, 155, 162
Mémoire sur la fermentation appellée alcoolique, 64
Mémoire sur la fermentation appellée lactique, L.P's 61, 130
Mer de Glace, LP's experiments at, 73-4, 80

Metchnikoff, Élie, 199; at Pasteur Institute, 204
Metz, 120
Meudon, LP's laboratory at, 176
Michelangelo Buonarroti, 162
Micro-organisms, LP's work on, 109
Microbes, 136, 207; method of reproduction, 151; theory of, 103-4
Microscopes, 68, 99; used in study of air, 70-2
Military conscription, 10
Milne-Edwards, Henri, 81
Mineralogy, 78
Minister of Agriculture, LP's report to, 141, 144
Minister of Public Instruction, 39-40, 47, 53, 63, 108; tribute to LP, 55-6, 205
Mississippi, 144
Mitscherlich, Eilhard, 26, 33-4, 36, LP meets, 46
Molière, Jean Baptiste Poquelin, 162
Le Moniteur Universel, LP's article in, 100
Montpellier, honors LP, 162
Montanvert, LP's experiments at, 73-4
Montrond, 123
Moscow, retreat from, 122
Mount Poupet, LP's experiment at, 73
Musset, Charles, 71, 81, LP's controversy with, 77, 80
Mycoderma aceti, LP's work on, 83

Napoleon I, 2-5, 31
Napoleon III, 44-5, 47, 105, 118, 149, 177; audience to LP, 79-80; defeat of, 119; honors LP, 95-6; interest in LP, 84, 108, 112-5; LP's report to, 86
National Assembly, increases LP's annuity, 166; votes LP life annuity, 131
Natural history, 69
Natural History Museum, Rouen, 67
Naumann, Maurice, 123-4
Needham, John Turberville, 68
Neurologists, 197
Nocard, I.E., on cholera mission, 168
Nord, Department of, 55
Normaliens, 119
Nicholas I, Czar of Russia, honors LP, 194

Nicolle, M., treated for rabies, 1–2
Nîmes, honors LP, 162
Nisard, Désiré, 106, 161

Of the Scientific Dogmatism of the Illustrious Pasteur, 165
On the Influence of M. Pasteur's Work on Medicine and Surgery, 136–7
Organic genesis, 71–2
Osler, Sir William, on theories of fermentation, 62
Oxygen, effect on bacilli, 136

Paget, Sir James, 158, 177
Palais royal, 22
Parasites, 93, 100–4
Paratartaric acid, 48–9; LP's discoveries with, 35, 48–50
Paris, 18, 123–4; description of, 12–3; LP in, 8–9, 13, 20–1, 24, 58–9, 126, 131, 145, 199; Pasteur family in, 50–1, 53, 83; siege of, 119–20
Paris Commune, 124–5
Paris Lycée, 134
Paris Pharmaceutical Society, awards prize to LP, 52–3; prize, 50
Pascal, Blaise, 162
Pasteur, Camille (LP's daughter), 82; death of, 94
—— Cécile (LP's daughter), 53; death of, 98
—— Claude Etienne (LP's great grandfather), 2
—— Denis (LP's ancestor), 2
—— Emilie, (LP's sister) 5, 7, 16
—— Jean Baptiste (LP's son), 44, 83, 202; enlists in *chasseurs*, 119; in Franco-Prussian war, 120–3; in Paris, 100
—— Jean Denis (LP's grandfather), death of, 5
—— Jean Henri (LP's grandfather), life of, 3
—— Jean Joseph (LP's father), 14, 35, 40, 66, 72; advice to LP, 17–8, 21–4, 27–8, 30, 32; death of, 92, disapproves of LP's travels, 51; early life, 3–4; learns mathematics from LP, 27; LP visits, 54; thanks Biot, 52
—— Jeanne (LP's daughter), 44, 66
—— Jeanne Etiennette (Roqui) (LP's mother), 4; death of, 35
—— Josephine (LP's sister), 5, 16–7, 35, death of, 44, studies mathematics, 30
—— Louis, advice to students, 206; apologizes to Guérin, 150; appointed to Lille, 54–5; at École Normale, 23–4, 29–30, 62–7, 94, 167; attacked by Academy of Medicine, 137–9, 150, 165–6, 186, 196–7; audience with Napoleon III, 79–80; award for experimental physiology by Academy of Sciences, 75; awarded annuity by National Assembly, 131, 166; awarded Cross of Legion of Honor, 52; awarded Cross of St. Anne of Russia, 194; awarded Grand Cordon of Legion of Honor, 157; awarded medal by Dumas, 161–2; awarded medal by Melun Agricultural Society, 162; awarded medal of Society of French Agriculturists, 151, awarded Paris Pharmaceutical prize, 52–3; awarded prize at Exposition of 1867, 105–6; awarded Rumford Medal, 58; benefit performance for, 193–4; birth of, 5; boyhood of, 5–6; controversy with University of Bonn, 120, 123–4; death of, 208; defeated for Senate, 131; defense of his work, 86; demonstrates discovery in crystallography, 36–8; devotion to family, 16, 92; discovers anthrax and chicken cholera vaccines, 151–2, 148–9; dismissed from École normale, 106–7; donations to support vaccination work, 193; early education, 8–9, 13–5; early mediocrity in chemistry, 18–9; elected to Academy of Medicine, 129; elected to Academy of Sciences, 77–9, 129, 160–1; fondness for children, 204; fondness for pigs, 165; genius

of, vii–viii, 101–2; germ theory, 71–3; health of, 116–7; homesickness of, 13–4; honored by Aubenas, 162; honored by Department of the Cantal, 166; honored by Dôle, 166; honored by International Congress of Hygiene, 163; honored by International Medical Congress, 157–8, 177; honored by Napoleon III, 95–6; honored by Nîmes, 162; honored by University of Bonn, 109; honored in Montpellier, 162; illness of, 53–4, 109–11, 196, 198–201, 203–8; in National Guard, 32; last years of, 203–8; letters to Marie, 49–50; marries Marie Laurent, 41–2; meets Mitscherlich, 46; paralysis of, 200; patriotism of, 6, 12, 32–3, 45, 108, 112, 118–20, 122–5, 127, 167, 201, 205; pedigree of, 2; philosophy of science, 96–7; professor at Sorbonne, 110; rabies treatment, 181–6; recreations, 18, 22–3; religion of, 82, 161–2, 203; research on anthrax, 133–9; *salon* of, 199; scientific technique, 91–3; searches for son, 121–3; sensitivity of, 6, 18, 145, 172–3, 194; talent for drawing, 8, 14–7; teaches at Strasbourg Academy, 40; teaches physics, 24; theses of, 30; tributes to, 186, 205–6; will of, 208; witnesses rabies treatment, 1
——Marie (Laurent) (wife of LP), 47, 50, 65, 98, 107, 114, 125, 155, 176, 196; advises Loir, 163; advises LP, 110–1, 149; assists LP, 114–6; devotion to LP, 66; lays flowers on Biot's grave, 79; LP's courtship of, 41–2, LP's letters to, 92; letters to LP's father, 58; protects LP, 113; searches for son, 121–3
—— Marie Louise *see* Vallery-Radot, Marie Louise (Pasteur)
—— Virginie (LP's sister), 5, 16–7, 35, 54, 84

—— family, 150, 189–90, 207, plaque on house of, 167
Pasteur Institute, in Australia, 201; inauguration ceremonies, 201–2; laboratories of, 204; LP buried in, 208; LP's apartments in, 203; LP's plans for, 198, 200–1; naming of, 195; *Normaliens* visit, 207; Rio de Janeiro, 204; site of, 195; tribute to LP, 205–6; work of, 196
Pasteurization, beginning of, 85–6, 110
Pébrine, disease of silkworms, 88–97, 100–5, 111
Pelletier, Louise, victim of rabies, 191–3,
—— family, 192
Pernin, 178
Peter, M., 165, 197
—— family, 166
Philomathic Society, LP's demonstration to, 78–9
Phylloxera, 86
Physics, 23, 29; LP's interest in, 21, 164
Plague bacillus, 206–7
Pointurier, (LP's teacher), 14, 16
Polarized light, 25–6, 30, 33–5, 38, 51, 78
Poligny, 121
Pommery, Mme., 201
Pont Gisquet, LP at, 97, 114
Pontarlier 120–1
Positivism, LP on, 161
A Posthumous Work of Claude Bernard, 141–2
Pouchet, Félix Archimède, 67, 69, 81–2, 132, LP's controversy with, 77, 80
Pouilly-le-fort, LP at, 156
Puerperal fever, LP on, 145–6
Putrefaction vibriones, 136

Rabbits, anthrax in, 134; LP's plan for controlling, 200–1; rabies experiments on, 173; susceptibility to cholera, 200–1
Rabies, deaths from, 193–6; early treatment of, 1–2, 171; human, LP treats, 181–6; LP's treatment for, 177, attacked, 194–8; LP's work on, 160, 170–9; vaccination for, 179–80

Racemic acid, 49–50, 56; LP's work on, 51–2
Rachel, Elisa Félix, tragedienne, 20, 194
Raulin, Jules, 76, 125; assists LP, 67, 113; LP's letters to 118
Redi, Francesco, 68
Redtencbacher, Ferdinand J., 49–50
Régiment Dauphin, 3
Reims, 201
Renan, Ernest, on LP, 161–2
Répécaud, LP's headmaster, 15
Researches on Dimorphism, LP's, 31
Rio de Janciro, Pasteur Institute in, 204
Roman Catholic Church, LP's devotion to, 82, 161–2, 203; Pasteur family in, 6
Romanet, LP's schoolmaster, 8, 10, 27–8, 31
Roqui, Jeanne Etiennette *see* Pasteur, Jeanne Etiennette (Roqui)
Rossignol, H., 156; on LP, 152
Rouget, swine fever, 160; LP's work on 163–5
Rousseau, Jean Jacques, 106
Roux, Émile, 144–5, 150, 192, 196, 206–7; assists LP, 135, 153, 155, 167; at Pasteur Institute, 204; award to, 157; defends LP, 196–7; on anthrax, 140; on cholera mission, 168–70; on diptheria, 206, on LP, 205; on rabies, 172, 186–9, 191
Rumford Medal, awarded LP, 58
Russians, given rabies treatment, 193–4

St. Etienne, citizens of, 106
St. Hippolyte-le-Fort, LP at, 113
St. Jacques du Haut Pas, 65
Sainte-Beuve, Charles Augustin, 106
Sainte-Claire Deville, Henri, 63, 100, 111–2, 118–9, 168, 202; death of, 157
Salins, LP in, 73; Pasteur family in, 3–4
Scheele, Charles William, 25
Science, applied, LP's interest in, 55–6; LP's philosophy of, 96–7, 128, 158; neglect of, in France, 108–9
Sedan, 119
Sédillot, Charles Emmanuel, on LP, 136–7

Seine river, 12
Semmelweiss, Ignaz, on puerperal fever, 146
Senegal, 144
Sens, LP in, 12
Septicemia, 164
Sericiculturists, honor LP, 162
Serres, Olivier de, 162
Sheep, anthrax in, 140; vaccination of, 152–5
Silk Commission, French, 109
Silk industry, honors LP, 162, LP's services to, 88–9, 117, 130
Silkworms, 122, 157; diseases, 87, 96–7, 112–3, 133; LP's book on, 115–6, LP's work on, 109
Smallpox, Jenner's work on, 149
Smolensk, 193
Society of French Agriculturists, award medal to LP, 151
Sorbonne, 163; LP at, 21, 24; LP honored by, 205; LP professor in, 110
Spain, silkworm disease in, 88
Spallanzani, Lazaro, 68
Splenic fever *see* anthrax
Spoilage, food, prevention of, 85–6
Spontaneous generation, theory of, 67 72, 77, 81–2, 126, 207; theory opposed by LP, 69, 70–3, 132–3, 142; work on by LP, 83
Stereochemistry, LP's work in, 27, 44
Sterilization, 146
Strasbourg, 107; LP in, 42, 118
Strasbourg Academy, LP at, 40, 53
Strauss, Isidor, 178; on cholera mission, 168
Studies on the Diseases of Silkworms, LP's, 116
Suez Canal, 105
Surgery, antiseptic technique in, 145, 166; LP's contribution to, 207
Switzerland, LP in, 73–4
La Sybille (ship), 110

Tannery, 4, 7
Tarnier, Stephen, 145
Tartaric acid factories, 48, 50
Tartaric acids, LP's work on, 56
Tartrates, 48–9; LP's studies of, 78
Le Temps, LP writes for, 200–1

Terrilion, assists LP, 191
Thann, 25
Theaters, 20, 30, 194
Thuillier, Louis, assists, LP, 163, 167; death of, 168-9; on cholera mission, 168-70
Tisserand, on rabies commission, 175
Toulouse, 71, 147
Tournon, LP appointed to, 28
Toussaint, Jean Joseph Henri, 147
Trieste, 114
Trocadéro, benefit performance for LP, 194
Turin, 165
Typhoid fever, 66, 98, 165-6

Udressier, counts of, 2

Vaccination, deaths attributed to, 196-8; experiments on, 152-5; rabies, 175, 186-90, 193-4; rabies, LP's failure with, 191-2; success of, 165
Vaccine, 204; anthrax, LP discovers, 151-2; chicken cholera, 151; for *rouget*, 163-4; LP's discovery of, 148-9; rabies, trial of, 181-6
Vaillant, Jean Baptist Philibert, 114
Vallery-Radot, Marie Louise (Pasteur) (LP's daughter), 82, 98, 102-3, 113, 121, 125; and Vallery-Radot, 131-2; assists LP, 99;
—— René, 150, 196; first meeting with LP, 131-2; LP with, 184-5; writes book on LP, 159-60
—— family, 205
Vaucluse, *rouget* in, 163
Veterinarians, honor LP, 162; oppose LP, 152-5, 165
Vercel, Jules, LP's school friend, 7, 11-3, 72-3, 142

Viala, Eugene, 167; assists LP, 144; on rabies, 187-8, 191
Vibrio, septic, 139
Vienna, LP in, 49-50
Villa Margharita, LP at, 196
Villa Vicentina, LP at, 114, 117-8
Villeneuve l'Étang, LP at, 207-8
Vinegar, LP's work on, 83
Vinegar makers, use LP's methods, 130
Virchow, Rudolph, 170
Viruses, LP's paper on, 163
Volga river, 144
Voltaire, François Marie Arouet, 106
Vône, Théodore, 181-2
Vulpian, Edmé Félix Alfred, 138, 202; on rabies, 175, 182

Weissenburg, 119
Widal, Fernand, 66
Wilhelm I of Prussia, 120, 123
Wine, diseases of, 82, 84-6, 98; fermentation of, 80; industry, importance in France, 83-4; LP's work on 84
Winegrowers, use LP's methods, 130
Winemaking, chemistry of, 56-7
Wines, experiments with, 110; pasteurization of, 85-6, 110
Wolves, rabid, 1-2, 7, 193-4

Yeast, 56, 60, 81; experiments with, 79-80; LP's work on, 56-7, 72-3, 85, 142-4
Yellow fever, LP on, 144
Yersin, Alexander, at Pasteur Institute, 204, 206

Zévort, Mme, 98
Zwickau, LP in, 48

FLORENCE NIGHTINGALE

Florence Nightingale

FLORENCE NIGHTINGALE

By JEANNETTE COVERT NOLAN

Illustrated by
GEORGE AVISON

The Junior Literary Guild and
Julian Messner, Inc.
New York

PUBLISHED BY JULIAN MESSNER, INC.
8 WEST 40TH STREET, NEW YORK 18

COPYRIGHT, 1946,
BY JEANNETTE COVERT NOLAN

Seventh Printing, April, 1956

PRINTED IN THE UNITED STATES OF AMERICA

CONTENTS

1	Lea Hurst—Summer, 1833	3
2	Holiday Season	15
3	Morning Incident	24
4	Growing Up	34
5	Young Lady of Leisure	44
6	Travels and Dreams	55
7	Glimpse of a Mission	65
8	First Freedom	73
9	The Call to Service	85
10	Journey and Arrival	94
11	A Lady with a Lamp	103
12	Crimean Days	110
13	Problems and Solutions	121
14	Scutari Winter	131
15	"The Daughter of England!"	143
16	Adventure's Ending	154
17	A New Summons	162
18	More Lamps Lighted	172
19	Heroine's Progress	181
20	At Home in South Street	191
21	Trials and Triumphs	200
22	Farewells	207

ILLUSTRATIONS

Florence Nightingale	Frontispiece
"Aren't you enjoying the party?"	7
Cantering along the narrow paths which wound through the clover fields	21
He endured the treatment with patience	31
She recorded it all in her diary	40
"Will you let me be a nurse?"	51
She and Sidney bent over the specifications	59
She wielded the heavy brush	69
The committee bowed to her imperious edict	82
Soldiers were dying of neglect	87
"The English nurse has come"	101
She stepped out upon the upper gallery	103
"Open the warehouse door!"	115
It was mostly hushed	129
"We've come to help you with the nursing"	132
There were large ships anchored in the harbour of Balaclava	143
She had to go on horseback	156
Promptly renamed him the Bison	167
She listened to what they said	173
This was their farewell	184
She might seem little and fragile	194
She witnessed the arrival of the Grenadier Guards	205
She was softer with the years	207

FLORENCE NIGHTINGALE

1

LEA HURST—SUMMER, 1833

FLORENCE LET THE heavy front door swing shut behind her. Then she crossed to the edge of the flagged terrace and paused a moment, frowning slightly. Her arms were filled with dozens of small paper-wrapped packages, each tied with a bit of red or yellow ribbon, and her cheeks were a little flushed from the effort of balancing this burden. She looked anxiously about, to see that nothing had been dropped; she looked again at the packages, her lips moving silently.

Reassured, she smiled and the frown vanished.

No, she had not miscounted; there would be a gift for every person at the party, no one had been forgotten—which meant that all the elaborate plans, her own, Mamma's and Parthe's, had worked out perfectly.

"And a good thing!" thought Florence who, at thirteen, had no patience with plans which failed.

The terrace was cool, shadowed by the stone walls of the house, mellow and vine-hung, rising up to the roof's pointed gables which were like so many conical, dark hats lined against the pastel blue of the sky and the fresh green of the summer trees. From here could be viewed the whole sweep of lawn, orderly, well-tended, luxuriant as bolts of green velvet unrolled in a draper's shop. But beyond the lawn lay the warm, sunlit meadow, overgrown with wild flowers and straggly with low stone fences, where today order abruptly ceased in a gay riot of flashing color and sound.

The party! What a celebration it was, this traditional gathering of the village schoolchildren for the annual entertainment at Lea Hurst, Squire Nightingale's Derbyshire estate. Since early morning the meadow had brimmed with merriment: songs, shouting, laughter so boisterous as to dim the roar of the Derwent River over there among its purple hills; games, dancing, a picnic luncheon spread on the grass under the alders. Now the afternoon waned, but festivities continued, and soon would come the climax of everything, the bountiful tea to be served on tables decorated with bunting and streamers—and finally the distribution of the "treats."

"I suppose," Florence thought, "it must be nearly tea time this instant, and Mamma will be wondering what's become of me." She glanced at the gold watch pinned to the ruffles of her cambric bodice. Four o'clock? She must hurry! Walking briskly, she started toward the hedge which bordered the lawn—and stopped.

On the far side of the thick boxwood someone was running and calling her name. "Florence? *Flo?*"

It was her sister's voice, and Florence waited. "Hello, Parthe!"

"Where are you, Flo?"

"Here, in plain sight." As Parthe darted through a gap in the hedge and appeared, out of breath and curls flying, Florence added calmly, "I was in the house, tying up the packages. Do you want me?"

"Yes." Parthe halted and pressed a hand to her heart. She was fourteen, a year older than Florence, but not so tall; an exceptionally graceful girl with delicate features and a complexion like English strawberries and cream. "Oh, I've *rushed*. Mamma sent me to fetch you."

"Why?" Florence asked. "Anything wrong?"

"Very wrong." Parthe nodded vigorously. "Libby Brown—you know her?"

"Of course, I know her; and her grandmother too—all the Browns."

"That Libby!" Parthe said, grimacing.

"But what's she *doing*, for heaven's sake, to distress you?"

"Oh, not me," Parthe said. "It's Mamma. Libby's doing nothing—that's the trouble. She's just *sitting*. And *moping*. She won't join in the contests or ride on the ponies. Papa volunteered to take her to the kennels to see the dogs—she wouldn't go. She won't talk to any of us or even to the other children. As you may imagine, poor Mamma is terribly upset by such behavior. Mamma can't bear it unless everybody is *happy* at the party. Everybody! So she told me to fetch you immediately. You're to *make* Libby happy—the stupid little creature!"

"Not stupid," Florence said. "Just shy and self-conscious. If you understand Libby—"

"*I* don't," Parthe said, "nor does Mamma. But you have that strange knack of understanding strange people—so you simply must go to the rescue, Flo. Give me the parcels. I'll get a basket for carrying them in, and I promise not to spill them. Hasten now, darling, on your errand of mercy, or whatever it is."

Florence surrendered the beribboned armload; she brushed back the brown hair from her shoulders and straightened her billowing skirts. "Where'll I find our moping Libby?"

"Hiding among the cabbages, probably. At least, I saw

her plodding in the direction of the kitchen garden a while ago. I wish you luck," Parthe said. "And don't pretend you mind, because you know you don't!"

As Florence turned and trudged along the path which led to the kitchen garden, she was both rueful and smiling. Always, it seemed, the difficult guests at Lea Hurst, the lonely or awkward ones, fell to her lot, to comfort and cheer. But Parthe's comment was true. Florence had enacted the role of rescuer so often that she didn't mind it. Perhaps she did, indeed, have a talent for understanding people.

"That might be a valuable thing to have," she thought.

Libby Brown was not among the cabbages. Libby had trailed from the vegetable beds into the apple orchard. When at last Florence spied her, she was crouched forlornly on a bench in the fence corner, a scrawny and unattractive child of eleven, her chin propped on doubled fists, elbows on knees. At Florence's approach, she scrambled up and curtsied.

"No, don't, Libby," Florence said, sitting down quickly. "What's the matter? Aren't you enjoying the party?"

Libby crimsoned with embarrassment, but she was frank. "Well, I'm not, Miss Florence, and that's a fact! Not that anyone's to blame except me. Your mother and father, Miss Parthe and everybody has been kind as kind. They've tried. But it's all too noisy, the boys pushing and the girls yelling as if out of their senses. I like being quiet, I'd rather be at home with Granny." She sighed. "I guess I'm just queer, or something."

"Oh, I don't think you're queer," Florence said soothingly.

"Don't you?"

"No, and I know how you feel. I like being quiet, myself."

"*Do* you?"

"Aren't you enjoying the party?"

"Yes," Florence said, "and whenever I want to be very quiet, I go upstairs to the old nursery. That's the quietest place in the world; only the dolls live there now. Libby, why don't you go up to the nursery with me? I'll show you the dolls and you can play without any interruptions or bothering; you can have your tea brought up and eat with the dolls."

"Would—would that be all right?" Libby's eyes brightened. She had heard of the collection of dolls in the Nightingale sisters' nursery.

"Oh, certainly," Florence said, getting to her feet. "Come."

Obediently, Libby slid off the bench and followed, her stout, square-toed boots scuffing the gravel, blissful anticipation dawning in her thin face.

The nursery, a spacious room with oak-beamed ceiling and mullioned windows, was on the top floor of the house; two flights of stairs had to be climbed to reach it. But Libby Brown didn't begrudge the exertion. From the moment the door was opened and she entered, Libby was in a state of enchantment, her shyness fading away as she trotted about, inspecting everything and pelting Florence with eager questions.

"How many toys! Are they yours?"

"Yes, mine and Parthe's."

"And books! And the little desks—do you have your lessons here?"

"Not any more." Florence had mounted a stool and was lifting down from a row of shelves the miniature trunks in which the dolls were kept. "We're too big now; we could scarcely fold our long legs under the desks, could we? We don't study much at Lea Hurst. This is our vacation. When we go back to Embley, lessons will begin again."

"Embley? Where's that?"

"In Hampshire. Embley's our other home, where we spend the autumn and winter."

"Every year?"

"Yes, every year."

"And the spring, Miss Florence?"

"Yes, unless we're staying in London then, as we often are."

"Are the lessons hard?"

"Awfully hard," Florence said. "History, mathematics, Latin and Greek. And Papa teaches us Italian. Papa is a *strict* teacher, much stricter than Miss Christie, our governess. He has us write essays, one each week, to improve our grammar and spelling."

"I wouldn't like writing the essays."

"I don't like them, either," Florence confessed. "Parthe's better at them than I am. Parthe's better at all the lessons."

"But why do you have another home?"

"Well, that's because of Papa." Florence jumped down from the stool and searched in a bureau drawer for keys to the trunks. "Papa is a Derbyshire man by birth; his people all lived in this part of England, and he dearly loves it. When he and Mamma were married, they settled at the Hall—Lea Hall, you know, just across the valley, the old farm which Papa inherited from his Great-uncle Peter Nightingale. But the farmhouse was inconvenient, and damp and cold and not very big, so Papa built Lea Hurst, this house. Then later he and Mamma were visiting in Hampshire and they saw Embley Park, and it was for sale, and they thought it was so beautiful that they must buy it—so they did."

"If *I* lived at Lea Hurst," Libby said, "I'd never go to Embley or anywhere else. I wouldn't *budge*."

"Wouldn't you? But Embley is very nice, too, and close to London, when Papa has to travel to the city on business."

"Nicer than Lea Hurst?"

"Maybe not. No," Florence said, "I couldn't choose between them, really. I almost cry when it's time to leave Lea Hurst in September—but, somehow, I'm every bit as sad at leaving Embley in the spring. Oh, Libby, the keys! Here, you may unlock the trunks and unpack them."

For the next quarter-hour, Libby, who liked being quiet, was quiet as a little mouse, exploring the contents of the trunks, carefully taking out and examining the dolls, which were of all sizes and varieties—big waxen lady dolls with wigs of golden hair; bisque babies with painted heads and jointed, muslin bodies; China dolls, French dolls, rag dolls stuffed with sawdust—while Florence stood by, watching.

Then Libby looked up, her expression bewildered.

"Why are so many of them *bandaged*? Are they *sick*?"

Florence smiled. "The bandaged ones are mine. Yes, they were always sick; or at any rate, I used to play they were. I always had them breaking their bones, or coming down with cholera or boils or rashes or something."

"But why?"

"So that I could put on poultices and plasters and give them medicine, and nurse them until they were well. Only I never allowed them to get entirely well—see, they have on their nightgowns—because that would have been so uninteresting."

"Were Miss Parthe's dolls sick, too?"

"Not at first. But they caught the diseases from mine, of course, though Parthe made an awful fuss about it."

"She didn't like to nurse them?"

"No, so I nursed them for her. But Parthe insisted on her dolls recovering *completely*, and wouldn't have it any other way. These are her babies, all dressed in their proper clothes."

"I like Miss Parthe's best," said Libby.

Florence picked up a rag doll and scrutinized it, her gray eyes tender with reminiscence. "This poor dear! She had a dislocated spine which I never could cure. She was my favorite. I practiced on her for ages."

"But, Miss Florence, I don't see *why*."

"Oh, because I wanted to be a nurse. I still want to be one. It's my ambition. I'm *going* to be!"

"A *nurse*?" Libby said. "You can't!"

"That's what Mamma tells me," Florence murmured. "That's what everybody says. But I will."

There was a short silence, and a tapping at the door. A white-capped maid peered into the room.

"Miss Florence, they've finished the tea, and Squire wishes you please to help with the treats."

"Thank you, Clemence. Will you bring Libby Brown a tray up here? Something special, and plenty of the raisin cake. You'll excuse me, Libby? You can manage by yourself."

"Oh, yes," said Libby confidently.

In the meadow, excitement was at fever pitch, with the young guests swarming around a central table which was presided over by Parthe and heaped high with the mysterious packages. Taking up a position opposite her sister, Florence thought that Libby's description had been accurate—the boys were pushing, the girls yelling as if out of their senses. As for Parthe, she looked utterly confused, like an old hen surrounded by a flock of unruly, capering chicks. But Florence saw that Mamma and Papa had remained serene. Seated in two large wicker armchairs behind the table, and somewhat separate from the milling throng, Mamma and Papa looked the **very** picture of benevolent, adult prosperity and might well have posed as the handsomest couple in the British Isles —as more than once they had been said to be.

With Florence's arrival on the scene, the passing out of the presents commenced; and as each child received his "treat"—it might be a ball or a tin horn, a set of dominoes or a wooden spade and pail—loud exclamations of delight burst forth.

"Oh, awful!" groaned Parthe, holding her ears. "What lungs they have! My word! But Papa's getting up now and it'll soon be over."

Yes, Mr. Nightingale was standing, clapping his hands. He made an announcement, "Children, we'll all sing together. *God Save the King.*"

They hushed, and then sang, " 'God save our gracious King!' "—all the verses of it, bravely and earnestly, with the Squire himself leading in a robust baritone, and the hills echoing the melody.

That was the end of the party, as everybody realized; the signal for farewells. Reluctantly everybody went home.

As the flurry of departures subsided, Parthe collapsed in the grass and leaned against Mamma's knee. "Isn't this a relief? Isn't the peace simply wonderful?"

"Are you tired, dear?" Mamma stroked Parthe's curls.

"I'm exhausted. I love the party, and I love it's being over."

"But it was very successful, wasn't it?" Mamma smiled, fanning herself with a wisp of lace. She turned to Papa. "William, don't you think it was successful?"

"Yes. Yes, indeed." Papa got out his own kerchief, a huge square of white linen and mopped his brow.

"Where's Florence? Ah, there you are, Flo. Come away, daughter, the servants will clear up all that mess on the tables. Well, were you satisfied with the event?"

"I don't know." Florence patted Papa's shoulder affectionately.

"What!" He slipped an arm around her waist. "You don't know?"

"It was all just fine. But—was it enough, Papa?"

"Why, Florence!" Mamma said, glancing up, astonished. "Whatever do you mean? I'm sure the children appreciated it, they had such a good time. I've never seen them so happy." She paused, her pretty face pink, her blue eyes clouding. "But you may be right. Maybe we *don't* do enough. We're so fortunate, we have so much. We must share—"

"Oh, Mamma!" Parthe said. "Flo's always having these odd notions. Pay no attention. Who could do more than you, or be more charitable and generous? The villagers adore you—we all adore you. You're the good woman of the Bible, the one in Proverbs who stretches out her hands to the poor and reaches forth to the needy, and everybody rises to call her blessed."

"Yes," Papa said. " 'Her price is far above rubies. Her husband praiseth her.' But is that what Florence means?"

"No, it isn't, Papa!"

"What *do* you mean?" Parthe said.

Florence hesitated. "I'm afraid I can't quite—well, for the children the party *was* enough—and you *are* just splendid to the villagers, Mamma, and they do love you. But, I mean, is it enough for *us*? Caring for the poor is now only a little part of our lives, something extra. But oughtn't we do it all the time?"

"And do nothing else? Oh, Flo," Parthe cried, "how silly! Why then we should have no time to ourselves."

"I suppose it is rather silly," Florence said. "But—"

"Libby Brown!" Parthe exclaimed suddenly. "Where *is* she?"

"Oh!" Florence said. "I forgot. She's in the nursery."

"She should have gone home with the rest of the children," said Mamma. "Her grandmother will be vexed."

"Never mind, my dear," said Papa. "I'll have one of the grooms drive Libby home in the pony-cart."

2

HOLIDAY SEASON

THE NIGHTINGALES were people of prominence not only in Derbyshire and Hampshire, but also in London; both Mamma and Papa had distinguished connections everywhere. Before her marriage, Mamma had been Frances Smith, daughter of William Smith, who for forty years was a member of Parliament, a man possessing wealth, social position, a large and satisfactory family, and an enviable reputation as the advocate of religious freedom and the protection of the underprivileged.

The William Smith country place was Jermyns, in Essex; there Mamma had spent the happiest possible childhood, growing up to be a charming and popular belle. In 1818 Mrs. William Smith had written to a friend, "Our beautiful Fanny is to marry young Nightingale." Everyone had thought it an excellent match.

At Jermyns, and at her father's London house, Mamma had learned to be a perfect hostess, and now nothing pleased her so much as to entertain visitors; indeed, she was famous for her hospitality. Perhaps Papa was less enthusiastic about the steady flow of "company" through the gates at Lea Hurst and at Embley—his interests were scholarly and agricultural, concerned with his books (especially the philosophical and religious books) and with his acres of land, which were tilled by tenant-farmers—

but he was devoted to his "beautiful Fanny," and very proud of her; he indulged her every fancy.

It was Mamma's wish that the two girls, Parthe and Florence, should have as secure and serene a youth as her own had been; she expected them to like the same pastimes; she hoped that they too would some day be the wives of worthy husbands and manage households similar to hers. In Parthe's case, these ideas of Mamma's seemed certain to bear fruit, for Parthe agreeably accepted them all. But about Florence, Mamma was not so sure.

As Parthe had said, Florence had odd notions. Was she also a little stubborn? Yes, Mamma and Parthe thought that perhaps she was—in a polite and sweet-tempered way, of course; which, as everybody knows, is the most wearisome sort of stubbornness to combat and overcome.

For one thing Florence often grew bored with the confusion which a houseful of even the best-mannered guests can create. Then she would take long, solitary walks through the fields and woods; or seek companionship with her pets, the ponies, the dogs, the ducklings, the tame squirrels scampering on the lawn. Sometimes she would go and sit in the chapel at Lea Hurst, thinking, losing herself in a dream of all the noble deeds she wanted to accomplish when she was older, wiser and more independent.

The chapel was a small structure which had been on this very spot since the days of Queen Elizabeth and it was really a part of the house, for Papa, who liked historical relics, had built Lea Hurst's strong stone walls right around the chapel. On Sundays a village Bible class met in the chapel, but on weekdays it was deserted, an interior swimming with pale yellow reflections of the sunshine outdoors, and so still that you could hear the branches of elms and oaks scratching on the roof.

Whenever Florence went into the chapel, she would think (for a while, at least) about God—because she enjoyed thinking about Him at any time, and it seemed to her particularly easy to believe and trust in Him here. She could even imagine that He was beside her, hovering close, and ready to listen to anything she might say to Him. She knew that, as Mamma and Papa had always told her, God was good; and the knowledge of His unfailing goodness made her yearn to do something (a really large and useful something!) toward the winning of His kingdom on earth. She hoped that God wouldn't object if she preferred to worship like this, alone in the chapel's seclusion, rather than by attending the regular Sunday church services—from which she occasionally absented herself on the plea of a headache. After all, the spirit of worship was what mattered, wasn't it, and not the form?

Having thought about God, Florence's attention would wander to other subjects, perhaps to Papa whom she loved so much. Not that she didn't love Mamma and Parthe also—of course, she did! But probably there was no harm in admitting that she was fondest of Papa, and felt a peculiar bond of sympathy with him.

Florence thought of Papa as an unusual man; and, to begin with, his name was unusual, because he hadn't been born a Nightingale at all. No, his parents were Mr. and Mrs. William Shore, and Papa had been named for his father; as William Shore he was known in his native Derbyshire, at the university in Edinburgh, and again at Trinity College, Cambridge, where he took his graduate degree. But his mother had been a niece of old

Peter Nightingale of Lea Hall, who wanted young William Shore to be the heir to his extensive estates; so, when he was twenty-one and no longer a minor in the eyes of the law, Papa had got his surname legally changed to Nightingale, as a tribute of gratitude and respect to the memory of Great-uncle Peter. After that, Papa was William Shore Nightingale; and now it was almost forgotten that his name had ever been anything else.

In fact, Papa believed that a name should *mean* something, everybody's name, and not be merely a tag, without rhyme or reason, which you must wear forever, whether you liked it or not; with this principle in mind, he had selected the names for his daughters. For the first three years of their married life, he and Mamma had traveled in Europe; they were in Italy, at Naples, when their first child was born, and Papa had said the baby must be called Parthenope, which was the name of the ancient Greek settlement originally on that site. Then, a year later, on May 12, 1820, at the Villa Colombaia, near the Porta Romana in Florence, a second little girl was born to the Nightingales.

"Her name," said Papa, "will be Florence."

Perhaps some people would have regarded this method of naming children as whimsical (and, in Parthe's case, rather *too* whimsical—though certainly Parthenope was better than Naples, which would have been strange, indeed!); but Florence approved of it, as she approved of everything Papa did. He was such a dashing figure of an English country-gentleman—sturdy and tanned, immaculately dressed in high white stock, plush-collared coat and tight-fitting trousers buckled down under the soles of his well-burnished boots. Papa was humorous and mild, never scolding; his daughters had never known him to be angry. Perhaps he was, if anything, too lenient in disposition; or perhaps he only seemed so because in his leisurely existence there were few occurrences to provoke him.

Somehow the school party was always a turning-point in the summer; afterward, the weeks fairly flew by, bringing nearer the time when the Nightingales, bag and baggage, servants and all, would move to Embley. As Florence had remarked to Libby Brown, the process was one to be viewed with mingled emotions. At Embley she would see many old friends, including various families of cats, spaniels and rabbits, and the horses in the stables; and she would be reunited with Miss Christie, the governess, who was a dear person. From Embley there might be a trip or two to Grandfather Smith's house in London. But Florence was sorry to think of Lea Hurst, empty and shuttered through the winter. How lonely it would be until the owners came again!

During the last week of August, Mamma made daily excursions to the village, for she could never have left without knowing that all the tenants were well provided with food, blankets and substantial clothing. It was regarded as a matter of course that Florence should accompany her and call on the invalids. According to Parthe's teasing comment, Flo always preferred ill people to healthy people—to an extent, this was true. In the basket on Florence's arm would be bunches of flowers, jars of broth or jelly, bottles of liniment; she knew just how to shake up a pillow, or brew a cup of tea or stir a pot of porridge. Her manner unhurried and soothing, she was content to sit a while by the sickbed, talking, telling a story, reading a chapter from the Bible.

But she did not like being thanked for such kindnesses; she shrank from compliments or praise. When old Granny Brown hailed her as an "angel child," she was quite wretched.

"Bless you, Miss Florence! Ah, what a grand little lady she is, what a gentle way she has with her!"

"I wish they wouldn't," Florence thought, blushing. "I'm not doing it for *that*."

If only the sick people could have been as silently receptive and unprotesting as were the sick dolls!

On the last day of the week, with all the villagers, ill or healthy, ministered to, Mamma gave Florence and Parthe permission to ride their ponies across the valley to Lea Hall, where Great-uncle Peter Nightingale had lived. They went in the afternoon, cantering along the narrow path which wound through the clover fields, then up the hill to the crest and the old, old gray stone house set in a thicket of giant rose bushes and clustering trees. The Hall had no occupants now; the girls got down from their side-saddles and walked all around and peeped through the bluish, cobwebbed windowpanes.

"From here," Parthe said, "I get glimpses of the staircase. Remember the twisted balustrade, Flo? Remember how we played on the steps when we were little?"

"Let's peep in at the kitchen," Florence said, "and remember Anthony Babington."

"And the conspiracy? Yes, let's!"

On tiptoe, hands shading their eyes, they looked into the kitchen, a room of ample proportions, with heavy-timbered roof and a huge stone hearth, equipped with copper kettles and roasting-spit.

"There's the trap-door to the attic chamber!" Parthe

exclaimed. "Can't you just imagine Babington's comrade, the young nobleman, hiding in the attic, waiting, quaking in his boots—being caught?"

Cantering along the narrow paths which wound through the clover fields

Florence nodded and began to speak, slowly, as though she recited a history assignment: "Almost two hundred and fifty years ago, when Elizabeth was on the throne, this house was known as Dethick. Then it was the home of Henry Babington and his son Anthony—"

"And it was larger, Flo," said Parthe, interrupting.

"Oh, yes. Much larger, very different, with turrets and balconies, galleries and ballrooms and an underground passage—"

"Which led to Wingfield Manor, where Mary Stuart, Queen of Scots, was kept a royal prisoner by Elizabeth!"

"Perhaps," Florence said. "Anyway, many people believed the passage led to Mary's prison. Young Anthony Babington was a stanch supporter of Mary Stuart; he had lived in Paris and there he pledged his fealty to her. When he returned to England he joined the secret organization which was plotting to release her, and often the meetings of the secret society were held here at Dethick."

"Right in this kitchen!" Parthe said. "And when the plot was discovered some of the conspirators fled to this house, and Elizabeth sent her soldiers to seek them here. Well, go on, Flo."

"At night the soldiers came," said Florence, "and burst open the door; and though they didn't find Anthony Babington himself, they did find others of the plotters, and seized them and dragged them off in irons. One man had crept through the ceiling trap into the chamber above, but somehow the soldiers knew it, and they got up on benches and forced up the trap-door, and so they captured him too. Then they went back along the road and presently they did find poor Anthony and arrested him; they took him to London—where he and all the society members were beheaded."

"Then," said Parthe, "Mary was tried and *she* was executed. Oh, what a tragic tale! Would you like to be a queen, Flo?"

"What? And have my head cut off?"

"Elizabeth's head was never cut off."

"But Mary's was. No, I should hate being a queen."

"Such terrible things don't happen nowadays. It mightn't be so bad," Parthe said. "Queens never have to work, you know."

"But I want to work, Pop."

"As a nurse, I suppose?"

"Yes. Why not?"

"Oh, you've been told so often, Flo! Nurses are never ladies. They're just dreadful *women*, slaving in dreary, dirty old hospitals—"

Now it was Florence who interrupted. "Hadn't we better go? Mamma said an early supper."

"Oh, yes," Parthe said, quickly diverted. "Early, because tomorrow we start for Embley. How lovely! You do like Embley, don't you, darling? Even if the village isn't so big? There are always a *few* invalids at Embley."

Florence knew that her sister was mocking her just a little, but she was not annoyed. Smiling, she swung up on the pony's back. Nothing Parthe said could annoy her. Nor could it shake her determination.

"Pop doesn't see," she thought. "She simply doesn't *see*."

3

MORNING INCIDENT

MR. NIGHTINGALE liked to drive in his own carriage all the way from Lea Hurst to Embley, taking his time and stopping frequently en route at the homes of friends or relatives in neighboring counties. Thus, the journey, though long, was never tedious—and the exact date and hour of arrival was of no slightest consequence, because the servants would have gone before, by more direct roads, to open and air the Hampshire house and put the furnishings in exquisite order.

The weather was fine, still warm but with an autumnal moistness and a transparent vapor shimmering above the bogs and heaths, the lakes and woods and flowering copses. When the carriage turned at last between the gateposts of Embley and bowled along the graveled lane and halted at the door, Florence thought that never had the immense Tudor house looked so stately and beautiful, or the gardens so luxuriant. Little wonder that Embley Park was a show-place, known as one of the most picturesque estates in all England! Immediately Florence was glad to be here.

The first thing she and Parthe did, after alighting and changing their traveling dresses for more comfortable clothing, was to run out over the lawn, through the rhododendron borders and hedges of azalea and laurel, to inspect the cypress tree on the front terrace. This was the "nursery tree," so called because it grew close to the house and towered high, its upper branches making a canopy of feathery foliage just outside the nursery windows. The nursery tree was old—Florence could not guess at its age—but even in her memory it had sheltered many generations of birds and squirrels; and under its trailing, tent-like boughs, Florence, at nine, had sat to write her autobiography, writing in French ("La Vie de Florence Rossignol") since, as Miss Christie had insisted, this would give her greater proficiency in the foreign language.

Fortunately, the nursery tree seemed now to be in good condition. "We must get some chestnuts and poke them into the holes in the bark," Parthe said. "For the nuthatches—who have probably missed us."

All that day and the next, the girls renewed acquaintance with old treasures and reminders of happy times in the past. There was, for instance, hanging in the hall the portrait of themselves and Mamma, painted by the artist Chalon, several years earlier. Pausing before it, they marvelled at what small children they once had been—

"But you were the taller even then, Flo," Parthe said. "See, I'm perched like an infant on Mamma's knee, while you're standing up like a real person. You do look intelligent! And so stern!"

"I was scared," Florence said. "Scared half to death, because the artist was a stranger. *You* look *pretty*."

They went into the library and got down their textbooks; and then, by the end of the week, Miss Christie had come and they were back at lessons. Almost before they knew it, a routine had been re-established and, under Mamma's expert management, the family life proceeded on smooth schedule. Every morning the Nightingales had prayers together, followed by breakfast and an interval in which Papa read the newspaper aloud at the table. Afterward, the girls went with Miss Christie to the schoolroom to study until noon, when luncheon was ready; then a short period of more study, this time with Papa, who drilled his daughters in history and Italian and talked interestingly about philosophy, of which he knew so much. In the late afternoon there was outdoor exercise before tea in the parlor at twilight; dinner in the evening, and probably some music in the drawing-room; lastly, more prayers and bedtime. Spare moments were devoted to reading or to fine needlework, such as embroidering. Parthe was learning to paint—or trying to, applying herself with diligence to brushes and canvas, palette and tubes of bright-hued pigments; but this was an inclination which Florence could not share. She would watch her sister, smile, suggest or criticize, then turn away to write letters—or add, in her carefully kept diary, further descriptions of "La Vie de Florence Rossignol."

And always there were to stay over Sunday, or longer (a week, maybe, a month) the inevitable visitors with whom Mamma loved to surround herself—Smith cousins, Shore cousins, relatives named Carter and Nicholson. Of them all, Florence liked best Papa's sister, dear Aunt Mai, who had married Mamma's brother, Samuel Smith. Aunt Mai and Uncle Sam were young, and the fact of their double relationship made them seem especially close and sympathetic; Florence was never anything but at ease with them. Indeed, she sometimes thought that Aunt Mai was the most amiable person in the world and Uncle Sam the most sensible. She could discuss with them the dreams she never mentioned to anyone else.

The village on the Park's outskirts was East Wellow; its vicar was the Reverend Mr. Giffard, a good friend of the Nightingales'—a special friend of Florence's. Making his parish rounds, Mr. Giffard never failed to stop in at Embley where he was heartily welcomed. Before his ordination as a clergyman, Mr. Giffard had studied medicine and whenever he called, Florence would engage him in conversations about the care of the sick and injured; unlike many other adults with whom she had contact, he seemed to think this interest not strange or morbid at all, but only natural.

Mr. Giffard was a fine horseman and enjoyed riding briskly over the Hampshire downs. Often he accepted Mr. Nightingale's offer of a mount from the Embley stables; then he would ask Florence to ride with him, and off they would gallop in the autumn sunshine.

One morning an incident occurred which was to linger long in Florence's mind—and in the tradition of East Wellow. Dashing over the billowing green downs, swerving at a hedgerow, the two friends drew rein and rested a minute to look at the pasture beneath them. Florence was breathless, laughing, her hair disarrayed, her hat fallen back on her shoulders. She said that she loved this view—

"Those are old Roger's sheep, Mr. Giffard. They behave so nicely, marching like soldiers, with Cap to guide them."

Mr. Giffard agreed. Yes, he himself had noticed the beautiful manners of Roger's sheep, the white pattern they made against the green pasture. "Roger is a lucky farmer to have such sheep—and a collie as smart as Cap to keep them in line as they graze. There are never any stragglers in the flock Cap tends."

But then Mr. Giffard paused, and gestured. "Miss Florence, something is wrong today!"

She stared at his pointing finger and was dismayed. Something was wrong, indeed! Today the pattern had not its customary neatness; the sheep were shifting, spreading out over the slopes, blundering about, bleating, straying. Cap, the clever collie, was not to be seen.

As they watched, Roger loomed into sight, in the middle of the flock. Roger was waving his arms like a windmill. "Hey!" he shouted. "Stop now—hey!"

"Come," said Mr. Giffard, and he spurred forward with Florence at his side. When he was within speaking range, he called out, "What's the matter, Roger? In trouble, aren't you?"

Roger glanced up, shaking his grizzled head. "That I am, sir. In desperate trouble. Can't get these animals to mind me at all. Plunge here and there they will, and never even look my way!"

"Where's Cap?"

"Ah, poor Cap!" Roger sighed. "Done for, I'm thinking."

"Done for?"

"Yes, sir. The devilish boys on yon farm stoned Cap; broke his leg, they did. He's a sadly hurt dog, poor Cap. I'll have to put him out of his misery."

"Oh, Roger!" Florence cried. "You're not going to kill Cap! You *wouldn't*!"

"Well, I'm afraid I must, missy." Roger tugged respectfully at his forelock, for this was the squire's daughter. "Yes, a bit of rope round his neck, one quick twist—but I'll never have another dog like him, because there never was his like!"

Florence turned from Roger to Mr. Giffard; tears were in her eyes: "Couldn't—couldn't we do something?"

Mr. Giffard looked thoughtful. "Is Cap in your shed now, Roger?"

"No, sir. In my house. Roped up, for he'll not let anyone near him. Snarls and snaps and shows his teeth. Ah, he's in pain, poor Cap! And these pesky sheep! See them go right out of bounds again! If you'll excuse me, sir and missy—" Shouting, Roger started once more in pursuit of the flock.

"Mr. Giffard?" Florence said. "You know so much about medicine. Couldn't we—"

He smiled and slapped his reins. "Perhaps. Come, Miss Florence."

They rode to Roger's house. The door was closed, locked; and from within sounded a violent barking which told of Cap's lonely suffering, his terror that someone would intrude to hurt him even more.

"I think Roger's neighbor will have a key we can borrow," said Mr. Giffard. "I'll get it."

Yes, the neighbor had a key which would fit. In a little while they had opened the door and were entering.

Cap lay stretched on the floor, trembling, rumbling out a hoarse protest of growls. But when Florence spoke to him—"Don't be frightened, Cap. We want to help you,"—he lifted his muzzle and feebly wagged his tail.

Mr. Giffard bent over the dog and very cautiously felt the leg which was badly swollen.

"Is it really broken?" Florence said.

"I'm not quite sure yet. Stand back, Miss Florence. He might bite."

"Oh, no!" Florence went down on her knees, stroking Cap's nose. "Why, we've been friends for years."

Mr. Giffard made his examination, and straightened. "The bone's not damaged. It's a dislocation and some torn ligaments. Serious, but not fatal; the poor chap ought not be destroyed. Hot compresses are the thing—"

"The kettle's on the stove! I'll boil the water!"

"But we have no cloth for the compresses."

"But we have!" Florence jumped to her feet. Old Roger's smock was suspended on a peg in the wall; she snatched it down, ripped it into squares, folded the squares into pads. "Mamma will give Roger another smock. Is this about the right size, Mr. Giffard?"

"Quite right. Now to heat the water! It may be rather a long-drawn-out process, Miss Florence."

"An hour?"

"Or longer. Will your mother be worried?"

"We won't think of that. Not yet," Florence said, smiling. "I can explain to Mamma."

So for more than an hour they applied the hot compresses to Cap's leg and he endured the treatment with patience, as if he understood that they intended only to help him. As the pain diminished, his tail thumped on the floor and he licked Florence's fingers, gazing at her with beautiful brown eyes.

Finally Mr. Giffard said they had done everything possible. "But there should be another treatment tomorrow."

"I'll come tomorrow," Florence said, "and every day until Cap is cured."

At noon they rode slowly homeward. Florence felt elated, jogging beside Mr. Giffard and chattering away more freely than ever before. This, she said, was what she liked—being useful. It was serving God, wasn't it, to work for the good of His creatures, whether these creatures were people or just dumb beasts?

"When I was a very small girl, Mr. Giffard—just six, I decided I was going to be a nurse, because that seems to me the best thing of all to be. I want to work in a hospi-

He endured the treatment with patience

tal, with only ill people around me; I want to make them well. Parthe laughs at me for that; she says nurses are dreadful women. But do they *have* to be dreadful? I don't think so! *I* wouldn't be!"

Mr. Giffard smiled at her eager young face. "My dear Miss Florence, you couldn't be dreadful. I can't picture you as anything except wholly charming. But—hospital work?" He paused. "You have no conception of what it is. How could you have, a little lady of your birth and breeding? I fear Miss Parthe's idea is very near the truth. Conditions in the hospitals are really disgraceful and the characters of the women who work there are not much better."

"Maybe," said Florence, "I could build my own hospital. Papa would build one for me. It need not be a large one. It would be *nice!*"

"Oh, I'm sure you would make your hospital nice. But nursing is scarcely the enterprise for a girl of your station, Miss Florence."

"Not even when I'm older?"

"I'm afraid not. You see, you are a gentleman's daughter."

"What difference does that make?"

"A great deal, perhaps." Mr. Giffard paused again. "It's all difficult to put into words; but in a society such as ours, there are conventions, rules. You say you want to serve God? How admirable! But you could do that in any one of a number of ways."

"What are they, Mr. Giffard?"

"Suppose you married an honest man whom you loved and then reared a family of fine, honorable children. You would then be serving God—"

"I don't think I will," she said. "I'll probably never get married at all."

Mr. Giffard laughed. "You may amend that notion later."

Florence made no response. She did not care to hear

what more the clergyman might have to say. She liked him, but he was mistaken about what she would do. Whoever opposed her was mistaken.

She rode silently, her eyes on the far horizon.

4

GROWING UP

THE YEARS HAD a way of passing, each one pleasantly like the one before. Lessons went on and were constantly more intensive, for Mr. Nightingale's aim was to educate his daughters thoroughly, so that as young ladies they could take their proper place in the cultured circle to which they had been born. But Mamma's training was no less rigorous; her girls must be prepared to marry well, rear families and preside over such houses as they had always known. They must be mindful of their obligations; must never forget the world's vast number of poverty-stricken folk. Charity, Mamma counselled, is the most becoming of all virtues.

The girls listened, believed and followed Mamma's example. But ever in Florence's thoughts flamed the conviction that charity, though beautiful, was not enough. Remembering the unfortunate, working for their betterment, should be one's *sole* occupation. She wished very much that she could see for herself the inside of some of these hospitals which people spoke of as appalling and intolerable. Why were not the hospitals reformed and made perfect? Could not their evils be corrected?

At Lea Hurst, in the brief summer months spent there, Florence took charge of the Bible class which met on Sundays in the quaint little chapel. She had for pupils girls no older than herself—yet very different in experience; they were servant girls, or youthful employees in mills from the towns roundabout who came to the country for a summer outing, some of them coming even as far as from Nottingham, where the big stocking mills flourished. Mr. Nightingale had thrown open his Derbyshire estate to the mill people; there they could camp out, tramp about at will, have a taste of fresh air and sunshine. When the church bells rang on Sunday morning, they could crowd into the chapel and hear Florence read God's word.

Slender and very grave, she would stand before her audience, her dark hair brushed in wings to frame her oval face, a knot at the nape of her neck—perhaps with a rose thrust into it, and another rose pinned to the wide lace collar of her fine silk frock. She would have removed her Leghorn bonnet of "coal-scuttle" size and style, and she wore no other ornaments than the flowers, for she wanted to be as much as possible like these girls in the class; she must talk to them intimately, as if she were one of them.

Yet she was conscious of the fact that she really was not one of them, an invisible chasm yawned between herself and them. They knew so much which she could not know, all the hard things of life, the rough corners and grim realities. Well, she would learn from them! She encouraged them to talk frankly of their labors, their problems. She was the audience then, drinking it all in, thinking. Perhaps she was secretly envious that none of these realities ever approached her except by hearsay.

Once Florence had the privilege of seeing Mrs. Elizabeth Fry, that valiant Englishwoman who was performing such miracles in the reforming of prisons and asylums for the insane. Mrs. Fry's career was well known; in the beginning she had been only a sort of Lady Bountiful to the poor and neglected in her immediate neighborhood. But, investigating farther, she had looked into Newgate prison; the female inmates there were miserably treated, utterly wretched, and she had resolved that something must be done for them and that she was the person to do it. Elizabeth Fry had the vision of a saint, the energy of a zealot. Accomplishing the reformation of Newgate, she carried the fight to similar institutions everywhere.

For Elizabeth Fry and her triumphs young Florence Nightingale had a feeling of awe and reverence. The astonishing thing was that Mrs. Fry's background was so very like Florence's. Elizabeth Fry's family was wealthy, her childhood had been sheltered. Yet, somehow, she had emerged from this background as a strong champion of actual, tangible good.

How had she done that, Florence wondered. What were the steps by which she had forged forward to her goal?

A rare and indomitable person, Elizabeth Fry! You thought of her—and contrasted the battles she had waged and won with your own lot in life, with all its easy circumstances. The weeks all flowing on so smoothly into years, each of which contributed to your benefit and enjoyment; Parthe's high spirits, Papa's solicitude, Mamma's tenderness; the well-managed house-parties at Lea Hurst, the picnics in the grove, the fetes on the lawn; luncheons and dinners at Embley; Christmas Eve and the villagers singing carols under the windows and then being asked in for a jolly supper of gingerbread, hot mince pies and eggnog at a table garnished with holly and mistletoe and silver coins, which were tokens for the singers. All this seemed designed to make you contented with things as they were, to distract you from doubts as to the rightness of the world. Why not just be swept along, unquestioning?

But Elizabeth Fry had rebelled. Some instinct had forced her to probe beneath the surface of her contentment, and what she saw there she must remember always.

Florence Nightingale would probe, too.

When Florence was seventeen, Queen Victoria acceded to the throne of England.

A dramatic event that was; the whole civilized world hummed with the news; at Embley Papa read all about it aloud to the group around the breakfast table. A girl donning the crown of the mightiest kingdom in the universe? And what a very young and unsophisticated girl! "Why, she is only eighteen; your age, Parthenope; only a year older than our Florence." And how plainly and modestly she had been brought up, in gloomy Kensington Palace, where she'd lived almost as a recluse, with just her mother, the Duchess of Kent, and her governess, the German Fräulein Lehzen, as companions.

Wasn't it true that Victoria had never slept a night away from her mother's room? Or been allowed to converse with any adult (friend, tutor or servant) except in her mother's presence? She hadn't known at all, or even suspected, that she was destined to be a queen. Not until she was twelve, when by means of a carefully arranged history lesson, her mother had told her what the future held in store.

Then Victoria had said solemnly, her first words, "I will be good."

The King is dead. Long live the Queen!

In the early hours of June 20, 1837, King William IV, Victoria's uncle, died. The Archbishop of Canterbury and the Lord Chamberlain were bearers of the tidings, posting to Kensington Palace in the shivery gray light of dawn, knocking portentously on the door, being admitted. Long live the Queen! She came walking down the great staircase, roused suddenly from her bed, clad in her padded dressing-gown and slippers. It was five o'clock, the world still and waiting, birds rustling in their nests, the east faintly streaked with pink.

She walked down the stairs, and the august messengers bowed low before her. "Your Majesty!" She was surprised, but very gracious, very dignified.

"I will be good."

A few hours more and the privy council had convened at Kensington, the usual oaths were administered to the Queen by the Lord Chancellor; all witnesses to these ceremonies were moved by the spectacle of Victoria's poise and self-possession. Here was a ruler deserving love and veneration! In the long chronicle of English monarchy, a new and better epoch had begun.

At Embley, as Papa read aloud, Florence thought about the Queen, who wanted most of all to be good, had pledged herself to goodness. The firm statement of intention was not difficult for Florence to understand; she knew what it was like to hear a call to duty and to respond with a vow. There had been that February day in this very year—February 7, 1839, it was; she would never forget it—when abruptly from somewhere a voice had spoken, telling her that she too was to be an instrument of destiny, divinely appointed. The voice was mysterious, not human; it may have been only the stirring of the wind; yet it spoke a clear summons. For so many years she had wished, with a child's indefinite, diffused longing, to serve God; she had talked of it to anyone who would not smile—and these listeners, even the politest of them, had never really known what she meant, their lack of comprehension had grieved her and encompassed her in a kind of groping loneliness—but now she was certain of God's call, because on February 7 she had heard it unmistakably and answered without hesitation.

Yes, she would serve God, and in the way of His selection—which, as it happened, was the way she herself preferred. The problem of Florence Nightingale's future was settled!

She recorded it all in her diary; the date, the soft yet commanding voice calling, calling. Like the young Queen, Florence had a mission.

"I could not pray for George IV," she was to write, later. "I thought people very good who prayed for him, and wondered whether he could have been much worse if he had not been prayed for. William IV I prayed for a little. But when Victoria came to the throne, I prayed for her in a rapture of feeling and my thoughts never wandered."

The Nightingales went abroad that autumn for it was time, Papa said, the girls had some foreign travel. They went to France and northern Italy, where they remained several months and were entertained by their numerous friends there. They were several more months in Switzerland, with a long stay in Geneva. It was Mr. Nightingale's idea that traveling had an educational value and was not to be undertaken merely for pleasure. His girls must concern themselves not only with the beauty of the scenery but also with the art, architecture, literature, people and laws of these European countries. They must keep industriously at their studies and make notes in their journals of everything they saw and did.

Perhaps Mr. Nightingale was unaware of the attention which Florence gave to the benevolent institutions

She recorded it all in her diary

in such cities as they visited or her burning curiosity to know more and more about hospitals, prisons and workhouses. Her eyes and ears were constantly open; she observed that here on the continent, as in England, the best and almost the only help extended to the poor, the insane, the diseased or indigent was through the Church and its religious orders, or through the exercise of private charity. The general public had not been roused to any enthusiasm for humanitarian efforts; those few public asylums which existed were places of filth, cruelty and squalor. In every nation the populace seemed to be divided into classes, with lines like fences drawn between. There were the aristocracy, the middle class, the great masses of the poor and oppressed—and only the exceptional person thought much about breaking through the fences and proclaiming the equality of all men's rights.

Genteel people, many of them, referred to the common folk as the "mob" or the "rabble," and assumed that their homes must be hovels, their habits repulsive. Those genteel people endowed with a conscience were not unwilling to assist the common folk to a better mode of life —certainly not! But they did so patronizingly, by way of charity, with the impulsive gesture of a lord flinging his full purse ino the outthrust hand of a beggar.

All this was to be seen in the slums of the world's big cities. Florence Nightingale saw it, and knew, at seventeen, that there were shameful flaws in the universal scheme of things. The flaws must be repaired! But how? The job was of huge proportions—and what could the single worker, toiling alone, hope for?

She would watch, inquire, find out.

It was the autumn of 1838 when the Nightingales left Geneva, going on to Paris to spend the winter. In the French capital they met Mary Clarke, a brilliantly intellectual Englishwoman whose home was a rendezvous for the most distinguished Parisian literary celebrities, and also for men of political fame. Invitations to Miss Clarke's *salon* were sought after; in her drawing-room gathered the elite, conversation scintillated and sparkled like diamonds. She had been instantly on terms of cordiality with all the Nightingales, a friendship which was to last through the years.

Because of Miss Clarke's courtesy in introducing them everywhere, the winter was an exciting one for Florence and Parthe, gay beyond any they had ever known before. Parthe especially threw herself heart and soul into the social program. But Florence too was blithely buoyant, feeling (as she said, somewhat apologetically) the "temptation to shine in society." The young gentlemen who took her in to dinner often had occasion to comment on the sharpness of her wit, her outbursts of humor and her keen appreciation of the ridiculous. She was never so pretty as Parthe; but her eyes were fine, under arched black brows; her features were delicate and sensitive; and her slim height set off to advantage all her new Paris-made costumes.

When in the spring of 1839 the Nightingales returned to England, they had been away eighteen months; and now they would not go directly to Embley or Lea Hurst. They must stop in London, Mamma said, for the "season." The girls must have piano and singing lessons with metropolitan masters, must attend a series of concerts and lectures, and see whatever dramas the London stage was offering. And they must be presented at court. Parthenope and Florence were now quite old enough, their mother thought, for a formal debut; they should have it at once—

As usual, Mamma's plans carried through. "Successfully!" she said. After this, every year they would spend the season in London—until (she probably added, to herself) the girls were properly married. Anyway, she had launched them.

They reached Embley in the early summer. Oh, how lovely it was, the grass and copses green, the shrubbery flowering, roses bending on slender stems in the garden, the nursery tree a haven for the nuthatches, the rhododendrons in lavish bloom.

"I shall always remember the rhododendrons as they look now," Florence thought. "I shall remember them even when I'm quite an old lady!"

Home, so dear, so beautiful—and so unchanged. That really was the astonishing thing, wasn't it? The unchangeableness of Embley and the life to be led there. You left it, were absent for ages; you came back, much more grown-up, your viewpoint broadened, and everything was the same! Somehow you were unprepared for that.

Precisely the same? Well, no. A few alterations had been made in the house itself, some interior decorating done, new bedrooms built. Now, as Florence recorded in a letter, Mamma could have here as guests "five able-bodied females with their husbands and belongings." But these differences were scarcely to be noticed, once the normal tempo of daily life had been resumed.

Embley was the same; when you drove to Derbyshire later, Lea Hurst would be the same, too. Even *tiresomely* the same. In both places luxury closed around you like a downy, warm blanket.

A beautiful blanket, yes. But rather excessively soft. Rather suffocating—wasn't it?

5

YOUNG LADY OF LEISURE

FLORENCE WAS TWENTY-ONE, then twenty-two. And what was she doing with herself?

Well, all the conventional and accustomed things. No more governesses, of course, and no more lessons. Papa was satisfied with his daughters' education, which was far above average. Indeed, they were extraordinarily cultivated young ladies, adept linguists, speaking several languages, including the Italian he'd taught them. In history, mathematics and philosophy they had a solid foundation; they knew a great deal about politics. They were sufficiently musical, anyway as much as fashion required them to be; and Parthe, at least, was interested in art. In their father's eyes they were superbly finished products. Henceforth they should study only as they chose.

Perhaps Papa would have been surprised, had he foreseen the trend which Florence's further studies were to take.

They had a few light tasks to be attended to daily—nothing arduous; rather, something like arranging the flowers or helping Mrs. Nightingale with her charity calls or embroidering an altar cloth for church, or mending their gloves. Then the girls were free to amuse themselves, to dance, sing, stroll with other young people of their own sort, to give fancy-dress balls, charades or tableaux. Once at Waverley Hall, the home of their Nicholson cousins, the Nightingale sisters took part in an amateur performance of *The Merchant of Venice*, directed by William Charles Macready, the eminent Shakespearean actor. Florence was Mr. Macready's stage manager on this occasion—most efficient, so everybody said.

But what of Florence's ambition?

It was not much advanced by the passing years. She continued to look after her villagers—a difficult thing because of the fact that as soon as she was constructively busy in Lea, the calendar dictated moving on again to Embley, or the other way round. After all, she knew this wasn't what a little girl had dreamed of those sunny afternoons in the old chapel, not what had been meant by a small, disembodied voice murmuring in her ear. This was but playing at something which should be done seriously. It was imitation, not reality; and the oppressing thought could never be quite shaken off.

La Vie de Florence Rossignol? She was still writing it, in her diary, in letters to many correspondents. But what was at first a vague distaste became a positive displeasure. The life of Florence Nightingale? The captivity, you might say! She loved her family—oh, yes! She loved her home. But the Lea Hurst hedgerows, the Embley rhododendron borders (if seen at a certain angle) curiously resembled fences with spiked tops, fences she couldn't get over or past. They gave her the feeling of being penned in, shut up within the narrow confines of a plush-lined jewel case. She must get out. She must!

Sometimes, in London for a week or month, her mood was more cheerful. London was an escape of sorts. In the country, she said, there was nothing beyond the necessity of "looking merry and saying something lively, mornings, noons and nights." In the city, "you can at least have the mornings to yourself."

You were spared, for instance, the ordeal of Papa's reading aloud at the breakfast table—

"To be read aloud to," Florence asserted, "is the most miserable exercise of the human intellect. Or rather, is it any exercise at all? It is like lying on one's back with one's hands tied, and having liquid poured down one's throat."

Not so bad for Parthe, perhaps. No, dear Pop could take refuge behind her sketching board while Papa ploughed methodically through the *Times* from the first page to the last. But Florence must sit, listening (or pretending to listen) and be bored.

The others didn't even guess what went on in her mind. That was the worst of it! Well, perhaps Papa understood, just a little, and was sorry. But Mrs. Nightingale and Parthe? Never! Was Florence pouting again, long-faced and silent? Why on earth couldn't she be happy? Hadn't she everything in creation to make her happy?

"It's a mystery!" Parthe declared.

"It's a disappointment," mourned Mamma, "to *me*."

Sometimes Florence solicited advice on how to conquer her dejection. Mary Clarke had a suggestion. Why shouldn't Florence write? A respectable calling for a lady, and Florence had literary ability, as shown in her letters.

"Write something," said Miss Clarke.

But Florence knew her own limitations; she wasn't cut out to be an author. "I think what is not of the first class had better not exist at all," she replied, "and besides I had so much rather live than write; writing is only a substitute for living. I think one's feelings waste themselves in words; they ought all to be distilled into actions which bring results."

She knew what life should be. Exactly. "Life is no holiday game, nor is it a clever book, nor is it a school of instruction, nor a valley of tears; but it is a hard fight, a struggle, a wrestling with the principle of evil, hand to hand, foot to foot." On the margin of a page of poetry, she scribbled her belief: "To find out what we can do, one's individual place, as well as the general end, is man's task."

If she had been a *man,* all would have been so easy for her! Then wealth and social position might have counted not as handicaps but as assets. Rich men's sons could be useful—in politics, for example. But to girls, to young ladies of Florence's kind, all such outlets for energy were forbidden.

Young ladies married; or, unmarried, remained at home. They were sweet, demure—and idle.

A summer visitor to Embley Park was Dr. Samuel Gridley Howe, the American, whose wife, the beautiful and talented Julia Ward Howe was to become a legendary figure in the United States as the author of the *Battle Hymn of the Republic.* Dr. Howe was an internationally famous philanthropist, working to alleviate the lot of blind people everywhere. One morning, as he walked in the rose garden, Florence went timidly up to him.

"Dr. Howe?"

He turned, smiling. "Yes, Miss Florence?"

"Will you answer a question for me? Frankly?"

"I shall be delighted!"

"If," Florence said, her voice very low and vibrant

with emotion, "if I should decide—*really* decide—to study nursing and devote all the rest of my life to nursing—do you think it would be a dreadful thing?"

"No, not dreadful." Dr. Howe stood, looking at the roses, his face grave now, as if he saw the depths of yearning behind the question. "Not dreadful at all. But —unusual, shall we say? In England whatever is unusual is likely to be deemed unfitting."

"Yes, I know. Everyone has told me."

"What everyone says has no effect upon you?"

"No. Because I want so much to be a nurse, I'm sure it is my true vocation! The wish, the hope, is all I care for in the world—" She paused, her grey eyes misty.

"Then," Dr. Howe said, "you must go on with it, without fear. Pursue and accomplish your aspirations. God will be with you."

Florence drew a tremulous breath. Here was advice she could accept! In the presence of this great humanitarian, she felt at ease, could speak unguardedly. She said that she had noted the achievements of the orders of nursing nuns in the Roman Catholic sisterhoods; for such women she had a profound admiration, since with them their profession was an entire religion and even life itself. But why was there not a Protestant organization of this type?

"My dear Miss Florence, there is Pastor Theodor Fliedner's establishment of deaconesses at Kaiserswerth in Germany. Have you not heard of it?"

She hadn't. Kaiserswerth? Stimulated by the mere thought that she was to have a new avenue to explore, she thanked Dr. Howe. He had helped her more than he would ever know.

That summer and the next, Florence gathered information about Kaiserswerth from all available sources, and frequently from the guests at Embley and Lea Hurst, many of whom were celebrities in one or another field of humanitarian endeavor—Sir Joshua Jebb, Surveyor of Prisons; Dr. Richard Dawes, dean of Hereford and educational reformer; Dr. Richard Fowler, experimenting at Salisbury with the open-air treatment of consumption; Mrs. Elizabeth Gaskell, recently coming into prominence with her published sketches of the Manchester slums. Now Mary Clarke was spending a month or two each year with the Nightingales; Florence consulted with her, and with Aunt Mai Smith, who was so faithfully interested.

The theory of nursing was uppermost in Florence's thoughts, something to ponder endlessly. Soon she had the chance for a brief practical experience. At Tapton Grandmamma Shore fell ill, and Florence was sent for. Grandmamma Shore was old and strong-willed; nobody else in the family could make her take her medicine. But she was fond of Florence. Maybe with Florence to care for her, she wouldn't be so unruly a patient.

Florence enjoyed the stay at Tapton in Grandmamma's house. To her cousin, Hilary Bonham Carter, she wrote that she hadn't been so nearly happy for a long time. "I am very glad to walk sometimes in the valley of the shadow of death as I do here." She was glad, too, when Grandmamma recovered.

It must have been at Tapton that she hit upon the wonderful idea of going to study nursing at the Salisbury hospital in Wiltshire. In secret she thought about it —how, having completed the course, she might get a small building in West Wellow, not far from home, and there found a nursing center, staffed by an English sisterhood of nurses which she would head. A fascinating scheme! If only she could get Mamma's consent—

She couldn't. Mamma was shocked. Florence at Salisbury hospital? Waiting upon strangers, dressing their wounds, bending over their beds, nursing them? Florence exposed to association with the regular nurses, uncouth men and ill-bred women who drank to excess (or so people said), used foul language and were obviously riffraff?

"No!" Mamma cried. "Oh, no!"

"Mamma is behaving," said Florence to Parthe, "as if her darling Flo had expressed the desire to be a scullery maid."

"Mamma is right," said Parthe. "Your idea is ridiculous."

Grudgingly then Florence gave it up. To Hilary Bonham Carter she wrote abjectly of her failure: "I shall never do anything, and am worse than dust and nothing. Oh, for some strong thing to sweep this loathsome life into the past!" Yet hope would not quite die. "The longer I live," she wrote in her diary, "the more I feel as if all my being was gradually drawing to one point."

Now Florence thought of asking Papa to get in touch with certain persons in London who could tell him the plain, unvarnished facts about hospitals.

"I am not averse to that," Papa said.

"If what you're told is not too bad, will you let me be a nurse?"

"If," Papa said cautiously, "I think a young lady of your rearing could adapt herself to such an atmosphere, I shall—well, countenance the possibility."

But the descriptions received were anything but reassuring. The stories of hospital life had not, it seemed, been exaggerated. There were vicious and degraded people admitted as patients. As for the nurses, both male and female, they were most reprehensible; scarcely any

"Will you let me be a nurse?"

among them had either good character or ability; they drank, they indulged in improprieties if not in downright immorality.

"Florence," Papa said, "no one stricken with illness ever goes voluntarily into a hospital—where, probably, the nurses can't even be trusted to give a dose of pills without making a mistake!"

"But the hospitals are always full of people."

"People who cannot afford to be sick at home. A deplorable thing, Florence!"

Yes, deplorable—and obviously not for William Shore Nightingale's daughter.

She was twenty-six now, and reading everything about Pastor Fliedner which came her way, snatching at any accounts she could lay hands upon. No tale had ever intrigued her so much.

Pieced together, bit by bit, it went back to 1833, when a Lutheran clergyman in the small German town on the Rhine had furnished the tiny summerhouse behind his own humble dwelling as a shelter for ailing and outcast women. Theodor Fliedner was a widely traveled man (indeed, he had tramped all over Europe and through England as an evangelistic preacher); in London he had talked with Elizabeth Fry. This must have been a meeting of kindred souls, for Fliedner's greatest pity was for the inmates of penal institutions, and especially for women who had suffered imprisonment and then been released as ex-convicts into communities which scorned and persecuted them. These were the poor creatures he most wished to help. Returning to Kaiserswerth, he patched the leaky roof of his summerhouse, made the interior clean and habitable; put in a cot, a chair, a table, let it be known that the place was ready for occupancy— and then prayed that God would send there some friendless wayfarer.

One cold night the first of his charges arrived, stumbling through the darkness, knocking. Herr Fliedner was asleep; his wife wakened him. In his coarse stockings, without boots, he opened the door.

"Welcome, my daughter."

During that winter, nine women came to the pastorage. It was evident that the flimsy sanctuary would have to be enlarged. Where, asked Fliedner's wife, would they get the money?

"The money? It will be provided *Liebchen*."

Somehow, in paltry sums from here and there, the money was provided. Nurses were secured for the ill women, nurses whom Theodor Fliedner himself painstakingly trained. Within three years, he had started a hospital in the wing of a deserted factory, equipping it with discarded odds and ends which he begged from the more prosperous folk of Kaiserswerth. Had he only six sheets for the hospital beds? Ah, but plenty of water to wash them in, and soap was so cheap! His nurses, the deaconesses, served not for wages but in fulfillment of a religious vow—though they could always leave, if they wished, and go back to ordinary life. Another year or two and he had a training school for teachers, an orphanage also; and now in twenty-five European cities his graduate nurses were beginning other hospitals, modeled after Kaiserswerth.

To Florence, Herr Fliedner's story was the one ray of light piercing the bleakness of her own frustration.

July 7, 1846, she wrote in her diary: "What is my business in the world and what have I done this last fortnight? I have read the *Daughter at Home* to Papa, and two chapters of Mackintosh; a volume of *Sybil* to Mamma. Learnt seven tunes by heart. Written various letters. Ridden with Papa. Paid eight visits. Done company. And that is all."

At Embley, October 7: "What have I done the last three months? They don't know how weary this way of life is to me—this *table d'hote* of people."

But she had been perusing the annual report from Kaiserswerth. "There is my home. There are my brothers and sisters all at work. There my heart is and there I trust will one day be my body, whether in this state or in the next, I do not care."

6

TRAVELS AND DREAMS

FLORENCE WAS TWENTY-SEVEN and going to Rome with her good friends, Charles and Selina Bracebridge. The Nightingale sisters offered differing reasons as to why Mamma allowed Flo to set out with just these two companions—a married couple, of course, yet no older than herself. Florence wrote to Hilary Bonham Carter that she hadn't been well: "All that I want to do in life depends on my health, which I am told a winter in Rome will establish forever." But Parthe, also writing to Hilary, confided that Flo had been indulging in "wearing thoughts," she was so pale, her sleep disturbed; duty had weighed too heavily on her conscience and she needed to rest her mind.

Parthe was a little worried about the boldness of Flo's venture—leaving home without her parents! It was a thing which Parthe herself would never have dared—or, for that matter, have enjoyed. When the solemn moment for farewells came, Parthe declared, "My heart is very full of many feelings." Still, she really didn't think that Flo would be harmed by the excursion.

"You must 'do' Rome thoroughly, Flo," Parthe said. "See everything that Papa and Mama saw on their wedding tour. And let us hear from you *often*."

Florence promised. No one must ever know how eager she was to get away!

For such travelers, Rome had many social diversions to extend; but Florence, with her studious temperament, would only sample these and devote most of her vacation to viewing the Holy City's art treasures. The great age, the hugeness and grandeur of Rome, its quality of being eternal and never-changing stirred her to the depths. In her letters home, as frequent and lengthy as Parthe could have wished, she told of how awed she was at beholding gigantic ruins, vast St. Peter's, the glorious sunsets over the wide Campagna, the incredible beauty of Michelangelo's paintings in the Sistine chapel.

Naturally enough perhaps, her thoughts turned to religion; she made a serious study of the Roman Catholic Church, its doctrine and ritual, even going so far as to enter the ten-day Retreat in the Convent of the Trinità dei Monti, where she became fast friends with the Superior, and acquainted herself with the organization and rules of the large school attached to the Convent. Observers wondered whether this reverent and intelligent Englishwoman might not be contemplating joining the Catholic faith—but, if so, her conversion never quite materialized. No, she would remain a Protestant, a member of the Church of England, but she would be always completely tolerant, respecting all sects, seeing the spiritual value in them all, hating bigotry and fanaticism.

In any denomination God could be served. And that alone was worth the doing.

In Rome the Bracebridges encountered some English friends, Sidney and Elizabeth Herbert, to whom Florence was introduced. No one, certainly not Florence herself, could have foreseen the significance of the meeting.

But Florence was at once attracted and impressed by

Sidney Herbert. Who would not have been? He was thirty-seven, recently married—yes, this was in fact his bridal journey, a long holiday between sessions of Parliament in which for fifteen years, almost from the time he left Oxford, he'd had a seat. He was a descendant of Sir Philip Sidney's sister and named for that gentle knight; Lord Pembroke was his half-brother, Wilton—the finest country residence in England—his home. To date his political career had been brilliant; he was perhaps the best-known among younger English statesmen. Indeed, all the virtues seemed combined in him. He was handsome; he had a keen intellect, chivalrous manners, a charming personality.

He had something else too, which Florence Nightingale was quick to perceive—an unwavering loyalty to goodness for its own sake, a purpose like a steadily burning fire to exert all his genius for the uplifting of his fellowmen. Clasping Sidney Herbert's hand, she recognized in him the man she herself would have wished to be—had not fate cast her in woman's inferior role.

After that chance meeting, the Bracebridges, the Herberts and Florence were almost constantly together, riding, driving, seeing galleries, a congenial group never lacking subjects for discussion.

"The most entire and unbroken freedom from dreaming I ever had," Florence later called it.

Elizabeth Herbert, blonde, vivacious, much younger than her husband, urged Sidney to tell about the hospital he hoped to build.

"A hospital? Florence will just dote on that!" Charles Bracebridge exclaimed. "Hospitals are her specialty."

Sidney glanced at her and Florence blushed. "Charles is teasing. But do tell us."

"It would be an infirmary for convalescents," Sidney said. "There are thirty-two villages on the Pembroke estates, several thousand people. I want an infirmary where these people of mine can recuperate after illness and be given the most modern medical treatment in the best possible conditions."

"His plans are all down on paper," said Elizabeth proudly.

"But I've much to do before I start building." He looked again at Florence. "Since your hobby is hospitals, Miss Nightingale, perhaps you'd come to Charmouth sometime and inspect the location and plans."

"Yes, I will," she said.

"Splendid! Just as soon as we're all in England again?"

"Make it a first order of business," Elizabeth begged. "And don't forget, Florence!"

Florence smiled. She would not forget. No danger.

With the Bracebridges she returned to England in the early summer, and shortly thereafter she went to Wilton for several days with the Herberts. Together, she and Sidney bent over the draughtsman's specifications for the convalescents' hospital.

Their first consultation. It would not be their last.

If only the "unbroken freedom from dreaming" might have been permanent! But no, she was back at Embley, back in the old Slough of Despond. She had expected that those months in Rome would cure her of her restlessness—Mamma had expected it; instead, the relief was temporary. A note of desperation marked the entries in her diary: "My God! What is to become of me? Everything has been tried, foreign travel, kind friends, everything." Everything, it seemed, except the one desire of her ardent heart—work! That she could not have, and for the most absurd of reasons, because it was unsuitable, because she was a lady!

She and Sidney bent over the specifications

Despite her protestations to Mary Clarke, she was writing a good deal now. Perhaps she might even write a book, which would be largely about the position of well-bred women in society. They were utterly useless, of that she was convinced, the merest parasites. Women were not supposed to need food for their heads and hearts; only their bodies were kept nourished.

What a humiliation it was, and what a wicked waste. Domestic duties? High-sounding words, yes; but actually just bad habits. Florence enumerated these bad habits: "Answering a multitude of letters which lead to nothing, from her so-called friends, keeping herself up to the level of the world that she may furnish her quota of amusement at the breakfast table; driving out her company in the carriage." This was woman's lot. A hateful one!

Women had no time to themselves—"never a half hour in all their lives (excepting before or after anybody is up in the house) that they can call their own, without fear of offending or hurting someone." Lucky the woman who could get an odd moment in which to work at something of her own choosing! Home? It was not a hallowed place, but a place of confinement, from which the sons of the family went away as soon as they could go, and daughters married, often without love, just to escape.

Such were the thoughts seething in Florence's mind as she sat, apparently quiet, in the drawing-room at Embley or Lea Hurst, her grey eyes observing each detail: the thick-piled carpet and damask-covered chairs, the softly gleaming silver and sparkling glass, the floor polished like a mirror; a white-capped maid tiptoeing in with the coffee tray, a liveried manservant shutting in the warm candlelight—shutting out the world which held work to be done, evil to be vanquished, suffering to be assuaged. Nothing, surely, could be more deadly than a drawing-room. Unless it was the clock on the drawing-room wall, ticking, slowly ticking, monotonous, irritating, with creeping hands measuring off the hours of another long, dull evening, measuring off eternity.

"Why are you so pensive, Flo? You're not saying anything tonight."

"I'm sorry, Mamma."

She was thinking of her book. Perhaps she would entitle one of the chapters "Is God in the Drawing-Room?" She knew the answer, right enough!

Mrs. Nightingale had been reading a novel. A very attractive story, such a sweet heroine.

Florence had read the book, too. "Probably the heroine was sweet because she had no family ties, no mother to make demands upon her."

Mrs. Nightingale was astonished and resentful. She said to her husband, when Flo had gone up to bed, that she had always been afraid it was a risk to let the girls study so much. "Not that I notice any bad effects in Parthe. But Florence is so—so—"

"Oh, she will settle down, my dear. Don't worry. She'll be marrying, making some man a good wife."

Upstairs, Florence also was wondering at the contrast between herself and Parthe. How could Pop endure it? "*I* can't! I simply *can't!*"

Nor would she marry. There had been chances, of course; eligible young men who came to court her. Only one of them she had ever considered seriously. He was a man already distinguished; Mamma, Papa and Parthe approved of him and would have smiled on the match. Florence admired him—even more, she took great and increasing pleasure in his companionship, found herself leaning on his sympathy. He had proposed, she had refused him, yet he persisted.

"I could be satisfied to spend a life with him," she

wrote. Yes, she could be *happy* with him. But wouldn't such happiness be just a form of selfishness? Perhaps she would only be fleeing from one drawing-room to another quite like it? If she married, her ambition would certainly go by the board—she could not face the prospect! Work, the kind of work she wanted, was infinitely more precious than a wife's happiness. That was "the true and rich life."

She knew that this determination of hers to live and die a spinster was a disappointment to her parents—to everybody. Once, a friend of whom she was fond had remarked to another friend, "Our dear Flo has just recovered from a severe cold, but I hear nothing of what I long for, that some noble-hearted gentleman, one who can love her as she deserves to be loved, prepares to take her to a home of her own." Well, that was news which her friends would never hear! Once Aunt Mai had suggested that a husband might in certain circumstances be an advantage. Had not Elizabeth Fry been helped by the fact that there was a Mr. Fry to encourage and support her? Florence was skeptical of this argument. Let others marry if it pleased them.

Love was not for her!

Yet she liked to talk with men, to listen to them—and to know that sometimes they listened to her. Dinner conversations were easy for her; she charmed her partners by the breadth of her information, the depth of her learning. Sometimes she amazed them.

"That daughter of Nightingale's, the younger one—very clever, isn't she? Very sharp, something of a bluestocking. Gets a chap to spouting on some topic of which he thinks he knows a lot; his *favorite* topic, geology maybe, Greek inscriptions, theology, something of the sort. Gets a chap to showing off a bit, preening himself—and then it's Miss Florence's turn, and in a moment she's proving that she knows far *more* about it. Well, well! A capital young lady—if she hadn't floored me with her Latin and Greek."

In the autumn of 1848 Florence's hopes soared suddenly to an ecstatic height. Mrs. Nightingale was going to Carlsbad, to take the waters there, her daughters must accompany her.

Carlsbad? Why, it was not far from Kaiserswerth. Not *too* far, anyway. Mary Clarke was now married to Julius Mohl, the eminent orientalist; the Mohls would meet the Nightingale ladies in Frankfurt—

"While you all go on to the baths, I shall be off to Kaiserswerth!" said Florence.

"Ah?" said Mamma, with lifted brows.

But it was not to be. Political troubles were brewing in Germany; Mr. Nightingale thought the trip unsafe, the plan was given up, and Parthenope and Florence went with Mamma to Malvern.

Florence was bitterly chagrined. Kaiserswerth, Pastor Fliedner, the deaconesses had seemed just within reach —and then slipped once more into the realm of the unattainable.

Seeing the shadow in her eyes, Mr. Nightingale said that he had no objection to Florence's spending several months in London where she might look over the hospitals and learn for herself what the nursing profession was like. She could put up at Grandfather Smith's house, or even in a decorous hotel; she might do a bit of charitable work in the Ragged Schools, those institutions which attempted to reform and educate wayward and destitute boys, gathered in from the London streets.

It was a compromise, but Florence accepted. She went to London and was briefly on the teaching staff of the Ragged Schools. Her pupils she spoke of as "my little thieves of Westminster"; they interested her. But her efforts at accomplishing much of good among them was somewhat hampered by her promise to Mamma that she would never be seen in public without an older woman or a trusted servant to convoy her. The "little thieves" responded to Miss Nightingale's cordiality—but they balked when confronted by her chaperon. The proprieties were against Florence.

Yet the months were profitable, for she was storing up quantities of information on hospitals in general, and prevailing methods of nursing. All her discoveries verified what she'd been told by the Reverend Mr. Giffard, by Papa, Mamma, everyone. Hospitals almost without exception were dirty, unsystematic, unsanitary, literally pesthouses where disease ran rampant and epidemics occurred periodically. Nurses, underpaid, recruited from the lowest classes, were often of the charwoman type; they could not read or write; they drank, stole, cheated, neglected their patients.

But whose faults were these? They must be laid at the door of a society which permitted them! They could be corrected!

Florence filled notebooks with her jottings as to how the whole lamentable situation might be revolutionized. Her scrutiny was critical, her vision clear.

Perhaps some day she would be able to do more than theorize. She existed only for that day.

7

GLIMPSE OF A MISSION

The Bracebridges were traveling again, this time to Greece and Egypt, and nothing would do but that Florence go with them. Only think, Selina said, of all the hospitals they might see en route; and Charles added that, returning, they probably would stop in Germany.

"What do you say, Florence?" asked the Bracebridges.

She said yes. Perhaps she would have said it anyway, for the old feeling of despondency was upon her and she was particularly displeased with the drawing-room clock; but the word Germany had an unique sound, it meant the magic attraction of Kaiserswerth. Maybe now she could set foot into that land of her visioning.

So, in the autumn of 1849, Florence left Embley for another glimpse of foreign countries, and once more Parthe voiced the hope that her dear sister would find a measure of peace, saying that Egypt might do for Florence what Rome had failed to do.

Mrs. Nightingale made no comment at all. She was almost ready to acknowledge herself baffled by the peculiarities of her younger daughter.

As was her custom, Florence took a great many books with her: "learned books," Parthe called them; and, traveling, Florence bought others, which she constantly studied, storing up a vast fund of information on mythology, history and folklore. Egypt was a place of infinite wonders; and though she must deplore the backwardness of its people and their system of laws, she admired the beauty of its scenery and wrote to Parthe long letters about the temples and tombs and statues. Of course, she made the opportunity to look into any charitable institutions seen in passing; at Alexandria she spent a good deal of time with the nuns of St. Vincent de Paul in their well-kept schools and the visitors' rooms of their convents. She wrote to Parthe that there were only nineteen of these noble religieuses, but they did uncomplainingly the work of ninety. The desert also interested Florence; she liked going out alone to watch the sunset. She told Parthe that she enjoyed poking her nose into the small villages which skirted the expanses of untracked sand. "I want to see how these poor people live."

It was April when the travelers reached Greece, and a political crisis was in process; but this did not curtail Florence's sight-seeing. At Athens she viewed the Parthenon by moonlight and said that nothing earth or heaven could produce would ever excel its loveliness. One day in the ancient city, inside a ruined temple, she performed a small act of mercy, rescuing a baby owl which had fallen from its nest and been snatched up by a party of yelling (and, Florence thought, probably cruel) street urchins.

The Greek boys would not give their catch to the slender Englishwoman who demanded it; but they were willing to sell.

"A farthing," Florence said, holding out the coin. "A farthing for the owlet?"

The boys nodded and clutched at the money. The tiny

bird fluttered to the ground, and Florence stooped and picked it up and put it into her pocket.

Selina Bracebridge, who had witnessed the purchase, was amused. "What now, Florence?"

"This is Athena," Florence said, "and she is going with us all the way. I shall take her in my pocket as a present for Parthe, who will simply adore her."

"But you have a cicada as a traveling occupant of your pocket," said Selina.

"Yes. I suppose Athena may eat the cicada. Well, it will only be the consolidating of two pets in one, and just imagine how happy Athena will be at Embley where there are oceans of mice to be had for the hunting."

Laughing, Selina said she feared that Athena was too much an infant to hunt as yet; but Florence, nothing daunted, said that Mamma's butler could provide the mice until Athena had grown old enough to feed herself.

Perhaps Florence's keenest pleasure in Athens was the time spent with American missionaries who conducted a school and orphanage there. Yet this had its depressing side, too. How worthless seemed her own existence when contrasted with that of the women missionaries. The thought greatly vexed her, and Selina Bracebridge felt that an attack of fever which Florence suffered just then was largely brought on by worry over what Florence described as her uselessness.

"Well," Selina said, "we shall soon be in Berlin; the hospitals in the German capital will lure you from the doldrums."

Florence did not reply, but thought that she wouldn't tarry long in Berlin, however fascinating were the hospitals. The distance from Berlin to Kaiserswerth was comparatively short, and from the moment of leaving England, Kaiserswerth had been her real destination.

July 31, a memorable day indeed, for Florence was at last in the little Prussian town, actually entering Pastor Fliedner's famous establishment, meeting the good man face-to-face. She wrote in her diary: "I could hardly believe I was there. With the feeling with which a pilgrim first looks on the Kedron, I saw the Rhine, dearer to me than the Nile." She was to stay a fortnight; the question was, she thought, how best to crowd into that brief interval all the many things she wished to learn.

Pastor Fliedner made her welcome and showed her over his buildings which now comprised a hospital of a hundred beds, an infant school, a penitentiary with twelve inmates, an orphan asylum and a normal school where school mistresses were trained. There was also the training school for nurses, housing a hundred deaconesses. Florence was given a blue cotton habit and a white apron, the deaconess' uniform which she donned proudly.

It seemed that cleanliness was the first lesson in the Kaiserswerth course for beginners; they scrubbed the floors.

"But you, Miss Nightingale, will not wish to scrub," said Pastor Fliedner, with a glance for Florence's well-groomed white hands which had never known such hard work.

Certainly she wished to scrub! Fetching soap and water, she got down on the floor and, with his eyes humorously upon her, she wielded the heavy brush. Finishing, she stood up, brushed her dark hair from her forehead and waited for him to speak.

"A very dirty floor, Miss Nightingale," he said, "and you have scrubbed it until it shines."

She wielded the heavy brush

She smiled, feeling strangely close to tears, as if she had won some knightly accolade.

A busy fortnight; and oh, such a happy one. "The world here fills my life with interest," wrote Florence to her mother. "We have ten minutes for each of our meals, of which we have four. We get up at five; breakfast a quarter before six. The patients dine at eleven; the sisters at twelve. We drink tea, that is, a drink made of ground rye, between two and three, and sup at seven. Several evenings in the week we collect in the great hall for a Bible lesson." Herr Fliedner's wisdom and knowledge of human nature were, she said, inspiring. "This is life. Now I know what it is to love life."

She did not add the thought so often in her mind—that here birth, breeding, station were as nothing and all that mattered was the willingness to work for others. Had Florence Nightingale been the lowliest commoner, Pastor Fliedner could not have accepted her presence more calmly. The deaconesses were entirely matter-of-fact, cool, kind, impersonal in their attitude toward this newcomer. If there was about her some odd distinction as, in her blue and white garments, she moved among them, they disregarded it. To them she was just another woman wanting to help. In their humble and self-effacing service of God, through the least of His creatures, she found the fulfillment of a desire long thwarted.

Only a fortnight of this deeply satisfying happiness—and then she must rejoin the Bracebridges who had been at Düsseldorf. But the riches gained could never be taken from her, and she knew that some day she would come back. "Left Kaiserswerth," she recorded in the diary, "feeling so brave, as if nothing could ever vex me again."

With her friends she went to Ghent and in a week she was writing out in pamphlet form her observations of Pastor Fliedner's accomplishments. The Bracebridges said they would remain in Ghent until she had completed her manuscript.

"Shall you publish it, Florence?" asked Selina.

"Yes, anonymously, when I'm in England."

She had no intention of publicizing her own experiences, but she wanted British readers to know about *The Institution of Kaiserswerth on the Rhine*.

By the end of August she was at home.

As she had predicted, Parthe greeted the little owl Athena with exclamations of delight, and apparently Athena was just as enthusiastic about her new mistress and Embley—where the butler was most obliging at foraging for young mice.

"You have tamed Athena so nicely," said Parthe to Florence, "that she sleeps regularly in my lap and can balance herself on my shoulder when I walk around. And her manners are charming!"

But a few weeks later this opinion of Athena's manners had to be temporarily revised. One morning Parthe came downstairs wearing a ruffled cap over her hair—just an ordinary white cap, but Athena, perched on the mantel, did not like it. With a hoarse cry and a flap of wings, the owl darted toward Parthe, seized a ruffled edge of the cap in her beak and twitched it off. Then Athena retreated to the mantel, sulking.

"Oh, you naughty bird," said Parthe, laughing. "You seem not a bit afraid of me. Perhaps you're not afraid of anything."

But this was another opinion which had to be revised. Some guest at Embley had given Mrs. Nightingale a large china owl in which a lighted candle could be set, the glow of the candle illuminating the green glass eyes of the china figure. At her first glimpse of this imitation of herself, Athena was resentful and frightened, and when Parthe put her down in front of those glittering eyes, she uttered shrieks of protest and flew away to the protection of the darkened drawing-room.

"She is mostly very sweet-tempered, though," Parthe said, "and I shall write her biography."

So Parthe took pen and ink and paper and started the life story of *Athena—an Owlet from the Parthenon*.

Neither the author nor the subject of this lively biography ever dreamed that the manuscript would be preserved as a precious exhibit in the British Museum Library because of its connection with the life of Florence Nightingale.

8

FIRST FREEDOM

"I AM THIRTY, the age at which Christ began His mission. Now no more childish things, no more vain things, no more love, no more marriage. Now, Lord, let me only think of Thy will."

This and other equally serious notations in Florence's 1850 diary betrayed the period of her very worst discouragement. She seemed out of tune with all her surroundings, the gulf separating her from her mother and Parthe was ever wider, and even dear Papa was disturbed by her behavior, the things she said and did—the things she could not avoid saying and doing!

She had never known a happy time, she reflected, except at Rome and at Kaiserswerth. "It is not the unhappiness I mind; it is not indeed; but people can't be unhappy without making those about them so. The thoughts and feelings that I have now I can remember since I was six. A profession, a trade, a necessary occupation, something to employ all my faculties, I have always felt essential to me. The first thought I can remember, and the last, was nursing work; and in the absence of this, education work, but more the education of the bad than of the young."

After numerous drawing-room ordeals, she wrote, "Oh, weary days, O evenings that seem never to end!

For how many long years I have watched that clock and thought it would never reach the ten. And for twenty or thirty more to do this!" Occasionally she would contrive to put forward the hands of the torturing clock, and flee a few minutes early from the family circle. "O how am I to get through this day," she asked herself each morning, "to talk through all this day? Why do I wish to leave this world? God knows I do not expect a heaven beyond, but that He would set me down in St. Giles', at a Kaiserswerth, there to find my work and my salvation in my work."

Yet in the midst of despair, she had recurrent flashes of rebellion. "I must *take* some things, as few as I can, to enable me to live. I must take them, they will not be given me." Silently she was arming for the break which must surely come; she would abandon hope of ever obtaining her mother's or Parthe's understanding, but she would try to hurt them as little as possible.

As for marriage, upon which she turned her back, she had years ago ruled against that, and it irritated her that Mamma, and even Papa, should still speak of it. Florence argued that she was now too old to marry; but Mamma said Pshaw! she herself had been thirty when she married William Shore Nightingale, and then she had chosen a husband six years her junior. Why, thirty was just a good age for marrying, and there were plenty of young bachelors who would bask in Florence's smile.

"No," Florence said. "No, please don't think of it."

At length she convinced her father of her absolute rejection of marriage, and with him she made a quaint sort of compact. "If," she pointed out, "I haven't changed my views within two more years, if at thirty-two I am still single, I shall deserve the same privileges you would have granted a grown son. Won't you let me lead then the kind of life I want?"

Rather anxiously Mr. Nightingale said he supposed so, for he had also been listening to his sister Mai, who had interceded in Florence's behalf. Yes, and he would settle an allowance on his dear Flo, because she must not feel poverty-stricken.

Florence thanked him. The compact would not be put down on paper, she said. "But I should like to call in Selina Bracebridge, Papa, and have her know the terms, so that she can vouch for my freedom, if it should ever be questioned."

After that, Florence somehow looked upon Papa as an ally and talked to him of how she should train and prepare herself for the future. Mrs. Nightingale and Parthe were going to Carlsbad for three months—it would be a chance, Florence said, for her to go to Kaiserswerth again.

"Very well," said Mr. Nightingale.

But as might have been expected, his wife was vigorously opposed. Bad enough, cried Mrs. Nightingale, that Florence should have published that pamphlet on Pastor Fliedner's project; many Britishers had guessed its authorship. Now if it were known that Florence was again at Kaiserswerth, for such a long time, three whole months, actually nursing in the hospital—what on earth would people *say*? Mrs. Nightingale cared terribly what people said, while Florence cared not at all.

"Why need anyone know, Mamma? I'll not mention it, if you don't."

"Nothing could prevail upon *me* to mention it. You think we might conceal your going from *everybody*?"

"Like the shameful thing it is? Yes, Mamma," replied Florence.

But concealment was a snare and a delusion, and after Mrs. Nightingale had entrenched herself in Carlsbad with Parthe and was drinking the waters, a letter from Florence said that the secret was out. It was all quite mysterious and not Florence's doing, but a few people did know that she was at Kaiserswerth. The Sidney Herberts, who were at Homburg, had paid her a visit. Refusing to think that Mamma could be really offended, Florence wrote often and lovingly of how busy she was—"until yesterday I never had time even to send my clothes to the wash"—of how she had taken the convalescent boys for beautiful walks in the country; how she was strengthened in body and heart.

"I know you will be glad to hear this, dearest Mum."

Mrs. Nightingale sighed, and was not glad.

Finally Florence wrote a long letter, appealing for her "beloved people's" sympathy.

Mrs. Nightingale was mute, having no sympathy to extend.

"Don't fret, Mamma," said Parthe. "As well that Flo is having this little fling; we can the sooner get her back to Lea Hurst."

Mrs. Nightingale wrote to the Mohls in Paris that she hoped "our dear child Florence" would be able to apply all the fine learning she had been acquiring—"to do a little to make us better. Parthe is much too idle to help and too apt to be satisfied with things as they are."

This second stay at Kaiserswerth was a milestone in Florence's life, everything which followed must be dated from those three months. Though she went docilely back to the leisure of Lea Hurst and Embley, she was bolder, much more assured, biding her time and knowing that she would eventually escape. Many of her friends in London were persons of prestige and influence: George Eliot, Elizabeth Barrett Browning, Lady Lovelace, who was Lord Byron's daughter. All were impressed with her intelligence, her air of quiet competence. "An earnest, noble woman," they called her, believing that she would some day achieve her ambitions. Lady Lovelace wrote a poem about her, the last stanza of which would be remembered later as an example of amazing prediction:

> "In future years, in distant climes,
> Should war's dread strife its victims claim,
> Should pestilence, unchecked betimes,
> Strike more than sword, than cannon maim,
> He who then reads these truthful rhymes
> Will trace her progress to undying fame."

In hours which would otherwise have been empty, Florence endeavored to formulate her rather unorthodox religious creed, writing it all out and then discussing what she had written with Papa, who had a taste for such self-analysis. She modestly titled these essays *Suggestions for Thought*.

"Shall we have your book printed, Florence?" asked Papa.

"Not now," she said. "Perhaps in a few years I'll print it privately."

According to the compact, she was to be permitted at thirty-two to start on her career—the nature of which was still vague, though certainly it would be some type of nursing. Therefore in the summer of 1852 she told Papa that she was going to Paris, where she would study in various Catholic orphanages and hospitals. But her mother had by no means sanctioned the compact, nor had she conceded defeat.

"You cannot travel alone, Florence. That I will not have!"

Florence said that Hilary Bonham Carter was going with her; the two younger women would travel with Lady Augusta Bruce, who was a lady-in-waiting to the Queen.

"Ah?" murmured Mrs. Nightingale, and for a week or two said nothing more. But then there was news that Florence's Great-aunt Evans was very ill. The journey *must* be postponed. "You would not be disrespectful to Great-aunt Evans, Florence?"

No, the trip would be postponed, Florence said, until Great-aunt Evans had improved.

Mrs. Nightingale made the most of the delay. "My dear, if you will give up Paris entirely, you may have that little old house on your father's Derbyshire estate—Cromford Bridge House—and convert it into a small hospital all your own. Doesn't that tempt you?"

"No," Florence said. "A small hospital of my own is not what I want now, Mamma. I am really going to Paris."

She went—and a letter from Mrs. Nightingale recalled her. Grandmamma Shore was sick again at Tapton, she begged for Florence. "You must come home and nurse her in her last illness."

Wearily Florence returned to England, to Tapton. It was in truth Grandmamma Shore's last illness; she was ninety-five and after a few weeks she died.

"You will have to assist with the funeral, Florence!"

"Yes, Mamma, I will."

She assisted with the funeral, and then repacked her trunk.

"Florence, you're not going back to France?"

"Yes, Mamma."

Mrs. Nightingale dissolved in tears. "Oh, please, my dear!"

"I am sorry if it grieves you, but I can't change the plan. I shall visit the Mohls in Paris. You are fond of them. You can trust them to protect me."

Mrs. Nightingale said sadly that she had always thought charity began at home.

In Paris again, Florence methodically set about her study, inspecting infirmaries and convents, seeing the work done by those of Pastor Fliedner's deaconesses who were nursing in France. She collected reports and statistics and compiled statistics where none had been before; she observed Paris surgeons in their clinics, she read case histories in medical libraries.

Every day, from morning to night, she was out, glorying in her sense of liberation, of being answerable only to herself. She was all over the city, in every nook and cranny, scorning to take a cab, instead riding on the omnibuses, rubbing elbows with the commonest folk—and how distressed Mamma would have been to know! In the evenings she could, if she wished, attend the social functions to which her host and hostess, Professor and Madame Mohl, were constantly invited and eager to escort her.

It was in Paris, the spring of 1853, that she was offered her first post of responsibility. The letter was from London. At 8 Chandos Street, Cavendish Square, the Establishment for Gentlewomen during Illness, which provided a home for sick governesses and other invalids or superannuated ladies of the "gentlewomen" class, was in need of a new superintendent. Miss Nightingale had been recommended. Would she accept?

Well, not at once. "It isn't precisely what I've wanted," Florence said to Madame Mohl, "but can I afford to be too critical?"

"I think you should take it," said Madame Mohl.

"Yes, so do I. I shall send a letter of acceptance."

The Establishment for Gentlewomen! How vividly Florence would remember her year there. Mr. Sidney Herbert was on the board, probably it was he who had proposed Florence's name—and had all the other board members been as level-headed as was Mr. Herbert, the new superintendent might have been spared much quibbling. But, alas, Florence found herself saddled with a committee of directors, most of whom were ladies of wealth and exalted rank looking jealously on their pet charity and suspiciously at Miss Nightingale.

"The Society of Fashionable Asses." That was the nickname Florence had for the committee; and in letters to Madame Mohl she told, with the sharpness and sarcasm which often tinged her pen, how she coped with them, skirmishing to get the upper hand.

"If you knew what the 'fashionable asses' have been doing, their 'offs' and their 'ons,' poor fools! There are no surgeon students nor improper patients at all, which is, of course, a great recommendation in the eyes of the Proper. The patients, or rather the Impatients, for I know what it is to nurse sick ladies, are all pay patients, poor friendless folk in London. I am to have the choosing of the house, the appointment of the Chaplain and the management of the funds as the F. S. A. are *at present* minded. But Isaiah himself could not prophesy how they will be minded at 8 o'clock this evening."

"The choosing of the house?" That meant the immediate moving of the institution from Chandos Street to Harley Street, and was an initial victory for Florence, who had insisted upon enlarged quarters. In ten days she accomplished the tremendous undertaking. But once installed at the Harley Street address, she faced other problems which bobbed up with astonishing rapidity.

A nursing home, Florence said, must have modern conveniences, such as bells ringing to summon the nurses, and an elevator, "a lift, in order that the nurse might not be merely a pair of legs." The committee had to be persuaded to these innovations, for there had been no bells or lift in Chandos Street.

Then Florence said that the rule forbidding the superintendent to walk with the doctors on their rounds must be revoked. Since she had been hired to assume full charge of the building, she would demand access to every part of it—yes, even to the operating room when surgery was in progress. The ladies of the committee were horrified. Only after debate would they assent, and then grudgingly.

But the knottiest problem concerned religion. The institution was Protestant, always had been, and must remain so. No Catholic patients, said the committee, could be admitted.

Miss Nightingale was instantly resentful. If that was the spirit of the place, she would have nothing to do with it—nothing! She would politely wish the committee good morning and withdraw. This issue was threshed out at prodigious length, while Florence stood firm.

Finally the committee agreed to lower the bars to Catholic patients.

"I shall take in Jews too," said Florence, who had no tolerance for any intolerance.

The committee bowed to her imperious edict

The committee groaned. "Not Jews?"

"Yes," said Florence, never budging an inch.

The committee bowed to her imperious edict.

Though frequently irritated, the new superintendent could laugh at her troubles. She seemed to have become a buffer between the "fashionable asses" and the staff of doctors—and out of favor with them all. But she learned to manipulate these factions, cleverly posing them one against the other, putting ideas into their heads, words into their mouths, and then letting them think that the ideas and the words had originated with themselves.

So, with somewhat the wiliness of the politician, she got things done, reducing friction to a minimum and seeking no credit or praise. The institution soon ran smoothly, and the inmates loved their efficient Miss Nightingale.

Florence often wrote to her father, telling him of her work; at his request, she sent the letters to Mr. Nightingale's London club. She did not correspond with her mother or Parthe, for the fact was that relations with them were more strained than ever. Mrs. Nightingale had hated the thought of Flo's being a superintendent—it was really dreadful! But if Florence just *would* be so queer, at least she could live with her family when the Nightingales came to London for the season. How much more comfortable she would be in a nice hotel than in that old asylum, or whatever it was.

Florence said no. At long, long last she was independent; the break she had made was "not likely to be repented of or reconsidered."

"But will you not come to Lea Hurst for a vacation this summer, Flo?" implored Parthe.

Florence said yes, and went for a few days in August, cutting short her holiday because of hearing that an epidemic of cholera threatened London. Hastening back to Harley Street, she looked out not only for her governesses but also for many cholera patients in the Middlesex Hospital. The epidemic subsided in the early autumn—and then it was that the interest of all London, and all England, and a great portion of the wide world centered suddenly upon incidents of the Crimean War, and Florence Nightingale heard the call of her particular and magnificent destiny.

9

THE CALL TO SERVICE

THE WAR WAS ONE which most observers (and eminent English historians among them) would have great difficulty explaining and justifying. The surface cause was Russia's policy of expansion and the wish of England to join with France in preventing the further encroachment of the Czar's armies upon Turkish territory. But the hidden and real cause was the age-old fear of nations that another nation may surpass it in power and conquest. In 1853 Russia had mobilized and occupied the portion of Turkey lying north of the Danube River; Russia had attacked and destroyed a Turkish squadron—very daringly, within sight of French and British warships stationed in the Bosporus. These acts seemed a challenge which England and France must answer with a declaration of war.

The campaigns which followed, on land and sea, were notable chiefly for their lack of military skill, the blundering of officials, the senseless sacrifice of troops and, finally, a peace in which it was realized that little of worth had been accomplished.

Early in 1854, to defend Turkey, England and France had dispatched an expeditionary force to Varna, a port on the Black Sea, fifty-seven thousand men, the largest body of troops ever sent to do battle on foreign soil.

When Russia saw this force, she edged away, dodging the fight. At about the same time, it became evident that the English and French soldiers must not be left at Varna because cholera raged there. Then the defending armies were somehow obliged to attack, instead. An invasion of the Crimean peninsula was decided upon, and Lord Raglan went out from England to command the Queen's men.

The first major engagement of the war was the Battle of Alma, which occurred September 20, 1854, six days after the landing of the British and French in the Crimea, and it was the result of this battle which so abruptly shocked England to what was happening in that far-off area—where, until now, things had seemed so slow, so uneventful and almost dull. Her Majesty's troops had been victorious; that is, they had fought with their usual brilliance and had taken their objective—but at a terrible cost! Even while England exulted in news of the triumph, the casualty lists began to arrive. So many brave men killed or wounded! Even worse were the reports of soldiers dying out there, dying by the hundreds, dying of neglect, because proper care was denied them, because medical supplies, good food, doctors and nurses had not been provided in sufficient amount—had, in fact, scarcely been provided at all!

William Howard Russell had gone to the Crimea as "special correspondent" for the London *Times*. He was an able newspaperman, his present mission was a novel one, for until he undertook the task, a "special correspondent" with an army in the field was a thing unknown. Mr. Russell with his own eyes had seen the Battle of Alma and its sad aftermath of needless suffering; he wrote back uncensored letters to the *Times*, which when printed made the country gasp with horror and remorse.

"It is with feelings of surprise and anger that the public will learn that no sufficient preparations have been made

Soldiers were dying of neglect

for the proper care of the wounded," wrote Mr. Russell. "Not only are there not sufficient surgeons—that, it might be urged, was unavoidable; not only are there no dressers and nurses—that might be a defect of system for which no one is to blame; but what will be said when it is known that there is not even linen to make bandages for the wounded?"

The Turks had turned over to the British a huge building in Scutari, which was a suburb of Constantinople, a building called the Barrack Hospital and here the wounded were being housed—as many of them, anyway, as survived the voyage from the Crimea to Turkey. But, mostly, the wounded died during the three hundred mile trip across the Black Sea, "expiring in agony," Mr. Russell said, "unheeded and shaken off, though catching desperately at the surgeon whenever he makes his rounds through the fetid ship." Those who lived to reach Scutari and the Barrack Hospital found themselves, with week-old wounds never touched by the hand of a medical man, shunted rudely into a cold, bare, echoing place where, as Mr. Russell said, "the commonest appliances of a workhouse sick ward are wanting," where "the men must die through the medical staff of the British army having forgotten that old rags are necessary for the dressing of wounds."

Mr. Russell had not misjudged the reaction of his public. His letters, appearing every day, were sensational, instantly arousing a storm of questions as to why these conditions prevailed. No nurses? Well, only a handful of very old pensioners, feeble old fellows who had been sent as an "ambulance corps," and were so far past the age for usefulness that they died themselves or fell sick and needed nursing. No hospital supplies? None, said Mr. Russell emphatically. "For all I can observe, these men die without the least effort being made to save them. There they lie, just as they were let down on the ground by their poor comrades, who brought them on their backs from the camp with the greatest tenderness, but who are not allowed to remain with them. The sick seem to be tended by the sick, and the dying by the dying."

Amid general indignation and excitement on the part of his readers, Mr. Russell's letters continued, "It is now pouring rain, the skies are black as ink, the wind is howling. Our men have not either warm or waterproof clothing . . . not a soul seems to care for their comfort, or even for their lives. These are hard truths, but the people of England must hear them. They must know that the wretched beggar who wanders about the streets of London leads the life of a prince compared with the British soldiers who are fighting out here for their country."

Of course, something must be done! At once! But what?

Mr. Russell drew a sharp contrast between his government and the French, "Their medical arrangements are extremely good, their surgeons more numerous, and they have the help of the Sisters of Charity who have accompanied the expedition. These devoted women are excellent nurses."

Well, why had not England some Sisters of Charity? The question had its first public asking in the *Times* of October 14. "There are numbers of ablebodied and tender-hearted Englishwomen who would joyfully and with alacrity go out to devote themselves to nursing the sick and wounded if they could be associated for that purpose and placed under proper protection." Once thrust forward, the query resounded the length and breadth of the British Isles. "*If nurses are needed, why can't we send them?*"

Then, in the minds of a few persons, a more explicit suggestion stirred. Henry Edward Manning (afterward Cardinal) wrote to the Bishop of Southwark to see if any sisters could be found for the East. "Why," said he, "will not Florence Nightingale give herself to this great work?" Already Lady Maria Forester had spoken to Miss Nightingale, if she would take out three nurses to Scutari, Lady Maria would pay all expenses of the group.

Perhaps Florence had been the very first to entertain this wonderful idea. After the most serious thought for the practical angles involved, she wrote from Harley Street on October 14 to Mrs. Sidney Herbert, her intimate friend whom she addressed as "My dearest," expressing her wish to go to Turkey, requesting Mrs. Herbert to lay the matter before her husband. There would be, Florence knew, many details to be smoothed out, permissions, grants of authority, official consents and credentials to be obtained—but she was anxious, indeed determined, to go, whether sponsored by the government or as a private agent, because "I do believe that we may be of use to the wounded wretches."

This letter to Elizabeth Herbert crossed in the mails a letter which Sidney Herbert had posted to Florence from Bournemouth, October 15, where he was spending the Sunday. Knowing nothing of Florence's inclinations, but pondering deeply, Mr. Herbert had come to the conclusion that there was just one way to remedy the lamentable situation. Nurses must be sent, they must be strictly supervised and directed—and Miss Nightingale was the only person in England who would be capable of organizing and superintending such a scheme.

His letter was very long and reasoned, for he had deliberated over every phase of it. He was quite aware that what he asked was amazing, even revolutionary— "none but male nurses having ever been admitted to military hospitals." He felt that Mr. Russell's stories were perhaps a bit exaggerated, for medical stores had been shipped to the Crimea in profusion, "by the *ton* weight;" and doctors had gone in the proportion of one to every ninety-five men. As to what had become of these tons of stores, these doctors, he could not surmise, but he was hopeful of their arrival. Still, the crying need was for nurses.

"I do not say one word to press you. You can judge for yourself which of conflicting or incompatible duties is the first, or the highest; but I must not conceal from you that I think upon your decision will depend the ultimate success or failure of the plan. Your own personal qualities, your knowledge and your power of administration, and among greater things your rank and position in Society give you the advantages in such a work which no other person possesses."

The government, Mr. Herbert said, would stanchly co-operate, the entire medical staff would be sworn to fullest assistance, everything requisite to the mission would be furnished in unlimited abundance. "I know you will come to a wise decision. God grant it may be in accordance with my hopes!"

Florence received Sidney Herbert's letter one day and, so swiftly did events trend, the very next day it was proclaimed from the War Office that Miss Nightingale, "a lady with greater practical experience of hospital administration and treatment than any other lady in the country," had been appointed by the Government as Superintendent of Nurses at Scutari, and had begun her work of organization as a preface to sailing for Turkey.

"Who is Florence Nightingale?"
That was now the question. Through the years, through

the prominence of her family, Florence had made a wide circle of friends, but she had never been a public figure. Overnight she had become the most talked-of person in England, the focus for national attention, her name on everyone's lips.

"Who *is* she? Tell us something *about* our heroine!"

Well, the newspapers could do that, and they got their information from the most reliable sources—from Mrs. Nightingale and from Parthe. Suddenly all conflict and stress in what had been at best an unsatisfactory relationship was forgotten; with pride Mamma and Parthe had spoken of the honor bestowed upon Florence, and had even displayed the War Office's letter to inquiring reporters. Mamma declared that she and Mr. Nightingale were ducks who had miraculously hatched a swan. Parthe said of dear Flo that "the way in which all things have tended to and fitted her for this is so very remarkable that one cannot but believe she was intended for it."

The *Examiner* and then the *Times* printed articles. Miss Nightingale was "a young lady of singular endowments, both natural and acquired. In a knowledge of the ancient languages and of the higher branches of mathematics, in general art, science and literature, her attainments are extraordinary. There is scarcely a modern language which she does not understand, and she speaks French, German and Italian as fluently as her native English. She has visited and studied all the various nations of Europe and has ascended the Nile to its remotest cataract. Young (about the age of our Queen), graceful, feminine, rich, popular, she holds a singularly gentle and persuasive influence over all with whom she comes in contact. Her friends and acquaintances are of all classes and persuasions, but her happiest place is at home, in the centre of a very large band of accomplished relatives, and in simplest obedience to her admiring parents."

Florence, if she read the articles, must have smiled rather ironically. Her happiest place at home? Her simple obedience to admiring parents? Picturesque, yes; but hardly exact. The newspapers, in a well-meant flood of enthusiasm, persisted in dwelling upon the sacrifice made by this charming and sensitive young lady, with her background of exalted birth and breeding, how she was forsaking assemblies, lectures, concerts, exhibitions and all the social pleasures of taste and intellect to which she was accustomed. Sacrifice? Absurd! thought Florence. The only thing in life she had ever desired was service of just the kind which was now at hand. It was what a little girl in the chapel at Lea Hurst had dreamed of, it was the very stuff of dreams and long suppressed yearnings.

It was opportunity—at last! And she had seized it!

10

JOURNEY AND ARRIVAL

"The selection of nurses, the finding of women equal to a task full of horrors and requiring, besides knowledge and good will, great energy and great courage, will be very difficult," Sidney Herbert had said to Florence.

He was quite right. There were but a few days for this business; even in the moment of her appointment Florence had shouldered a tremendous burden.

Her temporary headquarters were at Mr. Herbert's house, 49 Belgrave Square. An appeal for volunteers had gone forth, and here Florence interviewed all applicants. She was aided by Mrs. Bracebridge and another friend, Miss Mary Stanley; and often Parthe was present, sorting and packaging the vast quantities of knitted socks and shirts, the linen for bandages, which poured in from contributors throughout the Kingdom.

Parthe marveled at her sister's restrained manner. "In the midst of all this furious tumult and haste, you are calm as a May morning, Flo! You behave as if you were going, not to war, but just out for a walk in the park!"

Florence smiled. "What is there to be perturbed about?"

"Well, the War Office, the Military Medical Board, and half the nurses in London are waiting their turn to consult with you."

"Everything is moving nicely though, Pop—thanks to

my helpers. And everyone is so kind, rallying to a national emergency."

"Rallying to *you*," said Parthe generously. "Because you have fired the public's imagination as it never was fired before!"

Florence would have had to be much less clever than she was, not to see truth in this statement, and her heart was touched by the loyalty she encountered everywhere. Mr. and Mrs. Herbert were unwavering in her support; the Bracebridges had said they were going to Scutari, too; Uncle Sam Smith declared he would go as far as Marseilles; Aunt Mai had promised to respond to any demand Florence might make upon her time and effort. The people in the London streets were positive that Miss Nightingale was a saint who would soon have all the wounded British soldiers up and on their feet again. Nothing was too good for Miss Nightingale! Nothing was good *enough*!

Florence had thought of taking nineteen nurses with her, a party of twenty in all; but Mr. Herbert said there should be more. Forty was the number agreed upon, and now Florence must enroll them. She did not lack material; as Parthe had said, half the nurses in London seemed to be clamoring at the gates, besides scores of other women who had never before in their lives given a thought to nursing. But much of this material fell short of the standards Florence had set; the applicants must be carefully examined and weeded out, for she would have only the best.

In a small, quiet room of Mr. Herbert's house, she talked long and gravely with each volunteer.

"If," said Miss Mary Stanley, "anybody is disposed to criticize the nurses Florence accepts, I wish that person could see those she turns away. I didn't know there *were* such women! Money is what they're after, the only inducement. Just one has said she wanted to go because of a noble motive."

Parthe's comment was that Florence would choose well. "She'll not be concerned about their religions or their stations in society. Roman Catholics, Anglicans, Presbyterians—they are all the same to her; and she would every bit as soon have women of the laboring class as a lot of duchesses. What she desires is a group including all shades of opinion—just so the members will work together harmoniously and love God."

Meanwhile, Florence was not signing on her list the names of any duchesses; and several of the names sounded, and were, distinctly commonplace. When she found that further investigation would be but a waste of time, she notified Mr. Herbert of the list's closing. She had thirty-eight nurses and would see no more volunteers. For the most part, the thirty-eight were professionals, either Roman Catholics or Anglican nuns who were trained for their task.

Special Correspondent Russell had not ceased to send in his pitiful stories of the situation at Scutari, which seemed to go from bad to worse, and Florence felt that delay would be fatal. She had her own light luggage assembled, the Bracebridges and Mr. Sam Smith were ready, the accepted nurses anxious to be off. On October 21, the War Office announced that Miss Nightingale and her party would start that evening from London and would sail October 27 from Marseilles on the *Vectis*.

Only a few people came to bid the expedition farewell. Mamma and Papa were there, Parthe, the Herberts, a dozen or so of Florence's dearest friends. A still, cool autumn night, and everyone rather silent, eyes fixed on the expedition's leader, who stood tall, dignified and self-confident, well-groomed and dressed with simple elegance. As the train whistled a warning and good-byes were said, Florence kissed her parents and her sister and climbed aboard. She shed no tears, but smiled and waved her gloved hand.

She was very happy.

Mr. Sam Smith, writing home, said it probably was to be expected that confusions should arise, many arrangements be made "to keep forty in good humour." But Flo was most diplomatic with her flock. "She bears all wonderfully, winning everybody." Wherever she appeared, said Mr. Smith, there was nothing but admiration from high and low; the nurses already were quite in love with her and, because of her, were liking the journey.

When the steam packet on which they crossed the Channel came into the Boulogne harbor on the morning of October 22, the quay was thronged, for rumor of Miss Nightingale and her nurses had reached France and the populace of Boulogne wished to see and greet them. The scene was one of noise and gay color, and as Florence stepped ashore, she was surrounded by peasantwomen wearing crimson petticoats, bright kerchiefs and snowy caps like white-winged birds.

"Welcome, welcome, *les soeurs anglaises!*"

In a frenzy of excitement and joy, they surged forward, cheering these brave souls who were going out, as their own nurses had done, to a mission of mercy. Then other figures, husky, black-coated, yet feminine were pushing toward the travelers, snatching up the English bags, boxes and trunks, which they carried up the slope.

The women porters of Boulogne, and refusing to let Florence pay them, spurning almost with violence the fee she held out to them. "*Non!* You owe nothing. *Vive les soeurs!*"

Peasants and porters in attendance, the English party went to a hotel, where the landlord, the waitresses and chambermaids would not be paid or tipped, and the cheering was unabated. When the train left for Paris, Florence looked from her window at the grinning, gesticulating crowd.

"*Au 'voir!* Godspeed!"

There was a brief rest at Paris, then on to Marseilles. Florence purchased a great amount of stores in the French port. Though Sidney Herbert thought surely the supplies sent out from London would now be waiting at Constantinople, and though Dr. Andrew Smith, head of the Army Medical Department had said stoutly (and a little angrily) that the troops at Scutari lacked for nothing—nothing at all!—Florence had her doubts. Better to be on the safe side; and she had money with which to buy the things, food, beds, blankets, mattresses, medicines; her own money and sums donated by many patriotic Britishers.

The *Vectis* sailed as scheduled, October 27. It was a small, old-fashioned, uncomfortable vessel, but seaworthy, riding out storms, plowing doggedly through mountainous waves. Only a half-dozen of Florence's nurses had ever voyaged before; everybody else was frightened and seasick. Florence herself, normally a good sailor, felt none too well. In a letter to her parents and Parthe ("Dearest People") she told of her relief when, November 4, the ship dropped anchor at Constantinople:

"At six o'clock yesterday I staggered on deck to look at the plains of Troy, the tomb of Achilles, the mouths of the Scamander, the little harbour of Tenedos, between which and the main shore our *Vectis*, with stewards' cabins and galley torn away, blustering, creaking, shrieking, rushed on her way. We reached Constantinople this morn in a thick and heavy rain. Bad news from Balaclava. You will hear the awful wreck of our poor cavalry, four hundred wounded, arriving at this moment for us to nurse. (Later) Just starting for Scutari. We are to be housed in the hospital this very afternoon. Everybody is most kind. The wounded are, I believe, to be placed under our care. They are landing them now."

Finishing her letter, Florence went up again on deck, standing at the rail, scanning all that was visible of Constantinople. The harbor, known as the Golden Horn, was long and narrow, with the city curled around it, a city so large that it overflowed in three directions. Here, on twin banks of the Horn, were Stamboul and Galata; vast, uneven expanses of roofs and spires and minarets which thrust upward through the clinging gray mist of a chill, wet day. There, facing the Bosporus, lay Scutari, the Silver City which the Greeks had venerated, studded and wreathed with cypress trees, surmounted by domed hills; and, topping the tallest hill, the immense yellow quadrangle of the Barrack Hospital, with its square towers on four corners.

Gazing at that distant splotch of yellow among the hazy, drifting curtains of the mist, Florence thought of it as her domain, her sphere, toward which God had shown her the long, devious path. She was not afraid— no, her spirit did not falter, but was invincible as a blade of polished steel.

They were still landing the Balaclava wounded, a sorrowful procession straggling past below the rail of the *Vectis*. The world knew now what that battle had been.

The British attack upon the Russians' impregnable fortifications at Sevastopol, the charge of the Light Cavalry Brigade. With incredible gallantry, with the most foolhardy judgment, the Brigade had struck full-tilt, riding straight at the Russian artillery which was lined up, waiting, cannon yawning—and plenty of ammunition. The episode was as spectacular and fantastic as any ever to be chronicled in English military annals. It was an intrepid mass suicide which Alfred, Lord Tennyson would celebrate in verse. The Brigade had galloped, the Russian guns boomed—the Light Cavalry was slashed to ribbons, crushed, reduced to this litter of broken bodies carried on canvas stretchers.

> "Stormed at with shot and shell,
> Boldly they rode and well;
> Into the jaws of Death,
> Into the mouth of Hell,
> Rode the six hundred."

"Miss Nightingale?"

Florence turned from her thoughts of Balaclava's immortal slaughter. One of the younger nurses was behind her, a girl with pink cheeks and eager eyes.

"Miss Nightingale, when we do disembark, I hope there won't be any more waiting around. I hope we can go right to our work of tending those poor fellows."

"The strongest of you," Florence said grimly, "will be wanted at the washtub." (They must realize, she added to herself, that no sentimentalism, no romantic nonsense would soften the work. It would be hard, bitterly hard.)

Another hour, and the English party was put ashore to walk the steep quarter-mile road to the hospital. Miss Nightingale went first, marching into the building's cen-

"The English nurse has come"

tral courtyard which was so gigantic that twelve thousand men had been known to drill there at one time. Just through the doorway, she stopped.

The courtyard held such filth as could not have been imagined, the rotting carcass of an army mule, piles of amputated human arms and legs flung out the windows onto the pavement, which ran with blood.

Florence stopped—and called to a soldier orderly.

"This debris must be hauled away and buried."

The orderly paused, detecting a tone of command.

"This courtyard must be cleaned, the pavement scrubbed. *Immediately!*"

"Y-yes, ma'am."

On a cot inside the entrance, Sir Alexander Montgomery Moore, a British officer, had been trying to sleep and forget his aching wounds. The voices in the courtyard had wakened him.

"I think," said Sir Alexander to his nearest neighbor, "that the English nurse has come."

The neighbor nodded a head swathed with dirty rags. "It's Miss Florence Nightingale. She has come."

11
A LADY WITH A LAMP

FLORENCE OPENED THE DOOR and stepped out upon the upper gallery which stretched along three sides of the

She stepped out upon the upper gallery

building. She set down her lamp in the shelter of a pillar and pulled up the hood of her cape. The night was black, the sky mantled with low-hanging clouds pricked by an occasional star. The air was fresh and moist; she breathed it deeply and gratefully.

What a day this had been! Well, now it was behind her; there would be a meager interval to sleep—if she could. Then another day just as gruelling. She had no illusions about the days. She would have to take them as they came, one at a time, and do her best with them.

Neither had she illusions about the hospital. Rather, the two hospitals, for she had found that the General Hospital in Constantinople was also to be under her supervision. She must assign a few of her small nursing band to the General. She herself would stay here at the Barrack, keeping with her the more experienced women. Mrs. Drake was certainly a treasure, and Mrs. Roberts worth her weight in gold!

The Barrack, she knew now, after exploration, was simply that—a barrack, transformed to a hospital merely by the slapping on of a coat of whitewash. Its maximum capacity was 2,434 human beings and Balaclava had crowded it to the guards. Beneath these imposing yellow walls were cesspools and open sewers. The plumbing was woefully deficient—in fact, there was scarcely any plumbing at all, and no proper ventilation. The foulness of the interior atmosphere defied description—such a conglomeration of horrid smells! Rats and mice lived in the halls, vermin in the defective flooring. Yes, vermin crawled everywhere.

It was to this terrible place that soldiers, wounded in battle, were brought after a week-long voyage of neglect and suffering. Here they were unloaded, their garments stiff with drying gore, unloaded without ceremony, carried in and deposited, as if they had no more life in them than had that carcass of the army mule; most of them were laid on the bare floor because the few beds were occupied.

Wryly smiling, Florence remembered Sidney Herbert's vain hope that supplies would have arrived—and Dr. Andrew Smith's positive statement that nothing was wanting at Scutari.

Nothing? Florence could have made quite a memorandum of what was wanting. Hospital furniture, to start with, even the most ordinary and necessary pieces of furniture; beds, tables, chairs. After that, basins, buckets for water, soap, towels; and some candlesticks instead of the empty beer bottles now in use. Mattresses—oh, how she wished for mattresses! Mops, brooms, disinfectants, scrubbing brushes. "Scrub this courtyard," she had told the orderly. But there was not a scrubbing brush to be had anywhere. Not one. "I shall write to London for three hundred brushes," she thought. "It is not too many. Later I shall ask for more."

What about knives, forks, spoons, clean linen, hospital clothing? These men had no nightgowns. None at all. They lay in their dirty underwear and shirts, garments which were never washed. "Isn't clothing ever *laundered*?" she had demanded.

"Well," someone had said, "it is—at the rate of six shirts a month."

"You mean, six shirts a month for each man?"

"Oh, no, six shirts for *all* the men."

Hundreds, thousands of sick and dying men, and a monthly laundry of six shirts!

What about cotton, gauze, new bandages—bedpans?

Florence would have liked to present Dr. Smith with her memorandum of *essentials*, things needed now, just on the most cursory inspection, because you cannot manage a hospital without such things.

"Tomorrow," she said to herself, "I shall have the supplies I bought in Marseilles. How I wish I'd bought twice, ten times, as much! But, at least, tomorrow I shall have *some* supplies."

She thought back over the day, from the moment in which she had entered here. What had she done? First, there had been the parceling out of quarters, a vexing business because, though the Barrack was so large, it was now so full. One room, more spacious than the rest, was given to all the non-sectarian nurses as a dormitory; one medium-sized room was shared by the ten Roman Catholic nuns; the eight Anglican sisters had a somewhat smaller room. Something very small indeed, a cubbyhole, Florence had kept for herself and Mrs. Bracebridge. Charles Bracebridge and a young man who acted as Miss Nightingale's courier would sleep on divans in what was called the "sitting-room."

It did not really matter, Florence thought, if the members of her party were cramped and uncomfortable; they would be seldom in their rooms. But she was distressed for another reason. In the wards and the corridors, fever patients were thrown together with men who had not yet caught the fever.

"There should be separate areas for contagious cases. I shall rent a house somewhere nearby and move the fever patients into it."

This she would do with her own money. Silently she thanked Papa for the liberal allowance he had settled upon her; it would make possible many things which otherwise would have been impossible. Conceivably, her allowance from Papa might save many lives.

When the nurses had put down bags and boxes in their rooms, and changed into their uniforms and aprons, Miss Nightingale took them into the kitchen to prepare food for the sick men, some of whom were almost dead of starvation. The kitchen was equipped with huge kettles for boiling meat and vegetables; but no meat or vegetables were in the larder. There was very little foodstuff to cook that day. Well, a good store had been purchased in Marseilles and soon would be delivered from the harbour, and even now quantities of tea, rice, arrowroot, jellies for invalid diet were available—these Florence had brought in her luggage, never letting them get beyond reach.

After the patients were fed, the routine of wound-dressing began. Forty-five doctors comprised the medical staff, working in shifts, but the dressings to be done were unnumbered. Following after one of the surgeons, Florence herself attended to sixty-two patients, and then went from ward to ward, supervising, directing her subordinates. The surgeons were, as usual, amputating—not in a surgery or operating room; there was no such thing—but right out in the corridors, in plain view of everybody.

"I shall get a screen for this," Florence thought. "We must have a screen. The poor fellow who is to be operated on next is not helped by seeing his comrade die under the knife."

Soon, whenever she had an hour, she must write out some rules for the nurses. She intended that they must be strictly disciplined, for without discipline the best results could not be attained. The nurses must recognize and defer to her authority. She was their leader and she would be obeyed. But to enforce discipline, she would have to retain their affection and respect. They trusted her now; she must never do anything to lose their trust.

She hoped, too, to impress the doctors with her authority. Most of them she had liked in the first meeting. Most of them, she said to herself, were angels. A few were devils, heavy-handed men insensitive to the anguish of their patients. But all, she knew, were looking skeptically at Miss Nightingale, wondering what sort of person she was. It was an experiment, this admitting of women to a military hospital. She must convince them that it was a successful experiment.

There would be, she feared, some whom she could never convince, hidebound cynics, prejudiced medical men who would think of her as the rankest interloper and cry out against a government which would allow such absurdity—who might even be jealous of the Lady-in-Chief, which was the title Mr. Sidney Herbert had conferred upon her. But these reactionaries she must learn to ignore.

The night was darker now, every star obscured, rain was falling and the wind tugged at her skirts. She picked up the lamp and holding it before her, shielding the glow with her hand, she went through the door into the corridor, walking very softly and cautiously, making her way between the rows of huddled forms lying on the floor, seeing her shadow, tall and distorted, moving along the wall.

At the far end of the corridor, a young corporal, scarcely more than a boy, startled up from fitful napping and the incessant pain which had made him delirious. His eyes widened, and he lifted his battered body, propped himself on an elbow, staring incredulous.

"What—what's that?" he muttered hoarsely. "Why, it's a *lady!* A lady with a lamp!"

Then, strangely solaced, he slumped down again and slept.

12

CRIMEAN DAYS

THE BATTLE OF Inkerman occurred November 5, 1854.

In all the years which followed, the date would stand forth clearly in Florence Nightingale's memory because of what it had meant to her that year, at Scutari. Scarcely had she established the beginnings of some sort of routine, scarcely had she made a plan, when all was swept away with the influx of new patients.

There was but a half-hour's notice. "Get ready! More wounded are coming!" Then they were being borne in, five hundred and ten poor creatures, fallen before the Russian guns.

It was a time of frantic hurrying in the Barrack's corridors. Except for the Lady-in-Chief's poise, it would have been pandemonium. She refused to be dismayed. Did it seem that these men could not be accommodated? Well, they *must* be accommodated. Within eight hours, more than five hundred mattresses had somehow been pieced together, stuffed with straw, sewed up and placed on the floor; the men lying on the mattresses had been washed, their wounds had been dressed.

"A miracle!" said one of the nurses to Miss Nightingale. "We couldn't have done better in a London hospital."

Florence shrugged. "My opinion of London hospitals has never been high, but the worst of them is a garden of flowers compared to this."

Beneath an outward calm, she was worried, knowing that the voyage from the battle site, over unusually rough seas, had been a nightmare for the injured. The Turkish soldiers delegated as stretcher-bearers seemed needlessly callous and unfeeling—"the Turks, the very men for whom we are fighting!" Twenty-four of the wounded died during the day of their arrival. Dysentery, an implacable foe, had appeared in several of the wards.

Next day the surgeons performed hundreds of operations—for which no anesthetic was given. Though Sir John Hall, principal medical officer of the British Crimean forces, knew of this drug, its use was still in the experimental stages, and he did not favor it in cases of severe shock from gunshot wounds. Few men so disabled could survive the after-effects of chloroform, he said, and he would not risk losing patients in that way. Assisting the surgeons, Florence was astonished at the unshrinking heroism of the men. "It is really superhuman. We are steeped up to our necks in blood, yet they die or are cut up without a complaint!"

She wrote to a London acquaintance, "We have now *four miles* of beds, and not eighteen inches apart."

Yet at the end of that second day, she could reflect upon the good to be found even in the midst of appalling horrors. "I can truly say, like St. Peter, 'It is good for us to be here'—though I doubt whether if St. Peter had been here, he would have said so." Going her nightly rounds, she heard no groans, no murmurs of protest. Stoically, the men looked up at her, some of them smiled. "I was dreaming of my friends at home, ma'am." "I was dreaming of my mother."

The third day was a little bit easier and again Florence felt that she might eventually get the situation under control. But then the *Andes* made port with a ghastly freight.

The courier brought the word. "Five hundred and forty casualties. And two more ships loading at the Crimea."

Could they be housed in the Barrack? Yes, Florence said, there or in the General Hospital. "Let no soldier be told that we cannot take him in."

"But some Russian wounded are among the lot."

"We'll take in the Russians, too."

A dreadful pouring-in of shattered, mutilated men from the *Andes,* the other two vessels! Too many to be cared for, the doctors said; the more hopeful cases would have to be separated from those which seemed desperate. This weeding-out process was not to Miss Nightingale's liking. A life was a life; so long as a single breath animated a body, no effort should be spared.

"The five poor fellows lying in that corner, Sir John—can nothing be done for them?"

"Nothing, I fear."

"May I *try*?"

"Certainly. Try, if you will. It is futility."

She tried. Through the bleak hours between midnight and dawn, she worked over the five, feeding them with a spoon, bathing them, praying that they might gain a little strength. In the morning the surgeon examined them.

"They are in fair shape to be operated upon now."

"No longer hopeless cases?"

The surgeon shook his head. "I believe they may be saved."

There were additional troubles with which she must struggle. A tower room adjoining the nurses' quarters had been fitted up as an "extra diet kitchen," but daily the cook in charge reported that he had no foodstuffs beyond those Miss Nightingale herself had bought, which were almost depleted.

"Not a drop of milk, ma'am; and the bread is extremely moldy."

"Have we any butter?"

"None decent. What's here is mostly decomposed."

"Meat enough for broth?"

"Well, the meat is more like moist leather than like food. And we're waiting for potatoes; they're coming from France."

As the week passed, she knew what would be her two greatest obstacles. One was red tape; the other, a division of responsibility, the utter lack of co-ordination between departments. Conditions at Scutari were indeed scandalous, Mr. William H. Russell had portrayed them graphically; yet it would have been impossible to say who was at fault, whether committees or secretaries in London, or clerks and underlings in Constantinople. Perhaps the government as a whole was guilty. The result was all that concerned Florence Nightingale—and the result was chaos.

As Sidney Herbert had said, as many another cabinet member was declaring, supplies of all sorts had been sent in quantity to Constantinople, there was no excuse for such privations as the troops were suffering. But nobody knew whose liability these supplies were, nobody dared distribute them, since the duties of the various executors had never been defined. The casks and barrels and ton-weight containers at the Scutari wharf were enmeshed by the coils of red tape, forms, requisitions, regulations; the precious cargoes of supply ships were bound by sacred "service rules," which no one would question.

No one except Miss Nightingale. Asking for certain stores, she was told they had been received but could not be released to her—not without the procuring of endless signed papers. Such annoyances the Lady-in-Chief would tolerate only up to a point. She would run about from board to board, consulting this and that dignitary, complying with "service rules." But if too much put upon, she would (and frequently did) take the law into her own hands.

"I must have these stores. Why weren't they delivered to me?"

"Because the board hasn't inspected them, Miss Nightingale."

"Where is the board? No, don't answer. The board is not sitting just now. But my men are dying for want of these medicines, this lint. I must have them at once. Open the warehouse door."

"I can't, Miss Nightingale. I'd be court-martialed."

"No, I'll assume the blame. They can court-martial me. Open the door!"

Thus doors were opened to the grey-eyed, militant Lady-in-Chief.

The second obstacle was the attitude of some of the military officers. As she had foreseen, her presence here was resented by those who cherished tradition above the emergency's obvious need. "The Bird," they called her, these sulking adversaries; they laughed scornfully about the Bird and accused her of meddling. There was one ward at the Barrack in which the junior doctors were told by their superior to have nothing to do with Miss Nightingale, a very silly woman who insisted on getting things scrubbed (as if it mattered whether a hospital was clean!) and who "captured" the orderlies and coerced them to obey her.

"Open the warehouse door!"

Oh, yes, a thoroughly objectionable female, the Bird. Perhaps the most unpardonable, really maddening of her habits was that of always being right. You might dispute, argue with her, shout at her—and then circumstances would prove that she had facts, statistics at her fingertips and had been right all along. Of course, such a woman must not be countenanced. Whisper about her, harass her—ridicule her!

Quite conscious of this opposition, Florence could afford to ignore it. The majority of the doctors were friendly. As for the infantry and cavalry officers with whom she had contact, she seemed able either to dominate or defy them. Only this morning there had been an incident in which she demonstrated her talent for quelling impudence.

She had been crossing the courtyard with a can of arrowroot in her arms—and what a wonderful treasure it was, unearthed from the depths of one of those locked warehouses!—when the young captain of cavalry rode up, halting his horse so suddenly that the animal reared and pawed the air.

"Where did you get that can?" the captain thundered. "Who granted you permission to go rifling the army stores?"

She had attempted no reply. Saying nothing at all, she had stared at him.

After a few minutes, his gaze had shifted; flushed and discomfited, he had ridden on.

But such things were of small consequence, weren't they? By contrast, she could meditate upon the courtesy of Lord Raglan, British commander of all troops in the Crimean area, who had officially welcomed Miss Nightingale and promised his support and sympathy. The Senior Chaplain at Scutari also was a stanch ally, tirelessly lending himself to any task she proposed, even writing a letter back to her father in praise of her. And there were the Bracebridges, sustaining her with their cheerfulness, working like Trojans wherever she posted them, constantly telling her—telling everyone—that the good she had done and was doing was priceless. And her nurses, the members of her little band, had an absolute faith in the decisions of the Lady-in-Chief.

And her patients? They were the ones who counted! "My children"—she thought of them as that. "My poor, dear children!" Well, no sane person could have doubted how her children felt about Miss Nightingale, how pathetically they depended upon her, how glad and grateful they were to find in this alien land an Englishwoman, somebody from home, who gently and mercifully tended them, whose only wish was to comfort and cure them.

"Yes," said Florence, "we are getting on nicely in many ways."

Meanwhile, the violent controversy about the misfortunes of the Crimean wounded continued to rage in the columns of the London *Times,* and several observers ventured out to see for themselves what was happening at Scutari.

Early among the visitors was the Reverend Sidney Godolphin Osborne, with letters of introduction from Mr. Sidney Herbert. By chance, perhaps, the Reverend Mr. Osborne was escorted around the Constantinople hospitals by one of the doctors who would not acknowledge the true state of affairs. Repeatedly Mr. Osborne asked if he might not contribute some financial help, either from his own or other funds.

"No, no," replied the doctor. "We have everything. Nothing is wanting."

The assertion did not deceive Mr. Osborne. He had eyes in his head and, moreover, a measure of familiarity with medical and surgical practices. He saw at a glance that, had not Miss Nightingale been there, disaster would have overwhelmed Scutari. Returning to England, he reported her efficiency and industry—not forgetting to mention also the jealousy which somewhat hindered her labors.

Then Mr. Macdonald, appointed to administer the *Times* fund, came to Scutari. Mr. Macdonald had by now a vast amount of money to expend for the relief of the wounded. His first call had been at the London War Office, where he was cordially received but assured that the government had made ample provision and it was scarcely likely any further relief was needed at the front. Nevertheless, Mr. Macdonald thought he might as well proceed to the Crimea, an idea in which Mr. Sidney Herbert heartily concurred. So Mr. Macdonald sailed for Constantinople.

Here he was met with the same smiling, polite rebuff. Everything was progressing beautifully in the hospitals; the patients lacked for nothing. Slightly puzzled, Mr. Macdonald was wondering whether to go back to London, when he encountered a surgeon of the 39th regiment.

"If you have money, sir," said the surgeon, "for pity's sake, get our troops warm winter clothing! Their only uniforms are the linen suits issued to them under the hot sun of Gibraltar. Bitter weather is at hand. The men will be literally frozen to death! After that, look into the Scutari hospitals where the Englishwomen are nursing."

Mr. Macdonald straightway went into the markets and bought blankets and woollen clothing for the men of the 39th regiment. Then he turned his steps toward Scutari.

The officers he spoke with there were just as polite as those in Constantinople. They were interested to know of the money collected by the *Times* from an aroused and patriotic public. Amazing, splendid that so much had been subscribed. But there was no occasion to spend even a fraction of it on provisions for the army hospitals.

"We are abundantly well off!"

The most august of all the officers had what seemed an inspiration. "Why doesn't the *Times* dispose of its fund by building an English church at Pera?"

His fellow officers applauded. "A fine idea! A worthy cause!"

But, somehow, the English church at Pera had scant appeal to Mr. Macdonald—and anyway, he had resolved to see his mission through. "I should like to talk to Miss Nightingale, please."

Oh, the Bird? Dubiously they took him to the Lady-in-Chief.

"Miss Nightingale, I have come out here to offer the financial aid of thousands of your admirers. But now I am told that no aid is needed. Our soldiers have everything."

Florence's face was a study. "You have seen the Barrack hospital, Mr. Macdonald?"

"No. Only some of its staff."

She got to her feet. "Come with me."

They went through the wards and she showed him what had been done—and what remained to be done; the narrow rooms, the narrower corridors packed with rows of crudely constructed cots, mattresses hastily thrown together, improvised beds; the hundreds of men who had been washed and clad in clean garments; the hundreds more who were still half-naked, their wounds padded with bloody rags. In and out, up and down, covering the four miles of a veritable City of Misery, he followed her slim, graceful figure, watching the eyes of the men light with new hope as she passed, hearing her greet this one and that, never raising her quiet voice yet instilling with a sentence something of her own tremendous courage.

"This is what we have, Mr. Macdonald," she said at last. "Is it everything?"

When he made his report on Scutari, Mr. Macdonald had all the facts, and the *Times* fund would be spent wisely to accomplish good. He could not refrain from giving his impression of Florence Nightingale herself. She was an "incomparable woman," a "ministering angel." "The popular instinct was not mistaken which, when she set out from England, hailed her as a heroine."

Another black night, and the Lady-in-Chief was starting, as was her custom, on the half-hour's walk from the Barrack to the General Hospital. She always went, she couldn't have slept without knowing that there, too, the nurses had done their best. The path was unpaved and treacherous and she had with her an invalid soldier, who carried a lantern in his hand—the one hand which was left him after the Battle of the Alma.

"Steady on, Miss Nightingale!" The soldier swung his lantern in a flickering arc. "It's all rocks here."

"Yes, they say that from this spot the most beautiful view in the world is visible—in the daytime, I mean."

"You haven't seen the view then, ma'am?"

"Oh, no. I am never out except like this, at night. I should probably be too busy even to look."

She laughed a little, with a faint note of gayety. Mr. Macdonald was a friend; he would not forget. Supplies were on the way.

13

PROBLEMS AND SOLUTIONS

"I ALWAYS THOUGHT I might end my days as matron of a hospital," said Florence. "I never in wildest fancy thought I should end them as purveyor to a large part of the British army."

It was a foggy winter morning ("Inkerman weather," the soldiers in the Barrack said) cold, cloudy, drizzling; the Lady-in-Chief sat at a pine table in the central room of the nurses' quarters. She had been writing to Mr. Sidney Herbert and had paused to chat with Mrs. Bracebridge who was rearranging the shelves with which the walls were lined.

"If you didn't act as purveyor, we should be in a muddle," said Selina. "Someone must act, and the real purveyor has lost himself in snarls of red tape."

"Yesterday I foraged in the stores. It's a cruise I make almost daily and not sanctioned—but the only way I know of to get first-hand evidence of our stock."

"What did you find, Flo?"

"Very little. The things unfound were more numerous. No mops, no plates, no wooden trays—though the engineer is having them made. No slippers, no shoebrushes or blacking, no scissors for cutting the men's hair, no chloride of zinc—which I especially wanted."

"A gloomy prospect, isn't it?"

"Yes," Florence said, "but there is a brighter side. A

great many things have somehow come under my jurisdiction, so that I can dole them out where needed." Smiling, she looked about the room, which was neatly stacked with boxes, parcels, bundles of sheets and old linen, bolts of flannel; tubs of butter, sugar, bread; kettles, saucepans, books. "And here, Selina, is a notice that we're getting shirts, thousands of them, purchased with the *Times* money—yes, and getting them by requisition from the very official who a short while ago told Mr. Macdonald that we had more shirts than we could use! Bless Mr. Macdonald of the *Times!* And bless the Reverend Mr. Osborne and all other messengers of good will!"

Selina nodded emphatically; and Florence turned again to her letter, wrote a paragraph:

"I am a kind of general dealer in socks, shirts, knives and forks, wooden spoons, tin baths, cabbage and carrots, operating tables, towels and soap, small tooth combs, precipitate for destroying lice, bed pans and stump pillows. I will send you a picture of my Caravanserai, into which beasts come in and out. Indeed the vermin might, if they had but 'unity of purpose,' carry off the four miles of beds on their backs, and march with them into the War Office."

At that moment, a nurse entered and stood respectfully just inside the door. Florence put down her pen.

"Yes, Mrs. Drake?"

"Sago and beef tea for the fever cases in Ward Four, if you please, Miss Nightingale."

"Very well. Mrs. Bracebridge has them on her shelves."

Selina handed the containers of sago and beef tea to Mrs. Drake, who went out, her stiff skirts rustling.

"I suppose," Florence said, "the five big copper boilers haven't been mended?"

"Not yet."

"So we have only eight good ones? Lucky that we opened our two extra diet kitchens and fixed the three supplementary boilers on the main stairway."

"You did it," Selina said. "Quite alone, too. No one else would have thought of it. But you saw it was taking three or four hours to serve each meal, with the nurses trudging interminable miles between the wards and the old kitchen, and the food getting chilled—and the weaker patients, those who couldn't feed themselves, often going hungry. You have simply revolutionized the cookery methods in the Barrack, Flo."

"And you have done as much with the laundry methods."

"No. You and I together, my dear."

The laundry had indeed been a problem. There were in Scutari more than two hundred soldiers' wives who had no shelter, no livelihood, who faced a winter of utter destitution. Florence had said something must be done for them; and the generous Bracebridges had promptly collected a sum of money for their care. Using this fund and donating money of her own, Florence had rented a house for the women to occupy; and then abruptly thinking of the hospital laundry, she had asked Selina why the soldiers' wives could not be hired to wash the hospital bedding. After only a slight delay, proper laundry equipment was installed in the rented house and the vast washing project begun. Now Selina had been deputized to manage it; and though conditions could not be described as ideal, they were certainly much improved.

Florence finished and sealed her letter to Mr. Herbert. She would have had to stop writing anyway, because a group of orderlies waited at the door with requests or inquiries, and she knew that the customary rush of business had started. The nurses called this room the Tower of Babel; by late morning and then all through the rest of the day, it was besieged by people—by the nurses themselves, nuns, Turkish and Greek servants, French and Italian servants, British officers and surgeons. Everybody wanted to see and talk with Miss Nightingale; everybody was intent on his particular assignment, each spoke his own language. Sometimes also the Lady-in-Chief would hold here the "councils" over which she presided with firmness and dignity; and this was her office (at least, the only one she had) from which she had sent frequent reports to the government and to benefactors and supporters in England.

Many of the consultations were of the most serious import. Some were trivial—

"Good morning, Mrs. Lawfield. What can I do for you?"

"Miss Nightingale, excuse me, ma'am. I came out, as you know, prepared to submit to everything, to be put upon in every way. But there are some things, ma'am, one can't submit to."

"What things, for example?"

"There is the caps, ma'am, that suit one face and won't suit another." Mrs. Lawfield twisted a corner of her apron and looked very unhappy. "If I'd known, ma'am, about the caps, great as was my desire to come out to nurse at Scutari, I wouldn't have come, ma'am."

The Lady-in-Chief thought a moment. The costume she had devised for the Nightingale nurses was a gray tweed wrapper-like gown, a worsted jacket and, for outdoor wear, a short woollen coat and a brown holland scarf embroidered in red with the words "Scutari Hospital." The close-fitting cap was intended to give the wearer a sober, modest appearance; Miss Nightingale had not been bothered at all as to whether it was becoming.

How foolish of Mrs. Lawfield to bother! But she was such a good nurse—perhaps an exception should be made.

"I daresay you may go without the cap, Mrs. Lawfield."

"Oh, thank you, ma'am."

Completely satisfied, Mrs. Lawfield bowed and withdrew.

Also interrupting the stream of significant callers at the Caravanserai was Thomas. Twelve years old, a drummer boy, the pride of his regiment, the pet of the hospital, Thomas had fallen quite in love with Miss Nightingale. "I'm her man," he said, and had announced that he was ready to die for her—or, when the war was over, to forsake his drum and his military career, to go back to England with her.

"Well, Thomas?"

He saluted. "I just dropped in, Miss Nightingale, to tell you what my comrades are saying about you."

"What is that?"

"Before you came, they say, there was such cussin' and swearin' as you never heard; but since you came, it's all as holy as a church. You're the Angel of the Crimea, they say, and bad men can't be bad in the presence of an angel."

"Thank you, Thomas. I shall remember. But you had best run along now."

"Yes, ma'm," said Thomas.

The rush continued, all the many people who must bring their troubles and perplexities to Miss Nightingale and ask for remedy. Gradually they had realized that this was the one person they could rely upon; gradually, by steady pressure, she had established her authority here. She had done so by never sparing herself, never for an instant saying, even to herself, that she would not succeed. By what she knew to be superhuman effort she was accomplishing a work of reformation which to the world must have seemed impossible. But to her, failure had been the impossible thing; and she had always known she could not fail.

She liked to think that in all these weeks she had not allowed herself an hour's recreation, had denied herself proper rest and sleep and fresh air, that often mealtimes were passed over and forgotten while she toiled. To have given less than every ounce of strength would not have been enough—would not have been what God expected of her. For God was the only master she would acknowledge; she was His representative at Scutari; the work she did was His work. In that thought was all the reward, all the pleasure she desired.

"'Thy will be done'—"

In the evening, she revised again her disciplinary rules for the nurses. It was probably inevitable that, human nature being as it is, she should have been disappointed in some of the selections made back there, so quickly, in London. One young girl had been sent home almost immediately upon arrival; she was unqualified professionally, unfit morally. Much to the Lady-in-Chief's joy, her place had been taken at once by a Kaiserswerth nurse from Constantinople. Soon afterward, four more nurses were dismissed; they would not accept Miss Nightingale's rigid code and so she had felt she could not keep them on. A half-dozen she had transferred from the Barrack to the General Hospital. Now that she knew them well, she could estimate that of the original thirty-eight, only sixteen were really efficient at their job; but of these sixteen, five or six deserved (like Mrs. Lawfield) a rating of excellent.

Writing by lamplight in the Caravanserai, Florence outlined her ideas of nursing, of ward management. Every nurse, she wrote, should have undergone a course of training and should be, upon completing the course, subject to the direction of a female superintendent. The nurse must never think of herself as a rival of the doctor's, but must be wholly subordinate to the doctor, doing his bidding, heeding his instructions, never prescribing for a patient, never waiting upon a patient, except as the doctor specified. But nurses must not be regarded, by either doctors or persons outside the profession, as domestic servants—as housemaids; for they were never meant to be that, and theirs was a higher calling. A nurse's trained skill, her precious time, must not be wasted on such chores as the most unskilled slavey could as capably perform. The employment therefore of domestic servants and orderlies in a hospital must not be done away with.

Nurses must seek to exert a moral influence; they must always appear in the regulation uniform with the badge, must not trim their "bonnet-caps" with flowers or ribbons, must not have more than a small and designated amount of spirituous liquor to drink, could walk out only by permission, and then with their superintendent or in parties of three.

Though she didn't know it, Miss Nightingale was putting down the fundamental rules which, somewhat altered, would govern the nursing in military hospitals for generations to come.

"Flo! The post is here—and a letter for you!"

Florence looked up at Selina Bracebridge who had pushed aside the burlap curtain hanging in the doorway of the Caravanserai.

"A letter?"

"Forwarded by Mr. Herbert. It is dated 'Windsor Castle, December 6, 1854.'"

"Windsor Castle? From the Queen, Selina?"

Yes, from the Queen. Florence read it aloud:

"'Would you tell Mrs. Herbert that I beg she would let me see frequently the accounts she receives from Miss Nightingale or Mrs. Bracebridge, as *I hear no details of the wounded*, though I see so many from officers, etc., about the battlefield, and naturally the former must interest *me* more than anyone.

"'Let Mrs. Herbert also know that I wish Miss Nightingale and the ladies would tell these poor, noble wounded and sick men, that *no one* takes a warmer interest or feels *more* for their sufferings or admires their courage and heroism *more* than their Queen. Day and night she thinks of her beloved troops. So does the Prince.

"'Beg Mrs. Herbert to communicate these my words to those ladies, as I know that *our* sympathy is much valued by these noble fellows.—Victoria.'"

There was a little silence; then Selina said, rather tearfully, "God save the Queen!"

"I shall ask the Senior Chaplain to go from ward to

ward, reading the letter," Florence said. "Even the dying will want to know of Her Majesty's loving kindness."

When Selina had gone off in search of the Senior

It was mostly hushed

Chaplain, Florence took up her lamp to make her final round of the Barrack.

The place was pitchy black tonight; in some rooms, beneath a vaulted roof, like an eerie cavern; in the low-ceiled corridors, like a tunnel burrowing underground. It was mostly hushed, only an occasional stifled moan disturbing the silence; no other movement than an occasional figure tossing on a lumpy mattress, or unyielding cot, an orderly nodding in a chair, a nurse slipping softly by on noiseless feet. The cold wind buffeted at the windows and, far away, could be heard the dull roar of waves on the Straits of the Dardanelles—"like the sound of the Derwent," Florence thought, "when Parthe and I listened to it in our nursery at Lea Hurst, with the dolls!"

Through all the rooms she went, shifting a pillow here, straightening a blanket there, her shadow silhouetted in the ring of yellow which bobbed along the wall.

"The lady with the lamp!" It was a murmur running swiftly before the advancing ray of light; and men reached out to touch the shadow on the wall; and those who could, leaned forward to kiss the shadow as she passed.

14

SCUTARI WINTER

THE WINTER WAS hard and long in the Crimea. The British and French troops were entrenched around the Russian stronghold of Sevastopol; but sleet, snow and mud kept all armies at a standstill and the only military operations were a few siege skirmishes which could not be marked up as victories or defeats for either side. During those months disease was the principal foe of the British soldier, and disease had its many triumphs. Poorly fed and equipped, exposed to severe weather, the men by hundreds were sick with coughs, fever, pneumonia, dysentery.

Between the peninsular ports and Scutari, ships plied constantly, bringing more and more patients to Miss Nightingale's hospitals. Such arrivals Florence could cope with calmly enough—they were all in the day's work; but one ship which docked brought passengers of another sort, whose coming angered and disconcerted the Lady-in-Chief.

She was seated that day in the tower room at her table; she wore her usual costume, a black merino frock trimmed with black velvet, white linen collar, cuffs, apron and cap. She heard footsteps in the corridor, the curtain in the doorway was lifted. She glanced up—and saw her old friend, Miss Mary Stanley. Behind Miss

Stanley was a sizable group of feminine figures, dozens it seemed, dressed for traveling, luggage in their hands.

"Are you surprised, Florence?" said Miss Stanley.

"We've come to help you with the nursing"

"There are forty of us; we've come to help you with the nursing."

Florence got up. No, she was not surprised; she had been forewarned. But she was irate. Miss Stanley was a daughter of the Bishop of Norwich, she was a nurse of some experience and Florence had known her intimately for years. But Florence had not (and this was the point!) invited Miss Stanley to help at Scutari.

"You are here by Mr. Sidney Herbert's authority," Florence said coldly. "He sent you, after Mr. Bracebridge and the Reverend Mr. Osborne told him we were badly off and understaffed. But, of course, Mr. Herbert has no authority, and the gentlemen misinformed him. We are not badly off, we do not need more nurses. In fact, we are so crowded that we can't find quarters for you." She hesitated. "You may sleep here tonight, Mary; perhaps there will be a place for your party in the General Hospital. Later you can all be assigned to other hospitals in Constantinople, or somewhere."

When, rather abashed, Miss Stanley and her companions had withdrawn, Florence wrote furiously to Sidney Herbert. Yes, she had received his letter which said that Mary Stanley was leaving for Scutari. And now Miss Stanley had come. Meddling *women*? Well, what about meddling *men*? How dared anyone go over the head of the Lady-in-Chief to plan improvements at Scutari? Mr. Herbert must understand once and for all that, much as she liked him, Miss Nightingale would stand for no interference from him—or from any source. She had agreed to assume full management here; that she would assume and nothing less.

Her pen scratched over the paper. "You have sacrificed the cause so near my heart, you have sacrificed me, a matter of small importance now; you have sacrificed your own written word to a popular cry." Perhaps Mr. Herbert thought that, having found shelter for these forty poor wanderers, Miss Nightingale ought to resign?

She recalled to him how she had worked to gain the confidence of the medical officers; how by incessant vigilance, day and night, she had drilled her little band until now routine reigned where wildest upheaval had been before. Forty more nurses? To have women scampering about the wards of a Military Hospital all day long, which they would do were their numbers so increased would relax the discipline and increase their leisure. It would be both improper and absurd.

Yes, Miss Nightingale was thinking seriously of resigning!

Mr. Herbert wilted under this blast and was all apologies. People in England were enthusiastic and sentimental, he said, and probably had no idea of what the task at Scutari had been. He had acted impulsively; and at the behest, too, of Mr. Osborne, Mr. Bracebridge and other well-intentioned persons. But Florence must feel free to do just as she saw best. Miss Stanley and her whole party could be returned to England at Mr. Herbert's expense, and the incident closed.

Mrs. Herbert wrote to Mrs. Bracebridge, "I am heartbroken about the nurses, but I do assure you, if you send them all home without a trial, you will lose some really valuable women."

By the time these letters came, Florence had simmered down considerably and was thinking that a few recruits to her staff might be a boon. She reorganized the Barrack nurses, increasing the roster to fifty. Miss Stanley and the rest then went to hospitals at Koulali and Balaclava.

But between Miss Nightingale and Miss Stanley there was a definite estrangement and, parting at Scutari, they did not meet again. Florence had no regrets. Not this bond of friendship or any other could weigh in the balance with what she believed to be her duty. Individuals meant nothing—her cause everything!

With the men in the wards, her "children," Miss Nightingale was always infinitely compassionate and tender; but it was not in her character to take petty persecution without striking back, and more than once that winter she lashed out at her critics. In letters home she loosed her remarkable talent for sarcasm, writing mockingly of those physicians and military officials who still were not her friends, giving them satirical nicknames, pillorying them with single sentences of scorn.

The nurses, too, sometimes earned her wrath.

One day three of her staff appeared before her and announced that they were going to get married. So, in spite of the Lady-in-Chief's watchfulness, romance had flowered in the gloomy Barrack? She was incensed. Marriage was all very well in its place—which was not at Scutari. Some women must marry, perhaps. But not nurses! Why could they not see, these three stupid creatures, that only in serving God was their real hope for earthly happiness?

But the nurses went on and got married, just the same —as she had supposed they would. In such circumstances, her hands were tied, her superior insight of no avail; she could do nothing to prevent their folly.

She concerned herself with her patients and the condition of the Crimean army as a whole. It was pitiable, and showed all too plainly that something, somewhere, was very much amiss. The exhaustion of the ailing men unloaded at Scutari was evidence of gross error on somebody's part. Frost-bitten, thinly clad, half-starved, gaunt and hollow-eyed, they had been an easy prey to illness and were slow to recover. When discharged from the hospitals, these men would go back to their former wretched environment—and would probably soon be in hospitals again.

But even though the government's machinery for relief seemed to have bogged down, there still were private means of providing for the soldiers. Money in large sums had been sent to Miss Nightingale, from England, from Australia, New South Wales and New Zealand—thousands of pounds. If the dilemma was one of nobody's knowing that things were wrong, or nobody's caring sufficiently to straighten out the sad state of affairs, then Florence, who knew so well and cared with all her heart, was ready to step into the breach.

She urged Mr. Herbert to buy and ship immediately warm clothing for the Crimean troops; and she presented to him an incisive suggestion by which the meshes of red tape could be cut and supplies, including food, quickly transported to the front. Warehouses must be built, she said, and porters hired. In March, 1855, this suggestion was adopted and a road paved in the Crimea, so that freight thereafter was delivered to its destination without the old postponements and endless delays.

She said also that the hospital orderly system and the ambulance corps must be reorganized. She showed with statistics the faultiness of the army's purveying department, and how it could be made effectual. As for the military kitchen management and cookery, she contemptuously denounced it.

The army hospital's way of preparing a meal was to issue each man his day's rations, to wrap these rations in separate small bags of coarse cloth—and then to fling all the bags, hundreds of them, into huge boiling cauldrons. Of course, all the food which came out of the cauldron tasted alike, and none was fit to eat, especially in invalid cases where a delicate diet was essential. Miss Nightingale's extra diet kitchens corrected this difficulty at the Barrack and General Hospitals; and she demanded that her method be instituted elsewhere.

Some of these changes were made at once; many more were to be of benefit in the future.

Once during the winter, Miss Nightingale herself became a builder; it was a venture which earned her much criticism in hostile camps and just as much praise in others. Several wards in the Barrack were simply too dilapidated for further use, eight hundred beds were in these rooms from which all patients must be removed. Lord Raglan had told Miss Nightingale that many more patients might be expected soon, but not he—or anyone —would be responsible for ordering repairs.

This was a predicament calling for extreme measures. Florence engaged two hundred workmen and had the repairs made, paying the bill out of her own pocket. Somewhat later the War Department approved her action and reimbursed her.

Meanwhile in England, Lord Palmerston had been called to head the government as Prime Minister, and there were many cabinet changes. The offices of Secretary of State and Secretary at War were combined under Lord Panmure. Mr. Sidney Herbert was for a while Secretary for the Colonies, and then resigned, though he had not lost interest in the Crimean soldiers' plight or in Florence Nightingale's work. The new government appointed Lord Shaftesbury to investigate sanitation problems in the Scutari hospitals, and a commission was sent out for that purpose.

Lord Shaftesbury had a reputation as a humanitarian,

in his political career he had toiled always for the betterment of the laboring classes. Florence Nightingale had become acquainted with him when she taught in the Ragged Schools of London and Lord Shaftesbury was president of the Ragged Schools Union, a position he held for forty years. It was only natural, perhaps, that these two believers in reform should have identical views on the need for drastic reform of Scutari's sanitation facilities. When the commissioners had surveyed the Barrack, and thought about the death rate which rose appallingly in the winter months, the building of new sewers, flooring and walls was recommended—the very thing which Miss Nightingale had been urging for ever so long, and to which previous officials had turned a deaf ear.

Indeed, the commission worked swiftly and competently; Florence told Lord Shaftesbury it had "saved the army." One of its members, Dr. John Sutherland, was a friend with whom the Lady-in-Chief was to have a close future association.

Florence wrote to Parthe, "We have established a reading room for convalescents, which is well attended. The men are so glad to read. The officers look on with composure and say to me, 'You are spoiling the brutes.'"

The Barrack Hospital reading room was set up to provide leisure occupation for hours which, Florence knew, might otherwise be spent in drinking; and despite the skeptical smiles of the officers, she went on with it. Soon drunkenness among the soldiers was the exceptional rather than the usual thing. The officers said they could not account for this; a phenomenon, they said; and surely Miss Nightingale's reading room had nothing to do with it. The Bird was heard to say that she regretted having no trained teacher to start a course of study. Lessons for the soldiers? "Impossible!" exclaimed the officers.

Well, she would see about that.

As another experiment, she talked to the men on the subject of sending their pay home to their families. She had written this idea to the Queen, who transmitted her letter to the cabinet—where it was discussed. Some of the statesmen were for it; more were against it. The majority opinion seemed to be that "the soldier is not a remitting animal."

"Miss Nightingale," asserted one of the secretaries, "knows nothing of the British soldier."

She did not wait for the cabinet's sanction, but proceeded to create a Money Order Office, in which on four afternoons a month she received the money any soldier wished to forward to his home. Mr. Sam Smith was the receiving agent in England, passing on these allowances to the mothers, wives and children of the various soldiers. About £1,000 was taken in each month, and dispatched overseas. The idea spread, money order offices were opened in Constantinople, in Scutari, Balaclava and at the army headquarters in the Crimea. Within six months' times £71,000 was sent home. "All of it," Florence said, "money rescued from the canteen."

She tried in yet another way to rescue the soldier's pay from the canteen—by setting up the "Inkerman Café" on the Bosporus shore. She made the coffee house attractive and comfortable, and decorated it with a picture of the Queen, which Victoria had sent from Windsor Castle.

Encouraged by the popularity of the Inkerman Café, and convinced that she was not really "spoiling the brutes," she established classrooms in the Barrack, equipped them with books, games, music, maps, a magic lantern and stereoscope. When this project became known, everybody in England wished to contribute. The Queen and the Duchess of Kent made liberal donations; the government, through Sir Henry Storks, bought and equipped a second school building outside the Barrack —and two schoolmasters came from London to conduct the classes.

Florence's own faith in her "children" grew by leaps and bounds. "I have never seen so teachable and helpful a class as the Army generally. Give them opportunity promptly and securely to send money home, and they will use it. Give them schools and lectures and they will come to them. Give them books and games and amusements and they will leave off drinking. Give them suffering and they will bear it. Give them work and they will do it."

How did the men feel about Miss Nightingale? Listen to them as they talk together in the wards:

"Wonderful, she is, at cheering up anyone who's a bit low!"

"She's all full of life and fun when she speaks to us."

"If she were commanding our troops, we'd be in Sevastopol in a week!"

"Yes, and if the Queen should die, they ought to make Miss Nightingale the queen. 'Queen Florence!' How is it, mates?"

"Aye, aye! Queen Florence!"

A visitor from England in January, 1855, wrote that to see Florence in the Barrack made intelligible to him the saints of the Middle Ages. "If the soldiers were told that the roof had opened, and she had gone up palpably to Heaven, they would not be the least surprised. They quite believe she is in several places at once."

But in England, now and again, someone wondered if maybe Miss Nightingale was too broad-minded about religion. Was it so that she had no Presbyterian nurses at Scutari? A curious oversight! Hadn't she been quoted as saying that some of the Catholic nuns were the truest Christians she had ever met? Hadn't she written of the Reverend Mother Moore as her mainstay, "devoted, heart and head, to serve God and mankind?"

Was this Popery? Well, we must write to the London *Times!*

Echoes reached Florence. "They tell me," she commented in a letter to Mr. Herbert, "that there is a religious war about poor me in the *Times,* and that Mrs. Herbert has generously defended me. I do not know what I have done to be so dragged before the Public. But I am so glad that my God is not the God of the High Church, or of the low, that He is not a Romanist or an Anglican—or a Unitarian. I don't believe He is even a Russian, though His events go strangely against us. (N. B.—A Greek once said to me at Salamis, 'I do believe God Almighty is an Englishman.'")

The fact was that she made no distinctions on religious grounds between her nurses; and Miss Shaw Stewart, Mrs. Roberts and Mrs. Drake, Protestants all, were as much her favorites as were the nuns. She based her judgment solely on ability—and intolerance she had always detested.

It was spring at last and the number of cases at the Barrack so reduced that Florence decided to cross the

Black Sea to inspect the Balaclava hospitals. The trip might refresh her, for far from feeling satisfied with what she had done, she was haunted by the thought of what more she might have done.

She took with her a few companions; Mr. Bracebridge, Mrs. Roberts, two cooks, a courier, an invalided soldier and Thomas, the drummer boy.

May 5, she wrote home: "Poor old Flo steaming up the Bosporus in the *Robert Lowe* or *Robert Slow* (for an exceedingly slow boat she is) taking back 420 of her patients, a draught of convalescents returning to their regiments to be shot at again. What suggestions do the above ideas make to you in the Embley drawing-room? Stranger ones perhaps than to me, who, having been at Scutari six months today, am in sympathy with God, fulfilling the purpose I came into the world for."

15

"THE DAUGHTER OF ENGLAND!"

From the deck of the *Robert Lowe,* Florence saw the several large ships, the many small boats anchored in the

There were large ships anchored in the harbour of Balaclava

harbour of Balaclava. The shore and the landing pier were dark with people.

"Who are they all? Why have they gathered here?" she asked Charles Bracebridge.

In a moment she had her answer. These were friends, people who had heard of Miss Nightingale and her splendid work, who hoped now for a glimpse of Scutari's Lady-in-Chief. No sooner had her vessel steamed in than the welcome began, doctors and officials of Balaclava boarded the *Robert Lowe* to offer their respects and compliments. For more than an hour, Florence greeted her guests—and she was rather bored about it; she disliked such functions anyway; and what she really wanted was to go ashore and inspect hospitals. Lord Raglan, she was told, was scheduled to arrive shortly.

"I am sorry I cannot wait for him," Florence said, "but my errand is not of a social nature and I have no time to waste."

Thus, she missed the coming of the British commander. She went directly from the waterfront to the biggest of the hospitals where she started her tour of inspection.

But she did not wish to seem discourteous, and next day she set out on horseback with an escort to visit Lord Raglan at his headquarters in the camp of the besieging army.

The mare she rode was a beautiful creature, so light brown in color as to look golden in the sunshine, and so spirited that only an expert horsewoman could have kept in the saddle, as the party pushed forward along muddy paths which were noisy and crowded with refugees. This was spring, fine warm weather and the thousands of Crimean inhabitants made homeless by the war were on the move again after a winter of hardship and despair, streaming back toward the farms from which military maneuvers had driven them. Everywhere was tumult—straggling lines of oxen, sheep, cattle and mules, with their owners plodding behind; strings of carts and wagons, pulled by donkeys or by hand, laden with household goods, with grain sacks and crude farm implements. In the ditches beside the paths were overturned and abandoned conveyances, wreckage, rusty cannon left by retreating troops.

A scene of bedlam. But Florence rode without accident through it, though the golden mare often shied and reared and pranced skittishly.

"You are not afraid, Miss Nightingale?" queried an officer in her escort.

"Afraid?" She smiled. "I've ridden since I was a little girl." She thought for a minute of that little girl she had been, racing madly over the English downs, jumping fences—with Parthe as companion, or the Reverend Mr. Giffard or some other of those dear friends at home.

They went first to the village of Kadikoi, stopping to see the hospital there. Then they climbed to the top of a nearby hill which overlooked the approaches of Sevastopol. Alighting, they stood on the crest and Florence gazed down at the white tents which by thousands flanked the city walls. Puffs of white smoke billowed intermittently skyward, cannon boomed and muskets crackled fire. Sevastopol was beleaguered, was grimly resisting, but surrender was predicted.

Thomas scrambled over the rocks to stand beside Miss Nightingale. "The Russians can't last much longer," he said, his eyes bright with interest. "A wonderful sight, isn't it, ma'am?"

She shook her head sadly and turned away, knowing what the sight meant in human anguish, praying in her heart for the end of all fighting.

On the outskirts of the British lines was a hospital which she wished to inspect. Word of her visit had preceded her; as she went through the wards, the men received her with rejoicing. Lord Raglan was not there or in his headquarters. Unaware of Miss Nightingale's coming, he had gone off early to a distant area of the camp.

"But that doesn't matter," Florence said. She had now called upon him and exchanged courtesies—and she would have more time to spend with the sick and wounded.

Emerging an hour later, she was delighted to find a group of old acquaintances outside the hospital. These were former patients of hers at Scutari, men sent back from the Barrack to active duty, rallying around her now to shout their greetings.

"Miss Nightingale! Hurrah for the Lady-in-Chief!"

It was almost too much for the golden mare, who pranced and capered like a circus pony. But Florence's grip on the reins was steady, as she bowed and smiled.

A mile farther on, one of the escort officers said that they had best circle back toward safer terrain.

"Oh, no!" protested Florence. "Let us go up ahead."

"But the guns are firing, Miss Nightingale."

"I want a view of Sevastopol," she said, and while he hesitated, she pulled aside and trotted toward the city walls, and was at a point where the gates could be seen.

But here a sentry darted from ambush, waving his arms.

"Sharp firing! Turn away!"

"I am Florence Nightingale—"

"Just so!" cried the sentry. "The Russians would be glad to aim at you, ma'am."

She laughed. "Please let me go on. I'm not in the least afraid."

"No!" said the sentry, but then his arms dropped, for the lady was going on, unheeding. "Ah, well, if you must—"

"Miss Nightingale," said the escort officer, "I beg you to dismount and take refuge in that stone redoubt over there!"

Florence dismounted. The view from the redoubt was good, but still she was not contented. "I am going into the trenches."

The sentry was horrified. "The trenches? You will be killed!"

"Oh, I don't think so."

"Madam," said the sentry, "if anything happens, these gentlemen will witness that I did not fail to warn you of the danger."

She had been peering through a telescope; lowering it, she tied her cap strings, gathered her cape about her and smiled at him. "My good young man," she said, "more dead and wounded have passed through my hands than I hope you will ever see in the battlefield during the whole of your military service. Believe me, I am not afraid."

So she went into the trenches, walked through those deep and narrow gashes in the earth, stepped upon the ramparts, touched the gun carriages and the iron muzzles of the mortar cannon. Lastly she climbed up and sat a moment upon the center mortar.

One of her party, a Frenchman with an instinct for

the dramatic, cried out: "Behold the heroic daughter of England—the soldier's frend!"

A mighty burst of cheering rose from the trenches. "Bravo! Long live the daughter of England!"

"Henceforth this mortar shall be known as the 'Nightingale mortar!'" cried the Frenchman.

"Bravo!"

Now all the regiment had seen the valiant lady on the mortar, everyone was shouting: "It's Florence Nightingale! The Angel of the Crimea!"

The noise was so great that even the Russians inside the walls of Sevastopol heard and were startled. Florence herself was startled. Her face flushed with emotion, tears in her eyes, she got down from her perilous lookout.

"Miss Nightingale, we must go back to Balaclava—"

"Yes," she said quietly. "I am ready."

She was very tired that night—from the excitement and the long, rough ride, she thought. But in the morning, she was up and in the saddle for a trip to some convalescent huts located on the mountain slope, eight hundred feet above sea level. The sun was hot, with a brassy glare. All day the sun beat upon her and with evening a damp wind blew. She was quite exhausted; but next day she made the trip again, taking nurses who were much needed in the huts. For three days more she continued with her work of supervising the outlying infirmaries and convalescent posts—and then she could not continue.

She was ill. She had been stricken with that worst of scourges, Crimean fever.

The doctors in attendance were worried and ordered

that she be cared for in the mountainside sanatorium, where the pure air might speed recovery. They placed her on a stretcher and six soldiers, men whom she once had nursed, who knew and loved her, carried the stretcher through the streets of Balaclava and up the mountain road. Mrs. Roberts walked beside her, holding a white umbrella to shield Miss Nightingale from the pitiless sun; Thomas, weeping like a baby, marched behind and following Thomas was a doleful procession of mourning soldiers.

"Florence Nightingale is ill! She is near death!"

The tidings spread through Balaclava, echoed in Scutari. The patients in her own hospitals heard and buried their faces in their pillows, grieved and sobbing. The tidings were wafted to England, over the new electric cable recently completed. In London the message created consternation. Miss Nightingale ill? Dying, perhaps? This was a national calamity!

At five o'clock in the afternoon of a crucial day, two horsemen galloped to the door of the sanatorium and knocked. It was raining; their guttapercha cloaks were dripping wet, their hats sodden.

"We've come to inquire for Miss Nightingale," said one of them, to Mrs. Roberts who had opened the door.

"Hist! Don't speak so loud, my man!" Mrs. Roberts gestured for silence.

"Is Miss Nightingale here?"

"Yes, she is, poor lady—"

The visitor strode in, but Mrs. Roberts planted herself in the way. "No, you don't!"

"I must see Miss Nightingale."

"Oh, must you? And who are you?"

"Only a soldier, madam, but I've traveled long miles. My name is Raglan. Miss Nightingale knows me."

"Raglan?" Mrs. Roberts paused—and just then Florence called from her sickroom.

"It's Lord Raglan, Mrs. Roberts. Tell him I have a very bad fever, he must not see me."

Without more ado, Lord Raglan pushed by the nurse, went into the room and seated himself on a stool at the bedside. "I, too, am without fear," he said, "of fever or anything else, Miss Nightingale. I felt that I should never rest until I had expressed to you my thanks for all you've done and my wish that you may soon be well again." He stared at her, noticing how thin she was, her lips parched, her cheeks stained with unhealthy color. Was this to be her fate? Florence Nightingale, dying like this, her task unfinished? No, Lord Raglan did not think so. She would be spared. He got up. "Good-bye, Miss Nightingale. You will recover."

For twelve days more her condition was serious, but now the fever was receding, she was gaining a little strength. The doctors said that in a week she could be sent home to England.

"I am going home," she said, "to *Scutari*."

There was no arguing with the Lady-in-Chief. If she said she was going to Scutari, that was what she would do. The doctors sighed and summoned the stretcher-bearers. Down the mountain she was carried, and so to the port. At least, though, she could sail more comfortably than in a troop ship; Lord Ward's private yacht was in the Balaclava harbor and Selina Bracebridge, who had come in haste at the first news of Florence's illness, arranged for the use of this lighter, faster craft.

In June, only a little more than a month from the time

of her embarking for the Crimea, Florence saw again the lovely spires and minarets of Constantinople's skyline.

"I shall get well rapidly here," she said to Mrs. Bracebridge. "I am so happy to be back with my people."

Her people! All the men in the wards at the Barrack and the General Hospital wept their thankfulness and spoke her name with reverent awe. She had returned, their Angel—more slender and delicate than ever in figure, her hair cut short, with just the curling ends showing beneath her linen cap, her hands white and fragile—but walking with the same firm tread, smiling with the same tenderness, toiling with the same unflagging zeal for the welfare of her "children."

If one thing had been needed to intensify her popularity in England, this illness and recovery had been the thing. Florence Nightingale was now the most talked-of, the most famous woman in the world, a public idol, the object of universal admiration and acclaim. Songs with such titles as *The Woman's Smile, The Soldier's Cheer, The Shadow on the Pillow* appeared and were sold by the thousands of copies in music shops. Poems and artists' sketches of the Lady with the Lamp were printed, with both short and long biographies, in all the papers, from the smallest country journal to the publications of the great universities. Stationers brought out note-paper with her portrait as a watermark, or with a lithographed view of Lea Hurst; and there were scores of different pictures of her run off and sold by hawkers in the streets. China figurines in her likeness were on the counters of every shop, and tradesmen adorned their paper bags with sentimental pictures portraying her as she ministered to the wounded. Life boats, emigrant ships, streets, waltzes, puddings, articles of wearing apparel were named in her honor; and at fairs throughout the country and at seaside resorts were wax exhibits, sometimes life-size, depicting her at her merciful work. Race horses were named for her—"The Forest Plate handicap was won by Miss Nightingale, beating Barbarity and nine others"—and dozens, hundreds, of new babies were christened "Florence." Indeed, that magic name swept through the British Isles and the Empire, and so on around the globe, guaranteeing that a whole generation of Florences would grow up to keep green the memory of this first and noble Florence.

Lea Hurst and Embley became famous in her reflection, with gifts of every description pouring in (to be sorted and acknowledged by Parthe) and people driving or tramping out on Sundays to see the places where their heroine had lived. When it became known that Miss Nightingale did not intend to come home to recuperate but had said, "I will stand out the war with any man!", all these evidences of adoration were redoubled.

It boiled up at last in a huge public meeting held in London, the purpose of which was "to give expression to a general feeling that the services of Miss Nightingale in the hospitals of the East demand the grateful recognition of the British people." The *Times* said there never had been assembled a more brilliant, enthusiastic and unanimous audience. The Duke of Cambridge presided, and many representatives of the peerage were there. The common folk thronged in too, and overflowed the hall, and formed a vast crowd surrounding the hall, eager to hear the eloquent speeches of appreciation, eager to support any proposal of a testimonial.

Someone (perhaps the Duke of Cambridge) said that

Miss Nightingale had always wished to establish and maintain in her own land an institution like Pastor Fliedner's at Kaiserswerth. Therefore let it be resolved that a "Nightingale Fund" be raised, which would enable her to have in England a nurses' training school. Every person at the meeting, almost every person in the British Isles agreed to this suggestion. Mr. Sidney Herbert sent Miss Nightingale a copy of the resolution and told her how freely the contributions were already being made.

After receiving these communications, Florence answered rather coolly. She had not been especially pleased to learn of all the fuss and hubbub in England; she had never really wanted a public meeting held to pay her homage. She was, of course, not unmindful of the sympathy and the confidence which originators of the scheme had shown her—but unless she was to have sole control of the Nightingale Fund and the English Kaiserswerth she would not be interested. She would accept the proposal, yes. But her present work was such as she would never leave for any other. "I accept their proposal, provided I may do so on their understanding of this great uncertainty as to when it will be possible for me to carry it out."

Did she seem ungracious? She did not mean to. Perhaps it was only that she alone realized what she strove for—which was not recognition, but the feeling of having done God's will properly, in her own way—and *enough*.

16

ADVENTURE'S ENDING

SEVASTOPOL FELL TO the British and French armies September 8, 1855. This ending of the siege was really the close of the Crimean War. There would be a few more skirmishes before the signing of the peace in Paris the following March; but with the capitulation of beleaguered Sevastopol, Russia knew that she was defeated and her troops beat a gradual retreat.

The war was over—and what good was ever to be derived from all the fighting and bloodshed, perhaps no one in the world could say. But, anyway, it was over. Through the autumn months, Britain's expeditionary force was removed, bit by bit, from the Crimean peninsula and shipped back home.

But, as usual, the terrible aftermath of war remained to be dealt with; the maimed and mutilated men, the invalids in the Crimean and Scutari hospitals. These victims Florence Nightingale still regarded as her charge. Many friends, the members of her family, implored her to resign her position now and return to England. The Bracebridges, feeling that the pressure of work had slackened, were leaving—

"Please, Flo, come with us! You are not half so well as you pretend; your health is not what it was before that bout with the fever in the spring. Please, dear," said Selina, "let somebody else shoulder the burdens here!"

But Florence was not to be persuaded. True to an old promise, Aunt Mai Smith was starting for Scutari. "I'm staying, Selina," said Florence. "Aunt Mai will take your place as my special deputy. She will watch over me and my health."

Aunt Mai, arriving on the heels of the Bracebridges' departure, found her mission an arduous one. In letters she described the Lady-in-Chief's nightly activities, "She habitually writes till 1 or 2, sometimes till 3 or 4. We seldom get through even our little dinner (after it has been put off one, two or three hours on account of her visitors) without her being called away from it. I never saw a greater picture of exhaustion than Flo last night at ten . . . and she sat up the greater part of the night."

Such things as food, rest, temperature, Aunt Mai noticed, never interfered with Florence's performance of the task in hand. "She has attained a most wonderful calm and presence of mind. She is, I think, often deeply impressed, and depressed, though she does not show it outwardly. No irritation of temper, no hurry or confusion of manner, ever appears for a moment."

If she was depressed, it was because Florence foresaw that the winter would be harsh—in some respects, the difficulties might be even more numerous than those of a year ago. And so they were. Lord Raglan was dead now, an elderly man who had been worn out by the struggles and privations of the war. By some strange omission, the private and official instructions sent to him and defining exactly Miss Nightingale's position as superintendent of nurses had been mislaid or lost; and his successors, either indifferent or hostile to Miss Nightingale, said they knew nothing at all about it. Florence surmised that henceforth her work would be made as hard as possible for her; still, she could write pluckily to Mrs. Bracebridge, "We get things done all the same—only a little more slowly."

She had to go on horseback

Most of that winter she was in the Crimea. The weather was bad, with much snow, and she had to go on horseback or in a mule cart from one to another of the hospitals. It was hazardous traveling, and once the cart in which she rode upset among the ruts and snowdrifts, and she was tumbled out, battered and bruised. After this accident, she asked for and was given a hooded baggage car, without springs but drawn by a stout, sure-footed team, in which to make her rounds.

As she had expected, the several doctors and military officers who could never reconcile themselves to the Bird tried stubbornly to outwit and thwart her. But they had reckoned without Miss Nightingale's own stubbornness. She would not be outwitted or thwarted. She would not be stopped.

On one occasion, the enemy faction in a Balaclava hospital actually locked the doors against her—locked her out in the winter cold. She got a chair and sat down near the locked door, and having sent off a messenger for another key, she sat there all day, waiting, until at night the key was fetched. Then she went in. She was angry, yes. But she would have sat in that spot forever, if necessary, to gain entrance to the patients behind the door.

Sometimes the persecution took other forms; she had little or no food; her nurses had no beds and must sleep on benches in the office of a barrack. Perhaps the opposition thought such treatment would drive the Bird away. But she stayed, ignoring these things, as she said, *"for the sake of the work."*

"When people offend, they offend the Master before they do me," she said; therefore she would not "kick" or resist or resent, for that was not the Master's command. And, she added, "Is it even common sense?" She did not believe so.

By contrast were the reports reaching her from England where she seemed to be constantly more famous. The Nightingale Fund was growing enormously; the

Crimean soldiers had subscribed nearly £9,000, the Navy and Coast Guard almost as much. Jenny Lind had sung a benefit concert, the proceeds of which were contributed to the Fund.

In November Queen Victoria wrote Florence a letter filled with phrases of warmest admiration. "I am anxious, however," said the Queen, "of marking my feelings in a manner which I trust will be agreeable to you, and send you with this letter a brooch, the form and emblems of which commemorate your great and blessed work, and which I hope you will wear as a mark of the high approbation of your Sovereign!"

The brooch, a large enamelled badge, was stamped with St. George's Cross and the Royal Cipher, surmounted by a crown of diamonds and the word "Crimea." Around the edge was an inscription, "Blessed are the Merciful;" and on the reverse surface was a second inscription: "To Miss Florence Nightingale, as a mark of esteem and gratitude for her devotion to the Queen's brave soldiers. From Victoria R. 1855."

Florence had little taste for jewelry; her costumes were always unadorned, extremely simple; but she was proud of having earned her Sovereign's "high approbation," and so she wore the brooch Christmas Day when she went to dine at the British Embassy in Constantinople. It was a distinguished company, the men in colorful uniforms, the women beautifully and fashionably gowned—yet, somehow, Miss Nightingale in her white cap and plain black dress, the Queen's decoration at her throat, was the center of attraction, all eyes turned to her.

"I felt quite dumb," wrote another of the guests later, "as I looked at her wasted figure and short brown hair combed over the forehead like a child's. She is very slight, rather above the middle height; her face is long and thin, but this may be from recent illness and great fatigue. She has a very prominent nose, slightly Roman; and small grey eyes, kind, yet penetrating; but her face does not give you at all the idea of great talent. She looks a quiet, persevering, orderly, lady-like woman. She was still very weak and did not join in the games, but she sat on a sofa and looked on, laughing until the tears came into her eyes."

The weather moderated in March. Often on those early spring days Florence would stroll for an hour in the English burying-ground at Scutari. Many of her nurses had gone home now, the major part of the troops had gone and hundreds of convalescents; the hospitals were no longer crowded. But here were the soldiers who were never to see England again, it was of them Florence thought most earnestly—the dead.

Which among them had died needlessly? This was the question she brooded on; the needless deaths resulting from neglect and inadequacy of preparation and equipment. She remembered the shiploads of men brought from the battlefields, how poorly they had been clothed, how poorly nourished. That they should have suffered so was inexcusable; it was a wicked extravagance which should have been checked at the source. She had studied and pondered; and she had determined that what had happened in the Crimea must never recur. No other British soldiers must ever know such cruel treatment, such a tragic fate.

Something must be done! What? Perhaps the whole policy of a nation in regard to the maintaining of its armies must be revised, the whole system of the British

War Department be reformed. A colossal undertaking? Yes, but it could be effected.

Strolling, meditating, Florence Nightingale made a solemn vow—to herself and to God. Something would surely be done.

By midsummer the hospitals were almost empty, the four miles of corridors and wards at the Barrack, where wounded men had strained to catch a glimpse of a lady's flickering lamp, were deserted and echoing. The last duty had been discharged. Florence was sailing for England.

The British government had begged her to accept the use of a man-of-war for the voyage; she had said no, politely; she preferred to travel without flourish or pomp. She had reserved passage on a French ship and had signed the register as "Miss Smith." On the very day before leaving, she arranged for a huge cross of white marble to be erected on the mountain heights above Balaclava, on a peak not far from the sanatorium where she had lain so ill. This was to be her own tribute to the war's heroes, a shining cross with, at the foot, the carved supplication: "Lord have mercy on us."

With Aunt Mai and as "Miss Smith," she boarded the vessel. She had made no announcements of any sort, intended making none. In her portfolio was a letter which said that the regiments of the Coldstream Guards, the Grenadiers and the Fusiliers would send their three bands to meet her at the station and "play her home, whenever she might arrive, whether by day or night, if only they could find out when." But, wanting no bands, she had not told anyone about her journey.

From the French seaport she went to Paris, stopped for a night in a modest hotel and then was off to London.

"Miss Smith" was so inconspicuous in London that her true identity was never guessed. She got on a train which took her to the village station of Whatstandwell, and from there she walked alone to Lea Hurst.

She crossed the terrace of the big old stone house and rang the bell. The butler admitted her.

"Is it—it *is* Miss Florence!"

"Yes," she said. "I'm home."

"Certain persons have come in advance, Miss Florence. William Jones, a one-legged sailor lad; and Peter, a very little Russian boy—Peter Grillage, he calls himself. And a dog, Miss Florence; Rousch, a black Crimean puppy."

She smiled. "The spoils of war. I've said I would adopt William Jones and Peter Grillage; they have no people. The black puppy was given to me by the soldiers in the Barrack."

"They're all here. Miss Parthe is caring for them."

The butler bowed and stood aside, and she went past him—into the Lea Hurst drawing-room and the embrace of her parents and sister.

17

A NEW SUMMONS

"Now," Parthe said, "all that terrible time is behind you, Flo. Now you can rest."

They were in the morning room at Lea Hurst, Florence stretched out on a divan, scarcely listening to her sister's conversation, thinking not of what was behind but of what was ahead, a job to be done, a hard job—and how had she best attack it? In her diary only a few days ago, she had written, "I stand at the altar of the murdered men, and while I live I fight their cause." She had never meant anything more sincerely. Oh, how she hated stupidity, the false economy which had wasted so many lives, the false pride which would not correct its mistakes of judgment. With the Derbyshire sun cheerfully shining at the windows, she walked in memory the frosty winter corridors of Scutari, a lamp in her hand, the flickering rays playing upon bleakness and agony.

Parthe went on, "You can't imagine the people who have come to Lea Hurst this week, in carriages and on foot, hoping to see you. Hordes of people. The village is positively overrun. And all the lovely gifts! The workmen at Sheffield have sent you a set of beautiful cutlery; and there's that fine desk sent by our county neighbors. But I think the Duke of Devonshire's present is the very nicest —a silver owl! Quite like dear old Athena, this silver owl

A NEW SUMMONS

is; we must show it to Athena when we go to Embley. Flo, no other British subject has ever equaled your popularity. It is simply astounding!"

Florence smiled wryly. "At Scutari there were moments when the officials, to a man, would have burned me like Joan of Arc. But they knew they couldn't, and knew the War Office would not turn me out, because the English public was with me."

The butler entered with the mail. Since Miss Florence's arrival, the butler had obtained a bigger tray for the mail which was of tremendous proportions, stacks of letters and packages every day, and most of them addressed to this most popular of British subjects. Parthe took the letters and sorted them.

"Here is one from Sir James Clark in Scotland, Flo."

"Open it," Florence said. "Read it to me."

Parthe read. Sir James was asking Miss Nightingale and her father to be his guests during September at his house near Balmoral. He added that the Queen would be in residence then at Balmoral Castle close by; and the Queen had said she hoped to see Miss Nightingale.

Florence sat up suddenly. She recalled something which the Queen had said in the letter accompanying the jeweled badge, "It will be a very great satisfaction to me, when you return at last to these shores, to make the acquaintance of one who has set so bright an example to our sex." Would not this be the ideal opportunity to interest Victoria in the scheme which was obsessing all Florence's thoughts?

"Parthe, I shall accept Sir James's invitation!"

"But *can* you, Flo? Have you the strength to go to Scotland?"

"Of course, I'm going," said Florence. "It's a wonderful chance."

Lying there resting (or so, at least, Parthe believed) Florence thought of a scheme she had recently been devising. It was a thing so ambitious that any other person might well have shrunk from contemplating it. But Florence Nightingale was made of sterner stuff. She would be faithful to the vow repeated so often in the burying-ground above the Barrack in Scutari; what had happened must never happen again and the bitter lessons of the Crimea must be instilled now, before time swept the war into oblivion.

What would it mean to keep the vow? She did not know. But whatever it meant, that could be done. And must be!

She would need backing and reenforcements. She would be the Lady-in-Chief, but there would have to be captains to command, men distinguished and in high place, men she could count on.

Who? Well, Sidney Herbert. Yes, she could always count on him; like herself, his one thought was to establish God's kingdom on earth. Service was a religion to him, as it was to her. Dr. John Sutherland was another of the same stripe—Dr. Sutherland, the London physician who had been a member of the sanitation commission dispatched by Lord Shaftesbury to Scutari. Florence had liked Dr. Sutherland and recognized in him the reformer's temperament.

These two, then, to start with. And more, later.

Mr. William Shore Nightingale and his daughter Florence went to Sir James Clark's home, Birk Hall, September 19, 1856: and two days later Sir James drove his guests to Balmoral Castle and there introduced them to Queen Victoria and her husband, the Prince Consort.

It is only good manners to prepare for an afternoon's visit with royalty—Florence had prepared in more ways than one. Ever since she had known it was in prospect, she had resolved that this afternoon should be important, to herself, her plans, the nation as a whole. In these last several days she had been studying, poring over statistics, storing up information. When the Queen inquired about her work, she was ready with detailed answers.

She pointed out the fact which had so impressed her, that the soldiers were not properly cared for in peace times, and therefore went, undernourished and poorly clad and frequently half-sick, into war service. During the first seven months of the Crimean campaign, the mortality rate from disease alone had been sixty percent —"a rate, Your Majesty, which exceeds that of the Great Plague in London, a higher rate than the mortality in cholera." But even more dreadful to contemplate, the death rate among soldiers, young men between the ages of twenty and thirty-five, in peace times was double the civilian death rate—"in some London districts, the difference is much worse. Our soldiers enlist to death in the barracks!"

Surely a royal commission should be ordered, to look into the situation, and all the facilities which science and education had developed should be employed to remedy it. And immediately! Delay would be fatal. She denounced all who might advise delay.

"No one can feel for the army as I do. These people who talk to us have all fed their children on the fat of the land and dressed them in velvet and silk, while we have been away. I have had to see *my* children dressed in a dirty blanket and an old pair of regimental trousers, and see them fed on raw, salt meat, and nine thousand of my children—from causes which might have been prevented —are now in their forgotten graves. But I can never forget! People must have seen that long winter to know what it was!"

Miss Nightingale's eloquence was very moving; she spoke with intense emotion, and Queen Victoria believed her. A royal commission? But in England, a constitutional monarchy, the Crown cannot institute reforms which have not originated with its ministers. This, said the Queen, was something Lord Panmure, the Secretary of State for War, must sponsor. Since Lord Panmure was expected at Balmoral within the week, Miss Nightingale must stay and talk with him. Lord Panmure must be persuaded, and the Queen thought this could be more easily done if she herself were there to aid in the persuading.

Florence was not so optimistic about Lord Panmure. She had written to him just after her return from Scutari, wanting to put her suggestions before him, and his reply had been polite enough but very evasive. But if the Queen wished it, she would wait at Balmoral for him, and hope for the best.

That night, the Prince Consort wrote in his journal of Miss Nightingale's visit, "We are much pleased with her; she is extremely modest."

The Queen, in a letter to the Duke of Cambridge, wrote a comment which was destined to become a classic: "Such a clear head. I wish we had her at the War Office."

Florence's first encounter with Lord Panmure was, it seemed, a successful one. He was a large, burly Scotsman, with thick shoulders, a shaggy head, and a way of moving slowly and ponderously. Florence promptly nicknamed him the "Bison," and called him that in her letters

Promptly renamed him The Bison

to Sidney Herbert with whom she was in constant communication. She conferred with the Bison both at Balmoral and at Birk Hall; and it was agreed that she should write a report of her Crimean experiences, with notes on necessary reforms, this document to be considered by the cabinet. Soon after her departure from Scotland, Florence heard what the Bison's opinion of her had been in these meetings. Sir James Clark's son wrote to Miss Nightingale, "You may like to know that you fairly overcame Pan. We found him with his mane absolutely silky, and a loving sadness pervading his whole being." And Sidney Herbert wrote, "I forget whether I told you that the Bison was very much pleased with his interview with you. He says that he was very much surprised at your physical appearance, as I think you must have been with his."

"Perhaps," mused Florence, "Lord Panmure has pictured all lady reformers as freaks."

When the Bison's request had been seconded by Lord Palmerston, the Prime Minister, Florence launched at once into the assembling of material for her report. She went to London and took rooms at the Burlington Hotel in Old Burlington Street. Aunt Mai Smith accompanied her; and Florence gave her parents and Parthe to understand that she wanted no other chaperonage. As she had foreseen, this separation from her family aroused protests—especially from Mrs. Nightingale, who had fondly hoped that after so many adventures, Florence would now step back into the role of a dutiful daughter at home. But, having tasted freedom from family bonds, Florence had no intention of being trapped by them again.

As a matter of fact, her discontent at being at home, her resentment of any family claims made upon her, seemed to deepen as she grew older—perhaps because she thought of herself as an agent for service rather than as a woman, perhaps because she had not in her nature the longing for affection and warm personal relationships which most women know. Her capacity for love was great, but it was reserved for the human race, for the poor and abused and underprivileged; she chose not to expend it on individuals. The work she had done, and had still to do, was always uppermost in her heart and brain; she lived for that alone; everything else was superfluous, a distraction, every moment missed from her work an extravagance—almost a sin.

Friends were valuable only as they could be used to advance her work. Aunt Mai and Uncle Sam Smith were valuable because of their undeviating obedience to the demands of their niece's work. Her father she would see occasionally, in gratitude for the sympathy he had never failed to extend. As for Mamma and Parthe, they had not approved of Florence's work in the old days; and though their plaintiveness had melted away in the bright glow of her fame, they probably didn't approve of the work now. She felt that she owed them no debt of any sort. Obviously, she was not obliged to share existence with them.

Once settled in the Burlington Hotel (with Aunt Mai posted as a bodyguard, to keep off the curious folk who always haunt a celebrity) Florence began the selection of men she wanted as members of a royal commission to put through her reforms. Sidney Herbert must be chairman—she was sure of that! But the others must be painstakingly examined and each one pledged to carry out her ideas. As she had said, and as she honestly believed, no one on earth could "feel for the army" as she did, no one knew so well the faults in the present system. After weeks of correspondence and consultations, weeks in which her hotel apartment came to be known as the "Little War Office," she completed her roster of commissioners; and when at length Lord Panmure called on her, she was able to persuade him to the appointment of all but one of her nominees.

This in itself was a triumph; and much encouraged, Florence proceeded to write the report Lord Panmure had asked for.

A voluminous thing, that report! A monumental labor, a manuscript thousands of pages long, a full account of Florence's experiences in the Crimean War, but more than that—a medical history of the war, with chapters of figures and statistics and sections dealing with army diet and cookery, washing and canteens, commissariats and provisioning agents, the construction of army hospitals, the education and promotion of medical officers. No phase of those problems faced and solved at Scutari was omitted from the report; and in the final section the Lady-in-Chief summarized her suggestions for reform.

But though Florence wrote at prodigious length, she had finished before Lord Panmure was ready to name the royal commissioners. The Bison, she discovered, was indeed a slow-moving animal. To Florence, with her vigorous disposition and sharp temper, this tendency to procrastinate was maddening.

For months then she applied herself, with Sidney Herbert's connivance, to a process which she described as "bullying the Bison." She wanted action—at once; whereas the Bison seemed to have an aversion even to the thought of action. "Appoint the commissioners *now*!" she begged; the Bison answered that he had the gout in his hands, he could not write. Gout in his hands? Florence was enraged. "It is the flimsiest of excuses. Keep on bullying him!" she said to Mr. Herbert. "Threaten him. Tell him that unless he acts today, you will resign the chairmanship!" Mr. Herbert threatened—and the Bison only grunted.

But Florence held the trump card in this political game, and in the spring of 1857 she decided to use it. Suppose she should herself publish the story of the Crimean campaign—publish it from the housetops, so that the world would know of the British government's sins against the British army? She sent word to Lord Panmure that she would brook no further delay. "Sir, I shall go to the country with my story!"

As the Bison very well knew, the country was with Miss Nightingale. The last thing he could afford was to find himself pitted against her in a public airing of her cause. For Miss Nightingale was right. Simple justice was on her side. She was right, and the career of any man who opposed her now was at stake and would be forfeited.

So the Bison stirred. The Royal Warrant was issued, the commissioners named, the commission started its operations.

At her headquarters in Old Burlington Street, Florence chalked up another triumph. She had forced this action. But she was rather sure that her report would never be published, and therefore she arranged to have it printed and privately circulated at her own expense, as a matter of record—and as an instrument which, perhaps, she might have to use again.

She determined to see to it that the commission did not adopt Lord Panmure's tactics, but should push through its inquiry with all possible speed.

18

MORE LAMPS LIGHTED

WITH THE APPOINTMENT of the royal commission, Florence had made the first step in her program of reform. During the summer of 1857, she busied herself with the second step—that of forcing the commission to accept the specific aims set forth in her report. Four things she demanded: all army barracks must be rendered sanitary and livable; an army statistical department must be organized; an army medical school must be instituted; the entire army medical department must be revolutionized and reconstructed and all existing army hospital regulations revised to conform with her own scientific ideas. She could not, of course, be a member of the commission; as a woman, she was barred from any open participation in its labors. But she could control it—remaining behind the scenes and working through Sidney Herbert, Dr. Sutherland and the other commissioners, all of whom, with one exception, were sworn to her cause.

She was conscious of her powers. Not only was the Queen her avowed ally, but she had also the masses of the British people adoring and trusting her. Besides, she had so impressed herself upon the public mind that she was spoken of everywhere as infallibly versed in all questions of public service. The common belief was that whatever your problem, Miss Nightingale could solve it for you. She was wise, she was good, she had the love of humanity in her heart; and her experience was unlimited. Little wonder then that pioneers in every conceivable type of reform came to her with their own pet theories, asking for help, or that statesmen sought and deferred to her opinions.

She listened to what they said

They came to the Burlington Hotel, all these people who wished to see Miss Nightingale, and they waited in lines outside her door, hoping for the chance. Most of them she received, for a half-hour at a time; she listened to what they said and noted any of it that seemed sensible. If any man who might be of assistance to her stayed away, she sent for him—and he came as quickly as he could. She talked with the great and the near-great; England's Prime Minister was not too proud or too busy to respond to her summons.

Sidney Herbert was in consultation with her every day, and Dr. Sutherland quite as often. Indeed, these three composed the inner "cabinet" of Florence's "Little War Office"; and between the intervals of her larger meeting with an ever-increasing company of medical and social scientists, the small "cabinet" was in almost constant session. Yet even so, the Lady-in-Chief sometimes felt that Mr. Herbert and Dr. Sutherland could, if they tried, exert themselves a bit more in her behalf, and at such times she chided them.

Mr. Herbert had long ago acknowledged Florence as his guiding star and never protested. But Dr. Sutherland, a big jovial man, twenty years her senior, would on occasion tease her in fatherly vein about her impatience. "My dear Lady," he wrote once, replying to an angry note from Florence, "do not be unreasonable. I would have been with you yesterday, but, alas, my will was stronger than my legs. I have been at the Commission today, and as yet there is nothing to fear. I was too fatigued and too stupid to see you afterwards, but I intend coming tomorrow about 12 o'clock, and we can then prepare for the campaign of the coming week."

But if she seemed to drive these friends incontinently, she was no less exacting with herself. As Selina Bracebridge had said so long ago, Florence was not as well as she pretended to be and she began to show the strain of raddled nerves.

She had gone to Embley for Christmas and again for a few days in the spring—but her work had followed her there. Parthe declared that she quite hated the sight of the post with its long official envelopes addressed to Florence. But to Florence the official envelopes were an essential, the tools of her trade. Compared with what she was doing now, all she had accomplished at Scutari was the merest child's play, she said. Let Parthe and Mamma and Papa worry about her, if they must. That was not important. Only her work was important. There were many times when she was so exhausted that she lay for hours on the sofa in a sort of stupor, eyes shut, face pallid, scarcely breathing, as if she had fainted dead away—but if anyone dared say she was too ill for work, she would leap up and burst forth in tempestuous denial.

As the summer wore on and her health became worse, Dr. Sutherland pleaded with her to slacken the furious pace. With good-natured affection he told her that she was interested in everybody's sanitary improvement but her own. "Pray leave us all to ourselves, soldiers and all, for a while," he said. "We shall all be the better for a rest." Sidney Herbert added his voice to the argument, wouldn't she stop for a brief vacation? "I wish you could be turned into a cross-country squire like me for a few weeks!"

But no, she would not rest, would not stop. Instead, she started a new project, that of preparing a document in which she accounted for the administration of all funds and gifts sent to her during the war. She was taut with nerves, like a fine coiled spring that has been wound too tightly. Why, why, she cried, did people keep *pecking* at her? These admonitions, these warnings were echoes from the drawing-rooms of Embley and Lea Hurst; she had heard them since she was a child; and she would have none of them.

By autumn her illness was so marked that she at last consented to go to Malvern for treatment at the sanatorium there. Aunt Mai was her companion. When Malvern seemed not to benefit Florence, the two went on to other health resorts, dragging wearily from place to place. The doctors who examined her at this time were baffled by her case. Organically, they said, she was sound; but the years of over-exertion had shattered her nervous system; the doctors feared she must be an incurable invalid for the remainder of her life.

An incurable invalid? Florence was irate at the pronouncement. Learning in November that nurses were needed for the army in India, she wrote to volunteer her services—an offer made when she scarcely had strength to stand alone and, fortunately, the offer was refused.

A month later, Florence became convinced that she would soon die, and she set about ordering her affairs. She wrote a letter to Sidney Herbert outlining a course of action by which he could carry through her reforms, and expressing regret that she could not stay alive to "do the nurses," and to spend the money in the Florence Nightingale Fund with which she had hoped to found a training-school for her profession. Her inheritance she was leaving for the building of modern barracks, she said. She wrote also to Parthe, directing the disposal of all her personal belongings and keepsakes and asking that she be buried in the Crimea. She was sad at the thought of approaching death, but resigned to it because it seemed God's plan. "Perhaps He wants a 'Sanitary Officer' now for my Crimeans in some other world where they are gone."

She was still in her suite at the Old Burlington, for she preferred to die there in the midst of her work, rather than at either of her father's homes. But the weeks and the months passed and she did not die—and presently she was almost magically revived by the publication of the Royal Commission's report. Miss Nightingale's advice had been followed in every detail by the men whose appointments she had secured. Well, now that these things had been recommended, they must be put into effect!

Immediately she launched into this task, the final step in her program. Thin and white, propped up with pillows in her bed, she flung herself into the new work, writing, writing, studying charts and graphs, compiling statistics, calling statesmen to her for conferences—with slender, delicate fingers manipulating the policies of an empire.

In June, 1858, Parthe married Sir Harry Verney. The event meant little to Florence who was engrossed in matters of national portent and, as Aunt Mai said, working as if "each day may be the last on which she will have power to work." Writing to a friend, Florence commented that Parthe liked the marriage—"which is the main thing. And my father is very fond of Sir Harry Verney, which is the next best thing. He is old and rich, which is a disadvantage. He is active, has a will of his own and four children ready made, which is an advantage. So, on the whole, I think these reflections tend to approbation."

Perhaps the truth was that Florence had grown so far from her family that she could be touched only lightly by anything happening within the family circle. Parthe and her mother were almost like strangers to her; she had asked them not to come to the Old Burlington on their London visits, lest they disturb her at her work; and it was only infrequently that she ventured to Embley for a day or two, traveling in an invalid's conveyance and waited upon by Aunt Mai or by her friend, Mr. Arthur Clough, the poet, who had recently attached himself to Miss Nightingale's staff, somewhat in the role of errand boy or general factotum. With her father, Florence was more lenient, permitting him to call upon her at the hotel whenever he was in London. ("Dear Papa," she wrote, "I shall always be well enough to see *you* while this mortal coil is on me at all.") By special appointment, and sometimes as often as twice a day, he would slip into her room and sit beside the bed, talking to her for a full half-hour about religion and philosophy, those subjects which had always so fascinated him.

Now and then Hilary Bonham Carter came, or some other cousin, or the Bracebridges or Madame Mohl; and all were allowed a glimpse of Florence, leaning back among her pillows, and the counterpane covered with books, notebooks, writing paraphernalia. But mostly she saw only such persons as were working with her.

She did not see a great deal even of Aunt Mai who, as Parthe said, was the "dragon," posted outside her niece's bedchamber, warding off interlopers.

To an extent, and in a queer way, physical weakness became a protection to Florence, a haven from the interruptions and distractions which fret one who leads a more normal life, an economy measure to conserve time and energy. Uncle Sam Smith was in charge of her finances; she never had to bother about money or bills, for Uncle Sam made sure that she was comfortably maintained in the Burlington suite. Dr. Sutherland was always at hand, assuming the position of confidential secretary and taking over many taxing small duties. A request to speak to Miss Nightingale must first be scanned by Dr. Sutherland, who judged whether or not the request might be worthy of her attention. She saw no one whom she wished not to see; and yet she could turn away petitioners without offense, since it was well known that she was an invalid, struggling to perform a splendid and gigantic work and constantly working beyond her actual strength. There was Mr. Clough too, who asked for nothing more than the reward of serving Florence—in any way at all, who was happy just to fetch the mail, or write her inconsequential letters, or do up packages, or escort her on infrequent excursions in a closed carriage through the park.

To the British people at large Miss Nightingale was a lovely symbol, almost a legendary figure, a woman who had sacrificed (and continued to sacrifice) her youth, her ease, the pleasures of society, even her health in the cause of mercy. It was understood that she did not now appear in public, yet ever and again the rumor would get about that she *had* appeared, in the streets, in a restaurant or music hall. Then the woman who faintly resembled Miss Nightingale, who had been taken for her, would be surrounded by worshipful, sentimental throngs of folk who stretched out their hands to her, crying, "Let me stroke your shawl, ma'am! Please, ma'am, let me touch the hem of your skirt!"

When told of such incidents, Florence was humbly grateful—and vaguely irritated. She had never coveted fame or applause. She knew that she possessed genius, but she used it for the relief of God's creatures and she felt that she deserved no thanks.

Though she had many strings to her bow, many men of high rank in the realm at her beck and call, there was none like Sidney Herbert—probably history has never known a more unusual friendship than theirs. The association had in it no hint of romance; Mr. Herbert was happily married and his wife was that person whom Florence always addressed as "my dearest." Yet no two comrades ever shared so completely in ideals, ambitions and purposes as did Florence Nightingale and Sidney Herbert. On every question they saw eye-to-eye; together they saw each question whole, the talents of one supplementing the talents of the other.

Both were reformers born and bred; both were intensely religious; but of the two, Florence was the leader. Brave, chivalrous, unselfish and charming though he was, Sidney Herbert lacked the obstinate, ruthless, almost fanatical zeal which was so much a part of Florence's character. He regarded her as his superior in all things; she commanded and he obeyed. Several hours of every day he spent with her, and the times between their meetings he interspersed with notes and messages.

19

HEROINE'S PROGRESS

So SUPERBLY DID Florence manage her campaign that by 1861 every one of her proposed reforms had been effected and a new era in the welfare and efficiency of the British army had dawned. In the future there would be no such cruelties of neglect as had been endured by the troops in the Crimea. From this time forward, British soldiers wherever they were, would be quartered in barracks and hospitals which were correctly heated and lighted; their water supply would be ample and pure; their food would be properly cooked and their health constantly supervised.

Florence Nightingale was responsible for all these changes. Yet, having brought them into being, she was still not quite satisfied. The War Office itself had not been reorganized; she saw it as an old, outmoded, creaking machine, tied around with red tape which she had always detested—and she determined that it, too, must be reformed!

During most of the five-year period since her return from the Crimea, Sidney Herbert had been Secretary for War in the British cabinet, the indefatigable champion of all reform measures; and to him Florence now looked for assistance in her latest endeavor. Florence, in her sanctuary at the Burlington Hotel, would draw up the plans, which Mr. Herbert must then put into practice.

Root and branch, the War Office must be modernized; Florence did not doubt that together she and Sidney Herbert could bring it about.

There was, of course, antagonism from the start. Those men who had for years served in the War Office were instantly suspicious and set themselves to resist the reorganization. One among them, Sir Benjamin Hawes, the permanent Under-Secretary, was especially unfriendly to the idea of change.

"Our scheme," said Florence, "will probably result in Ben Hawes' resignation, and that is another of its advantages."

But Ben Hawes himself had no notion of resigning— not, at least, without a battle. He had long been a fixture in his job and meant to stay.

In the midst of the preliminary skirmishing, which Florence thoroughly enjoyed, Sidney Herbert suddenly fell ill. Or perhaps his illness was not so sudden, after all, for he had never been a physically robust man; he had been working without respite, and a year earlier he had been severely stricken with pleurisy. Anyway, he now was so far from well that doctors told him he must retire from public life, he must rest—or risk a total breakdown.

No news could have seemed more disastrous to Florence Nightingale, and she received it first with skepticism and then with resentment. Sidney Herbert retiring because of illness? But that was absurd! She herself had been ill all this while—so ill, indeed, that she scarcely ever rose from her bed! Yet she had never once thought of stopping work. Did the doctors say that Sidney Herbert had a fatal disease? What nonsense! "You know," exclaimed Florence, "I don't believe in fatal diseases." She sent for him and he came to consult with her, and she told him that he could not rest until the War Office had been reformed; the goal was so near, so very near, that he could not turn back now. He had been created a baron recently and as Lord Herbert he was entitled to a seat in the House of Lords. Why not, said Florence, give up his seat in the House of Commons and seek the comparative quiet of the House of Lords, remaining at the War Office, but taking things at a more leisurely stride?

Herbert reluctantly assented to this compromise. He would do as Florence said.

She was delighted. "One fight more," she cried, "the best and the last!"

So, for several more months, the fight went on—with Sidney Herbert's condition growing steadily weaker. Now he was attacked by fainting fits, and there were days when it was only by sipping brandy that he could keep on his feet. He listened as Florence spurred him on, cheering and encouraging him; but he knew finally that he had reached the end of his efforts. He would never be able to reform the War Office; and the dreadful moment had arrived when he must go to Florence and tell her of his failure.

He wrote out his resignation, and on July 9 he called at Florence's hotel to bid her good-bye before his departure for a hospital at Spa. Florence greeted him coldly, with reproaches. He said sadly that he was beaten.

"Beaten?" she repeated. "Don't you see that you've simply thrown away the game? And with all the winning cards in your hands! And so noble a game! Sidney Herbert beaten! Beaten by Ben Hawes! It is a disgrace—a worse disgrace than the hospitals at Scutari!"

This was their farewell, for he was never to see her again. On July 25 he was removed from Spa to his palatial and beloved home at Wilton, where a week later he died. His last murmurings before he lapsed into unconsciousness were of Florence.

This was their farewell

"Poor Florence! Poor Florence! Our joint work unfinished!"

What was her reaction to this calamity? She was wild with grief, she was inconsolable. Sidney Herbert dead? Gone—gone beyond recall? It could not be true!

But it was true, and when the fact was borne in upon her, she stifled her sobs and wrote long letters in praise of him, extolling his virtues as a friend, a Christian, an English gentleman. She wrote a memorandum on his achievements as an army reformer and sent this paper to Mr. Gladstone so that it might become a public record for all to read. Everything she herself had accomplished owed its success to Sidney Herbert, she said. Everything! He had been the "head and center" of it all. If remorse tinged her sorrow, if she felt that she had in any way hastened his collapse, she did not say so; but always afterward, whether in writing or speaking she referred to Sidney Herbert as her "dear master" and cherished his image in her heart.

The months which followed were difficult for Florence. Twice more misfortune struck at her. Arthur Clough died the next spring, a genuine bereavement, for the poet in his modest, self-effacing manner had made himself almost indispensable, each day doing dozens of small services and kindnesses to accommodate Miss Nightingale and lighten her burdens. Perhaps she hadn't sufficiently appreciated Arthur Clough or the quality of his devotion while he lived; but when he died she sorely missed him. She could not bear to open a newspaper lest she see his name in print and be reminded of her loss; and she sometimes wondered dismally whether she hadn't relied too much upon him and been "a drag upon his health and spirits."

Grief of another but no less poignant sort came to her from the most unexpected of all sources—from Aunt Mai Smith who, shortly after Clough's death, said that she must leave Florence and live again with her own family.

This to Florence seemed desertion—nothing else!—and she was wrathful. In vain Aunt Mai explained her reasons; she was now sixty-three years old, she said, and felt that she had earned a rest; her children and husband needed her; she wanted to be at home rather than posted, a "dragon," outside Florence's closed door. For these last four years, though every day in written communication with her famous niece, and only a few paces away, Aunt Mai hadn't *seen* Florence even once to speak to! Probably the loneliness of such an assignment had palled upon Aunt Mai; at any rate, she asked to be released.

Well, Florence could not hold Aunt Mai against her will, but she interpreted her going as disloyalty, as proof that she totally lacked understanding of the lofty causes for which Florence toiled. Evidently the business of reform meant nothing to Aunt Mai or she could not thus throw it all over at the slightest pretext. What fools, what utterly worthless creatures women were! In a towering rage, Florence wrote to Madame Mohl, pouring out the bitterness of her feeling against Aunt Mai. "I am sick with indignation at what wives and mothers will do out of the most egregious selfishness. And people call it all maternal or conjugal affection and think it pretty to say so."

But Aunt Mai left, just the same; and it was not until a very long time afterward that the breach was healed—and then only partially.

To "save something from the wreckage," Florence plunged into her work. It was her infallible refuge; it could not die, deceive or disappoint her. It was all that mattered in the world, and there was plenty of it to do. She sank herself in work, knowing that unlike human relationships it could never betray her.

Her activities during the ensuing few years were so many and varied as to defy enumeration, and to them all she brought that penetrating vision and intellectual skill which made certain their success.

The Civil War was then starting in the United States; and she was drawn into a correspondence with the American Secretary of War, advising him, providing him with statistics, rendering aid which was warmly welcomed and could not have been obtained elsewhere.

She published her *Notes on Nursing* and *Notes on Hospitals,* two detailed, instructive pamphlets which, printed and reprinted, were hailed as the clearest expositions on the subjects ever written, and were in reality the basis for all methods of modern treatment of the sick. No hospital was built in England without her inspection and approval of the plans.

She undertook and carried through to a victorious conclusion the introduction of sanitation in India, and the formation of a royal commission to do there what had been done for the British army at home. This was, if anything, a more enormous feat than any other she had attempted, a splendid labor of such scope as to affect and improve the lives of literally millions of people in that distant land where she had never been. She became the authority on all Indian matters for the British government; engineers and municipal officials sent her their plans for drainage and water facilities, and commissariat officials consulted her on soldiers' rations and victualing arrangements, and medical officers wrote to her for answers to their problems. Whatever progress was made in India was due in no small part to the imagination and sagacity of a bedridden woman in a London hotel room. For many years it was the custom for the newly appointed Viceroy, before he left England, to pay a visit to Miss Nightingale who would inform him concisely and accurately about the situation which he faced.

The foundation of the Nightingale Training School for Nurses was another event of this crowded, fruitful period. Since the time of its collection, the Nightingale fund had been invested in the name of a board of trustees, awaiting the moment when Florence should administer it. Now she chose St. Thomas' Hospital in London as the location for her school; she mapped the courses of study and started the first classes. Though she did not go to the hospital to witness her nurses at their routine, she kept the strictest account of them and was familiar with everything they did. As the school settled into smooth-running order, its graduates went out, like a body of apostles, carrying with them the knowledge they had absorbed and proving to the world how well they had been trained.

As a natural sequel to her training of nurses, Florence turned next to the appalling need for reform in English workhouses and infirmaries. This had weighed upon her since the long-ago days when she had taught in the London Ragged Schools and observed the piteous straits of the great city's paupers and destitute. It was among such people that the old-fashioned nurses held sway—the drunken, blundering and often immoral attendants hired by thoughtless public officials to preside over public institutions and the indigent poor for whom nobody seemed to have any real concern and who were powerless to better their circumstances.

In Liverpool an experiment in district nursing was being made and, as usual, Miss Nightingale was solicited for advice. But in this case, she gave more than advice; she co-operated by sending twelve of her St. Thomas' nurses to Liverpool where they not only set up a system of district nursing but took charge of the workhouse and converted it to a model institution. Within ten years trained nurses were serving in infirmaries all over the country and the old, vicious methods had faded into obscurity.

At the same time, while directing the Liverpool venture, Florence was exerting pressure for the enactment of new Poor Laws, so that the former evils could never recur. In this, as in everything, she was successful. "From the first," said one of her fellow-workers, "I had a sort of fixed faith that Florence Nightingale could do anything, and that faith is still firm in me, and so it came to pass that the instant that name entered the lists I felt the fight was virtually won."

It was an age for reform in England. A corner seemed to have been turned, an era left behind. The public conscience was waking from old apathy, the desire to remedy old evils was everywhere, stirring, in the air; the inherent rights of the common man were coming to be recognized.

Perhaps even without Florence Nightingale some of these advancements might eventually have been realized —slowly, after long, damaging delays. But to Florence Nightingale must go full credit for hastening the processes of reform, setting them in motion and then pushing them relentlessly toward the climax which conquered all obstacles to progress. Stubborn and fiery she was, striving for perfection and pleased with nothing less, imbued herself with a demon of industry and having the godlike ability to transmit her fervor to others, the personal magnetism of an evangelist, the sweeping eloquence of an exhorter. Thus, she was the principal exponent, the mainspring of all good things which the years of reformation produced.

La Vie de Florence Rossignol . . . Writing each night in her diary, she must frequently have thought of the first slim volume in the series, that one written in schoolgirl French for the governess, dear Miss Christie. The life of Florence Nightingale? What a glorious chronicle it had become!

The story of a heroine . . .

20

AT HOME IN SOUTH STREET

FROM THE MOMENT of Sidney Herbert's death, Florence had been dissatisfied with her suite at the Burlington Hotel. Somehow, it seemed haunted by memories of him. She seemed always to see his handsome, courtly figure seated beside her, to hear his voice. Also the ghost of Arthur Clough was there ("He used to tell me how the leaves were coming out," she said, "knowing that, without his eyes, I should never see the spring again!")—and the imagined presence of Aunt Mai. These three who had been so helpful and now had gone. "I am glad," she wrote (most sorrowfully), "to end a day which can never come back, gladdest to end a month."

For several years she moved about, seeking a home of her own in which to settle down, finally taking a house at No. 10 South Street, which her father leased for her and which, except for rare intervals, she was to occupy for nearly a half-century.

The house was small and pleasant, rather like a tower in structure, having four floors besides basement and attic. On each floor were two rooms, a big one with large windows facing south, a little one with northern exposure. On the ground floor was a dining-room, lined with bookcases, and a sunny, balconied drawing-room, Victorian in style, with more bookcases and a sofa upon which Florence reclined whenever she ventured downstairs.

The second-floor rooms were literally filled with books and boxes and cupboards of paper and files of correspondence which accumulated rapidly and were never destroyed. But Miss Nightingale's bedroom above was less businesslike and more attractive—a bright, airy, peaceful chamber with white walls and windows which had no blinds or curtains to keep out the light or obstruct the view. Here the furnishings were cheerful; a comfortable bed, tables and chairs conveniently located; pictures, a rose-shaded lamp, bowls of flowers sent up from the gardens at Embley and Lea Hurst in season.

On the top floor of the house was a guest room, and sometimes Florence had guests staying with her for a few days or a week. This did not necessarily mean that the guests were entertained personally by their hostess; usually they never laid eyes on her at all, but were granted the freedom of her hospitality—and read the notes she wrote them, which were brought by a maid or Dr. Sutherland.

As Florence said to Madame Mohl, "I am *obliged* (by my ill-health) to make Life an Art, to be always thinking of it; because otherwise I should do *nothing*."

The demands made upon her time and attention were constant, her mail was a vast flood of pamphlets, periodicals, letters. Her father had made her a liberal allowance, which was turned over to Mr. Sam Smith who paid the household accounts and distributed all surplus money at Florence's wish. Her way of living was so simple that she could give financial aid to many charities, and these she chose with care. But the begging letters, the appeals from every type of eccentric and crank, the ridiculous proposals of marriage which poured in upon her, Uncle Sam must deal with. The directions Florence scribbled to

Mr. Smith were characteristically definite: "Choke off this woman and tell her that I shall *never* be well enough to see her, here or *hereafter*."—"These miserable ecclesiastical quacks! Could you give them a lesson?"—"Dear Uncle Sam, please choke off this idiot."

All legitimate requests to see Miss Nightingale passed through the hands of Dr. Sutherland, who presided as her private secretary and chief steward in the drawing-room below. To Dr. Sutherland came at one time or another most of the dignitaries and celebrities, statesmen, scholars and politicians, reformers by the score, of England—and, indeed, of the civilized world—applying for an audience with the great lady whose approval or disapproval meant the difference between a cause's triumph or defeat. The truly unlucky applicants were those who never reached Miss Nightingale, whom Dr. Sutherland rejected at first glance. But what was the procedure for those more fortunate, upon whom Dr. Sutherland smiled rather than frowned?

Once told that you could see Miss Nightingale, a day and hour were set and you waited for your appointment. Then, at last, you were ushered to her upper room, you sat on a straight-backed chair at a proper distance from her bedside—she questioned you and you answered. Your conversation was strictly in the nature of an interview, nothing else, with no small talk, no wasted moments. You put your subject before Miss Nightingale, and almost instantly she had grasped it. Her mind was like a keen-edged knife cutting through complications to the gist of the matter. She might seem little and fragile lying there, but that was a deception. Only her body was fragile. Her intellect was quick, penetrating, strong; and whatever words you uttered had significance to her; she understood them, they were a part of her own information. You might have studied this thing, but you soon discovered that she too had studied it—and her knowledge probably went deeper than yours.

She might seem little and fragile

The conversation at an end, you rose and said goodbye and took yourself away, for there were others waiting, dozens of others, in a schedule divided for just such brief visits. And the lady must not be wearied!

One person at a time was admitted to the room. Miss

AT HOME IN SOUTH STREET

Nightingale received all her callers singly. For many years she never heard two other persons talking together or was included in a group where the talk was general. No person, even though a member of the household, ever entered the room by chance, no one ever appeared unexpectedly. If you saw Miss Nightingale at all, it was by express invitation and arrangement—and she, not you, determined the length of your visit.

When you were out of the room, you realized that quietly, courteously, tactfully, she had dismissed you. And that was that. Well, you would never forget her. Never!

After 1868 Florence toiled less strenuously at public reforms. The government had changed, many of her influential allies had retired; and though she still retained powerful contacts, she herself (as she phrased it) "went out of office." But she was industrious as ever, for now she could more closely supervise her training school for nurses.

This became her main activity. She saw to the moving of the institution to a better site, and then she took it in hand, much as if she were the headmistress of a girls' boarding school and the nurses her pupils.

She was very particular about the kind of young woman enrolling in training classes; she interviewed each candidate and it was only with her consent that one could be accepted. After these interviews, Miss Nightingale wrote down a memorandum of the impression made upon her by the visitor—what seemed to be this girl's attainments, what were her chances to be graduated and then to be useful in the world? Florence found such efforts gruelling and not always to her liking. "It takes a great deal out of me," she wrote to a friend. "God meant me for a reformer and I have turned out a detective." But it was, she thought, a duty which she must not shirk.

From her South Street home she exercised a remote control of all that went on in the school. Dr. Sutherland did the inspecting very regularly and thoroughly; from his reports, Florence drew her conclusions and checked upon the institution's welfare. She considered and dictated how the nurses should spend their holidays, she planned their futures, she had them come to her house, one at a time, for tea; she offered her guest room as a hostel for the matrons and teachers on their annual vacations.

She sent gifts of books and fruit to the nurses' dormitories and in summer the hospital was decorated with huge bouquets of rhododendrons from the Embley borders. Each January she wrote a New Year's address, which her brother-in-law, Sir Harry Verney, read aloud to the entire school in solemn assembly, in a hall garlanded with Lea Hurst evergreen boughs. The gentle wisdom of Miss Nightingale's words, delivered by Sir Harry, was a feature of the school calendar; and afterward, her address was printed and each nurse presented with a copy.

The detailed supervision lavished upon the students followed them as they went out into service; Florence kept her young women in sight, watching over them as a mother guards and guides her daughters. She corresponded with hundreds of them, receiving and answering thousands of letters every year from all corners of the globe where the Nightingale graduates were demonstrating the soundness of their training. Because of her efficiency and insistence upon an excellent preparation, the standards for nursing were raised throughout the British Empire and in many countries across the seas.

She had a profound conviction about the work of nursing—which in time led to a prolonged debate with those experts who were promoting the movement for passage of a Nurses Registration Act.

To Florence, nursing was first and last a religious endeavor, as much so as the vocation of a nun; she was unalterably against any dissenting opinion, she had nothing but scorn for persons who regarded it as a business, she shrank from hearing it spoken of as a profession. A nurse, she said, should feel that hers was a high and sacred dedication, in which she was charged with the care of souls. Thus, moral and spiritual motives must be the nurse's best equipment, religious aims her vital quality. Such intangibles could never be *registered,* could they? No!—and the woman who looked at nursing as primarily a means of livelihood was not worthy of being a nurse at all!

The refuting argument to such reasoning might be that Miss Nightingale's experiences had been extraordinary; in her own case, the necessity of earning a livelihood had been absent. She could well afford to say that wages and salaries were no factor; she had known only conditions of financial security, even affluence; she had never been paid for her work and did not want or need to be paid— by contrast, she had donated large sums to the work from her large income. But, if her ideas prevailed, would not nursing soon be an endeavor—or a business, a profession —limited in membership only to women who had both leisure and wealth in combination with a religious inspiration? How many such women were there? Where were they to be found?

Though she fought bitterly in opposition, the majority of trained nurses came to endorse registration, and Florence had to bow to the inevitable. But she was unreconciled. The whole matter annoyed and grieved her—it was like those instances when one of the Nightingale nurses married and Florence, furiously protesting, could do nothing to prevent the nonsense!

Strangely, perhaps, Miss Nightingale was never an advocate of feminism. Though herself an outstanding example of a woman who had contended against prodigious odds and carved out a career in fields always before barred to her sex, she had no wish to vote. The devious ways of politics all were known to her; the methods and policies of government were like an open book. Yet she did not favor the participation of women in either politics or government. In a day when the woman suffrage sentiment was born, and struggled into the ascendancy, she was unresponsive. Several of her women friends were ardent champions of the feminist cause—she would not embrace it. Indeed, she seldom mentioned it, but went on working for the uplifting and salvation of the human race as a whole, not discriminating between the sexes. Probably she had never thought of herself as downtrodden or victimized by men (nor had she been!) and in her various campaigns she had labored beside men, trusting them and conscious of her equality with the best of them.

If this was an old-fashioned attitude, so also was her antagonism for the theory of microbes, developed through the scientific research of Pasteur and Lister. Bacteriology was a study she would never undertake, the idea that disease was spread by germs seemed absurd to her. She had not met with microbes in the Crimea—

at least, she thought she hadn't. No, she had met only with dirt, lack of proper food, ventilation and sanitary facilities; from them, not from germs, sickness and misery had resulted. These things she had seen and could therefore believe. But had she ever seen a microbe? Certainly not! She would not then acknowledge the existence of microbes. Dr. Sutherland infuriated her by his interest, his belief, in them.

During the years she was increasingly dependent upon Dr. Sutherland's help and companionship, and often very impatient with him. She consulted him about everything, and begrudged those hours which he spent away from South Street. He had a house at Norwood and a little garden in which he liked to relax. Florence disapproved of both house and garden, and if he said he could not immediately do whatever she asked of him, she flung reproaches at him. Sometimes Dr. Sutherland rebelled at this tyranny; but usually he did as he was told. His good humor was such that he forgave Miss Nightingale's scoldings. "Thanks for your parting kick," he once wrote, "which is always pleasant to receive by them as likes it." And he retorted with teasing. When Florence asked him to fill in her census form and define her occupation, he wrote "None!"

As one commentator has said, Dr. Sutherland's wife, who also was devoted to Miss Nightingale, must often have welcomed home a very tired and exasperated man.

21

TRIALS AND TRIUMPHS

To FLORENCE NIGHTINGALE must be given much of the world's gratitude for the International Red Cross Society. This most wonderful of all humanitarian organizations was founded by the Swiss philanthropist, Henri Dunant, as an aftermath of the battle of Solferino.

Speaking in London in 1872, Monsieur Dunant said: "What inspired me to go to Italy during the war of 1859 was the work of Miss Florence Nightingale in the Crimea."

Appealed to for encouragement and help in the framing of the earliest Red Cross Convention, Florence had joined the movement immediately; the British delegates setting out in 1864 for the International Congress were armed with her written instructions which were meticulously followed in every detail. With the outbreak of the Franco-Prussian War in 1870, more calls reached Florence in her South Street seclusion.

Though from the first a party to the Geneva Convention, the British government had done nothing toward the actual formation of a Red Cross Society, but now this step must be taken. What was more natural than to look to Miss Nightingale for leadership? The temporary committee appointed in 1870 conferred with Florence; and largely through her whole-hearted co-operation, the British Red Cross Aid Society soon emerged as a reality.

Miss Nightingale said that had she not been confined to a sick bed, she would have volunteered for service on the battle front. As it was, she could work only as her physical impairments permitted—but she would do her utmost! Her letters read at public meetings brought forth rounds of deafening applause and incited a general enthusiasm for the infant organization.

Throughout the Franco-Prussian War, Florence was closely involved with the work of the Red Cross, both in England and abroad. Relatives and friends of hers were sent to inspect the hospitals of France and Germany, and their reports returned to her; Dr. Sutherland attended to much of the Society's correspondence; and Florence herself was diligent in the collection of money and gifts for war sufferers.

Of course, she was deluged with inquiries of all sorts. The French asked her for plans for field hospitals; the Crown Princess of Prussia begged for advice and assistance. Later the Crown Princess came in person to South Street—a visit which resulted in the introduction of Nightingale nurses into Prussian hospitals and a great improvement in German nursing methods.

Florence's sympathies were rather with the French in this conflict; but she was conscientiously impartial and strove for the alleviation of distress in both countries.

Now that she was "out of office," she wrote extensively on religious subjects, picking up again the *Suggestions for Thought*, that book begun so long ago, when it had seemed she was forever imprisoned in the Embley drawing-room, and almost forgotten in the crowded after-years. Now she wished again to analyze her own religion. She was a churchwoman, but had never gone much to church—as superintendent for the Harley Street "gentlewomen's" home, she used to hide on Sunday mornings so that the inmates would not be shocked to discover she was not a churchgoer. Her convictions were unorthodox, she knew, but very sincere and firm; she felt that she must crystallize and put neatly on paper her special creed, her confidence in God's infinite goodness.

In this she was urged on by Benjamin Jowett, the English scholar and theologian, master of Balliol College, Oxford, who had become perhaps her most intimate friend. Indeed, Dr. Jowett's cordiality compensated, to a degree, for the loss of Sidney Herbert, though this was an association of a different kind. Mr. Herbert had been Florence's partisan and collaborator; the master of Balliol sustained her with spiritual solace.

Yet even with Dr. Jowett's friendship to lean upon, and the series of voluminous letters they exchanged, and the expansion and clarifying of her *Suggestions for Thought*, she had many hours of utter dejection, when she was oppressed with the feeling of failure, futility. She was middle-aged, lonely; the isolation she had fostered and still clung to, did not bring happiness. Except when immersed in work, she had the nagging sensation of emptiness.

Insomnia troubled her; and at night, lying sleepless, she would reach for the pencil and notebook always on her bedside table and write memoranda of her reflections. Melancholy jottings they were, filled with doubt and self-reproach: "Oh, my Creator, Thou knowest that through all these 20 horrible years I have been supported by the belief that I was working with Thee Who wert bringing every one of us, even our poor nurses, to perfection."—"Oh, Lord my God, patience is very necessary for me, for I perceive that many things in this life do fall out as we would not."—"O Lord, even now I am trying to snatch the management of Thy world out of Thy hands." —"Too little have I looked for something higher and better than my own work."

In 1874 Florence's father died suddenly; and in the midst of mourning for him, she had to pause and see to legal and business affairs. Mr. Nightingale's sister, Aunt Mai Smith, was heir to his land and his two country houses, while his daughters, Parthe and Florence, inherited other properties. This meant that Mrs. Nightingale must be provided for. Mamma was eighty-six now, and Florence must be in part responsible for her. It was arranged that she should live in London with a nephew, but should have annual autumn sojourns at Lea Hurst.

Florence disliked the unavoidable interruptions of all such decisions. "Oh, God," she exclaimed, "let me not sink in these perplexities, but give me a great cause to do and die for! I am so disturbed by my family that I can't do my work."

But she and Mamma were now quite reconciled and on more affectionate terms than ever before. Mrs. Nightingale had ceased to be critical of this "swan" she had hatched. "You would have done nothing in life, Flo," she once said, "if you had not resisted me."

Florence was able to see her mother rather often in London and she visited her at Lea Hurst on several occasions. Once she rented a villa in Norwood and tried the experiment of their living together—which lasted for a period of a few weeks. The villa was painted red and was hideous; "like a monster lobster," Florence said, and she soon left it.

"This is the only time for 22 years," she wrote, "that

my work has not been the first cause for where I should live and how I should live. It is the caricature of a life!"

Mrs. Nightingale ended her days at Lea Hurst, a very, very old lady, whose mind had clouded. "Where is Florence?" she would ask. "Is she still in her hospital? I suppose she will never marry now."

As the years passed, Florence's health seemed to mend. The nervous malady disappeared; she was almost entirely well. After her mother's death, she never went back to Lea Hurst; but she saw something of Parthe, who, with her husband, had a house in South Street only a stone's throw distant from Florence's house. Sir Harry Verney's beautiful country place was Claydon, in Buckinghamshire; and infrequently Florence stayed there with her sister.

Florence had grown to be very fond of Sir Harry and had made friends with his children. Sometimes she drove in Sir Harry's carriage or walked in the park with him. In 1882 her health was so nearly normal that she accompanied Sir Harry to the opening of the new Law Courts—where she was recognized by Queen Victoria. "Look!" said the Queen, "Isn't that Miss Nightingale? It is, indeed!"

That same year she paid her first and only visit to St. Thomas' and with her own eyes saw the quarters of her nurses' training school. Again squired by Sir Harry, she witnessed the arrival of the Grenadier Guards at the railway station, fresh from their Egyptian campaign; and at Mr. Gladstone's invitation, she watched a military parade and review of the troops.

Her work in this period consisted of further reforms for India and a more comprehensive study of nursing problems; and she accomplished much of value, fearlessly forging ahead into new and untried paths of progress. It was only habit, perhaps, which kept her shut

She witnessed the arrival of the Grenadier Guards

away most of the time in her bright, airy upper room, the world shut out; she had come to prefer this sheltered solitary existence, finding in it peace, order, and a retreat from the acclaim which would surely have been heaped upon her, had she opened her doors to the normal activities of life.

In 1891, Dr. Sutherland died, and then except for servants, she was quite alone at No. 10 South Street. But Dr. Jowett, her nurses and privileged friends continued to call. And she was always busy.

Her interest in the British army never abated. Any reference to the splendid character of England's fighting man would bring a sparkle to her glance, a smile to her lips.

"The soldier," she would remark, "is a very expensive article!" But how admirable he was, how deserving of all that was done for him!

On Balaclava Day, October 25, 1897, she wrote greetings to the Crimean veterans, addressing them as "My dear old Comrades." During the Boer War, she helped again with the nursing program.

22

FAREWELLS

She was softer with the years, more amiable, her fiery mood mellowing.

She was softer with the years

Among the nurses at St. Thomas' were a favored few, young enough to be her granddaughters, with whom she was tender, endearing, nicknaming them as "The Pearl," or "The Goddess." She was thoughtful of all the young cousins in the family, and of Arthur Clough's children; she sent them presents and notes; she was "Ever your loving Aunt Florence." Advancing age made it necessary that she have a nurse to care for her, and she did not object. But at night, after the nurse had tucked her into bed, Florence would clamber out, patter into the next room and tuck in the nurse.

By her express wish she now lived very quietly, removed from stress and turmoil and well content to be, asking nothing but her precious solitude—and rest at last.

She refused to have her photograph taken and when she was besought to allow a statue of herself to be shown at Queen Victoria's Diamond Jubilee celebration in 1897, she replied, with a flash of her former temper, but smiling, "I won't be made a sign at an exhibition!"

Finally she yielded, and the statue was displayed.

"I hope it gets smashed!" said Florence.

The statue did not get smashed. Instead, it was decked each day with wreaths of flowers by people who delighted in the gesture of homage.

For though she was so old now, and the past slipping away into dimness, the century turning, Queen Victoria dead and Edward VII on the throne—though Florence Nightingale had renounced the world and its activities, she was still more than a memory to a nation which had adored her. She was still the idol she had always been. In December, 1908, England conferred upon her the Order of Merit, the greatest honor within the power of the realm to bestow, and the first time it had ever been offered a woman.

Sir Douglas Dawson, King Edward's emissary, brought the Order of Merit to her South Street chamber. There was no ceremony. Florence was eighty-eight, feeble; for months she had been rather vague about her surroundings, many things. Perhaps she didn't quite know who the gentleman was or why he had come. But she was polite, seemed to be appreciative.

"Too kind," she murmured. "Too kind."

She died August 13, 1910, between night and morning, falling asleep as usual and never waking. The government said she must be buried in Westminster Abbey —but the surviving relatives declined. Florence wouldn't have liked such pomp and circumstance; and, anyway, she had left directions about her funeral. It must be as simple as possible, she had said.

They buried her, then, at East Wellow, beside her father and mother, in the churchyard near Embley. Six stalwart army sergeants bore the flag-draped coffin along the country road, where the neighbors had gathered in a silent throng.

At the grave a hymn was sung, just one, but militant and challenging it was, appropriate to the day, the hour —to Florence Nightingale:

> "The son of God goes forth to war,
> His blood-red banner streams afar . . .
> Who follows in His train?"